The Two Horizons New Testamer

Joel B. Green and Max Turner, *General Editors*

Two features distinguish The Two Horizons New Testament Commentary series: theological exegesis and theological reflection.

Exegesis since the Reformation era and especially in the past two hundred years emphasized careful attention to philology, grammar, syntax, and
concerns of a historical nature. More recently, commentary has expanded to
include social-scientific, political, or canonical questions and more.

Without slighting the significance of those sorts of questions, scholars
in The Two Horizons New Testament Commentary locate their primary
interests on theological readings of texts, past and present. The result is a
paragraph-by-paragraph engagement with the text that is deliberately theological in focus.

Theological reflection in The Two Horizons New Testament Commentary takes many forms, including locating each New Testament book in
relation to the whole of Scripture — asking what the biblical book contributes to biblical theology — and in conversation with constructive theology of
today. How commentators engage in the work of theological reflection will
differ from book to book, depending on their particular theological tradition
and how they perceive the work of biblical theology and theological hermeneutics. This heterogeneity derives as well from the relative infancy of the
project of theological interpretation of Scripture in modern times and from
the challenge of grappling with a book's message in Greco-Roman antiquity,
in the canon of Scripture and history of interpretation, and for life in the ad-
mittedly diverse Western world at the beginning of the twenty-first century.

The Two Horizons New Testament Commentary is written primarily for students, pastors, and other Christian leaders seeking to engage in
theological interpretation of Scripture.

1 Peter

Joel B. Green

WILLIAM B. EERDMANS PUBLISHING COMPANY
GRAND RAPIDS, MICHIGAN / CAMBRIDGE, U.K.

Published 2007 by
Wm. B. Eerdmans Publishing Co.
2140 Oak Industrial Drive N.E., Grand Rapids, Michigan 49505 /
P.O. Box 163, Cambridge CB3 9PU U.K.

Printed in the United States of America

12 11 10 09 08 07   7 6 5 4 3 2 1

Library of Congress Cataloging-in-Publication Data

Green, Joel B., 1956-
    1 Peter / Joel B. Green.
        p.   cm.   — (The two horizons New Testament commentary)
    Includes bibliographical references and indexes.
    ISBN 978-0-8028-2553-7 (pbk.: alk. paper)
    1. Bible. N.T. Peter, 1st — Commentaries.
    I. Title.   II. Title: First Peter.

BS2795.53.G73   2007
227'.92077 — dc22

                                                              2007017999

www.eerdmans.com

Contents

Preface

The history of interpretation of 1 Peter has taken a number of fascinating twists and turns. For Martin Luther, it belonged to that small list of New Testament books that "show you Christ and teach you all that is necessary and salvatory for you to know, even if you were never to see or hear any other book" (*Preface to the New Testament* [1522]). For its pastoral tone, its depiction of Christians on a pilgrim journey, and its pronounced christological claims, the letter has gained some notoriety, but has hardly enjoyed the attention it deserves. Instead, it has served as an arsenal of texts to prove the doctrine of the "Harrowing of Hell," an exegetical tradition that dates back at least to the early second century but which gained special prominence in the medieval period (see 3:19; 4:6); or the priesthood of all believers (see 2:4-5, 9-10), central to the Reformers; or, more recently, the status of wives vis-à-vis their husbands (see 3:1-6) or the proper stance of Christians toward the state (see 2:13-16). This is unfortunate, since the considerable challenge of this letter has often suffered domestication in the hands of those who thus sunder this or that passage from the message of the letter as a whole.

This letter has also suffered from inattention since, among many Protestant interpreters, the light of the Pauline letters has tended to shine so brightly that 1 Peter has been relegated to the shadows of the New Testament — to a collection of letters impertinently and inauspiciously labeled by some as the Bible's "junk mail."

Given the contemporary church's ambiguous relationship to Christendom, 1 Peter begs for fresh consideration and renewed influence. I say "ambiguous" because, in some parts of the West, Christendom has already died a thousand deaths; in other areas of the West, including regions of the U.S. known as "the Bible belt" or even "the buckle of the Bible belt," Christendom is waning; and in much of the world — South America, Africa, and parts of

Asia especially — a new and robust form of Christendom is emerging. In these varied contexts, Christians and the Christian faith typically enjoy no privileged standing and their minority status may even invite social and political disquiet. Even in those locales where Christian faith remains a force with which to be reckoned, it is increasingly difficult in our world to ignore the difficult realities faced on a day-to-day basis by sisters and brothers in other places. As with the world of 1 Peter, so today we may come to understand better what it means to recognize and share in the "sufferings . . . being accomplished in the case of your family of believers throughout the world" (5:9). As followers of Christ learn to identify with our crucified-and-raised Lord, we may find in God's mercy a welcome message of living hope, in Christ the possibility of and pattern for a manner of life appropriate to those who dwell in a strange land, and in the Holy Spirit a sanctifying presence powerful to enable faithful witness. If so, we will have begun to embrace the message of this, Peter's word of encouragement and witness.

In preparing this commentary, I have been helped by many interactions — especially with students in my seminars on New Testament exegesis and systematic theology at Asbury Theological Seminary and with my Asbury colleagues, Dr. Chuck Gutenson and Dr. Ruth Anne Reese. Were someone to engage in an archeological study of this work, the influence of Dr. Francis Ian Andersen, friend and former colleague in Berkeley, would loom large, as would the many conversations that have resulted from my friendship with the co-editor of this series, Dr. Max Turner. I am happy to express my appreciation to all of these persons. I am also grateful to Asbury Theological Seminary for its provision of a sabbatical leave that allowed the much-needed time for the writing of this book. As always, Pamela's early dissatisfaction with the church's taken-for-granteds has served as an ongoing impetus to press on with the hard questions.

Abbreviations

A1CS	The Book of Acts in Its First Century Setting
AA	*American Anthropologist*
AB	Anchor Bible
ABD	*Anchor Bible Dictionary.* 6 vols. Edited by David Noel Freeman. New York: Doubleday, 1992.
ACCNT	Ancient Christian Commentary on Scripture, New Testament
AGJU	Arbeiten zur Geschichte antiken Judentums und des Urchristentums
AnBib	Analecta Biblica
ANRW	*Aufstieg und Niedergang der römischen Welt: Geschichte und Kultur Roms im Spiegel der neueren Forschung.* Edited by H. Temporini and W. Haase. Berlin: de Gruyter, 1972 -.
Apoc. Ab.	*Apocalypse of Abraham*
ATJ	*Asbury Theological Journal*
ASNU	Acta seminarii neotestamentici upsaliensis
b.	Babylonian Talmud
2 Bar	*2 Baruch*
BBR	*Bulletin of Biblical Research*
BDAG	Walter Bauer, et al. *A Greek-English Lexicon of the New Testament and Other Early Christian Literature.* 3rd ed. Revised and edited by Frederick William Danker. Chicago: University of Chicago Press, 2000.
BDF	Blass, F., A. Debrunner, and R. W. Funk. *A Greek Grammar of the New Testament and Other Early Christian Literature.* Chicago: Chicago University Press, 1961.
BECNT	Baker Exegetical Commentary on the New Testament
BETL	Bibliotheca Ephemeridum Theologicarum Lovaniensium

Bib	*Biblica*
BibInt	*Biblical Interpretation*
BibIntS	Biblical Interpretation Series
BRev	*Bible Review*
BSem	The Biblical Seminar
BT	*The Bible Translator*
BTB	*Biblical Theological Bulletin*
BZ	*Biblische Zeitschrift*
CBQ	*Catholic Biblical Quarterly*
ConNT	*Coniectanea neotestamentica*
CSS	Cistercian Studies Series
DLNTD	*Dictionary of the Later New Testament and Its Developments.* Edited by Ralph P. Martin and Peter H. Davids. Downers Grove: InterVarsity, 1997.
DNTB	*Dictionary of New Testament Background.* Edited by Craig A. Evans and Stanley E. Porter. Downers Grove: InterVarsity, 2000.
DPL	*Dictionary of Paul and His Letters.* Edited by Gerald F. Hawthorne, Ralph P. Martin, and Daniel G. Reid. Downers Grove: InterVarsity, 1993.
DTIB	*Dictionary for Theological Interpretation of the Bible.* Edited by Kevin J. Vanhoozer. Grand Rapids: Baker Academic, 2005.
ECC	Eerdmans Critical Commentary
EDNT	*Exegetical Dictionary of the New Testament.* Edited by Horst Balz and Gerhard Schneider. 3 vols. Grand Rapids: Eerdmans, 1993.
EKK	Evangelisch-katholischer Kommentar zum Neuen Testament
EPROER	Études préliminaires aux religions orientales dans l'empire romain
ExpTim	*Expository Times*
FB	Forschung zur Bibel
FCCGRW	First-Century Christians in the Graeco-Roman World
FilNT	*Filologia Neotestamentaria*
FRLANT	Forschungen zur Religion und Literatur des Alten und Neuen Testaments
GBS	Guides to Biblical Scholarship
HBT	*Horizons in Biblical Theology*
HNT	Handbuch zum Neuen Testament
HTKNT	Herders theologischer Kommentar zum Neuen Testament
HTR	*Harvard Theological Review*

HTS	Harvard Theological Studies
HUT	Hermeneutische Untersuchungen zur Theologie
IDB	*Interpreter's Dictionary of the Bible.* Edited by G. A. Buttrick. New York: Abingdon, 1962.
Int	*Interpretation*
ISBL	Indiana Studies in Biblical Literature
IVPNTC	InterVarsity Press New Testament Commentary Series
JBL	*Journal of Biblical Literature*
JETS	*Journal of the Evangelical Theological Society*
JHC	*Journal of Higher Criticism*
JSNT	*Journal for the Study of the New Testament*
JSNTSup	Journal for the Study of the New Testament Supplement Series
JTI	*Journal of Theological Interpretation*
JTS	*Journal of Theological Studies*
KTAH	Key Themes in Ancient History
LCL	Loeb Classical Library
L&N	*Greek-English Lexicon of the New Testament: Based on Semantic Domains.* 2 vols. Edited by Johannes P. Louw and Eugene A. Nida. New York: United Bible Societies, 1988.
LXX	Septuagint
MHT	Moulton, James Hope, Wilbur Francis Howard, and Nigel Turner. *A Grammar of New Testament Greek.* 4 vols. Edinburgh: T. & T. Clark, 1906-76.
MM	Moulton, James Hope, and George Milligan. *The Vocabulary of the Greek New Testament: Illustrated from the Papyri and Other Non-literary Sources.* Grand Rapids: Eerdmans, 1963.
MNTS	McMaster New Testament Studies
ModT	*Modern Theology*
mss.	manuscripts
NA^{27}	Nestle-Aland *Greek New Testament,* 27th ed.
NAB	New American Bible
NABPRSS	National Association of Baptist Professors of Religion Special Series
NASB	New American Standard Bible
NCBC	The New Cambridge Bible Commentary
NDBT	*New Dictionary of Biblical Theology.* Edited by T. Desmond Alexander and Brian S. Rosner. Downers Grove: InterVarsity, 2000.
Neot	*Neotestamentica*
NICNT	New International Commentary on the New Testament

NIGTC	New International Greek Testament Commentary
NIV	New International Version
NIVAC	New International Version Application Commentary
NJB	New Jerusalem Bible
NLT	New Living Translation
NovT	*Novum Testamentum*
NovTSup	Supplements to Novum Testamentum
NRSV	New Revised Standard Version
NSBT	New Studies in Biblical Theology
NT	New Testament
NTOA	Novum Testamentum et Orbis Antiquus
NTS	*New Testament Studies*
NTT	New Testament Theology
NTTS	New Testament Tools and Studies
OBO	Orbis Biblicus et Orientalis
OBT	Overtures to Biblical Theology
OCD	*The Oxford Classical Dictionary.* 3d ed. Edited by Simon Hornblower and Antony Spawforth. Oxford: Oxford University Press, 1996.
OT	Old Testament
OTL	Old Testament Library
OTP	*Old Testament Pseudepigrapha.* Edited by James H. Charlesworth. 2 vols. New York: Doubleday, 1983.
PSTJ	*Perkins School of Theology Journal*
QD	Quaestiones Disputatae
ResQ	*Restoration Quarterly*
RevExp	*Review & Expositor*
SABH	Studies in American Biblical Hermeneutics
SBEC	Studies in Bible and Early Christianity
SBL	Studies in Biblical Literature
SBLABS	Society of Biblical Literature Archeology and Biblical Studies
SBLDS	Society of Biblical Literature Dissertation Series
SBLRBS	Society of Biblical Literature Resources for Biblical Study
SBS	Stuttgarter Bibelstudien
SBT	Studies in Biblical Theology
SCB	*Science and Christian Belief*
SJLA	Studies in Judaism in Late Antiquity
SJT	*Scottish Journal of Theology*
SNTSMS	Society of New Testament Studies Monograph Series
SNTW	Studies of the New Testament and Its World

SOTBT   Studies in Old Testament Biblical Theology

TDNT   *Theological Dictionary of the New Testament.* Edited by Gerhard Kittel and Gerhard Friedrich. Grand Rapids: Eerdmans, 1964-76.

TDOT   *Theological Dictionary of the Old Testament.* 14 vols. Edited by G. Johannes Botterweck, et al. Grand Rapids: Eerdmans, 1974-.

Tg.   Targum

THKNT   Theologischer Handkommentar zum Neuen Testament

THNTC   Two Horizons New Testament Commentary

TLNT   *Theological Lexicon of the New Testament.* 3 vols. By Ceslas Spicq. Peabody: Hendrickson, 1994.

TNTC   Tyndale New Testament Commentaries

TynB   *Tyndale Bulletin*

UBT   Understanding Biblical Themes

WBC   Word Biblical Commentary

WUNT   Wissenschaftliche Untersuchungen zum Neuen Testament

WW   *Word & World*

ZBK   Zürcher Bibelkommentare

ZGB   Zürcher Grundrisse zur Bibel

ZNW   *Zeitschrift für die neutestamentliche Wissenschaft und die Kunde der älteren Kirche*

Orientation

Matters of Perspective

Pivotal questions surface in 1 Peter — pivotal for God's people then and now, and indeed in all times this side of the eschaton. What to do with Rome? What to do about Rome? What to make of Rome? For Peter, of course, "Rome" really was the issue: its sanctioned religions, its imperial and colonizing presence and practices, its world system, its matrices of honor and order. Even Peter understands that the problem is not Rome *per se,* though, and so he refers to Rome not by its real name but as "Babylon." That Babylon was a metaphor for Rome is clear enough from parallel usage (e.g., Revelation 18). Indeed, this identification was made transparent in the textual tradition of 1 Peter by a few minuscules that substitute "Rome" for "Babylon." "Babylon" was a cipher for a world power hostile to God, and, for Peter, this is what Rome had become. Peter thus highlights emphatically the problems of Christian life and witness in the presence of a world system not only out of step with God's purpose but actually set against it. "Babylon" appears in this letter at its close (5:13), where it serves to recapitulate Peter's perspective on the Christian "manner of living" developed throughout the letter. This reference to Babylon pulls back the curtain on the real context in which Peter's audience made their lives, focusing attention on the systemic character of harassment and the institutionalization of evil in patterns of sanctioned behavior and organizational structures that legitimate and propagate such behavior.

What to make of Rome? Among the available options, we might think of withdrawal into a kind of alternative community in which faithfulness to God is exercised in relative anonymity within the empire; or moving to the margins of population centers, to the underground, from which to execute attacks on the Empire, whether secretly or openly; or moving persons into positions of leadership of the cities, perhaps as esteemed benefactors, in order to participate innocuously in Roman society. Reflecting on the various expressions of Jewish faith in Roman antiquity, whether in Judea or the Diaspora, we find plentiful evidence of these kinds of tactics for "engagement" with Rome. The relevance of these models is not that Peter's audience was primarily Jewish, but that Peter paints his audience, like the Jews, as an exilic people, strangers in a strange land. Of course, these tactics for answering the question of "the Christian's place in society" have contemporary exemplars as well.

Scholarship on 1 Peter has tended toward choosing between two of these options.[1] Some have found in 1 Peter the basis for a benign presence in the world, accommodating to the institutions and conventions of society-at-large so as not to attract unwelcome attention. Others have found in 1 Peter a call to come apart, to the formation of a colony separate from the larger world, where holiness of faith and life might be practiced and modeled. Given the cultural contexts within which scholarship on 1 Peter has been practiced, perhaps such readings are only to be expected. Our own ecclesial traditions often help to shape how we read these texts, as do the typologies generally offered us for navigating the relationship of "Christ and culture."[2] Some might say that my own tradition presses in me in one or another of these directions, or perhaps threatens to pull me apart. A Wesleyan emphasis on prevenient grace urges me to find evidences of God at work in the wider world and to align myself accordingly; and so I am encouraged to take an optimistic view toward the world and to find pathways for participation in it. But a Wesleyan emphasis on holiness urges me to define myself over against the world, to find my identity in a negation of the world, and to locate myself in a community of others committed to holiness, a holy club. In fact, neither of these responses is particularly Wesleyan, and neither represents well the perspective of 1 Peter.

The difficulty we face, not least in the U.S., is one of perspective. Many of us are accustomed to imagining the church as an instrument of political and social change, and we imagine that we can wield the power of the state (in the wider world) or of our position (within ecclesiastical circles) in order "to build God's kingdom on earth." We easily overlook that the kingdom of God is God's, and that God has called us not to build but rather to serve the kingdom.[3] Many of us are accustomed to imagining that life as followers of

---

1. See further below, pp. 179-88.
2. I refer, of course, to Niebuhr, *Christ and Culture.*
3. This point is made emphatically and profoundly in Küng, *Church.*

Christ is a personal matter, or at most a matter to be discussed between me and my family or pastor or small group or that the public implications of Christian faith have to do with personal matters only. We have learned to render unto Caesar what is Caesar's and to God what is God's, not taking seriously enough that the realm of one's allegiance to God has no outer limits but reaches into nooks and crannies of all of life. Others of us have learned to view the world in us-them terms, the church against the world (or, more likely, the world against the church), with clear boundaries between the two, boundaries that ought not be crossed or at least, that have to be negotiated with care and skill. This, however, runs against the grain of Peter's own perspective on holiness-as-engagement. Or, to borrow words from Karl Barth first spoken in 1919, "Holiness in itself is no holiness whatever. From the safe and once lauded domain of religion we are beginning to look out on the world with real longing; for we suspect . . . that there can be no inside to that domain so long as there is no outside."[4]

What to make of Rome? The typical options we entertain do little or nothing to address the most basic of concerns here. This is because our tendency is to imagine that, whatever tactics we formulate, we can execute them by putting the politics of Rome to work for us. We will use the same instruments of influence, but we will use them better, and for a good and worthy cause. In their jointly authored *Resident Aliens,* Stanley Hauerwas and William Willimon hit the mark when they observe, "Christianity is mostly a matter of politics — politics as defined by the gospel."[5] Even if their perspective has proven susceptible to the charge that they promote withdrawal from the world, they are nonetheless right on this point. Indeed, this concern is central for 1 Peter.

1 Peter is about God and the ramifications of orienting life wholly around him. This entails refusing the conventions of honor and status that constitute Roman politics in favor of the valuations and judgment of the merciful God who has chosen and honored what the systems of this world have dismissed. To read 1 Peter is to be told not how we might think about God, but what God thinks of us. Here in 1 Peter is an invitation to adopt God's way of seeing things and to live accordingly; perhaps better, 1 Peter offers not so much an invitation as an exercise in formation in the character and ways of God. This entails allegiance to Jesus Christ, and not to Caesar, as Lord. And this has as its immediate corollary our awareness that Jesus' own rejection of the politics of Rome resulted in his suffering and death on a Ro-

---

4. Barth, "Christian's Place," p. 276.

5. Hauerwas and Willimon, *Resident Aliens,* p. 30. See further Hauerwas, *After Christendom?*

3

man cross *and* that his righteous suffering was not a denial but rather an affirmation of his status before God. What is more, this death was purposeful and meaningful, overcoming the powers of evil and effecting the transformation of persons from old and idolatrous ways of life, from wasting time feeding the insatiable desires of pagan life, to a life patterned after that of Christ, embodying the character of a holy God, demonstrating the possibility of faithful suffering — that is, suffering for righteousness rather than as punishment for sin, and blazing the pathway that leads through faithful suffering to glory. And it entails an openness to the empowering and transforming work of the Holy Spirit, the active presence of God in the midst of trying circumstances.

Because 1 Peter does not name tactics of resistance in terms explicit and recognizable to our ears, we may be tempted to imagine either that Peter counsels sectarian withdrawal from society or proposes optimism toward Babylon. What if, instead, we were to read this letter from the perspective of its central icon, the passion of Christ — that visible and horrible manifestation of what happens when life is lived according to God's view of the way the world really is? What if, instead, we were to read this letter from the perspective of its primary temporal orientation, the End — that actualization of God's purpose, the judgment, the vindication of the faithful, which undermines the claims of Babylon (in all its guises) to its own ultimacy or importance? Following the Christ who was crucified on a tree determines both internal and external relations; it is a profoundly political and missiological act (external) and a commitment to indwelling a terrain determined by the sanctifying Spirit and intramural hospitality (internal). The homeless people of God comprise God's household under construction, and a priesthood whose vocation it is to mediate God's presence wherever they find themselves. As they journey through suffering in hope of eschatological honor, they bear witness in the present to the coming new age.

Matters of Introduction

Using a standard formula, 1 Peter describes itself as "a brief letter" written to encourage its recipients and to testify concerning the grace of God (5:12). Who was this author? Who were these recipients? What was their situation? Matters of "introduction" typically concern such questions. I will have more to say on these and related issues in the framework of the commentary itself or in the context of the "theological horizons" that follow the commentary proper. By way of preliminary orientation, however, let me show my hand on some of the anticipated introductory questions.

1 Peter is cast in the form of a letter — complete with the identification of the person of the author ("Peter, apostle of Jesus Christ") and addressee ("the chosen, strangers in the world of the diaspora," 1:1) in its introduction, and the expected greeting (from "Babylon," that is, from Rome) in its conclusion (5:12-14). Its lack of greater specificity in its address and its opening reference to a series of contiguous regions of Asia Minor ("Pontus, Galatia, Cappadocia, Asia, and Bithynia," 1:1) mark it as a circular letter (cf. Acts 15:23-29; Col 4:16). This was a form otherwise known in Israel's Scriptures and in Second Temple Jewish literature, where it was used to address the people of God in particular locales — "the Jews in Egypt" (2 Macc 1:1–2:18) or the Jewish exiles in Babylon (e.g., Jer 29:4-23; 2 *Bar* 78–86; cf. Jas 1:1). Of course, in the case of 1 Peter, the "diaspora letter" has its origin *in* Babylon rather than its having been sent *to* Babylonian exiles.

The letter might seem to vacillate on the question of the ethnic identity of its authorial audience. The form of the letter and its opening reference to the diaspora (1:1) suggest an audience of Jewish Christians. This conclusion would be supported by the letter's dependence on the Scriptures of Israel and its repeated identification of its readers with appellatives used of Israel. What is more, persons outside of the community are called "Gentiles" (2:12; 4:3). Finally, given the letter's attribution to the apostle Peter, it may be of interest that, according to Paul, Peter's mission was to the Jews (Gal 2:7).

On the other hand, repeated references to the pagan character of their background strongly intimate that most of those in the audience assumed by the letter were Gentile (see 1:14, 18; 2:10, 25; 4:3-4). The comment that, prior to their conversion, the readers of 1 Peter had neither faith nor hope in God likewise urges their identification as Gentiles (1:21). These considerations speak decisively in favor of our identifying the first audience of 1 Peter as communities of Christians in which persons of Gentile background would have predominated.

What of evidence to the contrary? With respect to the importance to this letter of Israel's Scriptures, three observations invite reflection. First, to say that the majority of the first audience of 1 Peter was comprised of Gentiles is not to say that all were Gentiles, and we can imagine that Jewish Christians within the communities to which this letter is addressed would have been able to draw ongoing attention to the scriptural allusions and echoes that dot the landscape of the letter. Second, the person or persons who conveyed the letter across the area of Asia mentioned in 1:1 ("Pontus, Galatia, Cappadocia, Asia, and Bithynia") would have served not only as letter-carriers but also as performers of the letter, interpreting it to these groups of Christians. We can imagine their attending to the interplay of the letter with its scriptural intertexts. Third, it should not be forgotten that Israel's Scriptures comprised *the* Bible of those early Christians, so that we would be mistaken were we to suppose that even Gentile converts would not have been progressing in their intimacy with the words of Scripture.[6] With regard to the locus of his mission, Peter himself is known to have had a ministry within the Gentile world (see Acts 10:1–11:18; 15:7-11; 1 Cor 1:12). Finally, 1 Peter employs as a central motif the identification of Israel and the church, with the result that normal usage of such terms as "Jewish" or "Gentile" cannot be assumed. The people of God envisioned in this letter is none other than "Israel" — so this document's "Jewishness" intimates less a description of the ethnic origins of its implied audience and more a clarification of its readers' status before God.

Peter describes his audience as "aliens" and "strangers in the world," foreigners in this sense: their commitments to the lordship of Jesus Christ have led to transformed attitudes and behaviors that place them on the fringes of their communities. This is not because they set out to distance themselves from their contemporaries; rather, they have become the victims of social ostracism, their allegiance to Christ having won for them slander, animosity, and vilification. Previously they have participated in the mainstream of Greco-Roman society ("discharging the will of the Gentiles," 4:3), but their segregation from prevailing attitudes and practices has now marked them as social misfits worthy of contempt. 1 Peter was written to address Christians in such circumstances as these — not so much to resolve the enigma of the suffering of God's people as to give significance to their distress and to articulate how best to engage a world set against those allegiances, attitudes, and actions that are consistent with God's agenda.

By whom was this letter written? In spite of the clear identification of the author as "Peter, an apostle of Jesus Christ" (1:1), doubts about Petrine authorship continue to linger.[7] This is primarily because the author of 1 Peter evidences relatively superior facility in Greek (relative, that is, to other forms of NT Greek),[8] employs Israel's Scriptures in their Greek rather than Hebrew form, and manifests some training in the canons of Greco-Roman rhetoric. In short, it is doubted whether Peter the Galilean fisherman would have been

---

6. Compare, e.g., the level of familiarity with the Scriptures and their interpretation that Paul assumes of a predominately Gentile church in 1 Corinthians 10.

7. Indeed, Richard announces that "modern scholarship, employing linguistic, social, and theological factors, is virtually unanimous in arguing for pseudonymity" ("Honorable Conduct," p. 413).

8. From her quantitative textual analysis, Jobes musters evidence suggesting that arguments based on the quality of the Greek of 1 Peter are overdrawn; she concludes that the author of 1 Peter would have been a person whose first language was not Greek (pp. 325-38).

capable of authoring such a document. The force of such considerations is mitigated, however, by conventions governing the writing and sending of letters in Roman antiquity — including the use of secretaries, the correlative anachronism of the modern portrait of the autonomous author, and the practice of shaping letters through multiple drafts.[9]

The imposition of theological factors as evidence against Petrine authorship has little to commend it, based as it is on a circular argument. Noting that there is little in 1 Peter that one might regard as *distinctively* Petrine, the conclusion is then reached that 1 Peter could not have been authored by the apostle. Given the historical issues attending other evidence for our knowledge of Peter's distinctive theology, however, we must admit that we have little by which to measure whether 1 Peter provides us with a genuinely Petrine theological message — unless, of course, we allow 1 Peter to stand as evidence. This is all the more true when we recognize that those who, at least in part on theological grounds, deny the authorship of 1 Peter also deny that the apostle penned the only other NT document claiming Petrine authorship, 2 Peter; critical scholarship tends likewise to dismiss the possibility that we have access to Peter's theology either by means of the Petrine speeches reported in the Acts of the Apostles or in those few references in the canonical Gospels where Peter speaks. Accordingly, we are left to a handful of references in the Pauline epistles (see 1 Cor 1:12; 3:22; 9:5; 15:5; Gal 1:18; 2:7-11), which tell us almost nothing about Peter's theology.[10] I will have more to say about the theological relationship of 1 and 2 Peter in a section devoted to "1 Peter and the New Testament,"[11] but here have need only to point out that arguments against Petrine authorship based on theological considerations have no traction.

In fact, the high degree to which the message of 1 Peter finds a home in the NT as a whole actually comprises a profound rhetorical move on the part of the apostle. Experiences of hostility and challenges of pluralism from outside the church provide Peter with the occasion for articulating what is common ground within the church. Antagonism toward the church from beyond its borders provides the occasion for solidifying the church's center in relation to the ancient purpose of God, for drawing out the continuity from Israel of old to the contemporary life of God's people, and for remembering that the primary orientation of faithful life is the God and Father of our Lord Jesus Christ. We should not be surprised, then, if 1 Peter participates fully in the

---

9. See Richards, *Secretary;* idem, *First-Century Letter Writing.*

10. Moreover, whereas in Galatians Paul has it that Peter was "an apostle to the circumcised" (2:8), in 1 Corinthians he provides evidence that Peter's mission included Gentiles (1:12).

11. See below, pp. 234-39.

emerging Christian consensus and emphasizes the common ground of the faithful as they look for places to secure their feet in the struggle for faithful witness.

Assuming that the figure of Peter stands immediately behind the writing of this document that carries his name, this would require that the letter originated prior to his martyrdom (i.e., prior to *ca.* AD 64-65). Scholars seeking to locate more precisely the historical situation about which Peter is concerned in this letter have sometimes pointed to the period of the persecution of Christians under Nero in the 60s. This would make sense of references to malice and the "fiery ordeal," as well as the general feeling of apprehension that characterizes the document as a whole (e.g., 4:4, 12, 16). Such specificity actually introduces more problems than it solves, since this would require Peter to have addressed for his audience in Asia Minor a situation in which he himself (and not they) would have been embroiled. The Neronian persecution, after all, was localized in the vicinity of Rome itself, but 1 Peter implies that it is the Christian population of the Anatolian Peninsula that is caught up in slander and scorn. Peter nowhere implies that the persecution being experienced by his readers carried with it the legitimization of Roman decree. Instead, Christians in the first-century Mediterranean world would have attracted widespread, but localized ill will for their failure to participate in the religious celebrations that permeated Roman culture — some in honor of the goddess of Rome herself, *Roma,* others in honor of the emperor and his divine attributes, and so on.

If it is impossible to associate the historical situation of 1 Peter with official persecution under Nero, the same may be said of other actions against Christian believers under the emperors Domitian (AD 81-96) and Trajan (AD 97-117).[12] The presence of unofficial harassment instigated by the populace in areas throughout the empire is easier to imagine, even if it is also more difficult to use as a means of dating 1 Peter. It is of interest, though, that the Book of Revelation, written in the mid-90s, takes an even less generous view of the Roman government than does 1 Peter. Although himself engaged in criticism of Rome and the empire, Peter is under the impression that the government is capable of rendering justice on those who do evil and praising those who do good (2:14). John's analysis leads to another conclusion. He views the empire as a blasphemous power that has set itself over against the will of God and thus against the people of God. Since the audiences of 1 Peter and Revelation overlap significantly (see Revelation 2–3), it may be that John wrote at a time

---

12. Koester, e.g., attempts to tie the letter's composition to the Domitian persecution (*Early Christianity,* p. 294).

when relations with the Roman world had further deteriorated. This again would support an earlier rather than later dating of 1 Peter.

In fact, the situation presumed by 1 Peter is easy to place throughout the Roman Empire and therefore difficult to pinpoint more precisely on a timeline. Periods of hostility toward Christians, such as that experienced under Domitian, were only intensifications of a more pervasive menace toward foreigners, especially from the East, with their nontraditional religions. The flow of immigrants from the East into Rome was like sewage dumped in a grand river, according to the Roman satirist Juvenal, writing in the early second century (*Saturae* 3.60-65). Lucian of Samosata (born *ca.* AD 120) wrote a sneering account of a person who had converted to and then rejected Christian faith. Therein, he speaks of "the man who was crucified in Palestine because he introduced this new cult into the world" and describes Christians as "worshiping the crucified sophist" *(The Passing of Peregrinus)*. More to the point, what Peter describes is not an imperial action against the church or any other government-sponsored decision against Christians, but trouble from "the Gentiles" — that is, from Roman society in general, from which Peter's audience had, through their dispositions and behaviors, distanced themselves (see 4:3-4). The suffering of Christ "on the tree" (2:24), pointedly emphasized in 1 Peter, would have attracted special antagonism from Romans. For example, a crude graffiti cartoon probably dating from the early second century portrays a young man worshiping a donkey-headed human figure on a cross. In what may well be the oldest depiction of "Christ crucified," the Greek caption mocks, "Alexamenos worships [his] god." Though dating from the early second century, this iconographical and literary evidence brings to the surface general attitudes and practices of harassment from earlier times. In the earlier years of the church's spread, too, Christians would have distinguished themselves from the general populace by their nonparticipation in public festivals (cultural affairs imbued with religious, political, and social consequence). Failing to associate themselves with these religiocultural activities, their behaviors would have been perceived by the general populace as atheistic, perhaps even bordering on unlawful. Failing to participate in these activities, they would have been charged with bringing upon their communities the disfavor of the gods. Their presence within communities of the empire, including the Anatolian peninsula, would have attracted negative attention, too, on account of the political and economic ramifications of those practices (cf., e.g., Acts 16:19-24; 17:6-7; 19:23-41).[13]

---

13. For surveys of the evidence, see Goppelt, *Apostolic and Post-Apostolic Times,* pp. 108-17; Moule, *Birth,* pp. 152-76; Achtemeier, pp. 23-36; Holladay, *Introduction,* pp. 701-05.

Because of the general ubiquity of such forms of social pressure on Christ-followers in the larger Roman world and the lack of further historical specificity concerning a particular outbreak of persecution within Peter's letter itself, our reading of the message of 1 Peter would not be unduly altered were we to locate its origins later in the first century. First Peter's use of "Babylon" as a byname for Rome may point to such a later occasion, since this designation for Rome gained currency in the last three decades of the first century. Of course, dating the letter during this period would rule out the possibility of Peter's direct involvement in its content, in which case one might posit another leader associated with the apostle within the Christian communities of Rome. Early or late, the same social setting is plausible — namely, social ostracism as a form of persecution instigated by popular sentiment.

Hence, the possibility that 1 Peter was written after the apostle's death, perhaps by some member of a "Petrine circle,"[14] cannot be dismissed out of hand. If 1 Peter was written by persons associated with the apostle, then it is easy to recognize among them such noble intentions as their concern to preserve and appropriate the apostle's message, all the while appealing to his authority.[15] More significant is the identification of the apostle Peter as author of the letter — an identification which, from a canonical perspective at least, is important for its "authorization" of the letter and the letter's message.

Although I regard Peter as the genuine author of this letter, in my comments I will not attempt to construct a portrait of the historical Peter and his theology beyond the evidence we find in the letter itself. The possibility of constructing a "theology of (the historical) Peter" on the basis of the two NT letters bearing his name, 1 and 2 Peter, is tempting, but complicated by concerns about the authorship of 2 Peter.[16] This exercise would run aground, too, on methodological questions due to the occasional nature of these two letters: as occasional documents, they provide evidence only for those aspects of Petrine thought deemed important for the particulars addressed by the let-

14. See the different perspectives of Elliott ("Rehabilitation") and Horrell ("Petrine Circle").

15. See, e.g., Achtemeier, pp. 39-43. I do not regard the inclusion of 1 Peter in the canon as either dependent on or proof of its authorship by the apostle, since I do not regard authorship as a determinative criterion for canonicity. Consider, e.g., the circularity of some arguments for the inclusion of Hebrews (which must have been written by an apostle since it was clearly canonical), or arguments against the inclusion of the *Gospel of Peter* — based not on questions about its authorship but on its lack of conformity to the rule of faith.

16. Elsewhere I have shown why, particularly on grounds of genre, I regard 2 Peter as having been written in the name of, rather than by, the apostle Peter (Achtemeier, et al., *Introducing the NT*, pp. 527-31).

ters, not for the whole of Peter's thought. What is more, an attempt of this sort would fall outside the scope of our more narrow interests in the commentary itself, though I will return to the potential of finding in 1 and 2 Peter a coordinated Petrine witness when I address, below, the relation of 1 Peter to the wider NT.[17]

Similarly, although in the course of the commentary I will refer to Peter's audience, I am not concerned only with Peter's historical audience (or "authorial audience"), but also with whether we are ready to read 1 Peter as a letter addressed to us — that is, whether we are ready to allow our dispositions and behaviors to be so transformed that we experience, on account of our faith, conflicted presence in the world, and to embrace as our own the vision of God Peter develops in this letter. Are we ready to read 1 Peter as our book?

Together with the Book of Revelation, 1 Peter is unrivaled among NT documents for its concern with questions of Christian identity, constitution, and behavior in a hostile world. For 1 Peter, Christian communities must struggle with how to maintain a peculiar identity as God's people in the midst of contrary cultural forces. This is accomplished by identifying with Christ, both in his suffering and in the promise of restoration and justice. Through maintaining their allegiance to God the Father, theirs is a living hope certified by the resurrection of Jesus to life and animated by the Holy Spirit. Their inheritance is nothing less than eschatological salvation.

17. See pp. 234-39 below.

Commentary on 1 Peter

1:1-12

The opening to 1 Peter identifies this document as a letter for wide distribution (an encyclical or circular letter, often referred to as a "general" or "catholic" letter) and more particularly as a "diaspora letter."[1] The general purpose of such letters is well-summarized in the description of a Hellenistic Jewish letter that mirrors 1 Peter in form from roughly the same time period: "a letter of doctrine and a roll of hope" to strengthen those in exile (2 *Bar* 77:12).[2]

Words typically associated with "diaspora" include "exile," "trauma," "expulsion from the homeland," "refugees," and the like. "Punishment," too, comes to mind. The aforementioned letter, 2 *Baruch,* admits early on that the scattering of God's people was the result of divine chastening: "For we had sinned against him who created us, and had not observed the commandments which he ordered us" (2 *Bar* 79:2). We read similarly of Jerusalem in Lamentations, that "the LORD has made her suffer for the multitude of her transgressions; her children have gone away, captives before the foe" (1:5).[3] That is, "diaspora" easily fosters bitter and doleful images, "offering a bleak vision that leads either to despair or to a remote reverie of restoration."[4]

Although Peter's audience may well have experienced their diasporic status in bleak terms, Peter begins immediately to interpret suffering and ostracism in essentially hopeful terms. They are chosen by God (1:1), he insists, born anew into a living hope (1:3). Throughout this opening section, Peter

1. For the form, see 2 Macc 1:1–2:18; Jer 29:4-23; 2 *Bar* 78–86; Jas 1:1.
2. Translation from Klijn, "2 Baruch," p. 648.
3. Unless otherwise noted, citations of biblical texts other than 1 Peter are derived from the NRSV.
4. Gruen, *Diaspora*, p. 232.

underscores the theological context of the lives of these "strangers in the world of the diaspora," directing attention to the aim and work of God in these circumstances.

What Peter does not say is almost as important as what he affirms. First, he provides nowhere any hint that the affliction and misery of his audience is the consequence of their sin or God's judgment. Such categories simply have no place in his letter. Nor does he take the route of other diaspora letters of painting the resolution of contemporary misfortune in terms of God's striking out against their enemies: "But you know that our Creator will surely avenge us . . . according to everything which they have done against and among us" (2 *Bar* 82:2). Nor does he deny the validity of the experiences of his audience, as though they were not really experiencing the life of refugees. The issue is not *that* or *what* they are suffering, but rather how to make sense of it. Hence, 1 Peter concerns itself from the very beginning with issues of Christian identity and formation, constitution and behavior. This is profound theological work.

1:1-2

1:1 Peter, apostle of Jesus Christ, to the chosen,[5] strangers in the world of the diaspora in Pontus, Galatia, Cappadocia, Asia, and Bithynia, 2 according to the foreknowledge of God the Father, in the sanctification of the Spirit, because of the obedience and sprinkling of the blood of Jesus Christ: May grace and peace be multiplied to you.

With his letter opening, or "greeting," Peter draws himself and his audience onto a series of maps — relationally, geographically, and, above all, theologically. In deceptively compact statements, he also sets the stage for what will follow in the remainder of his letter.[6] How well Peter was known to Christians of the Anatolian peninsula is unknown;[7] we have no evidence that he was a

---

5. Both adjectives (ἐκλεκτοῖς [*eklektois*, "chosen"] and παρεπιδήμοις [*parepidēmois*, "strangers"]) are substantival, describing in complementary (if seemingly oxymoronic) ways the identity of the addressees. A small minority of mss. (א* sy) insert "and" (καί, *kai*) between them, the effect of which would be to disallow the possibility that "chosen" might be read as a modifier for "stranger."

6. For detail regarding how as a introduces motifs to be developed further in the letter, see Tite, "Compositional Function"; idem, *Compositional Transitions;* Elliott, pp. 321-22.

7. By the time of Peter's writing, Bithynia and Pontus would have comprised a single province, suggesting that Peter is referring to five regions rather than five provinces. The long-

missionary in the regions named and he provides almost nothing by way of personal reminiscence in the letter itself (though see 5:1). What is important at this juncture is simply this: his identification as "apostle of Jesus Christ," which marks him as the authorized agent of Jesus Christ and qualifies his message as originating with Christ.[8]

Peter spends far more energy identifying his audience, and this marks one of the most important contributions of the letter — namely, to press upon them, indeed, to form them in, their true identity. He does so by inscribing them into the world of Israel's Scriptures and the record of God's relationship with his chosen people, and by characterizing their lives in relation to God the Father, the Holy Spirit, and Jesus Christ — that is, in trinitarian terms.[9]

That they are "strangers in the world of the diaspora" will have come as no surprise to Peter's audience.[10] As Gentile Christians, this language might have been foreign to them, so deeply rooted is it in the world of Israel's history, but the trials of foreigner status, the erosion of identity and roots, and the endurance of slander rather than praise — these would have been familiar indeed. That Peter's audience was not violently torn from their homes and paraded to alien lands does not lessen the reality of their status in the world. "Diaspora" has become a metaphor for social ostracism and other forms of harassment and is associated with notions of exile.

That is, Peter's "strangers" are not "Jews" living among "Gentiles" in the expected sense of these terms, as though the author were concerned with their ethnic or nationalistic status. Attempts to find in Peter's descriptive terms a reference to his audience's economic status founders similarly on a problem of category. One's social status was a product of numerous intersecting considerations, relative income or access to the means of production being only one of them. In fact, there is no basis within the letter itself for

---

standing conclusion that the order in which these areas appear represents the travel route of the letter's carrier (recently, see Hemer, "Address") has been rendered improbable through the reexamination of the evidence by Seland; he concludes that the propagation of 1 Peter would have involved multiple carriers on multiple routes (*Strangers*, pp. 28-36).

8. That is, the phrase ἀπόστολος Ἰησοῦ Χριστοῦ (*apostolos Iēsou Christou*, "apostle of Jesus Christ") expresses a genitive of origin. For Peter's self-identification as a marker of social distinction, see Campbell, *Honor*, pp. 35-36, 42.

9. Compare Matt 28:19; 1 Cor 12:4-6; 2 Cor 13:13; Gal 4:6; Eph 4:4-6; 2 Thess 2:14-16; Jude 20-21.

10. παρεπίδημοι (*parepidēmoi*, "stranger" or "alien" dwelling in a foreign land) appears in 1 Peter in 1:1 and in tandem with πάροικοι (*paroikoi*, "alien" or "stranger") in 2:11. There is no apparent distinction between these terms in Petrine usage (see Chin, "Heavenly Home").

suggesting that Peter's audience occupied any rung on the ladder of economic measurement other than would have been characteristic of the mainstream of people living in Asia Minor. Rather, these are people whose commitments to the lordship of Jesus Christ have led to transformed dispositions and behaviors that place them on the margins of respectable society. Their allegiance to Christ had won for them animosity, scorn, and vilification. Their lack of acculturation to prevailing social values marked them as misfits worthy of contempt.[11]

Debate has tended to focus on whether "strangers in the world of the diaspora" should be read metaphorically or literally (i.e., with reference to social status).[12] Although well-intentioned as a way of undermining a purely "spiritual" reading of Peter's address, as though the phrase referred merely to persons on a journey to their true home in heaven,[13] the dichotomy, metaphorical versus nonmetaphorical, is itself wrongheaded. Metaphors pervade the whole of everyday life, and our day-to-day conceptual systems operate in terms that are fundamentally metaphorical. In other words, "metaphor" has to do with how we conceive of the world and not simply with how we represent the world linguistically.[14] In the present case, "diaspora" is self-evidently metaphorical, since Peter's largely Gentile audience will not have been confused with Jews displaced from their homeland. "Strangers," too, would have roots in Israel's story (e.g., Gen 15:13; 23:4; Exod 22:21; 23:9; Ps 39:12). Additionally, given the imaginative structure of the human mind, metaphors like "stranger" or "diaspora," so easily traceable in the Scriptures of Israel and Israel's experience of exile, are not stagnant or frozen, but are subject to blending and, then, fresh comprehension.[15] Consequently, we can easily make room both for the development of the metaphor prior to the writing of 1 Peter (say, influenced by descriptions of proselytes in the Second Tem-

---

11. Debate on the identify of Peter's "strangers" (or "aliens") has focused on Elliott's important work, *Home for the Homeless*, which argued that Peter's audience shared a marginal existence prior to their conversion, a viewpoint that falters on the evidence of 1:1 (which suggests that marginal status and divine election are conjoined [cf. Feldmeier, *Christen als Fremde*]) and evidence within the letter that their estrangement derives from their status as Christians (e.g., 4:14-16). Elliott's greatest contribution was to undermine any reading that failed to account for the day-to-day social circumstances of Peter's addressees. For criticism and alternatives, see, e.g., Feldmeier, *Christen als Fremde*; Bechtler, *Following in His Steps*, pp. 64-83; Seland, "πάροικος καὶ παρεπίδημος"; idem, *Strangers*, pp. 39-78; Chin, "Heavenly Home."

12. Nonmetaphorical — e.g., Elliott, *Home for the Homeless*; followed by McKnight, e.g., pp. 23-26. Metaphorical — e.g., Davids, pp. 46-47; Furnish, "Elect Sojourners"; T. Martin, *Metaphor and Composition*; Feldmeier, *Christen als Fremde*.

13. For this reading, see, e.g., *TLNT* 3:43.

14. Cf. Lakoff, "How the Body Shapes Thought"; idem, "How to Live with an Embodied Mind"; Lakoff and M. Johnson, *Metaphors*.

15. Fauconnier and Turner, *Way We Think*, especially pp. 39-57.

ple period),[16] for the formation of a new "blend" in the letter itself (so as to give the notion of "stranger" a surprisingly positive spin, even to the point of promising that "strangers" will share in God's own glory [1:7]), and for the universalizing of the theme to all Christians (as in the *Epistle to Diognetus*, quoted below).

For persons thus branded as "not at home," intimate with day-to-day cancerous slander and calamity, the temptations are several: to embrace the dispositions and practices conventional in the wider world (i.e., the threat of assimilation and defection) and to query one's status before God chief among them. (We do not easily correlate rejection within the human family with honorable status before God.) Crucial challenges therefore include negotiating and maintaining community boundaries, identity formation and coherence, and finding positive, redemptive meaning for diasporic life.[17] Peter will address the issue of boundaries and behavior in his repeated calls to holy and honorable living, but for now focuses on concerns with formation and meaning.

The terms "stranger" and "diaspora" are joined by a third, "chosen," in 1:1. This underscores Peter's indebtedness to the story of Israel (e.g., Deut 7:6; 14:2; Isa 41:8-9; 49:7), which highlights, on the one hand, God's gracious selection of his people and his faithfulness to them, exemplified prototypically in Exodus, and, on the other, the concomitant status allotted them as a consequence of divine election. Says the LORD, "You have seen what I did to the Egyptians, and how I bore you on eagles' wings and brought you to myself. Now therefore, if you obey my voice and keep my covenant, you shall be my treasured possession out of all the peoples. Indeed, the whole earth is mine, but you shall be for me a priestly kingdom and a holy nation" (Exod 19:4-6). In the background, too, we may hear reverberations of the story of Abraham, the prototypical "stranger" chosen by God. "Now the LORD said to Abram, 'Go from your country and your kindred and your father's house to the land that I will show you. I will make of you a great nation, and I will bless you, and make your name great, so that you will be a blessing" (Gen 12:1-2).[18] Accordingly, the concept of "stranger" is for Peter interwoven with motifs associated with election, such as call and vocation, covenant, and journey. To be God's people is to be "on the way" under his care and leadership.

The believer, then, is never really "at home," as the second-century *Epistle to Diognetus* puts it:

16. So Seland, "πάροικος καὶ παρεπίδημος"; idem, *Strangers*, pp. 39-78.

17. See Smith-Christopher, *Exile.*

18. For Abraham's status as "stranger" see Genesis 11; 12:10; 17:8; 20:1; 21:23, 34; 23:4. For his election, see Gen 18:19; *Apoc. Ab.* 20:6. See further, Schreiner, "Election," pp. 450-51.

For Christians are no different from other people in terms of their country, language or customs. Nowhere do they inhabit cities of their own, use a strange dialect, or live life out of the ordinary. . . . They live in their respective countries, but only as resident aliens; they participate in all things as citizens, and they endure all things as foreigners. Every foreign territory is a homeland for them, every homeland foreign territory. They marry like everyone else and have children, but they do not expose them once they are born. They share their meals but not their sexual partners. They are found in the flesh but do not live according to the flesh. They live on earth but participate in the life of heaven. They are obedient to the laws that have been made, and by their own lives they supersede the laws. They love everyone and are persecuted by all. They are not understood and they are condemned. They are put to death and made alive. They are impoverished and make many rich. They lack all things and abound in everything. They are dishonored and they are exalted in their dishonors. (5:1-14 [LCL])

In many ways, what makes 1 Peter difficult to read as Christian Scripture is this initial attempt on the part of Peter to identify his audience. First Peter is addressed to folks who do not belong, who eke out their lives on the periphery of acceptable society, whose deepest loyalties and inclinations do not line up very well with what matters most in the world in which they live. This is not the sort of life that most people find attractive. In terms of our ability genuinely to understand 1 Peter, all of the linguistic skills we might develop, all of the material on historical background we might accumulate — none of this will make up for the basic reality that, as a whole, we resist the possibility that this letter is addressed to us, that we might be cast as "nobodies in the world." The problem is theological. What separates us from 1 Peter is not "the strange world of the Bible" as much as its unhandy, inconvenient claims on our lives. Commenting on Peter's greeting, The Venerable Bede recognized that we who can truly say that we are but travelers on this earth are in a position to believe "that the Letters of blessed Peter were written to us as well and to read them as having been sent to us."[19] 1 Peter invites a reading among those who are ready to embrace the identity and status of exiles in the dispersion.

The three prepositional phrases of v. 2 modify Peter's identification of his audience as "chosen" and "strangers." Alien status does not contradict di-

---

19. Bede, pp. 69-70. Though he underestimates the degree to which 1 Peter counsels a posture of resistance in the wider world, van Rensburg ("Christians as Resident and Visiting Aliens") demonstrates the importance of the stranger motif for contemporary Christian faithfulness. See also Moy, "Resident Aliens."

vine election, but is the outgrowth (1) of God's purpose, (2) of the Spirit's sanctifying work, and (3) of the redemption of Christ (himself rejected among humans but chosen by God [e.g., 2:4]). These phrases are coordinated so as to make sense of the apparent oxymoron contained in the juxtaposition of these two categories: chosen by God, strangers in the world.

(1) The paradoxical status of the believers to whom Peter addresses himself is in accordance with the foreknowledge of God; in the same way, we will learn, Jesus was "chosen before the creation of the world" (1:20).[20] This refers less to notions of predetermination and more to the divine purpose as a basic hermeneutical principle that will pervade the letter as a whole. Divine choice and alien status are deeply rooted in God's purpose as this comes to expression in the Scriptures, so the dissonance of present life, chosen by God but held in contempt in society, is neither a surprise to God nor a contradiction of his plan. Peter will demonstrate that the way of Jesus Christ was the path of suffering and glory (e.g., 2:20; 4:13-14; 5:1, 10), that the model of Jesus Christ interprets and is interpreted by the Scriptures of Israel (cf. 1:10-12, 19 [Isa 52:13–53:12]; 2:4-10 [Ps 118:22; Isa 8:14]; 2:21-25 [Isa 52:13–53:12]; 4:1-2, 17), and that this pattern is characteristic of those who follow in his footsteps (e.g., 4:12-14; 5:10).

(2) In the second phrase, the Holy Spirit is identified as the agent of God's power, oriented toward the work of "making holy" — a motif of significance elsewhere in the letter (1:15, 16, 19, 22; 2:5, 9; 3:15). Typically, the preposition ἐν *(en)* in the phrase ἐν ἁγιασμῷ πνεύματος *(en hagiasmō pneumatos)* is read instrumentally, "by means of the sanctification of the Spirit," so that the emphasis falls narrowly on the activity of the Spirit. The interest here in alien-status in the diaspora, though, invites a different line of questioning: Where might believers find their "home"? In this case, "in" (ἐν) would refer to boundedness within a container, whether spatial or temporal, or a state or condition, drawing our attention to the fact that, just as the letter begins by locating its audience in the diaspora, so it ends with a climactic declaration of their true domicile. Their life is "in Christ" (5:10, 14) — a life defined throughout the letter in christological terms with particular reference to the redemptive and exemplary journey of Jesus through suffering to exaltation. Recalling Peter's concern to map the location of his audience, we might press for a reading of "in the sanctification of the Spirit" as a close semantic cousin of that other "place," "in Christ." To put it differently, "because of the obedience and sprinkling of blood of Jesus Christ," Peter's audience has been relo-

---

20. πρόγνωσις *(prognōsis,* "knowledge in advance") appears in 1 Peter only in 1:2; the verbal form, προγινώσκω *(proginōskō,* "know in advance"), appears only in 1:20.

cated in a new space: "in the realm of holiness engendered by the Holy Spirit"[21] — emphasizing the activity of the Spirit and its results in the lives of the chosen.

(3) The relationship of the second and third prepositional phrases is usually articulated as cause and effect: the sanctifying work of the Spirit is for the purpose of obedience and sprinkling of blood. This view founders on the question, What might it mean to say that sanctification results in "the sprinkling of the blood of Jesus Christ"? The usual response is to fracture the sentence, relating "obedience" to God's chosen people as subject but "blood-sprinkling" to Jesus Christ as subject. This reading is confused grammatically.[22] However, if we take εἰς (eis) as causal ("because of") rather than telic ("with the result that"), and Ἰησοῦ Χριστοῦ (Iesou Christou, "of Jesus Christ") as a subjective genitive, we achieve the translation, "because of the obedience and sprinkling of the blood of Jesus Christ."[23] Held together in tandem, then, are the totality of Jesus' life of faithfulness to God and the sacrificial quality of his death — both together treated as redemptive. Indeed, it is precisely because of Jesus' obedience that he could serve as the sacrifice, since, in the sacrificial system, an unblemished animal served as an analogy for the election of Israel set apart for life in relationship to and service of God (cf. 1:19; 2:22).[24] Within this system, sin and death are transferred to the sacrificial victim, its purity and life to those who receive the benefits of the sacrifice. Working within this economy, Peter declares that Jesus wipes away sin and its effects through his obedient life and death. This reading coheres with Peter's larger emphasis on the exemplary and redemptive faithfulness of Christ, demonstrates the interrelation of christology and pneumatology in Peter's theology, and accentuates the balance in these three phrases, which then focus

21. Thus, taking πνεύματος (pneumatos, "of the Spirit") as a genitive of production; for this construction, cf. Wallace, *Greek Grammar*, pp. 104-06. For the possibility of an identification of the Spirit as "the sphere within which" in this phrase, see also Furnish, "Elect Sojourners," p. 5.

22. Drawing on the background of the notion of "sprinkling of blood" in Exod 24:3-8, Achtemeier (p. 89) theorizes that Peter refers to "the sanctifying action of the Spirit to the end that they be the people of a new covenant, which like the covenant of Israel entails obedience and sacrifice, in this case the sacrifice of Christ," but this does not overcome the grammatical issue.

23. See the argument in Agnew, "1 Peter 1:2," adopted also by Elliott, p. 319. For causal εἰς, see Mantey, "Causal Use of *eis*"; idem, "On Causal *eis* Again"; Dana and Mantey, *Manual Grammar*, pp. 103-5 (R. Marcus ["On Causal *eis*" and "The Elusive Causal *eis*"] discounts Mantey's extra biblical references, but not this usage); BDF §207; MHT 3:266-67. Compare the Vulgate (*in obedientiam et aspersionem sanguinis Iesu Christi*) and Wycliffe ("bi obedience, and spryngyng of the blood of Jhesu Crist").

24. On the sprinkling of blood in the sacrificial cult see, e.g., Lev 5:9; 16:15.

on the activity of God, the Spirit, and Jesus Christ. That the Spirit's work here is for the purpose of the believer's obedience is widely held.[25] The interpretation adopted here does not vacate Peter's letter of this notion, but instead asserts from the very beginning the basis of the life of the chosen in the life of Christ.

1:3-12

3 Blessed be the God and Father of our Lord Jesus Christ, who in accordance with his great mercy has given us new birth into a living hope through the resurrection of Jesus Christ from the dead, 4 into an imperishable, uncorrupted, and unfading inheritance, reserved in heaven for you[26] 5 who are guarded by God's power through his faithfulness[27] for a salvation ready to be revealed at the last time. 6 In this you rejoice, even if now for a short time it is necessary that you are distressed by various trials, 7 in order that the testing of your faith (more precious than gold, which, though perishable, is tested by fire) may be found to result in praise and glory and honor at the revelation of Jesus Christ — 8 whom, though you have not seen, you love; in whom, though you do not now see, you have faith, and you rejoice with inexpressible and glorious joy 9 for you are receiving the goal of faith, your[28] salvation. 10 Concerning this salvation the prophets, who prophesied concerning the grace that has come to you, searched and explored, 11 inquiring into what person[29]

---

25. E.g., D. Peterson, *Possessed by God,* pp. 64-65.

26. Some mss. substitute "you" for "us" in v. 3 (1241 *pc*), or "us" for "you" in v. 4 (p[72vid] *pc* vg[ms]), presumably in order to achieve consistency of reference.

27. The phrase διὰ πίστεως *(dia pisteōs)* is usually taken as a reference to faith in God, a characteristic of Peter's audience which, then, serves as "the instrument whereby the divine protection becomes reality" (Achtemeier, p. 97). Arichea thinks the object of this faith is Jesus Christ ("God or Christ?" p. 414) — a view that finds no support in this context, oriented as it is around God — but he still assumes that the faith in question is that of Peter's audience. Horrell has raised the possibility that the subject of πίστεως *(pisteōs)* is God (i.e., πίστεως is a subjective genitive; see his "Whose Faith(fulness)"), a reading that is not only possible grammatically, but also meshes well with the otherwise heightened emphasis on God's faithfulness in 1:3-12.

28. The pronoun "your" is omitted by some witnesses (e.g., B), and "our" is read in others (1505 *pc* bo[ms] or[lat]). A similar problem with pronouns appears in vv. 3-4 and subsequently.

29. τίς *(tis)* could be read adjectively (thus, "which or what sort of time"). Michaels (pp. 41-43) argues that OT and Second Temple Jewish literature was more likely to query the time and circumstances of the anticipated salvation, but this does not account for the interest in *this* context of identifying Jesus as Messiah (1:1, 2, 3, 7); nor does it account for the hermeneutical problem introduced here — namely, where do we find in "the prophets" testimony to the "sufferings coming to Christ." In other words, it will not do simply to argue from OT and Jewish usage what we should expect of Peter here, since it is obvious that Peter is set on showing how to

or what sort of time was meant[30] when the Spirit of Christ which was in them was testifying in advance to the sufferings coming to Christ and his subsequent glories. 12 It was revealed to them that they were not serving themselves but you in these matters — matters that have now been announced to you through those who evangelized you through the Holy Spirit sent from heaven, matters on which angels yearn to gaze.

The introduction to the letter continues with what is in Greek a single sentence, running from 1:3 to 1:12 — rendering this whole section a declaration of and elaboration on God's mercy. Rhetorically, vv. 3-12 function for Peter's letter as the *exordium,* the purpose of which is to create a good atmosphere, preparing the audience to receive the instruction that will follow and introducing the main elements of the letter.[31] As doxology, 1:3-12 is less prayer and more proclamation, a celebration of God's gracious character and activity as the means by which to make sense of the paradoxical life of Peter's audience. As such, it situates the contemporary struggles of Peter's audience within the interpretive matrix of God's agenda, reminding them that their current situation is the result of their having been transformed in accordance with God's mercy, demonstrating that their lives are following the pattern of Jesus' career, and authenticating the movement from present suffering to future glory by anchoring it in Spirit-inspired prophetic witness. Multiple terms are used to identify the true situation of Peter's audience — "new birth," "living hope," "heavenly inheritance," and "salvation" (three times!) the most explicit among them — and these establish the basis of eschatological joy and continuing faithfulness. Although this section comprises a single complex sentence, it is easily divided into three units, each oriented toward salvation: vv. 3-5, introduced by the blessing formula and concluded with reference to "a salvation ready to be revealed at the last time"; vv. 6-9, introduced by the relative clause "in which," and concluded with reference to "your salvation"; and vv. 10-12, introduced by the phrase, "concerning this salvation."

Throughout, Peter maintains an unwavering focus on the situation of his addressees: their new birth, their distress, their trials, their testing, their

---

read "the prophets" christologically. Moreover, Kilpatrick has shown that, both in 1 Peter and in NT practice more generally, τίς *(tis)* is otherwise always a pronoun (3:13; 4:17; 5:8) ("1 Pet 1:11").

30. In what is probably an example of unintentional scribal error, several mss. (p⁷² ℵ A B* C etc.) support a reading that combines the imperfect active ἐδήλου *(edēlou)* with the following article τό *(to)* to form the imperfect middle ἐδηλοῦτο *(edēlouto).*

31. Tite, *Compositional Transitions,* p. 52; Thurén, *Argument and Theology,* pp. 90-91. 1:3-12 grounds the arguments to be developed throughout the letter; see Kendall, "Literary and Theological Function."

love, their faith, their joy, and the grace that had come to them. Obviously, however, a rehearsal of their current circumstances is incomplete without situating the present within the grand mural of God's character and activity. In v. 2, God's actions are consistent with his wisdom and intention ("according to the foreknowledge of God the Father"); to this Peter now adds an emphasis on God's "great mercy" as the source of his salvific activity. This declaration is seamless with the OT portrait of God's lovingkindness (חסד, *ḥsd*), which connotes spontaneous kindness and acts of generosity grounded in dispositions of compassion toward those in need, a characteristic of God which grounds divine-human relations in God's generous initiative and sustaining faithfulness culminating in the powerful, restorative activity of God on behalf of humanity. In the OT, the mercy of God is exhibited in his compassionate response to the cries of Israel, in his redemptive initiative in rescuing Israel from slavery, in their transformation by him into a people, in his choosing them from among the nations, and by his gift of Torah by which their relationship would be sustained.[32] Analogously for Peter, God's mercy is on display in his transformation of people by giving them new birth into a living hope.

The identification of God as "Father of our Lord Jesus Christ" is rare and appears in the NT only in doxological contexts (Rom 15:6; 2 Cor 1:3; Eph 1:3; Col 1:3; 1 Pet 1:3). However, this affirmation is deeply rooted in the gospel tradition, wherein both Jesus and God bear witness to Jesus' filial relationship with God (e.g., Matt 7:21; 10:32-33; Mark 1:9-11; 9:7; 14:36; Luke 2:49; 10:21-22). By means of this father-son predication, the god to whom Peter refers is identified as the God known to us in Jesus Christ, and Jesus is noted for his obedience to his Father as well as his capacity to represent God and to make known his beneficence. Indeed, to refer to Jesus as "Lord" in the Greco-Roman world of 1 Peter is to encourage thoughts of Jesus as (divine) benefactor and (royal) savior, as well as to invite an understanding of Jesus in terms reserved for Yahweh in the OT.[33] It is not too much to say that, with this claim regarding the lordship of Jesus Christ, Peter has put his finger on the problem confronting his readers: Naming Jesus Christ as Lord undercut the lordly claims of the

---

32. In the LXX, ἔλεος (*eleos*, "mercy") is the customary translation of חסד (*ḥsd*, "lovingkindness"). Mercy is intrinsic to Yahweh's character: note the self-revelation and repeated affirmation of Yahweh as "a God merciful and gracious" in Exod 34:6-7; Num 14:17-19; Deut 5:9-10; 7:9-13; Pss 77:9-10; 86:5, 15; 103:8-12, 17-18; 111:4; 116:5; 145:8-9; Joel 2:12-14; Jon 3:10-4:3; Neh 9:17-19, 31-32; 2 Chr 30:9. On חסד, see Andersen, "Yahweh, the Kind and Sensitive God"; Clark, *Word* Hesed.

33. See *TLNT* 2:341-50. Cf. Furnish, "Elect Sojourners," p. 7: ". . . decisively in him have God's ways and purposes been revealed to the elect."

emperor and the imperial cult, tore followers of Christ away from the idol worship that pervaded everyday life in the world of Rome, and thus distinguished believers as aliens in their own communities. Although undeniable, the exalted status of Jesus Christ in 1 Peter should not be overemphasized, since whatever Peter says concerning Jesus is cast within the more expansive framework of the supremacy of God the Father.[34]

Jesus' sonship is here lumped together with the parental status of God in relation to believers. Rather than referring to his audience as "children of God" (as in Paul — e.g., Rom 8:14-21; or John — e.g., John 1:12-13), Peter announces that God has caused them to be born anew (on which see further, below). To speak of God as "Father" directs attention to God's faithfulness to his promises and to the beneficence of God available in Jesus — or, more particularly, "through the resurrection of Jesus Christ." Hence, although both Jesus and believers find their identity in relationship to God, they do so in different ways. Whereas Jesus' relationship to God is immediate, the fatherhood of God in relation to believers is mediated through Jesus Christ.[35] The present context has it that the faithfulness of God the Father is evident in the past, in God's raising Jesus from the dead; is on display in the present through his guarding believers for salvation and the evangelistic offer of grace; and can be trusted with regard to the future, with respect to the salvation that will be revealed at "the last time."

Complementing this portrait of God's faithfulness is the way Peter identifies God as the primary actor throughout this section. He has given new birth, raised Jesus from the dead, reserved an inheritance, guarded his people, and sent the Holy Spirit. Conspicuous, too, is the christocentrism of Peter's doxology. Christ appears in each of its three subunits (vv. 3, 7-8, 11), with particular focus on the pattern of Christ's life, from suffering to glory. Additionally, the Holy Spirit is identified as "the Spirit of Christ" (v. 11), an expression that could refer either to "the Spirit testifying concerning the Messiah" or to "the preexistent spirit of Christ." Since it is otherwise clear that Peter assumes the preexistence of Christ (1:20), the latter is the more likely reading.[36]

---

34. Selwyn, pp. 75-78; Hurtado, "Christology," pp. 173-74.

35. Although Thompson *(Promise of the Father)* does not work with 1 Peter, her observations are nonetheless apropos Peter's presentation. See the discussion in Lategan, "Social Transformation," pp. 108-9.

36. So, e.g., Achtemeier, pp. 109-10; idem, "Christology," pp. 145-47. Michaels ("Catholic Christologies," pp. 275-76) observes other instances in 1 Peter where God the Father and Jesus Christ are interchangeable (e.g., 5:19-11 with reference to eternal power and glory). Against this conclusion, Dunn (*Christology,* pp. 159-60; "Jesus — Flesh and Spirit," p. 152) draws attention to the ambiguity of Peter's language: (1) Even if πνεῦμα Χριστοῦ *(pneuma Christou)* is a

In other words, Peter speaks of Jesus Christ as the one whose activity was manifest long ago through the Holy Spirit, and this means that Peter speaks of Jesus at the very point at which we might have anticipated that he would speak of God (cf. 4:14). Peter thus characterizes Jesus Christ as sharing in the very identity of God,[37] so that the trinitarian language of 1:2 receives further elaboration in 1:3-12.

If Peter's purpose in 1:3-12 centers on understanding theologically the present experience of his audience ("distressed by various trials"), then how Peter portrays God is primary. Contained within his portrait of God, and as an outgrowth of God's mercy, is Peter's emphasis on "new birth." Hence, it is important that we trace the multiple, interrelated ways he develops this new reality: (1) "new birth" as a conversion of the imagination, (2) the temporal boundedness and eschatological alignment of "new birth," and (3) the

---

subjective genitive ("Christ's Spirit"), the identification of the Spirit with Jesus is to be traced to his resurrection. The prophets of whom Peter writes are Christian prophets, and so "the Spirit of Christ" would serve as a post-Easter reference — a reading that would take the forecasted "suffering" as a reference to those who follow Christ (Selwyn, p. 136: "the sufferings of the Christward road"; cf. Warden, "Prophets"). (2) If, on the other hand, πνεῦμα Χριστοῦ *(pneuma Christou)* is an objective genitive ("Spirit prophesying about Christ"), then the Spirit is not identified with Christ. However, both the parallel of οἱ περὶ τῆς εἰς ὑμᾶς χάριτος προφητεύσαντες *(hoi peri tēs eis hymas charitos prophēteusantes,* "who prophesied concerning the grace that has come to you," v. 10) with τὸ . . . προμαρτυρόμενον τὰ εἰς Χριστὸν παθήματα *(to . . . promartyromenon ta eis Christon pathēmata,* "testifying in advance to the sufferings coming to Christ, v. 11), and the parallel use of πάθημα *(pathēma,* "sufferings") in 4:13; 5:1 intimate that the sufferings of Jesus Christ are in view here. This, then, undermines any possibility of seeing Christian prophets in 1:11, since they would not have been able to testify to the sufferings coming to Christ in advance of his passion (see further, Jobes, pp. 98-101). Whether πνεῦμα Χριστοῦ *(pneuma Christou)* is an objective or subjective genitive (or epexegetical: "the Spirit that was Christ") is debatable, of course, but we should not allow Pauline usage to predetermine Petrine (contra Dunn), and, as Elliott has observed, the two ideas are not necessarily competitive: "The Messiah whose spirit spoke through the prophets earlier has now been revealed as Jesus, the Messiah/Christ (1:19-20) who himself was 'foreknown before the foundation of the world' (1:20)" (p. 346).

37. It is not enough to refer to Peter's christology as "functional," then (contra Richard, "Functional Christology"). Bauckham *(God Crucified;* cf. Thompson, *God,* pp. 17-55) has rightly complained that discussion about NT christology has been handicapped by its presumption of the categories "ontological" versus "functional." Where Bauckham is less helpful is in his apparent lack of awareness of long-standing controversy around what constitutes "identity" (e.g., R. Martin and Barresi, "Personal Identity"; Rorty, ed., *Identities;* K. Berger, *Identity;* Bynum, *Metamorphosis);* the move from notions of "what I do" or "what I am" to "who I am" is surprisingly complex. I am using "identity" in the sense of continuity in terms of a network of relationships and narrative of interactions, together with an emphasis on functionality that refuses any dichotomy between performance and sentiment (or character).

christological basis of "new birth," which locates the new birth within God's ancient purpose.

(1) *"New birth" as conversion of the imagination:* Granted that the phrase "conversion of the imagination" is alien to 1 Peter, it is nonetheless helpful shorthand for grasping Peter's basic emphasis. By "imagination," I mean "a basic image-schematic capacity for ordering our experience,"[38] a life-world employing patterns of thought that are at once *conceptual* (a way of seeing things), *conative* (a set of beliefs and values to which a group and its members are deeply attached), and *action-guiding* (we live according to its terms).[39] The issue is this: life-events do not come with self-contained and immediately obvious interpretations; rather, we conceptualize them in terms of imaginative structures that we take to be true, normal, and good. As a rule, the world-at-large casts a thick, dark cloud of despair over experiences of suffering, distress, trials, and alien status. Peter insists that such experiences on the part of his audience must be read according to a radically different pattern of thought — one that grows out of new birth. "New birth," then, is a dramatic metaphor for the decisive transformation of life that has come in accordance with God's mercy and by means of the resurrection of Jesus. What Peter announces, then, is a conversion of the imagination: personal reconstruction within a new web of relationships, resocialization within the new community, and the embodiment of a new life-world evidenced in altered dispositions and attitudes.[40]

The metaphor of new birth (see 1:3; 2:2-3) is related to others found in the biblical and extrabiblical tradition — for example, new creation (Isa 65:17; 2 Cor 5:15), being born anew or from above (John 3:3, 7), adoption (Rom 8:14-17), rebirth and renewal (Tit 3:5), and portrayal of entry into the community of the faithful as resurrection (1QH 3:19-23) — and is reflected in subsequent rabbinic discourse concerning proselytes: "One who has become a proselyte is like a child newly born" (*b. Yebamoth* 22b).[41] For Peter, "new birth" has three results (indicated by three clauses, each beginning with εἰς [*eis,* "into" or "for"]): "a living hope," "an inheritance," and "salvation" (vv. 3-5). The notion of "inheritance" borrows from and builds on the divine promise of the land to Abraham and his lineage, to Israel (Gen 12:7; Num 26:53-56; Deut 26:1; Acts 13:19), a commitment grounded in Yahweh's ultimate claim to ownership of the land. However, unlike the land promised to Israel, occupied by the people

---

38. M. Johnson, *Body in the Mind,* p. xx; cf. Bryant, *Faith and the Play of Imagination,* p. 5.

39. I have borrowed this formulation from Flanagan, *Problem of the Soul,* pp. 27-55.

40. On this model of conversion, see Meeks, *Christian Morality,* pp. 18-36; Snow and Machalek, "Convert"; N. H. Taylor, "Social Nature of Conversion."

41. See Goppelt, pp. 81-83.

but now lost to the nation, this inheritance is "imperishable, uncorrupted, and unfading." Moreover, the identity of the community of God's people will no longer be tied to a geophysical location; neither will their hope be oriented toward restoration of the land. Like "new birth," this metaphorical use of "inheritance" enjoyed wider usage, as in the transcendent reality identified as redemption (Eph 1:14) or salvation (Heb 1:14).

We should not be fooled into thinking that Peter's message is unconcerned with present realities simply because its focus seems so fully transcendent and future. Such a misconception is aided by those translations that refer to "the salvation of your souls" in v. 9 (e.g., NASB, NIV, NLT), however unintentionally belittling embodied life in the present by allowing the notion that Christian hope resides in a future life with God in a disembodied heaven. To the contrary, ψυχή (*psychē*, "life" or "vitality," sometimes translated as "soul") is, in the biblical tradition, what one *is* rather than what one *has*; accordingly, Peter's reference would be to the salvation of persons (and not parts of persons).[42]

Although various forms of body-soul dualism were available in the world of 1 Peter, the often-repeated view that Greek thought was dualistic is an unfortunate hyperbole that fails to account for the diversity within the Hellenistic world;[43] and, in any case, the monism of the Scriptures of Israel would have presented a significant countervoice to dualism.[44] In 1 Peter, ψυχή (*psychē*, "life," "vitality") appears in 1:9, 22; 2:11, 25; 3:20; 4:19 — in contrast to σαρκικός (*sarkikos*, "belonging to this world") in 2:11, but never in relation to σάρξ (*sarx*, "flesh, physical body, etc."); σάρξ is juxtaposed with πνεῦμα [*pneuma*, "spirit"] in 3:18; 4:6). Christ is the guardian of your ψυχαί ("lives," 2:25), just as God is guarding "you" for a salvation ready to be revealed at the last time (1:5), and those who suffer entrust their ψυχαί ("lives") to God (4:19). In 3:20, ψυχή obviously refers to "persons." Generally for Peter, however, σάρξ concerns "life as it reflects and/or pertains to this world" (1:24; 3:18, 21; 4:1, 2, 6) and ψυχή connotes "life as it reflects and/or pertains to the world to come." The dualism with which Peter operates, then, is eschatological and not anthropological.[45]

---

42. See, e.g., Dautzenberg, "Σωτηρία ψυχῶν"; Davids, p. 60. More generally, Stone, "Soul"; J. B. Green, "Restoring the Human Person"; and for lexicography, Seebass, "נפשׁ" (especially the excursus on "The Translation 'Soul'" [pp. 508-10]).

43. See J. P. Wright and Potter, eds., *Psyche and Soma;* and the summary in D. B. Martin, *Corinthian Body*, pp. 3-37.

44. See Warne, *Hebrew Perspectives.*

45. For a different assessment, see Feldmeier, "Seelenheil."

In language reminiscent of Jesus' counsel to his disciples in the face of martyrdom (Mark 8:35), Peter speaks of human life as it is directed toward and guarded by God. Moreover, Peter's language contains no hint of salvation as escape from or abandonment of this life, but focuses instead on God's future promises.[46] For Peter, then, the character of the future casts its shadow backward, impinging resolutely on the present. Knowing God's future changes everything, for it alienates those who share this hope from those who do not; it generates conflict around what has ultimate value; and it provides the foundation for appropriate response in the present: continued faithfulness (v. 9) and, especially, joy (vv. 6, 8).[47]

In large measure, this is the importance of Peter's drawing out the saving significance of the resurrection of Jesus Christ, for, in the later OT and contemporary Jewish literature, "resurrection" referred above all to the divine inauguration of a new world order. Three interrelated motifs help to structure our understanding: (A) Resurrection signals the restoration of Israel. (B) Resurrection marks God's vindication of the righteous who have suffered unjustly; having been condemned and made to suffer among humans, the righteous will in the resurrection be vindicated before God. (C) Resurrection marks the decisive establishment of divine justice; injustice and wickedness will not have the final word, but in the resurrection will be decisively repudiated.[48] To proclaim the resurrection, then, is already to proclaim a new world, and to call for a "conversion of the imagination."

(2) The temporal boundedness and eschatological alignment of "new birth": Peter's introductory blessing is littered with time-oriented terms: "time" (καιρός, *kairos*, vv. 5, 11), "in the last time" (ἐν καιρῷ ἐσχάτῳ, *en kairō eschatō*," v. 5), "for a short time" (ὀλίγον ἄρτι, *oligon arti*, v. 6), "at the present time" (ἄρτι, *arti*, v. 8), and "now" (νῦν, *nyn*, v. 12). On the basis of these and other, less explicit chronological markers (e.g., προμαρτύρομαι, *promarturomai*, "to testify in advance," v. 11), a timeline or plotline is easily constructed. With this, Peter declares that the present is the time of both distress and trials on the one hand, evangelism and grace on the other, and, significantly, that the present time of marginal status in the world is constrained temporally. As the Venerable Bede observed with respect to v. 6, "He says, *for*

---

46. See N. T. Wright, *Resurrection*, pp. 456-66.

47. See Kendall, "1 Pet 1:3-9." In spite of T. Martin's arguments favoring a reading of ἀγαλλιᾶσθε (*agalliasthe*, "rejoice") as a present indicative with future meaning ("1 Pet 1:6, 8"), Peter is counseling eschatological joy in the face of present distress (see 4:12-13; compare Hab 3:18; Matt 5:11-12; cf. Dautzenberg, "Σωτηρία ψυχῶν," pp. 270-71).

48. Cf., e.g., Hos 6:1-3; Ezek 37:1-14; Isa 26:19; Dan 12:1-3; K. L. Anderson, "Resurrection," pp. 47-90; N. T. Wright, *Resurrection*, pp. 85-206.

a little while, . . . because when the eternal reward is given, everything that appeared hard and harsh in the midst of the tribulations of the world will appear brief and light."[49]

Peter's opening blessing thus couches the whole of the letter in a particular understanding of "the times." In *the past,* God gave Peter's audience new birth — that is, a reconfigured relationship to himself as their Father and a transformation of life-world that refocused their lives around a future inheritance. *The future,* when Jesus Christ is revealed, signals the cessation of "various trials" and marks the time when God will reveal salvation, will reveal Jesus Christ in final glory, and will give believers their inheritance. Not long from now, Peter advises, his audience will share in the praise, glory, and honor that would otherwise be reserved for God alone (cf. 5:1, 4). That is, at the last time, they will be vindicated. Between past and future, *the present* is known for its onerous trials. At the same time, God's power is *presently* guarding those under duress who, in spite of appearances, are "receiving the goal of faith": salvation. Thus, although the metaphor of "new birth" is for Peter set within the framework of life as strangers in this world, it nonetheless makes personal and brings forward into the present God's end-time salvation.[50]

Additionally, the past was marked by prophets who queried the identity of the person and character of the time intended by the Spirit in their testimony to the suffering and glories of the Messiah. There is no longer any need for such puzzling, however, since, as Peter bears witness, the person of the Messiah is none other than Jesus, and the previously enigmatic time is none other than that which takes its character from his career, with suffering giving way to glories. "Glories" (plural) is rare in this context,[51] but apparently refers to the series of events that mark Jesus' vindication and participation in the glory of God: resurrection (1:3), ascension/enthronement (3:22), and final revelation (1:7). On account of Jesus' death and resurrection, the present (νῦν, *nyn,* v. 12) is also marked as the time of "grace" and announcement of good news. In this context, "grace" refers to the substance of salvation, with an emphasis on that element of salvation already present.[52] In light of a future readied and reserved by God, believers embrace the grace they have received and are thus enabled to nurture hope for an inheritance that is future, as well as love for and faith in Jesus Christ who is presently hidden.

---

49. Bede, p. 73. More fully, see the discussion of "temporal liminality" in Bechtler, *Following in His Steps,* pp. 127-35.

50. See Feldmeier, "Wiedergeburt."

51. The plural of δόξα (*doxa,* "glory") is used substantively of heavenly beings in Jude 8; 2 Pet 2:10. For the present sense, the singular is expected (e.g., Luke 24:26; 1 Pet 4:13).

52. Cf. 2:19; 4:10; K. Berger, "χάρις," pp. 459-60.

Present trials, we should understand, are not in spite of but are the consequence of the new birth. The imagery of "new birth" implies a new life-world, but, to continue the metaphor, it also introduces the need for growth and maturation, for growing into salvation (cf. 1:14-16, 22-23; 2:2-3). Peter's use of the term "trial" (πειρασμός, *peirasmos*, v. 6), which can refer to diabolic temptation just as easily as divine test, introduces this paradox: With the potential for both glory and tragedy, the very process that can develop and deepen human life (testing) is the one that can stunt and corrupt human life (temptation).[53] Knowing "what time it is" and orienting oneself appropriately to God's future are pivotal for responding faithfully in the context of testing.

(3) The christological basis of "new birth": "New birth" is thoroughly christocentric in character. First, "new birth" is the consequence of the resurrection of Jesus Christ. Second, the new life into which one is born has as its paramount exemplar the life of Christ. If the suffering of Jesus did not disqualify his status as God's Son and as Lord, then neither does the misery of life as strangers in the world render Peter's audience as ineligible for their status as God's children. Rather, affliction, paradoxically, brands them as faithful followers of the Christ who suffered, and, if this is true, then they can be assured that, just as they share in his suffering, so they will share in his glory.

Peter's christological claims are grounded in a theological hermeneutic — that is, a mode of understanding that takes seriously how theological commitments shape or order our reading of Scripture. In this case, the suffering-and-vindicated Christ and the Scriptures of Israel are mutually informing, with Peter providing a case study in how the Scriptures must be read: (1) as "testifying in advance to the sufferings coming to Christ and his subsequent glories" and (2) in continuity with the faith communities comprising Peter's audience, a continuity made possible by the Holy Spirit.[54] Which prophetic words does Peter have in view? We are not told, nor can we find among the

---

53. Moberly, *Bible, Theology, and Faith*, p. 240. See Gaventa, *From Darkness to Light*, pp. 142-43.

54. Schutter rightly identifies vv. 10-12 as "a hermeneutical key" (*Hermeneutic and Composition*, pp. 100-109), but unnecessarily complicates the discussion by centering his interest on Peter's alleged "*pesher*-like exegesis." Swete anticipated much of the discussion on the use of Scriptures of Israel by NT authors when he wrote, "This context is the *locus classicus* for the New Testament doctrine of Messianic Prophecy" (*Holy Spirit*, p. 261). Thus, emphasis would fall on proof of Jesus' messiahship grounded in scriptural prophecy (classically, Lindars, *NT Apologetic*). However, Peter is not working to prove Jesus' messiahship (which he and apparently his audience take for granted [1:1, 2, 3, 7, etc.]) but to show how to read the Scriptures ecclesiologically — that is, so as to legitimize, form, and direct the life of God's people.

prophets plain and direct precedent for messianic suffering. Later, Peter will demonstrate how to read Isa 52:13–53:12, which concerns the suffering Servant of Yahweh, in messianic terms (cf. 2:21-25), but this is not the direction he takes here. Instead, what Peter provides is a theological pattern by which to order the prophetic witness.

This does not mean that the words of the prophets were devoid of revelatory value before Christ; after all, God made known to them that their words were forward-looking (v. 12). It does mean, though, that their words lacked the clarity provided them when set alongside the career of Christ. Even more so, it means that Peter finds an essential unity in the outworking of God's purpose, from the Scriptures of Israel to the community of Christ's followers — a unity that coheres in the one God, Yahweh, who raised Jesus from the dead; and in the Holy Spirit, who inspired the prophets of old and the evangelists who proclaim the message of the prophets as good news.[55]

Recalling our earlier emphasis on imaginative structures, we see here the importance of recognizing and embracing the fabula (or story behind the story) of rejection leading to vindication, suffering to glory.[56] Peter thus provides a particular way of articulating the beginning, middle, and end of the biblical story. The story of salvation finds its locus here: the prophets, who prophesied in advance, testified to the sufferings destined for Christ and the subsequent glory. How do we know this is the "true" story? How do we know that this reading of the story is true? They prophesied through the Spirit, and the gospel message, which embodies this story, was brought by means of the Spirit. In short, Peter presents the Holy Spirit in a way congruent with the work of God's Spirit otherwise in the literature of Second Temple Judaism as the enabler and guarantor of authentic exegesis of Israel's story, Israel's Scriptures.[57]

This exegesis functions, first, to tie the exemplary and salvific life of Jesus Christ into the ancient purposes of God found in Scripture,[58] and, then,

---

55. The importance of Peter's witness on this matter is suggested by the contemporary debate regarding the nature of the OT's discrete voice as God's word (cf., e.g., Watson, *Text and Truth;* Seitz, *Word without End;* and the exchange between the two in Seitz, "Christological Interpretation"; and Watson, "OT as Christian Scripture").

56. The importance of the suffering-glory pattern for 1 Peter is widely recognized — e.g., Richard, "Functional Christology," pp. 130-39 ("For our author, Jesus is the image of suffering and glory" [p. 133]); Schutter, *Hermeneutic and Composition* (e.g., p. 123, speaking of the "'suffering'/'glories' schema"); Pearson, *Christological and Rhetorical Properties.*

57. E.g., in Josephus and Philo, at Qumran, and in Sirach; see Levison, "Holy Spirit," pp. 512-13; idem, *Spirit,* pp. 254-59. More generally, see J. B. Green, "Faithful Witness in the Diaspora."

58. The work of the prophets — "searching and exploring" (v. 10), "inquiring" (v. 11) — parallels that of seeking out the Lord and his decrees in Ps 119:2 (118:2 LXX).

to tie the lives of these "strangers" into the life of Jesus Christ. Inexorably linked in the consequent passion theology are the sufferings of Christ and his followers, who are thereby assured that their suffering will have a redemptive effect and will lead to glory and honor from God just as Jesus' suffering did.[59] This is the interpretation of things inspired by the Spirit.

We should not imagine that Peter is unique in the way he engages in the theological task here. Scholars have traced numerous points of contact between the form, language, and theology of Peter's letter and that of other Christian figures. The word-linkage in 1:6-7 (an example of *gradatio*) that crescendos from suffering to "praise and glory and honor when Jesus Christ is revealed" is reminiscent of Rom 5:3-5; Jas 1:2-3. An analogous emphasis on faith in the absence of what can be seen is found in John 20:29; 2 Cor 5:7; Heb 11:27, just as other NT writers bear witness to the unfulfilled longing of OT prophets (e.g., Matt 13:17; Luke 10:24). We can find parallels for joy in the midst of suffering (e.g., Luke 6:22-23) and for the imagery of new birth (e.g., John 3:3, 7), as well as analogues of Peter's emphasis on eschatological transformation (e.g., 1 Cor 15:52-54) and his theological hermeneutic (e.g., Luke 24:25-27). Many other examples might be given, the effect of which need not be to urge that Peter is lacking in theological creativity nor that he was literarily dependent on other NT texts.[60] Instead, we might learn from Peter an important lesson regarding the theological task. Theological work in the midst of the challenges of living as strangers in the world is not well-served by driving wedges between and among Christian communities or traditions; more appropriate is the work of reflecting on and articulating what is common ground within the church. Challenges to the church from the outside provide the occasion for solidifying the church's internal identity, tracing its roots in the ancient purpose of God, drawing out the continuity from Israel of old to the contemporary life of God's people, and remembering that the primary orientation of faithful life is toward the God and Father of our Lord Jesus Christ. Hence, Peter's rhetoric and message are inscribed deeply into the saga of Israel and participate fully in the emerging Christian consensus as he explores the significance of the great mural of Israel's story, interpreted now through the pivotal events of Jesus' passion and resurrection, and emphasizes the common ground of the faithful as they look for places to secure their feet in the struggle for faithful witness.

59. See Brox, p. 63; Campbell, *Honor*, pp. 55-56.

60. Historically, examination of the points of contact between Peter and other NT writers has been motivated by an interest in demonstrating or refuting literary dependence, sometimes in the service of discussion of the authorship of 1 Peter; cf., e.g., Best, "1 Peter and the Gospel Tradition"; Selwyn, pp. 365-466; Herzer, *Petrus oder Paulus*; Metzner, *Rezeption*.

Although Peter's blessing is a lengthy celebration of God's faithfulness and goodness, the situation of his audience occupies center stage throughout. Engaging one obstacle after the other, he dispenses with what might otherwise be regarded as impediments to their realizing their hope. God is faithful and will remember his promises. Their inheritance will never perish or corrode or fade. Their testing is nothing but a means of maturation and identification with Christ and so produces faithfulness. The prophecies were not mistaken, but are assured by the Holy Spirit. In the end, new birth grounds the assurance that duress and trials do not keep the believer from God's power and glory. In fact, the status that Peter's audience enjoys accords unsurpassed privilege to them: as God's children they are the beneficiaries of things the ancient prophets never understood and angels long to see. Their lot is neither despair in the face of suffering nor passive waiting for the end. As salvation is the goal of faith, so the present provides the arena for active faithfulness for those straining toward God's future.

1:13–2:10

From the indicative mood ("is") that characterized 1:3-12, Peter moves to the imperative ("ought"), a change marked by the opening conjunctive "therefore" (διό, *dio*). Peter's "blessing," with its celebration of God's mercy and careful identification of Peter's audience within the overarching plan of God, thus functions as the warrant for these words of exhortation. The section as a whole has as its boundaries a dual emphasis on "call" or "election" (1:15; 2:9-10; cf. 1:20; 2:4, 6) and holiness (1:15-16; 2:9; cf. 2:5): having been called by God, Peter's audience must now live into their call to be God's people, holy in every aspect of life. The introduction of the next unit of the letter is signaled by the use of direct address (that is, the vocative case) in 2:11: "beloved" (ἀγαπητοί, *agapētoi*).

In his biblical theology of exile, Smith-Christopher observes that "a stronger sense of 'community identity' arises under circumstances of minority, stateless existence."[1] Given Peter's description of his audience as people "dwelling in a strange land" (1:17), we are not surprised that Peter works to form a community consciousness at home in the Jewish diaspora. This requires attention to two distinct but related boundary measures: an emphasis on solidarity and a concern with distinguishing characteristics.

First, throughout this unit, members of Peter's audience are epitomized

---

1. Smith-Christopher, *Exile,* p. 141.

with familial language and terms of endearment: "children" (1:14), "brotherly love" (1:22), "born anew" (1:23), "parentage" (or "seed," 1:23), "newborn babies" (2:2), "to mature as children" (2:2), and "house/household" (2:5). The relational language used of God, "Father" (1:17), is further evidence of this motif. Other appellatives Peter uses for his audience include "holy/royal priesthood" (2:5, 9), "holy nation" (2:9), and "God's (own) people" (2:9, 10). These descriptors establish, assert, and uphold a strong semantics of solidarity, belonging, and election within the communities of the letter's destination.[2]

Second, as exilic identity is a matter of disciplined life oriented toward survival as a distinct people, so, in the present, members of Peter's audience are to embody the call to Israel in Exodus and Exile to be holy. Indeed, the nature of familial relations emphasized by Peter gives rise to expectations regarding conduct becoming this family whose Father is God. As obedient children, a priestly people, a holy nation, they were to embrace the ecclesial and missional vocation to be "holy" (that is, "different," or "distinctive") in the world (1:15-16; 2:5, 9). Dispositions and behaviors grounded in the identity of God's people are encouraged (1:13, 14, 17, etc.), while dispositions and behaviors characteristic of their former lives are negated (1:14, 18). Interestingly, Peter does not engage in invective rhetoric with respect to the ways of life of his audience's contemporaries. Holiness is not measured in units of negation of whatever characterizes "the world," but (negatively) in differentiation from one's former ways and (positively) in imitation of God. Either way, Peter's audience is marked as "different." This is important for two reasons — because in the household of the Roman Empire, status was achieved via conformity to conventional habits of life, so "being different" was evaluated negatively as deviance, and because persons liberated by the precious blood of Christ orient their lives toward the God who is different. Living at the confluence of these two realities, Christian existence can only be characterized as "dwelling in a strange land" (1:17). Though chosen and precious in God's valuation, such persons are nonetheless rejected by those outside the faith (2:4, 7-8).

1:13-21

13 Therefore, having readied your mind for action, practicing vigilance, you must set your hope completely on the grace coming to you at the revelation of Jesus Christ. 14 As obedient children, no longer being shaped by the desires that marked your former time of ignorance, 15 you yourselves must rather become holy in every

2. Cf. Fasold, *Sociolinguistics*, pp. 1-38.

aspect of life, just as the one who called you is holy, 16 for it is written, "You shall be holy, because I am holy." 17 Since you call upon a Father who judges impartially, each according to his or her performance, you must live with reverent fear during the time of your dwelling in a strange land, 18 knowing that you were liberated from the emptiness of your inherited way of life — not by such perishable things as gold or silver, 19 but by the precious blood of Christ, like that of a lamb without blemish or defect, 20 who was chosen before the creation of the world, yet revealed at the end of the ages because of you 21 who through him are faithful[3] to God, who raised him from the dead and gave him glory so that your faith and hope are in God.

With v. 13, Peter moves from describing the new perspective held by those who have been reborn to an exhortation centered on a new way of life.[4] This new perspective, summed up in the phrase "living hope" (v. 3), serves as both presupposition and persistent mindset for Peter's audience. This is indicated by the two participles that modify the main verb "to set your hope" in v. 13: "having readied your mind for action" (aorist, indicating action before the main verb) and "practicing vigilance" (present, indicating action contemporaneous with the main verb). With the patterns of thought counseled in vv. 3-12 thereby assumed, faithful life is cast within eschatological horizons calling for ongoing diligence or vigilance.[5] The opening of v. 14, "as (ὡς, *hōs*) children," also evidences the perspective from which the world is viewed or action taken[6] — in this case, from the perspective of those who have been given new birth (v. 3). The section as a whole, vv. 13-21, begins and ends with reference to "hope" (vv. 13, 21) and is centrally focused on "behavior, conduct, or way of life" (vv. 15, 17, 18). The accent on hope is carried over from the previous section (v. 3), but the emphasis on "way of life" is introduced for the first time, signaling early in the letter a pronounced interest in the nature of faithful life and ethical comportment in the world.[7] Clearly, Peter anticipates that hope will be displayed in changed life.

---

3. πιστεύοντας (*pisteuontas*) is read by p⁷² ℵ C P Ψ 1739 𝔐, πιστεύσαντας (*pisteusantas*) by 33 *pc*, and πιστούς (*pistous*, adopted by NA²⁷) by A B *pv* vg. Although the participle is thus well-attested, the adjective has good support and is the more difficult reading.

4. See Feldmeier, *Christen als Fremden*, pp. 138-42.

5. See 4:7: "The end of all things has come, so keep a disciplined mind and exercise vigilance" (σωφρονήσατε οὖν καὶ νήψατε, *sōphronēsate oun kai nēpsate*); 5:8: "Remain vigilant! Stay alert"! (νήψατε, γρηγορήσατε, *nēpsate, grēgorēsate*).

6. BDAG 1104-5.

7. On the importance of ἀναστροφή (*anastrophē*) and its semantic cousin ἀγαθοποιΐα (*agathopoiia*) in 1 Peter, see Elliott, *Elect and the Holy*, pp. 179-83.

This section can be further divided into three subsections, each related to one of three active verbs: on account of the mercy of God (vv. 3-12), believers are urged *to set their hope* completely on the coming grace (v. 13); on account of the holiness of God, believers are *to become holy in every aspect of life*, setting aside their former cravings (vv. 14-16); and, on account of the Father's impartial justice and the liberation effected by Christ's sacrificial death, believers are *to live in reverent fear* (vv. 17-21).[8] The whole is set up by Peter's celebration of God's mercy and faithfulness in vv. 3-12, however. This is clear from the first word, διό *(dio)*, an inferential conjunctive that identifies a causal chain from God's faithfulness to new birth, and from new birth to a new way of living. The present section is further related to the letter's opening blessing by its recollection of such important motifs as hope (vv. 3, 13, 21), revelation (vv. 5, 7, 13, 20), grace (vv. 10, 13), the resurrection and glory of Jesus (vv. 3, 11, 21), and the related metaphors of the Fatherhood of God, the new birth, and status as children (vv. 3, 14, 17). Given the degree of thematic coherence between these two sections, vv. 3-12 and vv. 13-21, the emphatic appearance of Peter's concern with conduct is all the more striking.

Peter's instruction is set within and determined by a temporal map that permeates these verses.[9] Events (or conditions) that figure centrally in the scheme by which Peter orders the lives of his audience can be arranged on a timeline as follows:

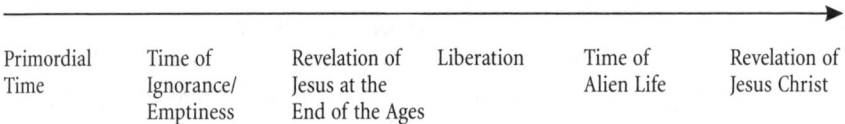

Primordial Time	Time of Ignorance/ Emptiness	Revelation of Jesus at the End of the Ages	Liberation	Time of Alien Life	Revelation of Jesus Christ

(1) Primordial Time (1:20): Perhaps using a traditional christological formulation,[10] Peter inscribes the sacrificial death of Jesus into the timeless plan of God. In doing so, then, Peter underscores and expands on what is al-

---

8. Many translations transform Peter's participles into imperatives. Without discounting the possibility of the imperatival participle, whether in 1 Peter or elsewhere, Snyder calls into question its alleged pervasiveness in this letter and offers criteria for discerning its presence ("Participles and Imperatives"). I am largely following his analysis.

9. A version of what follows has appeared in J. B. Green, "Narrating the Gospel."

10. Note, e.g., the use of εἰδότες + ὅτι (*eidotes* + *hoti*, "knowing" + "that") in v. 18 and the carefully balanced couplet and the μέν . . . δέ (*men . . . de*, "on the one hand . . . on the other") clause in v. 20, among recent scholars, cf. Strecker, *Theology,* pp. 628-30; Chester and Martin, *Theology,* pp. 108-9. Bultmann suggested a reconstruction of the original "hymn," relocating v. 20 in relation to v. 18 ("Bekenntnis- und Liedfragmente," pp. 10-12, 14). Pearson (*Christological and Rhetorical Properties,* pp. 97-111) identifies vv. 18-21 as "a composite of formulary materials."

ready known to his audience (v. 18: "knowing that"). Building on the undeveloped but assumed premise of Christ's preexistence,[11] Peter urges that God's own agenda and initiative stand behind Jesus' redemptive work. To put it differently, the sacrificial death of Jesus must be taken seriously as providing insight into the very nature of God.[12]

The purpose of Peter's affirmation is given at the close of v. 20: the selection of Christ before the foundations of the world and his revelation at the end of the ages was "because of you." That is, Peter (1) assures his audience that the plan of God finds its goal in the community of the faithful and, in this way, (2) confirms the location of his audience, whose lives might be characterized as marginal in the world-at-large, as nonetheless at the heart of God's will. Not unlike the work of Hellenistic historians and consistent with Jewish voices, Peter urges that, beneath the surface of day-to-day events, divine guidance is at work.[13]

Additionally, given the premium placed on what is old in the world of 1 Peter ("the old is better"),[14] Peter's affirmation puts in the strongest possible terms the significance of the way of life he has set before his audience. Far from being subject to dismissal as newfangled, this life is grounded in unparalleled antiquity. Because Peter otherwise counsels his audience to put aside their former desires and inherited way of life (vv. 14, 18), it was imperative that he provide a sensible substitute, with sensibility measured in terms of age.

(2) Time of Ignorance/Emptiness (1:14, 18; cf. 2:11; 4:3-4): Turning first to the description of the former life of Peter's audience in v. 14, "ignorance" is often a catch-phrase for "Gentiles" unable to recognize God in spite of transparent evidence of his goodness (Wis 13:1) and, living apart from Torah, unable to differentiate right from wrong (Wis 14:22). In the NT, however, "ignorance" characterizes those, Gentile or Jew, who do not know the God revealed in Jesus Christ (i.e., "the God and Father of our Lord Jesus Christ," 1:3; see Acts 3:17; 17:30) and, therefore, whose knowledge of God can only be distorted. "Ignorance" is less the state of "lacking information," more the pro-

---

11. Cf. Ignatius, *Magnesians* 6:1: "Jesus Christ, who was with the Father before the ages and has been manifest at the end" (LCL); Hermas, *Similitudes* 9:12.2-3: "The Son of God is older than all his creation . . . he has been revealed in the last days . . ." (LCL).

12. So Gunton, *Actuality of Atonement*, p. 149.

13. See Squires, *Plan of God*, pp. 15-36; *Odes of Solomon* 4:14: "For all was manifest to you as God, and was set in order from the beginning before you" (Charlesworth, "Odes of Solomon," p. 737); *4 Ezra* 6.1-6; more generally, e.g., Gen 50:20.

14. With reference to Greek, Roman, Hellenistic-Jewish, and early Christian literature, this motif is explored in Pilhofer, *Presbyteron Kreitton*.

found failure to grasp the character and purpose of God. Misconceiving the nature of God and life before God, they were blinded to what God was doing. Consequently, the resolution of "ignorance" is never simply "the amassing of data" but a realignment with God's ancient purpose, a theological transformation. This is exactly what Peter's audience has received: new birth into a living hope.

In the Greco-Roman world, "desire" (ἐπιθυμία, *epithymia*) appears in moral discourse — already in Plato but more recently especially among the Stoics, in Hellenistic Jewish literature, and in Christian writings — with such generally negative connotations as "insatiable cravings" or "lust."[15] As a generic vice almost universally condemned, "desire" marked "the former time of ignorance." In the present text, desires rooted in ignorance belong to the past, so should no longer shape or form (συσχηματίζομαι, *syschēmatizomai*) Peter's audience; in its place, imitation of God's holiness is expected. For Peter, "desire" and "holiness" appear as opposing forces each capable of drawing persons into its orbit, conforming human character and actions to its ways and so sculpting human life. Paul similarly wrote, "Do not be conformed to this world, but be transformed by the renewing of your minds" (Rom 12:2).

Condemnatory rhetoric is also used of the former life of Peter's audience in v. 18, where their "inherited way of life," is dismissed as "empty" or "futile." In Peter's world, this is a stunning conclusion. For example, although Cicero might have been hesitant on philosophical grounds to support Roman cultic practices, he nevertheless supported them on account of their antiquity and in order to maintain political stability (e.g., *De Divinatione* 2.75). Roman culture valued what was handed down from generation to generation, not least religious tradition, but Peter assigns those customs to the category of idolatry. It is difficult to exaggerate the seriousness of Peter's claim. According to pervasive sentiment, to break from one's ancestral religion was to invite disaster in the form of recriminations from the gods thus scorned. Accordingly, those who set aside ancestral traditions invited contempt for undermining the fabric of society by engaging in nonconformist behavior. It is no wonder, then, that the liberation that comes through the death of Christ (a liberation that is explicated in terms not of "deliverance from bondage to sin," say, but from an idolatrous way of life) has as its effect a time of "dwelling in a strange land," of alien status (v. 17).[16]

15. E.g., Plato *Phaedrus* 83b; Epictetus 2.16.45; 2.18.8-9; Wis 4:12; *4 Macc.* 1:22; Rom 1:24; Jas 1:14-15

16. On πατροπαράδοτος (*patroparadotos*, "handed down from ancestors," *hapax* in biblical Greek), see van Unnik, "Critique of Paganism"; on the problem of departing from ancestral tradition, van Unnik, pp. 140-41; Talbert, "Plan of 1 Peter," p. 145.

Peter's description of the former lives of his audience characterizes them unmistakably as Gentiles (that is, as predominately Gentiles). This is because a theologian like Peter, who otherwise so positively construes Israel, could hardly speak of the "former time" of Jews or their "inherited way of life" in such damning terms. If they were primarily Gentile, then all the more did they need both to be inducted into the story of Israel (a major concern of 1 Peter) and to have their lives sculpted anew.

(3) The End of the Ages (1:20): In locating "the end of the ages" subsequent to what Peter describes as the "time of ignorance," I am breaking from a strict chronological ordering; almost certainly, the advent of Jesus predated the pagan lives of most or all of his audience. What seems crucial to acknowledge, though, is that their *awareness* of Jesus' advent at the end of the ages, so important to our writer, for whom the revelation of Jesus was "because of you," has interrupted their former lives. Existentially, then, if not in a strictly chronological sense, this ordering of events and conditions is appropriate. For Peter, the advent of Jesus Christ constitutes the midpoint in a history that spans the period from creation to the final revelation of Jesus Christ; as such, no telling of the narrative of God's election and redemption is true that does not pass through and take its meaning from the death and resurrection of Jesus.

The notion of "the end of the ages" is a commonplace in Jewish apocalyptic texts of the Second Temple Period, even if those interpretations of "the end" might differ markedly. Two motifs from that literature are of interest to us on account of their repetition here: the anticipated resurrection of the dead (marking the restoration of Israel) and an expected time of affliction or woe (marking the onset of the messianic age). In 1 Peter thus far, the resurrection of the dead has come into play in vv. 3 and 21, and suffering is the lot of both Jesus (vv. 2, 11, 19) and God's people, Peter's audience (vv. 6, 7, 17). The revelation of Jesus of which Peter writes in v. 20 thus refers to the advent of Jesus, and especially his passion and resurrection, by which the End has been inaugurated. This portrait is only enhanced with the reference to God's honoring Jesus by raising him from the dead and giving him glory in v. 21, the orientation of which is toward the present — that is, toward calling forth trust and hope in God.[17] What is more, reading Peter against the backdrop of contemporary Jewish apocalyptic thought, we learn that the suffering of believers is nothing less than a participation in the Messiah's own suffering, by which

---

17. Hence, even though Peter accentuates the significance of Jesus' mediation of salvation in vv. 18-19, center stage still belongs to God the Father, who remains the primary actor. As faith and hope are the consequence of God's having raised Jesus from the dead (vv. 3, 21a), so faith and hope have as their object God.

God actualizes his salvific purpose. The sufferings of Jesus and his followers together constitute the birth pangs through which the new age emerges. Upon reflection, this is not surprising.

> Integral salvation is not posthistorical. It is realized in a liberation process that involves conflict. All historical liberation, even the liberation brought us by Jesus Christ, occurs in the context of a covenant of suffering, pain, and death between human beings and God. Suffering is the price we have to pay for the resistance the fatalizing systems put up to each and every quantum leap in history. God spares no one this suffering, this sacrifice — not even his well-beloved Son. But this is not "harmless," meaningless suffering. It is pregnant with meaning. It is part of a liberation project.[18]

This interpretation of suffering in relation to the end of the ages is not unique to Peter, but is found in the Gospels of Matthew and Mark, in Paul, and in Revelation; indeed, it was known from earliest Christian times.[19]

This is not to say that, for Peter (or the rest of the NT), the death of Jesus is like any other human passing. We have here an early intimation of a motif Peter will develop more fully in his letter, that the suffering of believers is "effective" in God's plan. In the present context, however, the "effectiveness" of Jesus' death is worked out in a way unparalleled in descriptions of the misery of Jesus' followers in this letter. His is an atoning death effective for the liberation of God's people. This, together with his resurrection from the dead, marks a decisive turning point in human history, inaugurating the end of the ages. Peter's audience thus lives in the time associated with the appearance of Jesus Christ, the end of the ages. In terms of Peter's timeline, the pressing question is whether people conduct themselves accordingly.

(4) Liberation (1:18-19): For Peter's audience, "liberation" lies in the past (aorist participle), driving home once again that God has already acted decisively in their lives: to give them new birth (v. 3), to evangelize them (through the sending of the Holy Spirit, v. 12), and to liberate or redeem them. Liberation is grounded in the work of Christ, and Peter conflates three images as he articulates the atonement theology of this text: (a) "liberation" or "ransom," (b) "lamb," and (c) the combination of "blood" and "[a lamb] without blemish or defect."

(a) The importance of "liberation" derives in the OT from God's liberating (or ransoming) Israel from enslavement in Egypt (e.g., Exod 6:6; 15:13;

---

18. Boff, *Passion*, p. 125.

19. For relevant background in Second Temple Judaism and in the NT, see Allison, *End of the Ages;* Allison does not involve 1 Peter in his study, however.

Deut 7:8; Isa 43:1; etc.). However, ransom in this sense is effected without concern for payment (cf. Isa 52:3!), whereas Peter observes that the liberation of believers comes with a price: not "such perishable things as gold or silver" but "the precious blood of Christ." This opens the door to possible influence from practices associated with human affairs — recovering a person or property through the payment of a "ransom" — in the LXX (e.g., Lev 25:25, 48-49) and in the Roman world (e.g., of prisoners of war).[20] Peter had precedent for blending these two portraits of "ransom" in the words of Jesus in Mark 10:45, a text that builds on Isa 52:13–53:12.[21] Later, this Isaianic text will figure prominently in Peter's christology (e.g., 2:21-25).[22] "Liberation" is a virtual stand-in for "salvation" (though 1 Peter uses "salvation" to describe present and future realities rather than a past event in the life of the believer [1:5, 9, 10; 2:2]).

(b) The image of the "lamb" takes us more specifically into the tradition of the Passover sacrifice (Exodus 12) — so central to Israel's history and identity — and its appropriation within early Christianity (e.g., John 1:29, 36; 1 Cor 5:7). Celebrated annually, Passover both memorialized and reappropriated for generations of God's people God's election and great act of deliverance.

(c) The reference to "blood" and the phrase "without blemish or defect" recall Israel's economy of sacrifice and attribute atoning significance to Jesus' death. As in texts associated with Paul (Rom 3:25; 5:9; Eph 1:7; 2:13; Col 1:20), "blood" must be understood symbolically (since the mode of Jesus' execution was not particularly bloody) as shorthand for "purification offering" (e.g., Lev 4:1–6:7; 6:24–7:10; see Leviticus 16), the focus of which is on cleansing the effect of sin. In a signal text, Lev 17:11-14, the shedding of blood — regarded as the substance of life and therefore as sacred to God — signifies the offering of the lives of those for whom the sacrifice is made. In this system, the life of an unblemished animal substitutes for blemished human life, and this had effi-

20. See further, *TLNT* 2:424-28. Based on his work with the Delphi inscriptions, Deissmann drew attention to the importance for Pauline studies of sacral manumission, whereby a slave might gain emancipation through the "solemn right of fictitious purchase by some divinity" (*Light from the Ancient East*, pp. 319-30 [p. 322]); others have suggested the potential influence on 1 Peter as well (e.g., Michaels, p. 64). The significance of this practice for early Christian atonement theology is questionable, though, both because the notion of "slave of the god" is not found in the Delphi material and because atonement theology allows no room for self-redemption; see further Bartchy, *First-Century Slavery*, pp. 121-25; Barth and Blanke, *Philemon*, pp. 47-49.

21. For discussion, see Lohse, *Märtyrer und Gottesknecht*, pp. 117-22; Stuhlmacher, "Vicariously Giving His Life for Many"; McKnight, *Jesus and His Death*, pp. 159-75. Cf. 1 Tim 2:5-6; Tit 2:14.

22. See Pearson, *Christological and Rhetorical Properties*.

cacy in the restoration of right relations with God. The author's qualification of Christ's blood as "precious" marks a profound, if easily overlooked, theological move. Reckoned by human criteria, Jesus' death on a tree (2:24) was anything but honorable, so mention of his passion could easily evoke valuations of humiliation and scorn.[23] In a manner consistent with his emphasis on God's choice of Jesus (1:20) and the subsequent declaration of Jesus as rejected among humans but "chosen and precious (or honored)" before God (2:4, 6), Peter declares that Jesus' death, however ignominious in the Roman world, actually bears divine approval. The imagery Peter borrows from Israel's economy of sacrifice thus portrays the honorable death of Jesus as effective in wiping away sin and its effects.

Interestingly, in 1 Pet 1:18-19, sin and its consequences per se are not the focus of redemption; "the emptiness of your inherited way of life" is. This suggests the potency of the desires of that former life, a suggestion that gains leverage in Peter's admonition against allowing oneself to be shaped or formed by them. "Liberation" belongs to the larger semantic domain of salvation understood in terms of war.[24] Recent advances in neuropsychology have highlighted the importance of cultural context and social interactions in the formation of our "selves."[25] Biblical texts like the one before us give expression to the same reality, with the result that we should not be surprised that an "inherited way of life" and its "desires" could present themselves as forces against which God has undertaken battle.

Drawing deeply from the well of Israel's life and moving effortlessly among Israel's images of reconciliation and rescue, Peter forges an atonement theology the focus of which is liberation from slavery, not to Egyptians but to an inherited way of life that is empty and characterized by insatiable cravings and idolatry.

(5) Time of Alien Life (1:17): Peter uses the term χρόνος *(chronos),* "a period of time during which some activity occurs,"[26] twice in this section, in both instances with reference to the time during which believers live (vv. 17,

---

23. The quandary presented by the shame of the cross of Christ was widely recognized — e.g., 1 Cor 1:23; Phil 2:8; Heb 9:22; Justin, *1 Apologia* 13.4 ("They say that our madness consists in the fact that we put a crucified man after the unchangeable and eternal God, the creator of the world"); Lactantius, *Institutes* 4.26 ("Why, if he was God, and chose to die, did he not at least suffer by some honorable kind of death? Why was it by the cross, especially? Why an infamous kind of punishment, which may appear unworthy even of a man, if he is free, although guilty?").

24. See J. B. Green, *Salvation,* pp. 63-92.

25. E.g., Reyna, *Connections;* Siegel, *Developing Mind.*

26. καιρός *(kairos)* appears in vv. 5, 11: "a definite or favorable time."

20). They refer to the present differently, however. In v. 17, Peter writes of "the time of your dwelling in a strange land," while in v. 20 he writes of "the end of the times (or ages)." The juxtaposition of these two descriptions is parabolic of the deeper reality to which his audience must attend, namely, that the last days, inaugurated by the death and resurrection of Jesus, can only be, for those who have been born anew, a time of living as strangers, never really at home. Apart from this verse, the noun παροικία (*paroikia*, "temporary dwelling among strangers") occurs in the NT only once, in Luke's description of Israel's "stay in the land of Egypt" (Acts 13:17). The parallel between the two is apt, especially when it is recognized that παροικία *(paroikia)* functions within Second Temple Judaism already as a metaphor for exilic life (e.g., *3 Maccabees* 7:19); recall the closely related phrase "strangers in the world of the diaspora" (1:1), which likewise speaks to a socioreligious situation as outsiders, subject to day-to-day cancerous slander and bedevilment.

With three imperatives, Peter sketches the shape of expected conduct in this temporal and social context: "set their hope" (v. 13), "become holy" (v. 15), and "live in reverent fear" (v. 17). Together, these constitute a response of resistance centered on an alternative structuring of time and formative narrative, a rejection of ancestral and contemporary conventions for behavior, and allegiance to a competing god/God; embodied in characteristic practices; and made possible by a liberation that reverberates with echoes of the story of Israel's exodus from Egypt, that prototypical expression of Yahweh the Warrior.

The directive regarding hope (v. 13) presumes transformed ways of thinking and is clearly set within an eschatological horizon. My translation "having readied your mind for action" masks the idiom Peter employs, reminiscent of the Passover ritual (e.g., Exod 12:11) and the eschatological teaching of Jesus (Luke 12:35): "gird up the loins (of your mind)."[27] Peter assumes that his audience has readied their minds for action and, indeed, that they are already "practicing vigilance." In other words, they have already embraced a new way of seeing things and are nurturing new patterns of thought on account of their having been born anew; and so he presses them to orient and commit themselves fully to the consummation of God's purpose. This "grace" is a semantic double for the "salvation" mentioned in vv. 5, 9.

27. The idiom is familiar among folk who in preparation for physical activity must first secure their robes; thus, "to gird the loins" meant "to ready oneself for action." The metaphor appears in the OT (e.g., 2 Kgs 4:29; 9:1; Jer 1:17; Nah 2:1). I draw particular attention to Passover because of the manifest interest in Exodus and Passover in this context and to the Lukan text on account of the similar eschatological focus and Peter's otherwise well-known indebtedness to the gospel tradition.

The directive regarding holiness (v. 15) is a call to be shaped by God's holiness as opposed to being shaped by "the desires that marked your former time of ignorance."[28] As such, this directive has as its warrant the holiness of God, together with the essential human vocation to imitate God (or to reflect the image of God). Intimately related to the call to holiness is the identity of Peter's audience as "obedient children" (v. 14) and reference to their "faithfulness" (v. 21). In the Greco-Roman world, obedience is one of the presumed characteristics of children, and this extends to those for whom God is Father. In other words, the call to holiness arises only in the context of the new status God has given his people in causing them to be born anew (v. 3). Similarly, in the wake of their exodus from Egypt, Israel is told, "So you shall remember and do all my commandments, and you shall be holy to your God. I am the LORD your God, who brought you out of the land of Egypt, to be your God: I am the LORD your God" (Num 15:40-41). The importance of these observations is to remind us that holiness is gift, grounded in relationship with God, before it is command.

The scriptural grounding for Peter's call to holiness appears to have been drawn most directly from Lev 19:2: "You shall be holy, for I the LORD your God am holy."[29] The larger context of Leviticus 19 is reflected in 1 Peter as well — in the collocation of the call to holiness and the admonition to revere (φοβέω, phobeō) one's parents (father and mother in Lev 19:3; Father in 1 Pet 1:17); in the analogy of context, concerned as it is in both instances with distinguishing God's people from the ways of the wider world;[30] and, above all, in Peter's phrase, "in every aspect of life." As Leviticus 19 has it, holiness extends indeed into the nooks and crannies of life: family and community respect (vv. 3, 32), religious loyalty (vv. 3-8, 12, 26-31), economic relationships (vv. 9-10), workers' rights (v. 13), social compassion (v. 14), judicial integrity (v. 15), neighborly attitudes and conduct (vv. 11, 16-18), distinctiveness (v. 19), sexual integrity (vv. 20-22, 29), exclusion of the idolatrous and occult (vv. 4, 26-31), racial equality (vv. 33-34), and commercial honesty (vv. 35-36).[31] This is a holiness of engagement, not of withdrawal.[32]

The directive regarding living with reverent fear (v. 17) has two war-

28. The antithesis is registered by the sentence construction of vv. 14-16: ὡς . . . ἀλλὰ κατά (hōs . . . alla kata, "as . . . but according to"); see Tite, *Compositional Transitions*, pp. 68-69 (though Tite erroneously refers to "imitating the holiness of Jesus Christ," whereas 1 Peter is here concerned with conformity to the holiness of God).

29. Cf. Lev 11:45; 20:7, 26; Num 15:40

30. See Lev 11:44-45; 20:26; G. L. Green, "Use of the OT," 285.

31. This way of reading Leviticus 19 is borrowed from C. J. H. Wright, "OT Ethics."

32. See J. B. Green, "Identity and Engagement."

rants: "you call upon a Father who judges impartially" and knowledge of one's liberation from the futility of an inherited way of life. The latter certifies that the believer is free to live a life other than one enslaved to the past. The former is subject to serious distortion and deserves careful attention. "To call upon" is the language of prayer (e.g., Acts 2:21; 9:14; 22:16); "to call upon a Father" may borrow language from the Lord's Prayer (Matt 6:9; Luke 11:2; cf. Rom 8:15; Gal 4:6; on God as "Father" see above, pp. 23-24.) Today, the reference to the Father as impartial in judgment might suggest notions of God's lack of bias, his neutrality or objectivity in matters of justice. To the contrary, even if the pages of the LXX are dotted with references to divine (and human) impartiality (e.g., 2 Chron 19:4-7; Wis 5:18; Sir 35:15-16), we ought not imagine that the scales of divine justice are blind. After all, the God who liberated Israel from Egypt is the God who directs his people to show regard toward and partiality on behalf of the alien, the orphan, and the widow — that is, the oppressed and marginal.[33] The idiom Peter employs is "to acknowledge someone's face" or "to show favor," particularly with regard to rank or status. The point, then, is that God is not swayed by the canons of prestige prevalent in Peter's world (e.g., sex, age, ancestry, landed wealth, the status of one's circle of friends), accounting instead for one's "performance" (ἔργον, *ergon*). On this point, Peter's perspective is again subject to distortion, since in our world it is easy enough to imagine a dichotomy between what one "is" and what one "does." In the world of Peter, however, one's deepest allegiances and one's character were on display through one's practices.[34] Indeed, Peter defines expected performance with reference to behavior ("you must live") that exhibits a particular sentiment ("with reverent fear").

Another possible distortion of Peter's message is that we imagine that he points to God's judgment as itself motivation for fearful living.[35] This is countered by reference to God as Father, connoting images from Scripture of faithful beneficence rather than threatening judgment; by Peter's reference to the manner of divine judgment in order to counter concerns with social standing in his world; by the grounding of holiness in the initiative of God and of performance in transformed character; and finally by the fact that "fear" (φόβος, *phobos*; cf. 1:17; 2:18; 3:2, 14, 16) in this context has to do not with intimidation, anxious dread, or terror but with the fundamental orien-

33. E.g., Lev 19:9-10; 23:22; Deut 14:28-29; 24:19-22; 26:12; cf. Jas 1:27.

34. See the programmatic comments in Di Vito, "Old Testament Anthropology"; K. Berger, *Identity*, pp. 70-81.

35. This seems to be the perspective of Denney, for example; he writes with reference to 1:17 that sanctification "is required in view of the account they must render" (*Death of Christ*, pp. 91-92).

tation of one's life toward God, according the highest value to one's relationship with God so that it determines all else.

(6) Revelation of Jesus Christ (1:13): Peter actually begins his exhortation in vv. 13-21 with the end of the story: "the [end-time] revelation of Jesus Christ." This serves two immediate purposes. First, it continues his interest in the eschatological horizons of life for those who have been born anew (vv. 3, 4, 7, 11), thus providing a reminder that vindication is the certain successor to the suffering of the faithful. Second, Peter employs a literary device known as "backshadowing," which posits that the pattern of history is revealed, that the nature of the end is known, and that the present can be evaluated accordingly.[36] This means that Peter can interpret the present in light of his convictions regarding the future and can direct his audience to live their lives in ways determined by that future, in hope (vv. 13, 21).

What agenda is served by this concern with "the times," this attention to the emplotment of God's story? First, recalling that Peter's audience is primarily Gentile and therefore unskilled in rehearsing the story of God's dealings with Israel, Peter works to introduce and to induct them further into a particular way of construing their history that is deeply rooted in the eternal plan of God and that takes seriously the formation and maintenance of God's people Israel through Passover, exodus, and the pattern of reconciliation through sacrifice. As cognitive scientist Mark Turner has observed, "narrative imagining is our fundamental form of predicting" and our "fundamental cognitive instrument for explanation."[37] For Peter, the only true categories for making sense of daily existence are determined by a particular narrative, the scriptural story. Second, remembering that we tell stories not only to make sense of the world but to form identity and community, we see that, in selecting these particular events and in ordering them in this particular way, Peter is set on constructing the identity of the communities to which he has addressed himself. Although we would never confuse Peter's letter with a narrative text, his concern with marking the times suggests an agenda like that of those who use narrative to represent history. In this way, he orients his audience toward the future consummation of God's plan at the same time that he grounds their identity in a divine strategy that predates creation itself. He is already working to collapse the self-evident historical distinctives between Israel of old and these communities of Jesus-followers in the service of a theological unity that conjoins old and new. On account of the initiative of God,

---

36. See Morson, *Narrative and Freedom*, pp. 234-64 — who, however, takes a dim view of this "foreshadowing after the fact."

37. Turner, *Literary Mind*, p. 20; cf. Bruner, *Making Stories*; Eakin, *Making Selves.*

manifest in the passion and resurrection of Jesus, these communities stem from the same roots. They are one. The result is a strong sense of continuity with the past, a secure place within the arc of God's gracious purpose, and a firm basis for projecting oneself into a future made certain in Jesus' resurrection from the dead. Third, this concern with future and past has present significance. Peter's attention to "the times" carefully articulates the nature of present-day existence — not as an anomaly in God's story, nor as a challenge to God's faithfulness, but as an opportunity for identification with Christ and for putting into play the human vocation to imitate the holiness of God.

1:22–2:3

22 Having set yourselves apart through obedience to the truth[38] for the purpose of unpretentious familial love, you must love one another deeply[39] and unceasingly, 23 having been given new birth not from perishable seed but imperishable, through the living and enduring word of God[40] — 24 since "all humanity is like grass and all human glory like the flower of grass. The grass withers and the flower falls off, 25 but the word of the Lord endures forever." This is the word that was proclaimed to you as good news. 2:1 Therefore, having set aside every evil and every deceit, and pretenses and jealousies and all slander, 2 like newborn babies you are to yearn for the pure milk of the word so that in it you may grow up into salvation,[41] 3 since you have tasted that the Lord is gracious.[42]

38. The addition of διὰ πνεύματος (*dia pneumatos,* "through the Spirit") in P 𝔐 1^vid vg^ms is probably theologically motivated, to clarify that obedience is through the Spirit (see Metzger, *Textual Commentary,* p. 688). The phrase is missing in p^72 ℵ A B C Ψ, etc.

39. Literally "from the heart." The modifier καθαρᾶς (*katharas,* "clean") has significant external support (e.g., p^72 ℵ* C P Ψ, etc.), but is absent in A B vg. "Clean heart" appears elsewhere in the NT in Matt 5:8; 1 Tim 1:5; 2 Tim 2:22, and this sentiment may have influenced the text of 1 Peter here (see also Rom 6:17); see Michaels, p. 72 (who regards it as an interpolation, but hypothesizes that it might have been omitted accidentally on account of the repetition of κα- [*ka-*] in καθαρᾶς καρδίας [*katharas kardias*]).

40. Some external evidence supports the insertion of "forever" (εἰς τὸν αἰῶνα [*eis ton aiōna,* e.g., P 𝔐] or εἰς τοὺς αἰῶνας [*eis tous aiōnas,* 1838 *pc*]), probably under the influence of v. 25a. The Greek text is ambiguous, with the result that "living and enduring" could modify either "God" or "word." The context argues for the latter, since the ensuing scriptural citation from Isaiah concerns the enduring character of the word. See further LaVerdiere, "Grammatical Ambiguity."

41. 𝔐 omits εἰς σωτηρίαν (*eis sōtērian,* "unto salvation"), an emendation most likely motivated by the sentiment that attaining through growth what is usually spoken of as an eschatological gift was theologically unacceptable. The phrase is found in all of the earliest and best mss.

42. External evidence is divided on whether the text should read "gracious" (χρηστός

Within the larger section that runs from 1:13 to 2:10, this textual unit is held together by its heightened focus on the "word [of God/the Lord]" (1:23, 25 [2x]; 2:2), around which the logic of this text turns.[43] Other points of contact between 1:22-25 and 2:1-3 include concern with pretentiousness (1:22; 2:1), new birth (1:23; 2:2), and the pronounced and pervasive new emphasis on the integrity of relationships within the community of disciples. Already known for calling upon God as Father (1:17), they are now recognized as sisters and brothers, a kin group. Additionally, the behaviors that Peter negates in 2:1 ("every evil and every deceit, and pretenses and jealousies and all slander") have their positive alternative in the deceptively simple directive in 1:22: "love one another." Although the appearance of the coordinating conjunctive "therefore" might suggest the beginning of a further subsection in 2:1, the implications Peter wants to draw in 2:1-3 are grounded above all in 1:22-25. Hence, I am treating 1:22–2:3 as a single unit, while at the same time recognizing the close connection these verses have with earlier emphases — for example, holiness/purification (1:2, 15, 22), obedience (vv. 2, 14, 22), causing to be born anew (1:3, 23), perishable–imperishable (1:4, 18, 23), and proclaiming the good news (1:12, 25).

As in 1:13-21, so here, Peter's directives are organically related to and, indeed, grow out of his declaration of his audience's new life. In the present text, the participles in 1:21, 23 (perfect tense) and in 2:1 (aorist), and the causal clause in 2:3 ("since you have tasted"), provide the temporal and circumstantial base for his two directives: "you must love one another" (1:22) and "you are to yearn" (2:2), respectively. The indicative grounds and gives rise to the imperative — or, better, Peter recognizes that new practices are inevitable and therefore expected outgrowths from the internalizing of new commitments and dispositions.[44] In Peter's calculus there can be no dichotomy between character and performance. This sentiment is hardly unique. According to Matthew, for example, Jesus proclaimed that "every good tree bears good fruit, but the bad tree bears bad fruit" (7:17), and Paul writes, "[y]ou reap whatever you sow. If you sow to your own flesh, you will reap corruption from the flesh; but if you sow to the Spirit, you will reap eternal

---

[*chrēstos*, p⁷² K L, etc.]) or "Christ" (χριστός [*Christos*, ℵ A B C Ψ]). It is difficult to imagine a deliberate substitution of "gracious" for "Christ," but not vice versa; either emendation is possible through accidental substitution due to an error of hearing, however. "Gracious," alluding to Ps 34:8 (33:9 LXX), is the preferred reading.

43. Less obvious textual markers include the segregation of v. 22 from v. 21 by asyndeton (cf. Brox, p. 85).

44. For my understanding of "practices," I am largely dependent on Bourdieu — e.g., *Logic of Practice* and *Practical Reason*.

life from the Spirit (Gal 6:7-8). The commonsense character of this agronomic proverb should not mask the fact that, for Peter, practices reflecting a transformed life, and the transformed life itself, are the results of God's kindness and initiative.

A map of the overall structure of this segment of Peter's letter is instructive for identifying its central concerns.[45]

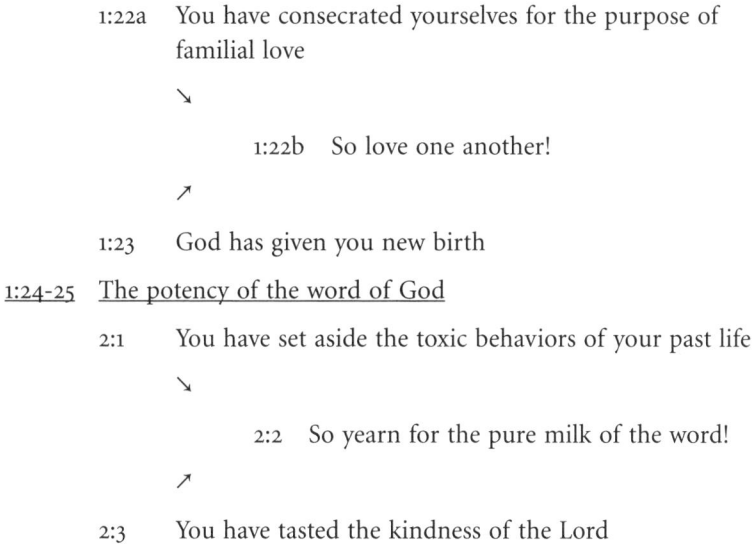

> 1:22a   You have consecrated yourselves for the purpose of familial love
>
> ↘
>
> 1:22b   So love one another!
>
> ↗
>
> 1:23   God has given you new birth
>
> 1:24-25   The potency of the word of God
>
> 2:1   You have set aside the toxic behaviors of your past life
>
> ↘
>
> 2:2   So yearn for the pure milk of the word!
>
> ↗
>
> 2:3   You have tasted the kindness of the Lord

This outline is helpful in demonstrating the relationship between Peter's directives and their accompanying dependent clauses. It also highlights two crucial features of Peter's argument: (1) an expansive understanding of conversion and (2) a pronounced emphasis on the efficacy of the word.

(1) Conversion: The phrases in 1:22a, 23; 2:1, 3 refer, albeit in different ways, to the same moment: conversion. All are cast in the past and provide the basis for a life befitting those born anew. "Setting apart" or "(moral) purification" (1:22) signals a cutting off from the past, a "setting aside" (2:1). As we have seen (above, on 1:3), "new birth" is a dramatic metaphor for a decisive transformation of life (1:23).

The short phrase in 2:3 provides an example of Peter's exegesis, in this case an interpretation of Ps 34:8: "Taste and see that the Lord is good." The

---

45. For related and alternative attempts to represent the structure of this text, see Thurén, *Argument and Theology,* pp. 116-19; Evang, "ἐκ καρδίας ἀλλήλους ἀγαπήσατε ἐκτενῶς"; Prasad, *Christian Way of Life,* pp. 350-58 (including criticism of Evang).

points of contact between 1 Pet 1:3–2:3 and the psalm are many, including the call to hope and to exult in the Lord, the call to revere him, a context of living as strangers (LXX Ps 33:5: παροικία, *paroikia*, "abide among strangers"; see 1 Pet 1:17), the expectation of divine liberation, and an admonition against evil speech.[46] While the psalmist issues an invitation ("Taste!"), Peter claims a past reality ("you have tasted," with reference to the saving work of God [1:3]); what those in the past could only anticipate but not fully understand, Peter's audience has received (1:10-12). In an adroit maneuver, Peter moves this salvific moment in a christological direction. Having substituted "Lord" for the LXX's "God" in Isa 40:8, he recalls his identification of Jesus as Lord in 1:3 and so opens this text to a reading in which the "word" is the good news concerning Jesus (1:25), the Lord whose goodness has been tasted (2:3). As in 1:11, then, Jesus stands in the place of God.

Interestingly, the phrases Peter uses to identify this life transformation dramatically anticipate recent historical and social-scientific study of conversion.[47] First, conversion in antiquity might refer to both event and process and connote either transition from one religion to another or moving deeper into one's own religion. These various senses are present here. Note Peter's reference to past acts with ongoing effects (see the use of the perfect tense in the verbs ἁγνίζω, *hagnizō*, "consecrate, purify" [1:22] and ἀναγεννάω, *anagennaō*, "give new birth" [1:23]), the use of the aorist in 2:1, 3 (ἀποτίθημι, *apotithēmi*, "put off"; and γεύομαι, *geuomai*, "yearn"); and the melding of the human-biological and horticultural images of seed (1:23) and growth, especially in the image of "growing up into salvation" (2:2). For Peter, salvation "is something toward which we are moving, not something for which we are merely waiting."[48]

Second, conversion entails autobiographical reconstruction — signified transparently by Peter in the image of rebirth and emphasized earlier in 1:14, 18. Third, conversion is a profoundly social act; indeed, for Peter's primarily Gentile audience, conversion would have had immediate and far-reaching social consequences, entailing withdrawal from pagan behaviors and segregation from many of the particulars of day-to-day social life. In

46. See Snodgrass, "1 Peter II.1-10," pp. 102-3; Schutter, *Hermeneutic and Composition*, pp. 44-49 (who is overly critical of the earlier work of Bornemann, "Taufrede des Silvanus"); G. L. Green, "Use of the OT," pp. 280-82.

47. For historical material, see, e.g., Goodman, *Mission and Conversion;* Finn, *From Death to Rebirth;* Rousseau, "Conversion." Some of the relevant social-scientific literature is surveyed in Davis and Rambo, "Converting"; see also Snow and Machalek, "Convert"; N. H. Taylor, "Social Nature of Conversion"; Meeks, *Christian Morality.*

48. Michaels, "Going to Heaven," p. 251.

fact, given Peter's catalog of ways in which his audience suffers mistreatment from those outside the community of believers (e.g., 2:12; 3:9, 16; 4:14-16), we can hear him insisting that their treatment of one other within the community must not reprise the behavior of outsiders who malign Christian believers.

Closely related, fourth, conversion involves incorporation into a new community with its distinguishing practices, signified in the present text with the imagery of no longer clothing oneself (ἀποτίθημι, *apotithēmi,* "take off [as with clothes]"; cf. Rom 13:12; Col 3:8; Jas 1:21) in evil, deceit, and the like (2:1), but giving oneself rather to deep and unceasing love for those within the community. To "love" (ἀγαπάω, *agapaō*) entails a group ethos of solidarity and loyalty, an essential disposition favoring others in the community and so a refusal to harm them, a commitment to harmony within the group. This emphasis on the community of believers is underscored by the collocation of familial terms, together with metaphors of new birth and newborn babies; the converted are children, who constitute a family, with God as Father (1:2, 3, 17).[49] Of special interest is Peter's use of the term φιλαδελφία (*philadelphia,* "brotherly love"). A common image in early Christian discourse,[50] familial love would have particular importance in the sort of world assumed by 1 Peter, in which a strong sense of "family" identity would serve to counter the more pervasive experience of "strangerhood."[51] It is not surprising, then, to find similar language in 2:17 and 5:9 (ἀδελφότης, *adelphotēs,* "brotherhood," "family of believers"); and 3:8 (φιλάδελφος, *philadelphos,* "sibling love") and a related sentiment in 5:14: "Greet one another with a kiss of love."

Fifth, new life grows out of and is centered in the word of God. Or, as Peter claims, their obedience is to "the truth." This is another way of saying that conversion includes the adoption of a new symbolic universe — not one among many possible ways to construe reality, but the valid one, the one that corresponds to the way things really are, for Peter, from the perspective of the gospel. New life puts on display the transformation of believers' patterns of thought, a transformation that is generated and cultivated by the word of the Lord.

---

49. See van Rensburg, "Salvific Metaphors," pp. 387-88.

50. See, e.g., the use of φιλαδελφία (*philadelphia,* "brotherly love") in Rom 12:10; 1 Thess 4:9; and the more extensive use of brother–sister terminology in the NT. Writing at the close of the second century, Tertullian observed, "We are designated by the name of brothers. . . . How much more worthily are they called brothers who have recognized a common father in God" (*Apologia* 39.8-9). On familial imagery in early Christian discourse, see, e.g., Moxnes, ed., *Constructing Early Christian Families.*

51. Osiek and Balch, *Families,* p. 190.

A suggestive parallel to the aggregate of images Peter has gathered here comes from Luke 8:1-21, with its concern with sowing seeds and growth, Jesus' explicit identification of the seed with the word of God (or gospel), and Jesus' declaration that his siblings are those who hear and perform the word of God.

Through the amassing of adjectives in this text, Peter draws attention to the radical character of conversion. It is not enough to say "familial love," but he must qualify this love by insisting that it allows no room for play-acting (1:22; cf. 2:1); indeed, it was a commonplace in the classical world that the premier danger to mutual love is hypocrisy.[52] "One another" statements dot the landscape of early Christian discourse.[53] Peter's directive to "love one another," which repeats the idea of "familial love," identifies that love as "from the heart" and unceasing. Rather than counseling his audience to put aside their former ways of life, as he did in 1:14, 18, Peter now names some of those behaviors (2:1), not by way of providing an exhaustive catalog of vices but using these (punctuated with the threefold appearance of "all") to represent forms of behavior that oppose the ethos and practice of love to which he has just called them. By embracing love and avoiding these sanctioned behaviors, believers demonstrate themselves to be genuine members of the holy community.[54] A comparison with a text from the Dead Sea Scrolls is instructive: "I will not keep Belial within my heart, and in my mouth shall be heard no folly or sinful deceit, no cunning or lies shall be found on my lips. The fruit of holiness shall be on my tongue and no abomination shall be found upon it. . . . I will cause vanities to cease from my lips, uncleanness and crookedness from the knowledge of my heart" (1QS 10:21-23).[55] As in 1 Peter, so at Qumran, what flows from the human mouth is inseparable from the human heart (cf. Jas 3:6). Just as "your former times of ignorance" were characterized naturally by certain desires (1:14), so the dispositions of the reborn are internalized deeply, operative at a preconscious level, and naturally exhibited in mutual love.

---

52. Cf. Konstan, *Friendship*, 153-56.

53. E.g., "love one another" (Rom 12:10; 13:8; 1 Thess 4:9; 1 Pet 3:8; 4:8; 1 John 3:11, 14, 23; 4:7, 11-12; 2 John 5), "honor one another" (Rom 12:10), "live in harmony with one another" (Rom 12:16; 15:5; cf. 2 Cor 13:11), "greet one another with a holy kiss" (Rom 16:16; 1 Cor 16:20; 2 Cor 13:12; cf. 1 Pet 5:14), "be kind to one another" (Eph 4:32), "forgive one another" (Eph 4:32), etc. See Lohfink, *Jesus and Community*, pp. 99-106.

54. On this function of vice lists, see Meeks, *Christian Morality*, pp. 69-71. Peter thus departs from the usual form, which pairs lists of vices and virtues (for background, see Charles, "Vice and Virtue Lists"); in his case, the prescribed virtue is "love" — highly prized in the Greco-Roman world (e.g., Plutarch, *On Brotherly Love*).

55. Trans. Vermes, *Dead Sea Scrolls*, p. 114.

(2) The Efficacy of the Word: From a cursory perspective, reflection on "the word" in 1:23b-25 appears parenthetical to the directives Peter puts forward in 1:22; 2:2. Closer examination moves "the word" to center stage. Terms for "word" (λόγος, *logos,* and ῥῆμα, *rhēma*) may appear only in 1:23b, 25, but associated expressions are used in 1:22 and 2:2. In the phrase "obedience to the truth" (1:22), "obedience" is semantically related to "faith(fulness)" (see 2:7-8) and "truth" is a stand-in for "gospel." This reading of "truth" is suggested not only by Pauline and post-apostolic usage, but also by Peter's reference to new birth by means of the word in 1:23 and to the preaching of the gospel in 1:25.[56] The phrase in question in 2:2 is "pure milk of the word."[57] Elsewhere in the NT where the content of the Christian faith is represented as "milk," we find the connotation of nourishment fit for the worldly or immature (1 Cor 3:1-3; Heb 5:11-14). Here, however, we find no hint at all of disappointment on the part of Peter on account of the lack of spiritual growth among his audience. Nor, in referring to them with the simile "newborn babies," does he castigate them for any developmental deficit. The focus is not on their spiritual youth but on Peter's imperative that the intensity of their desire for the word be modeled on a newborn's craving for milk. In short, the three parts of this textual unit — 1:22-23a, 1:23b-25, and 2:1-3 — each carry forward an emphasis on the word — not the "word of Scripture" *per se,* but the word as good news, the gospel concerning Jesus Christ.

This emphasis finds its center in 1:24-25 with the use of Isa 40:6-8, a text borrowed from a context in which the word of God finds expression in the mouth of the herald of good news (Isa 40:9). Isaiah 40 is particularly apropos Peter's concerns, since the Isaianic passage addresses Israel in exile, discouraged, with an acclamation of God's faithfulness and the gospel of restoration.

---

56. E.g., Gal 5:7; Eph 1:13; Col 1:5; 2 Thess 2:10, 12-13; cf. the expression "the canon of truth" or "rule of truth" in Irenaeus, Clement of Alexandria, Hippolytus, Tertullian, and Novatian. In *Against Heresies,* Irenaeus writes, "But as we follow for our teacher the one and only true God, and possess his words as the rule of truth, we do all speak alike with regard to the same things, knowing but one God . . . who in these last times manifested his own Son . . ." (4.35.4). On "truth" and "gospel" as synonymous in this context see Goppelt, p. 125; Prasad, *Christian Way of Life,* p. 344; *TLNT* 1:74-75.

57. λογικός *(logikos)* is sometimes translated "spiritual" (e.g., NAB, NIV, NJB, NRSV), a translation recommended by BDAG 598. The suffix -ικος *(-ikos)* suggests the sense of "belonging to" or "pertaining to" (MHT 2:377-79) — in this case, then, "pertaining to λόγος *(logos)*" and so inviting the reading, "pertaining to verbal communication." The context demands this reading (cf., e.g., McCartney, "λογικός"; Achtemeier, pp. 146-47; Elliott, pp. 400-401); for lexical analogues, see McCartney, "λογικός," pp. 131-32. For an alternative but not contradictory view, see Jobes, pp. 132-41: "food that corresponds to the reality of their new life" (p. 136).

The parallel with 1 Peter at this point could not be more appropriate, since Peter has already spoken of prophets who testified in advance concerning the good news (1:10-12) and now moves immediately to claim that the word of the Lord was proclaimed as gospel — i.e., the good news of the word regarding Jesus Christ (1:25b).

The chief significance of the Isaianic citation lies in the contrast between the transience of human life and honor and the enduring nature of the word of the Lord. (A declaration of the fleeting character of "honor" is striking in Peter's world, ordered as it was around honor and replete with consideration of public opinion.) Peter's logic exploits this comparison. That is, he draws on the OT text not as a warrant for his argument, but for its explanatory value. If the seed from which they were begotten was perishable, then their fate would surely be that of the grass and its flower, which withers and falls off. But if the word of God, the good news, is living and everlasting, and if believers have been given new birth through his word, then the life into which they have been reborn is unending and their love for one another can endure as well. In short, the word of God, the good news, is efficacious in generating, cultivating, and sustaining new life. How might the word serve in this way? For Peter, obedience to the word comprises conversion; it is through the word that new birth is given; the word is the substance of the good news; and, now, believers are to live into the word: having set themselves apart for the purpose of familial love, they must love; they must yearn for the word; and it is in the word that they will grow up into their salvation.

2:4-10

4 Coming to him, a living stone — rejected by humans but in God's perspective elect, honored — 5 you yourselves also as living stones, a spiritual house, are being built to be a holy priesthood, in order to offer spiritual sacrifices acceptable to God through Jesus Christ; 6 for it stands written in Scripture, "Look! I am placing in Zion a stone, a cornerstone, elect, honored, and whoever believes in it will never be dishonored." 7 For you who believe, then, there is honor, but for those who do not believe, "the very stone that the builders rejected has become the head of the corner," 8 even "a stone that causes stumbling and a rock that causes offense." Disbelieving the word, they stumble — which is the end to which they were appointed. 9 You, on the other hand, are an elect clan, a royal priesthood, a holy nation, a people for God's possession, so that you might announce the wondrous acts of the one who called you out of darkness into his marvelous light — 10 you

who once were not a people but are now the people of God, who once were not shown mercy but now have been shown mercy.

This last unit of the larger section of Peter's letter that runs from 1:13 to 2:10 draws together its major threads into a climax focused on both the identity and the vocation of Peter's audience. These threads have to do above all with sketching an interpretive canopy under which to relish in their corporate status before God, a status that is theirs not so much in spite of their having experienced rejection in the world, but on account of it. In order to accomplish this end, Peter weaves together the witness of Israel's Scriptures and the career of Jesus, so that the OT is understood christologically on the way to its ecclesiological appropriation. In other words, Peter's task is not to read the Scriptures christologically but to show how a christological reading of Scripture guides the church in the formation of its identity and pursuit of its mission. To put it differently, and more accurately, Peter reads the situation of his Christian audience from the perspective of the career of Jesus Christ, and the career of Jesus Christ from the perspective of the Scriptures — specifically, from the scriptural plot line concerned with the vindication and glory of the rejected and suffering righteous.

1 Peter 2:4-10 is segregated by the forgoing material by asyndeton (the absence of conjunctive markers), but clearly related to it. The relative pronoun ὅς *(hos),* translated here as "him," has as its antecedent "Lord" in v. 3, ensuring that we understand that the "Lord" to whom Peter refers in his allusion to Ps 34:8 is Jesus Christ. Additionally, the emphasis on consecration and purity in 1:22; 2:1 is prerequisite to the identification of Christians as the spiritual house, or temple, in 2:5. But the integrity of the present unit is urged by the introduction of the stone-midrash in 2:4-8 and the repeated interest in divine election (vv. 4, 6, 9), priestly service (vv. 5, 9), holiness (vv. 5, 9), and the overwhelmingly theocentric character of this text (in which God is explicitly named in vv. 4, 5, 9).

With regard to structure, vv. 4 and 5 set the theme for this unit, on which Peter then expands in vv. 6-10. Thus, vv. 4 and 5 borrow the vocabulary of the biblical texts cited and appropriated in vv. 6-8 (Isa 28:16; Ps 118:22; Isa 8:14), building on a series of basic polarities: honor–shame, choose–reject, belief–disbelief. Christians, introduced as "living stones" in v. 5, then become the special focus of vv. 9-10, which also draw on biblical texts (Isa 43:20-21; Exod 19:5-6; Hos 2:23).[58]

---

58. Cf. Thurén, *Argument and Theology,* p. 127; Bechtler, *Following in His Steps,* pp. 186-87; Bauckham, "James, 1 and 2 Peter, Jude," pp. 310-11.

Scholars in recent years have recognized the importance of the values of honor and shame in the ancient Mediterranean world.[59] Increased sensitivity to concerns with social standing has focused our attention on a number of related factors:

- how status is allocated — via ascription (factors over which we have no control, such as family lineage or gender) or performance (factors over which we do have control, such as education or expressions of piety or bravery),
- an elevated concern with one's public face (as opposed to self-image), which functions as an implicit form of social pressure — as Aristotle remarked, "For there are many things that shame before such people [i.e., our neighbors] makes us do or leave undone. And we feel more shame when we are likely to be continually seen by, and go about under the eyes of, those who know of our disgrace" (*Rhetoric* 1385a) — as well as the use of shaming techniques, such as name-calling (see the vituperative use of "Christian" in 4:16) or public ostracism or malice (cf. 2:12; 3:9, 16; 4:14-16), as forms of social control,
- the concomitant social reality that honor accrued to those whose behavior conformed to accepted norms, and, therefore,
- the determinative significance of identifying the "public" in relation to which honor will be measured.

Although 1 Peter is replete with terms from the semantic domain of honor and shame,[60] they especially congregate in 2:4-10, including ἀποδοκιμάζω (*apodokimazō*, "judge someone or something unworthy and thus to be rejected") in vv. 4, 7, ἔντιμος (*entimos*, "honored, esteemed") in vv. 4, 6, εὐπρόσδεκτος (*euprosdektos*, "acceptable") in v. 5, καταισχύνω (*kataischynō*, "dishonor, put to shame") in v. 6, and τιμή (*timē*, "honor") in v. 7. We would be mistaken, though, were we to reduce the significance of Peter's present concern with honor and shame to word usage and sociological categories. What is especially critical is how Peter manipulates those categories as he seeks to sculpt the identity of his audience theologically.

First, he articulates the basis for judgments concerning honor and shame. Basic and inseparable questions in the determination of status in-

---

59. See, e.g., Finley, *World of Odysseus;* and, among the many available introductions to the role of this "pivotal value" in NT studies, Moxnes, "Honor and Shame"; deSilva, *Honor,* pp. 23-93.

60. Elliott demonstrates the pervasiveness of this terminology in an appendix to his essay, "Disgraced yet Graced," pp. 174-75.

clude: On what basis? And in whose perspective? If public sentiment is at stake, then it is important to know who comprises one's reference group. Already in Greco-Roman antiquity, we find diversity with regard to these conventions. Various subcultures — Jews in the diaspora, for example, or philosophical schools — defined what was honorable in various ways. "In such a world, it became essential to define carefully who constituted one's group of significant others — those people whose approval or disapproval mattered — and to insulate group members from concern about the honor or dishonor in which they were held by outsiders."[61] First Peter 2:4-10 is a profoundly theocentric text, with human valuations dismissed in favor of divine and with God's valuation regarded as decisive and ultimate (e.g., vv. 4, 5, 9, 10). Perhaps not surprisingly, then, the measures so important for determining status in the wider world of 1 Peter are irrelevant. Genealogy, gender, congenital defect — these typical canons of prestige are not even mentioned. Nor is it that an interest in ascribed honor simply gives way to acquired honor, or performance. Instead, what matters is God's choice, his election, his appointment. Status in the new community to which Peter is addressing himself is above all else an expression of God's grace.

"Performance" is a concern, but it is rather narrowly circumscribed. It has to do with whether one adopts God's valuation of people and things, developed here in terms of belief or disbelief in the gospel (vv. 6-7). Those who disbelieve are like builders who reject the stone chosen by God. This immediately identifies God as the arbiter of status, an emphasis that is furthered in two ways. On the one hand, those who believe are honored (v. 7) and "will never be dishonored" (v. 6), whereas for those who disbelieve, there is only stumbling and offense (v. 8). In other words, status vis-à-vis God is based on how one responds to Jesus Christ, whether with faith or rejection. V. 8 borrows from Isa 8:14, a passage that warns against following the ways of the nations and thinking their thoughts, lest Yahweh himself become a cause for stumbling, a trap, and a snare (Isa 8:11-15); this Isaianic echo serves to fill out the meaning of "disbelief" in a way that makes sense in 1 Peter (see 1:14, 18; 2:1). The Greek text of v. 7a is elliptical to a fault, with the result that it could refer to Christ as the honored one, or to believers who either have or will have honor. As trust is (or is not) in Christ and since this faith is the basis for the status of humans before God, Peter is surely claiming here that honor is extended to believers. The present tense does not rule out the future, and, given Peter's emphasis on the present Christian community and its living hope, it is

---

61. deSilva, "Honor and Shame," p. 520; cf. Eilberg-Schwartz, *Savage in Judaism,* pp. 195-216.

best to read honor as a present gift that will extend into the eschaton.[62] On the other hand, God's purpose is at work with respect to both believers and disbelievers. The former are chosen by God as progeny of elect stock (v. 9), while the fate of the latter, "stumbling," has been predetermined by God (v. 8). The result of refusing the gospel is that its subject, Jesus Christ, is experienced as an obstacle. Faith, then, has a hermeneutical role, allowing one to see what could otherwise not be seen. From a point of view illumined by conventional wisdom, Jesus and his followers are humiliated, rejected, ostracized, but from a perspective radiated by the passion of Jesus, they are God's elect, honored. This means that faith and unfaith are matters of human volition, but the consequences of faith and unfaith have been preset.[63]

Given the way in which Peter sets two kinds of builders over against each other — the God who is constructing a "spiritual house" or temple and those humans who reject the cornerstone of that temple — it is difficult not to hear in the background a basic critique of idolatry, the religious frontispiece of Greco-Roman life. Not only were idols made with human hands (e.g., Ps 115:4; Acts 19:26), but temples made with human hands could never serve as a dwelling place for God (e.g., Acts 7:48; 17:24).

Second, Peter articulates a key presupposition concerning the status of Jesus Christ, and he does so by drawing on the implicit authority of the Scriptures to speak on God's behalf. Isa 28:16, cited in v. 6, is set within an oracle of judgment that gives way to the promise of a new community, a promise to be realized as God restores his people and institutes his righteous rule.[64] The *Targum on Isaiah* takes this promise in a messianic direction, an interpretation that is helped along by an expectation well-documented in Second Temple Judaism of a new temple built by the Messiah.[65] The whole participates in

62. Hence, Achtemeier presents us with false alternatives when he writes, "To argue that it represents honor given now, not at judgment day . . . , is to trivialize the honor and ignore the total context of both passage and letter" (p. 161, n. 149). The analogy with the honoring of Jesus Christ, who is presently rejected by disbelievers but honored by God (presumably past, present, and future!), encourages a view that what is at issue here is whether the perspective of humans or of God is decisive in the determination of one's status. See further, Bechtler, *Following in His Steps*, pp. 187-88, n. 7.

63. As the narrator of Lewis's *Magician's Nephew* has it, "For what you see and hear depends a good deal on where you are standing: it also depends on what sort of person you are" (p. 125). See Elliott, p. 434; Feldmeier, *Christen als Fremde*, pp. 182-83.

64. Childs, *Isaiah*, pp. 208-10.

65. This expectation can be traced to readings of 2 Sam 7.13. God establishes the Davidic dynasty, whereas a Davidid builds the Temple. See Zech 6:12-13; *Tg. Nebiim* Zech 6:12-13 ("Behold the man whose name is Messiah, destined to be revealed, installed in office, and to build the temple of Yahweh . . ."); *Tg. Nebiim* Isa 53:5 ("And he will build a house of holiness . . ."); *1 Enoch*

a motif we find elsewhere in the Scriptures of Israel — namely, the difference between how God and humans value things (e.g., 1 Sam 16:7; Isa 55:8-9: Mark 8:33). In this case, what human builders reject (ἀποδοκιμάζω, *apodokimazō* — also used in Jesus' predictions of his rejection as a synecdoche for his passion: Mark 8:31; Luke 9:22; 17:25) God has chosen and esteemed.

The metaphorical contrast could hardly be more stark. A "cornerstone" is not only the stone set at the corner of two intersecting walls (as the name implies), but is one prepared and chosen for its exact 90° angle, and so the basis for the construction of the whole building. Choosing the right corner is basic not only to the aesthetics of the building but also to its stability and longevity. Obviously, as they set out to build, God (and those who adopt God's canons of valuation) and those who reject Jesus have radically different bases for appraisal.

Adding to the significance of this contrast is the contradiction resident in Jesus' career, a contradiction that would be self-evident to inhabitants of the wider Roman world. What separated the form of Jesus' execution from other forms of capital punishment was not the physical pain associated with crucifixion but the shame attached to it. Executed publicly at a major crossroads or on a well-trafficked artery, naked, denied burial, and left as carrion for birds and beasts, victims of crucifixion were subject to vicious ridicule. The Gospel records themselves make this clear — focusing as they do on myriad attempts to dishonor Jesus: spitting on him (Matt 26:67; 27:30; Mark 14:65; 15:19), striking him on his face and head (Matt 26:67; Mark 14:65; Luke 22:63), ridicule (Matt 27:29, 31, 41; Mark 15:20, 31), insults (Matt 27:44; Mark 15:32; Luke 22:65), and derisive mocking (Mark 15:16-20, 29-32; Luke 22:65; 23:11, 35-37). Seneca justifiably concludes of death by crucifixion:

> Can anyone be found who would prefer wasting away in pain dying limb by limb, or letting out his life drop by drop, rather than expiring once for all? Can any man be found willing to be fastened to the accursed tree, long sickly, already deformed, swelling with ugly weals on shoulders and chest, and drawing the breath of life amid long drawn-out agony? He would have many excuses for dying even before mounting the cross.[66]

Juxtaposed with this horrible reality is Peter's reference, in this context, to Jesus as Lord (1:3; 2:3), that "name . . . above every name" (Phil 2:9).

90:28-29 ("Then I stood still, looking at that ancient house being transformed. . . . I went on seeing until the Lord of the sheep brought about a new house . . ."); J. B. Green, *Death of Jesus,* pp. 278-80; Sanders, *Jesus and Judaism,* pp. 77-90; and, more broadly, McKelvey, *New Temple.*

66. Seneca, *ad Lucilium* 101; trans. Hengel, *Crucifixion,* pp. 31-32.

Third, having identified God as the decisive broker of honor and having demonstrated God's norms of valuation in his election and honoring of Jesus Christ, Peter goes on to develop the identity of his Christian audience in terms of imitation of Christ. Crucially, he does so not in terms of what his audience must become but in terms of what they already are. The parallel between Jesus and Peter's Christian audience is not complete, but it is significant:

Jesus	*Peter's Audience*
a living stone	living stones
rejected by humans	(implicit: rejected by humans)
in God's perspective, elect	in God's perspective, elect
in God's perspective, honored	in God's perspective, honored

Those who "come to him," "a living stone," themselves become "living stones" who share in his fate, both among humans and before God. In normal usage, a stone is "living" if it is in its original place, a usage that is out of place here, since this "living stone" has been dressed for its use in construction.[67] Peter has grounded the "living hope" of Christians in the resurrection of Jesus (1:3), suggesting that "living" refers here to Christ's having been raised from the dead, who extends this life to believers, the "reborn." Again, however, it is not that Jesus and Peter's audience are "equals." It is clear, for example, that the community of Jesus' followers comprise a temple that has him as its corner-stone — that is, that carefully prepared rock that ensures that the building is true. Additionally, the "spiritual sacrifices" they offer are acceptable to God *through* Jesus Christ. Moreover, as we have seen, their identification with Jesus is rooted in their response of faith to the gospel. Here, then, is the basis for instruction to which Peter will return again and again (e.g., 2:21-22; 3:9): You share in Jesus' identity, so respond to your antagonists as he did (knowing that it is God's evaluation that matters).

Fourth, appropriating for his audience a number of historic designations associated with Israel, Peter extends to them an incomparable honorifics of identity:

Spiritual House, Temple (v. 5).[68] With particularly vivid imagery, Chris-

---

67. So Achtemeier, p. 154.

68. Elliott argues that οἶκος *(oikos)* refers to "house(hold)" rather than "temple" (pp. 414-18; idem, *Elect and the Holy*, pp. 157-59). See, however, Best, "1 Peter II, 4-10," pp. 280-81. For use of οἶκος *(oikos)* for "temple," cf., e.g., Luke 6.4, 11.51, 19.46, Acts 2.2, 7.47-49. It is difficult to escape a reading of "temple" here given the confluence of related terms: οἰκοδομέω *(oikodomeō)* in relation to the "house (of God)" (v. 5; cf. 1 Chron 17:4, etc.), "priesthood" (v. 5), ἀναφέρω *(anapherō)*, with reference to offering a sacrifice (v. 5; cf. Lev 17:5; Isa 57:6; etc.), "spiritual sacri-

tians are represented as "living stones," components of a "spiritual house." Rebirth entails incorporation into a new community.[69] This is the new temple, the building of which was to accompany the restoration of Israel; this is the temple whose glory would outstrip that of the former temple (Hag 2:9).[70] In this case, the community of the faithful (and not individual believers) is itself the temple, which marks the community as sharing in the glory of God, as consecrated to God, as the residence of the Spirit (see above on 1:2), and as a symbol of God's power and presence.

Holy Priesthood (v. 5). Christians are being built up to the end that they are a holy priesthood. The purpose of this priesthood is to offer "spiritual sacrifices," a likely reference to holiness of life (1:15) and mutual love (1:22)[71] — an extension of the notion of "sacrifice" reminiscent of prophetic directives (e.g., 1 Sam 15:22-23; Jer 7:21-23; cf. Rom 12:1). Neither here nor in v. 9 can we find a basis for the Reformation doctrine of "the priesthood of all believers," not because the doctrine lacks warrant (see, e.g., 4:10-11), but because Peter's emphasis is not on the priestly role of each believer but on the priestly identity of God's people.[72] Emphasis falls therefore not on the priestly role of believers within the community of believers, but on the priestly identity and role of the community of believers in the world-at-large.

Elect Clan (v. 9). Peter uses the term γένος *(genos)*, which in the Jewish diaspora referred to a recognizable ethnic group sharing both ancestry and custom.[73] This appellation is surprising since the γένος *(genos)* of which Peter writes is comprised of persons otherwise unrelated, but is nonetheless apropos his Christian audience on account of their diasporic existence (1:1, 17), the common behaviors that characterize them (thus far, 1:14-17, 22; 2:2; see further, 2:11–3:7), their having become an identifiable people through new birth

---

fices" (v. 5), and consecration/holiness (1:22; 2:1, 5, 9). Although each of these terms is subject to an alternative sense, their confluence comprises strong evidence in support of a reference to the Temple. Of numerous parallels in the LXX, Goppelt mentions Judg 17:5; Isa 56:7 (p. 141).

69. This is emphasized in Feldmeier, 87-88; idem, "Wiedergeburt."

70. On the "new temple," see McKelvey, *New Temple,* reprised in McKelvey, "Temple." That Qumran provided a precursor to the notion of temple-as-community was argued especially by Gärtner, *Temple and Community,* though see now the critical comments in Schmidt, *How the Temple Thinks,* pp. 132-97.

71. Though holy life and mutual love are suggested by the immediate context in 1 Peter, a wider canvassing of the NT would add martyrdom, mission, praise, prayer, and giving (cf. Best, "1 Peter II, 4-10," pp. 287-88; Walton, "Sacrifice and Priesthood," pp. 138-41)

72. See the excurses in Schweizer, pp. 46-47; Brox, pp. 108-10; also Elliott, *Elect and the Holy,* pp. 166-69.

73. Barclay, *Mediterranean Diaspora,* pp. 402-13.

74. See Meyers, *Exodus,* pp. 145, 147.

(1:3, 23), and their status as God's people through their election and induction into Israel's story. Irrespective of present circumstances that might hint otherwise, they share with Jesus their having been chosen by God (1:1, 20; 2:4, 6). The phrase itself "elect clan" (or "chosen people") appears in Isa 43:20, a text with other parallels in vv. 9-10. Isaiah identifies Israel as God's chosen people in relation to exodus and restoration from exile, naming the Lord as the one "who makes a way in the sea, a path in the mighty waters," and as the one who provides for his people on the wilderness journey and in the midst of adversity (Isa 43:16-20). Peter reconceives the Isaianic text in order to refine the identity of his audience. In an important sense, though, this declaration of the honored status of God's people is foremost a celebration of the God who has made them a people.

Royal Priesthood and Holy Nation (v. 9). Alluding again to the narrative of God's mighty deliverance of his people from bondage, Peter borrows language from Exod 19:6. This is a reminder that God both hears the cries of his people in distress and acts to rescue them, entering into covenant with them. Importantly in both contexts, Exodus and 1 Peter, the resultant bond is communal in nature: between God and a people (again, not an individual). This bond entails a communal vocation, a mission; in the exercise of its priestly role, this people exemplifies God's holy character and propagates his will.[74]

A People for God's Possession (v. 9). Although Peter's language does not replicate the terminology of the OT, analogs do appear in Exod 19:5 ("my treasured possession") and Isa 43:21 ("the people whom I formed for myself"). The association with the twin notions of God's care for the distressed and the formation of God's people in exodus and restoration is important for 1 Peter, as is this emphasis on God's initiative in claiming his people and the high value he has placed on them. For Peter, his Christian audience, having been liberated by the precious blood of Christ (1:19), is all the more precious to God.

The responsibility that accrues to a community thus named comes at the end of v. 9: "to announce the wondrous acts of the one who called you out of darkness into his marvelous light." Similar language used to describe the reformation of Israel — "chosen people" and "the people whom I formed for myself" — leads to a similar vocation: "to declare my praise" (Isa 43:20-21). In Peter, however, "praise" is expanded to include not only vertical language (worship) but also horizontal (proclamation), and has been given a particular content. This is God's mighty deeds, and especially the act on which Christian conversion is based — namely, the saving death of Jesus Christ and God's having raised him from the dead (1:3, 18-19, 23). The move from darkness to

75. See Elliott, p. 442.

light is a typical metaphor for conversion (e.g., Acts 26:18; Eph 5:8; 1 Thess 5:5; cf. Rom 13:12; 2 Cor 4:6) with roots in representations of exodus and return from exile (e.g., Pss 107:10-13; 118:27; Isa 42:16; 58:10).

The consequence of God's salvific work and choice is the creation of a people that previously did not exist (v. 10). In naming his children Lo-ruhamah ("shown no mercy," Hos 1:6) and Lo-ammi ("not my people," Hos 1:9), Hosea had pronounced judgment on Israel, but also anticipated a reversal when his children would be renamed Ruhamah ("shown mercy," 2:1, 23) and Ammi ("my people," 2:1, 23). Borrowing these categories from Hosea, Peter deploys language used of the judgment and restoration of Israel to designate the significance of the conversion of his now-Christian audience — thus highlighting further the embeddedness of Christians in Israel's story with the result that the Scriptures of Israel are seen more and more as the account of their heritage — and to celebrate the saving and generative mercy of God.[75]

Writing of Israel in Exodus with words now also at home with reference to the Christian community in 1 Peter, Childs aptly summarizes:

> Israel is God's own people, set apart from the rest of the nations. Israel as a people is also dedicated to God's service among the nations as priests function with a society. Finally, the life of Israel shall be commensurate with the holiness of the covenant God. The covenant responsibility encompasses her whole life, defining her relation to God and to her neighbors, and the quality of her existence.[76]

One might say, then, that Peter has studied the past with an eye to serving the present and especially to showing the continuity between followers of Jesus and Israel of old. It is in that story that Christians will find their true identity and learn the way of faithfulness. Indeed, Achtemeier observes, "In 1 Peter, the language and hence the reality of Israel pass without remainder into the language and hence the reality of the new people of God."[77] Peter collapses the historical distinctives between ancient Israel and contemporary Christians in favor of theological unity, but not in order to deny the importance of history. Rather, in a world in which great age is honored,[78] he roots this "elect clan" in the antiquity of the relationship between God and Israel.

76. Childs, *Exodus*, p. 367.

77. Achtemeier, p. 69; see further idem, "Christology"; idem, "Newborn Babies." Note, however, that Achtemeier does not mean by this to suggest that Jews are thereby excluded from God's new people.

78. See, e.g., Pilhofer, *Presbyteron Kreitton*.

2:11–4:11

This major unit within the body of 1 Peter is set off from the preceding material, first, by the direct address with which it opens: "Beloved." This is paralleled in 4:12 — which, then, opens the next section of the letter. In addition to this explicit discourse marker, these boundaries are also suggested by parallel references to the glory of God in 2:12 and 4:11, forming an *inclusio,* and the presence of a benedictory acclamation in 4:11: "To whom be glory and the power forever and ever. Amen" (cf. 5:11). The movement is from Peter's focus on *identity* in 1:13–2:10 (summarized in 2:11: "aliens and exiles") to this lengthy emphasis on *exhortation.*[1] As a people whose perspective on the world is that of a stranger in the world, how should Peter's Christian audience live? What manner of life befits aliens?

As with the rest of the letter, this section is heavily theocentric (θεός, *theos,* "God" appears nineteen times), ensuring that the whole of life is structured in relation to God's will, mapped according to God's perspective, provisioned and enabled by God, and directed to God's glory. References to Christ (Χριστός, *Christos*) are also plentiful (seven), and this section is home to two significant christological passages (2:21-25; 3:18-22), with special emphasis given to his passion and vindication. It is here that Peter takes pains to interpret the suffering of Christ as redemptive, exemplary, and effective. Peter also adds to his already well-developed emphasis on the pattern of suffering and glory. In Peter's hands, this provides not only christological affirmation but also a promise to his Christian audience that if they follow Jesus' example their own suffering will be effective and lead to their vindication.

Within these theological and christological boundaries, though, Peter's focus remains on the context within which his Christians readers live and on the shape their lives are to take. This context is signified paradoxically. On the one hand, they live as "aliens and exiles" (2:11) "among the Gentiles" (2:12), where they experience·defamation, harshness, and suffering (2:12, 18-19; 3:9, 14, 16; 4:1); theirs is a minority status void of power and prestige (2:18; 3:1; 4:3-4). On the other hand, they live "in Christ" (3:16), with the result that their lives are to be determined by his. Three sets of terms used to describe this life are of special interest:

ὑπομένω (*hypomenō,* 2:20). Because this term is usually translated "endure," we might be led to imagine that Peter counsels longsuffering, forbearance, or some other expression of passivity in the face of trials. More appro-

---

1. παρακαλέω, *parakaleō,* "to encourage, exhort, urge," appears in the letter for the first time in 2:11 (also 5:1, 12).

priate translations, which account for both Greek tradition and LXX usage, would be "show unyielding perseverance or courageous steadfastness in the face of opposition."[2] That is, Peter encourages *resistance* — active, not passive; determined, but not violent. It is incumbent on the interpreter of this extended section of the letter to ask, What shape might this resistance take?

ἀγαθοποιέω *(agathopoieō, 2:15, 20; 3:6, 17)*. The term itself, "do good" or "do what is right," is rather vague since it does not carry within itself the standard by which to measure what is good or right. In an important sense, though, this is precisely the purpose of this long section of Peter's letter, to sketch what constitutes good behavior (in opposition to "evildoing" [κακοποιέω, *kakopoieō*, 2:12; 3:17]), summarized in 4:2 as "living . . . by the will of God."

ἀναστροφή *(anastrophē, 2:12; 3:1, 2, 16)*. Peter modifies "way of life" as "good" (2:12; 3:16), reverent and pious (3:1-2), and "in Christ" (3:16).

These references are related above all to Christian behavior in the world at large, but Peter also devotes attention to intramural relations, set with the eschatological horizons of his announcement that "the end of all things has come near" (4:7-11). Pervading this general portrait of the social practices that are to characterize Peter's Christian audience is an ethics of engagement, what Volf calls "soft difference."[3] That is, Peter navigates a via media, refusing such alternatives as revolt, withdrawal, or assimilation.

2:11-12

11 Beloved, I urge you as aliens and strangers in the world to avoid worldly cravings that wage war against life, 12 by maintaining[4] your honorable way of life among the

---

2. See Radl, "ὑπομένω"; *TLNT* 3:414-20.

3. Volf, "Soft Difference." This is disputed territory in Petrine studies, with the lines marked off especially by Balch (whose position is that Peter counsels social integration; see his *Let Wives Be Submissive;* idem, "Hellenization/Acculturation"; idem, "Household Codes") and Elliott (who argues that Peter urges a more sectarian identity capable of resisting pressures toward social conformity; see his *Home for the Homeless;* idem, "1 Peter, Its Situation and Strategy"; idem, *Social Science Criticism,* pp. 70-86). See the criticisms and alternative views of Feldmeier, *Christen als Fremde* (distinct from but engaged with Roman society); Talbert, "Plan of 1 Peter" (internal cohesion and social adaptability); Bechtler, *Following in His Steps,* pp. 109-78 ("liminal existence" presents an ambiguous relationship to society-at-large); Richard, "Honorable Conduct" (dual identity as both insiders and outsiders is mediated by the realization that all are God's creatures deserving of honor); Seland, *Strangers,* pp. 147- 89 ("a rather high acculturation" modified by commitment to obedience to Christ as the primary value of life).

4. With Achtemeier (p. 172), I am reading ἔχοντες *(echontes)* as an adverbial participle of means.

Gentiles, so that, whereas[5] they slander you as evildoers, from observing[6] your honorable deeds, they might glorify God[7] on the day of visitation.

This brief textual unit not only opens this major section of the letter (2:11-4:11), but functions as its descriptive heading. With 2:13, Peter moves into a more detailed examination of the contours of the "honorable life" he counsels here, employing the form of the "household code" so pervasive in Roman antiquity. As behavior is the visible expression of a group's shared and mutually reinforcing thought patterns for making sense of the world, and as practices flow out of their shared deepest allegiances and dispositions, so Peter begins now to widen the angle of his lens to explore the way of life that displays the identity of his Christian audience. Of course, since practices also shape dispositions and the imagination by which life in the world is ordered (see above on 1:3), what Peter encourages here is also formative of identity.[8]

Peter summarizes the identity of his audience in four ways:

(1) Though highly stylized,[9] his use of the term "beloved" in direct address is nonetheless consistent with and demonstrative of his admonition regarding mutual love in 1:22 (also 3:8; 4:8). Typically, address forms are governed by either of two semantic fields, *power* and *solidarity*[10] — with the former governed by status inconsistencies, the latter by intimacy and shared fate. They generate and cultivate particular relations. Bourdieu remarks, "Terms of address and reference . . . contain the magical power to institute frontiers and constitute groups, by performative declarations . . . that are invested with all the strength of the group that they help to make."[11] Peter's ad-

---

5. BDAG (p. 329) reads the ἐν ᾧ *(en hō)* clause with ἐν *(en)* taken as a marker of circumstance — thus, "whereas they slander," but notes that it is difficult to distinguish between this usage and "marker of a period of time" (i.e., "when" or "while") (on the temporal relative clause, see Moule, *Idiom Book*, p. 133; BDF §383; Achtemeier, p. 177). "Whereas" incorporates the clear sense that slander is a current reality while also accounting for the contrast between slander and giving glory.

6. Some witnesses (A P Ψ 33 𝔐) read the aorist ἐποπτεύσαντες *(epopteusantes)* rather than the present participle. The present participle is the more difficult reading; it is also well-attested (e.g., p⁷² ℵ).

7. One important witness (p⁷²) inserts ὑμῶν *(hymōn)* so that we would read "your God," presumably under the influence of Matt 5:16.

8. As Hillary of Arles recognized, Peter's concern with behavior "serves to unite all the members of the church in one overall harmony" (*Introductory Commentary on 1 Peter;* cited in Bray, p. 91).

9. Cf. Rom 12:19; 1 Cor 10:14; 15:58; 2 Cor 7:1; 12:19; Phil 2:12; 4:1; 1 Thess 2:8; Heb 6:9; Jas 1:16, 19; 2:5; 1 Pet 4:12; 2 Pet 3:8, 14, 17; 1 John 2:7; 3:2, 21; 4:1, 7, 11; Jude 3, 17, 20.

10. See R. Brown and Gilman, "Pronouns"; Fasold, *Sociolinguistics,* pp. 1-38.

11. Bourdieu, *Logic of Practice,* p. 170.

dress, then, encodes a social relationship of intimate kinship and solidarity between himself and his addressees. Whatever else might be said of his status as an apostle (1:1) and elder (5:1), he moves ahead with his instruction without hinting at any status inequality.

(2) Peter has already identified his audience with a cognate of the term πάροικος (*paroikos*, "alien," "stranger") in 1:17 (παροικία, *paroikia*, "stay among strangers"), and used the term παρεπίδημος (*parepidēmos*, "stranger") in 1:1. He now joins these two semantic cousins, thus presenting a hendiadys (two words to describe one thing) for "non-citizen" or "people of the diaspora" — that is, "a transparent distance in relation to society, a distance from its values, ideals, institutions, and politics."[12] In Gen 23:4, Abraham uses the same combination to describe himself, and it is worth recalling that Abraham had the status of someone without land holdings on account of the vocation given him by God. In the same way, the cost of discipleship for Peter's Christian audience is that they were rendered "aliens and strangers" in their own home communities.[13]

(3) In a related move, Peter identifies his audience as living "among the Gentiles." Given that many of Peter's audience would have been drawn from the ranks of the Gentile world, this may seem an odd move. However, we have just seen in vv. 9-10 how Peter applies Israel's own self-descriptors to Christians (e.g., "a royal priesthood, a holy nation"). In the same way, he now uses the collective term "the Gentiles" in a manner analogous to Israel's own usage. Whereas Israel deployed the term in designations of non-Jews (people who lived outside Torah), so in Peter's hands "Gentiles" can refer to all who do not follow Jesus. Interestingly, although in normal usage (i.e., with reference to "non-Jews") in the Second Temple Period "Gentiles" were those from whom Jews segregated themselves and on whom God's end-time judgment would fall, the traditions and ways of the Jews were attractive to some Gentiles, and Jews could be hospitable to the inclusion of Gentiles as sympathizers and proselytes.[14] The discrimination suggested by such us-them labeling, then, need not be absolute — a fact that is already inherent in the priestly

---

12. Feldmeier, *Christen als Fremde*, p. 22. See T. W. Martin, *Metaphor and Composition*, pp. 191-92.

13. On the problematic debate regarding a "literal" or "metaphorical" reading of "aliens and strangers," see above on 1:1. In his lengthy discussion of 2:11 Seland finds that, drawing on the social world of proselytes, Peter thus identifies his audience in relation to their social estrangement as converts in a hostile world (*Strangers*, pp. 39-78, 130-32).

14. For separation from Gentiles, see, e.g., Ezra; Nehemiah; Tob 1:9; 3:10; *Epistle of Aristeas* 139, 151, 277; for judgment, Sir 36:1-17; *1 Enoch* 48:7-10; 63:1-12; and for evidence related to the attraction of Gentiles to the Jews, see Feldman, *Jew and Gentile*, pp. 177-415.

role assigned to the Christian community in 2:4-10 and will become even more apparent throughout the letter.

(4) The present context of Peter's audience is marred by their being slandered as evildoers. This is the first explicit reference to the hostility directed against Christians in this letter, though it is anticipated in the prior use of language connoting marginal existence and identification with Jesus in his suffering. What constitutes "evil"-doing is, of course, in the eye of the beholder, and there is evidence already in the NT that Christians were subject to such accusations on account of their resistance to Roman conventions, their topsy-turvy worldview, and their missionary activity (e.g., Acts 16:20-21; 17:6-7; 19:24-27).[15] In 4:4 Peter will observe, "They are surprised that you no longer join them in the same excesses of dissipation, and so they blaspheme." In other words, Christians were "evildoers" because they were different; on account of their practices they did not fit in. In a world concerned with public standing, a particularly effective means of marginalizing one's opponents and reducing their wider influence is the smear campaign.

If this is the reality within which Christians live, what exhortation does Peter provide? They are "to avoid worldly cravings" by "maintaining an honorable way of life." Importantly, "life among *the Gentiles*" ought still to be "life *among* the Gentiles": engagement and witness, not withdrawal and isolationism. "Avoid cravings" is well-known advice found already in Greek moral philosophy (see above, 1:14). Though in moral literature, "cravings" is often discussion in relation to the object of one's desire, Peter takes another route, modifying "desires" in two ways: they are worldly, and they engage in war against life. The point of his contrast could not be more stark, for he pits one form of life against another — life as it reflects or pertains to this world (σαρκικός, *sarkikos*) and life as it reflects or pertains to the world to come (ψυχή, *psychē*).[16] Orienting one's life eschatologically ("a living hope," 1:3) is the means by which one creates distance from a life branded by the desires of this age.[17] How does one determine what lifestyle is "honorable" (καλός,

---

15. According to Tacitus, Nero was able to direct blame for starting the fire of Rome onto Christians since they were "loathed for their vices" (*Annals* 15.44, LCL).

16. See above on 1:9.

17. Thus, Bede, p. 89: "He suitably calls them *newcomers and strangers* that they may the less subject their mind to earthly affairs the more they remember that they have a fatherland in heaven. For there is accustomed to be this difference in this life between the elect and the condemned: that the elect as strangers and exiles now look for a fatherland in the future and are less pleased with the passing joys of the present the more they hope to receive future joys without end and to reign with Christ for ever; but the condemned on the other hand have their fatherland here and know how to yearn after the pleasures of this life alone. . . ."

kalos)? In the Roman world, obviously, this would be determined by the mores of public opinion, so that prevailing conventions provided a strong means of social control. In the preceding textual unit (2:4-10), however, Peter has demonstrated that it is not the opinion of society at large that is decisive and ultimate, but rather the perspective of God. He is the one who elects and honors what humans deprecate and reject. What is already clear is that this life is not "shaped by the desires that marked your former time of ignorance" and is characterized by holiness (1:14-16). More specifics regarding what constitutes "honorable behavior," the character of life which God approves, comprise the subject of the rest of this major section of the letter, 2:13–4:11.

Before outlining the shape of those honorable practices, though, Peter comments on their effect in relation to "the Gentiles." In a formulation reminiscent of Matt 5:16 and undoubtedly dependent on the same tradition going back to Jesus, Peter writes of the effectiveness of Christian behavior. In his theology of witness,[18] honorable deeds point beyond themselves — not only to the allegiances and dispositions of those doing the acting, but to the God whose call determines those dispositions and to whom those dispositions are directed. Christian witness is effective in leading outsiders to glorify God. The question is whether this result is realized in the present, through the conversion of disbelievers, or at the eschaton, when those whom they slandered are recognized for their faithfulness to God with the result that disbelievers come to glorify God. Might this be a false dichotomy? Reflected in Phil 2:10-11, the latter option also appears in the scene of final judgment in the Jewish book of Wisdom, probably dating from the first century BC:

> Then the righteous will stand with great confidence in the presence of those who have oppressed them and those who make light of their labors. When the unrighteous see them, they will be shaken with dreadful fear, and they will be amazed at the unexpected salvation of the righteous. They will speak to one another in repentance, and in anguish of spirit they will groan, and say, "These are persons whom we once held in derision and made a byword of reproach — fools that we were! We thought that their lives were madness and that their end was without honor." (Wis 5:1-4)

The conclusion that Peter likewise refers to final judgment is urged by Peter's concern otherwise with eschatological judgment (1:5, 7, 13; 4:7, 14, 17; 5:1) and by the phrase he employs, "day of visitation." This is one of myriad ways of re-

---

18. See Senior and Stuhlmueller, *Biblical Foundations for Mission*, pp. 297-302; Köstenberger and O'Brien, *Salvation*, pp. 237-43.

ferring to "day of the Lord" — in the OT a day of judgment (e.g., Isa 13:6-9; 34:8-12; Jer 46:9-12; Ezek 30:1-9; Obad 15-18; Zeph 2:1-15), a phrase popular among early Christians with reference to the eschaton (Acts 2:20; 1 Cor 1:8; 2 Pet 3:10; *Barn.* 15:4).[19] This does not vacate this text of its evangelistic import, however, since, on the last day, both believers and unbelievers will glorify God; the question is whether they will do so as an extension of their faith or as a contradiction of decisions made in the present life.

2:13–3:12

With 2:13, Peter begins a lengthy section with significant points of contact with the household code (sometimes known by its German designation, *Haustafel*), known throughout the Greco-Roman world, including Hellenistic Judaism and the NT.[20] Characterized by their focus on obligations of submission and reciprocity within the extended family — wives-husbands, slaves-masters, children-parents — they embodied basic values in Roman culture. Obligations to the state also factor in some examples of the form. Because they were based on the fundamental understanding of the human community assumed and propagated by the Roman Empire, any attempt to threaten their categories would be viewed as a threat to the glue of the empire itself.

For Rome, the household was regarded, as Cicero put it, as "the seed-bed of the state";[21] the orderliness of household relations was both a model for and the basis of order within the empire (with persons "assigned a precise place in a vast system of orders, classes, tribes, and centuries");[22] and Rome regarded itself as a household with the emperor as *paterfamilias.* The center of the Roman world was, first, the home,

---

19. Among the numerous synonymous expressions: "the day" (1 Cor 3:13; Heb 10:25), "that day" (Zeph 1:15; Zech 3:10; Luke 10:12; 2 Thess 1:10), "the day of vengeance" (Isa 61:2; 1QS 10:19), "your day" (2 *Baruch* 48:47; 49:2), "the day of great judgment" or "great day of judgment" (1 *Enoch* 10:6; 98:10; *Jubilees* 5:10), "the day of the wrath of judgment" (*Jubilees* 24:30), "the day of the Lord's judgment" (*Psalms of Solomon* 15:12), "the great day" (Jude 6), "the day of God" (2 Pet 3:12), "the last day" (John 6:39-40), "the day of the Mighty One" (2 *Baruch* 55:6), etc.

20. In the NT, cf., e.g., Eph 5:21–6:9; Col 3:18–4:1; 1 Pet 2:13–3:12. Regarding issues of background, see the helpful summary in Bauman-Martin, "Women on the Edge," pp. 259-63. This introductory section borrows heavily from Achtemeier, Green, and Thompson, *Introducing the NT,* pp. 524-26.

21. Cicero *On Duties* 1.53-55; cited in Gardner and Wiedemann, *Roman Household,* p. 2.

22. Nicolet, "Citizen," p. 26.

from whence the world took shape; by extension, Rome performed this function, ordering life, setting boundaries: everyone with a place, everyone in their place.

According to the NT evidence, Christian theologians did not merely absorb Roman household codes into their common life, but "baptized them," adapting them to the demands of their faith commitments. Christian innovations included the call to *mutual submission* as an interpretive heading for the household code (Ephesians), the introduction of the phrase *"in Christ"* by way of formulating a new set of behavioral norms, and *adaptation* of the household code to particular social scenes. In this way, the use of household duty codes functioned as rhetorical devices for communicating particular responses in particular social settings. Apparently, the struggle with community identity among believers led to adaptations of normal social institutions as this numerically rather insignificant group of persons, Christians, explored means for faithful existence as a minority movement within wider society.

By way of introduction to the household duty material in 1 Peter, let me make three general observations. First, this section appears immediately after a major shift in the structure of the letter, marked by the use of the address "Beloved, I urge you . . ." in 2:11. Peter has thus turned from an elaborate description of the theological and social identity of his Christian audience to the behaviors that appropriately flow from that identity and help to shape it further. The behavioral distinctives he begins to enumerate with 2:13 are concrete ways in which his audience is to relate to a social situation in which they are cast as "aliens and strangers." For this reason, it might be argued that Peter has adopted the form of the household duty code in order to encourage these Christian believers to adapt themselves more fully to Roman society and so to demonstrate the character of the Christian community as essentially orderly and law-abiding;[23] accordingly, he would be urging them for the sake of their own survival to give up some of their distinctives and to embrace more fully practices deemed honorable in the ancient Mediterranean. But such a reading of the household code in 1 Peter would require that we view this section of the letter in unbending tension with the rest of the document. What is crucial elsewhere in the letter is that one do what is honorable in the sight of the Lord; repeatedly, too, Peter warns his readers to expect nothing less than hostility and slander. More likely, then, this section of the letter has the opposite force. It is designed to warn against compromise with Roman social values even though failure to

---

23. So Balch, *Let Wives Be Submissive;* cf. Woyke, *Neutestamentlichen Haustafeln,* pp. 47-48.

do so will invite further suffering. This interpretation is born out by the two further considerations.

Second, Peter's household code lacks the formal parallelism typically associated with this literary form. True, husbands are mentioned alongside wives, but the amount of material devoted to wives is far out of proportion to the instruction directed toward their counterparts; and slaves are without counterpart in this list. What is more, directives to all Christians in 3:14-16 are modeled closely on, if not quite identical to, Peter's directives to wives in 3:1-6 (see below, on 3:14-16). In other words, Peter's directives are more far-reaching than we might first imagine, bursting through the narrow embankments of instruction to Christian subgroups like slaves or women so as to address the Christian community as a whole.

Third, at the center of 2:13–3:12 is a section extolling the example of Christ, so that the whole of Peter's household code can be understood in terms of an inverted parallelism:

> 2:13-17: instruction for everyone
>   2:18-20: instruction for slaves
>   2:21-25: the example of Christ
>   3:1-7: instruction for wives (and husbands)
> 3:8-12: instruction for everyone

Peter's instructions thus pivot on the example of Christ, who suffered unjustly and did not reciprocate with abuse, but rather entrusted himself to the God who judges justly. By emphasizing slaves and wives, and correlating their recommended behavior with that of Christ, Peter paints his audience generally as persons without power and privilege in society-at-large — the very thing we would expect of a people otherwise characterized as "aliens and strangers" (1:1, 17; 2:11).[24] Christians should expect to be treated as those who are powerless in household relationships, knowing, however, that their appropriate conduct would have a redemptive effect akin to that of Jesus. His death had the effect of restoring those who had gone astray; analogously, their maintenance of Christian behavior in the midst of unjust suffering might bring to faith those who presently abuse them (see 2:12; 3:1).

---

24. It is therefore difficult to follow Winter when he finds in 2:14 a reference to Christians receiving public accolades as civic benefactors (*Welfare of the City*, pp. 25-40).

2:13-17

13 Be subordinate to every human institution²⁵ on account of the Lord — whether to the emperor as superior, 14 or to the governors as those sent by him to render justice on those who do evil but to praise those who do good, 15 for thus it is the will of God that you, by doing good, silence the ignorant talk of foolish people 16 — as free people and not as persons having freedom as a pretext for evil, but as God's slaves. 17 Honor all people. Love the family of believers. Fear God. Honor the emperor.

With the imperative to "be subordinate" in v. 13, Peter begins to sketch the nature of alien existence in the world in which his Christian audience finds itself. With v. 18, he will move from this focus on the expected behavior of all Christians to the particular responsibility of (household) slaves; at the end of this household code, in 3:8-12, he will return explicitly to address all.

Peter's instruction in this unit is difficult to follow on account of the complexity of the sentence that runs from v. 13 to v. 16. Simplifying for the sake of clarity, his admonition boils down to this: "Be subordinate to every human institution on account of the Lord, as free people, as God's slaves." The intervening material in vv. 13b-15 and 16b is parenthetical to and explanatory of his primary directive, and v. 17 explicates further the place of Christians in the world.

Although it is often translated "submit," Peter's opening imperative ὑποτάγητε *(hypotagēte)* is best understood as the negative of "withdraw" rather than an alternative to the exercise of power or rebelliousness. Finding and occupying responsibly one's place in society, not resignation, is more to the point.²⁶ That this subordination is not ultimate has been ensured already by the apostle's use of another term, "obedience" (ὑπακοή, *hypakoē*), in relation to God and the gospel (1:2, 14, 22). Here, in its barest form the imperative to "be subordinate" is further qualified by three phrases: "on account of the Lord," "as free people," and "as God's slaves." Clearly, the claims of humans and human institutions do not supplant the claims of the Lord. Indeed, though in the Roman world Caesar was named "lord," Peter speaks of Jesus as Lord in v. 13, immediately prior to his reference to the emperor, ensuring the priority of the claims of the Lord Jesus Christ (cf. 1:3, 25; 2:3, 3:15).

One of the basic polarities descriptive of human relations is "slave or

---

25. Or "to every human creature."

26. Hill, "Liturgical Formulations," p. 55; Senior, "Conduct of Christians," pp. 429-30; Meeks, *Morality,* pp. 38-39; Goppelt, *Theology,* p. 168: "At its core the directive did not address itself in opposition to rebellion but to the flight of emigration. It wanted to say primarily: enlist yourselves in the given institution!"

free." As the Roman jurist Gaius wrote in the late second century AD, "The first division of humanity is into free and slaves" (*Institutiones* 1.9; cf. Gal 3:28; John 8:33). For this reason, it is startling to find both descriptors attributed to Peter's audience. The Greco-Roman world knew the notion of freedom encapsulated in the axiom "live as you like" or "do as you please" (compare the Corinthian slogan "All things are lawful for me" [1 Cor 6:12]). But the rise of the city-state motivated discussion around the relationship of freedom and law. The values of freedom on the one hand, integration into a given order on the other — these stand in apparent competition. For the Greeks and then the Romans, a characteristic resolution to this tension asserted that, "since the law (of nature) is good and since no one desires to do what is bad, the only person who is truly free and does what he wants is the one who does what is good and thus follows the law." Pressing further, even in Greek philosophy, "god" could be associated with the "true law,"[27] and this provides a useful background for making sense of Peter's seemingly paradoxical phrases, "as free people" and "as God's slaves."

In the context of this letter and against the backdrop of Peter's portrayal of Christian life in terms of exodus imagery, however, still more can be said. First, a "free person" (as opposed to a slave or even a "freed person") was one *born* into freedom, a status Peter now claims for his audience (irrespective of their social station in the Roman world) on the basis of their having been born anew (1:3; 2:2).[28] Second, deeply embedded in the exodus tradition is the notion that God's liberation of Israel was for the purpose of service: "Let my people go, so that they may serve [λατρεύω, *latreuō*; NRSV "worship"] me in the wilderness" (Exod 7:16; see 8:1, 20; 9:1, 13; compare Luke 1:74). Freedom is for service, as Levenson claims: "The point of exodus is not freedom in the sense of self-determination, but *service*, the service of the loving, redeeming, and delivering God of Israel, rather than the state and its proud king."[29] Not surprisingly, then, key to the metaphor of "slavery" in the NT, whether to Christ or to God, is that of absolute devotion.[30] Third, Peter's earlier image of liberation now comes into fresh focus. Liberation was *from* "the emptiness of your inherited way of life" (1:18), *from* those "desires that marked your former

27. Jones, "Freedom," p. 856; with regard to the standard definition of freedom as "doing whatever one wants," Jones refers to Aristotle *Politics* 5.9.1310a; Cicero *Officiis* 1.70, etc. For additional background, see Raaflaub, "Freedom in the Ancient World"; Nestle, *Eleutheria*.

28. Gaius *Institutiones* 1.9-11: "The first division of humanity by the law of persons is into free and slaves. The free are divided into freeborn and freed persons. The freeborn are free by birth, freed persons by manumission from legal slavery."

29. Levenson, "Exodus and Liberation," p. 152.

30. See Harris, *Slave of Christ.*

time of ignorance" by which his audience had previously been formed (1:14). The picture is that of a power at work to shape and to enslave — indeed, a power that "wages war" against life (2:11). In its stead, another power is at work, the call to holiness made possible through the death and resurrection of Jesus. Thus, liberation is *for* divine service, *for* holiness.

It is "as free people" who are "slaves of God" that Christians are able to subordinate themselves to human institutions. Subordination is thus an expression of freedom, not of coercion. What is more, any potential claims of human institutions to wield ultimate authority are mitigated, even denied, at the outset by Peter's locating his directives under the umbrella of obedience to God.

Whether subordination is to "every human institution" or to "every human creature" is unclear. κτίσις *(ktisis)* usually refers to "creation" or "creature" in biblical Greek, but can refer to the result of human creative effort, such as the founding of a city.[31] Human institutions are suggested by references to the emperor and his appointees in vv. 13b-14, but "humans [in general]" are suggested by the potentially parallel admonition in v. 17: "Honor all people." In either case, the emperor is defined in human terms (no small claim in light of the development of the imperial cult in the world of 1 Peter),[32] and the role he and his representatives are to exercise is circumscribed as rendering justice to those who "do evil" and rewarding those who "do good."

"Doing good" (ἀγαθοποιός, *agathopoios*) is unlikely to refer simply to "living as a good citizen" nor to anything so exalted as assuming the role of a public "benefactor" whose "praise" might come in the form of monuments and memorials. After all, Peter uses the verbal form of this noun (ἀγαθοποιέω, *agathopoieō*) with respect to the performance of slaves (2:20) and of wives (3:6) and as an impetus for (wrongful) suffering (3:17), and these do not point us in the direction of public service and patronage. Moreover, "doing good" is set in opposition to "doing evil" in vv. 14-15 and to "sinning" in v. 20 — contrasts that do not point us in the direction of public benefaction. Nor does evidence within the letter regarding the makeup of Peter's audience encourage our finding among their number many persons so well-placed and with the necessary funds.[33] More simply, Peter is thus insisting that, when practiced well, the role of these public officials was both balanced

---

31. On the latter, see MM 362; BDAG 573.

32. Cf. Fishwick, *Imperial Cult.*

33. See Seland, *Strangers,* 176-80; Jobes, pp. 174-76; Achtemeier, pp. 184-85. Van Unnik thought in terms of living up "to the standard of first-class citizens" ("Good Works," p. 99; see pp. 99-106), a view that anticipated Winter's proposal that "good works" refers to public benefaction ("Public Honoring"; idem, *Welfare of the City,* pp. 25-40).

and responsive to the actual performance of those over whom they judged. In such a context, God's will is that Christians live lives marked by goodness and in this way pull back the curtain on the misjudgments of others. (Vv. 14 and 15 thus recapitulate and expand on v. 12.) These "others" need not be particularly bad people, but Peter does portray them as lacking in perception — operating with a deficit of good judgment and with an erroneous view of God, their "ignorant talk" no doubt derived from the ignorance characteristic of those who have not experienced new birth (1:14).

In staccato style in v. 17, Peter names four overarching expectations of those who "do good" according to the will of God. Mutual love is characteristic of the Christian community (literally, "brotherhood" — see on 1:22).[34] Reverent fear is due God alone (see above on 1:17), a further denial of the divinity of the emperor. Most stunning, though is that the same verb, "honor" (τιμάω, *timaō*), names the Christian obligation both to emperor and to all. Regarding the emperor, Peter's directive represents no less than what is expected of all living under imperial rule; this is expected, given the emperor's superior status (v. 13). On the surface, Peter might seem to be abdicating the rule of Christ for the rule of Rome. Almost with the same stroke of the pen, however, Peter writes "Honor all people." It is hard to imagine a more devastating critique of the Roman way, for with the pairing of these two directives Peter has flattened the status pyramid of the Roman world. He has just made one's response to the slave next door no less than one's response to the emperor. Without saying so explicitly, Peter has thus cast his Christian audience as imitators of the Father who exercises impartiality in judgment (1:17).

2:18-20

18 Household slaves, subordinate yourselves[35] in all fear to your[36] masters — not only to those who are good and considerate, but also to those who are harsh; 19 for

---

34. ἡ ἀδελφότης (*hē adelphotēs*) appears in the NT only in 1 Pet. 2:17; 5:9, and in the LXX in 1 Macc 12:10, 17; 4 Maccabees 9:23; 10:3, 15; 13:19, 27. The potential association with 4 Maccabees is especially interesting, since it refers to a social context not unlike that of 1 Peter — namely, a minority group struggling with the majority. In 4 Maccabees, ἡ ἀδελφότης (*hē adelphotēs*) suggests not only the sense of "(the character and heritage of) the family of believers," but especially "the family of believers called to faithful testimony in the face of hostility."

35. Following Snyder ("Participles and Imperatives," p. 197), I am reading ὑποτασσόμενοι (*hypotassomenoi*) as an imperative.

36. The second person plural is understood, but has been added by ℵ and a few other witnesses.

this is commendable,[37] if someone endures pain, suffering unjustly, because of one's consciousness of God.[38] 20 For what credit is it if you endure when you sin and are beaten? Rather, if, when you do good and suffer, you endure, this is commendable before God.

In the context of Peter's household code (2:13–3:12), Peter seemingly moves now from general instruction aimed at his Christian audience (2:13-17) to address household slaves in particular. A parallel focus on wives (and, almost as a footnote, to husbands) will appear in 3:1-7. The effect is an ostensible particularization of the more general directives in 2:13-17 — that is, vv. 18-20 show how the admonition "to honor" everyone is to be worked out in the particular case of household slaves.

Three telling observations indicate that, with this focus on household slaves, not all may be as it seems, however. First, the form of the household code as this is represented in parallel Christian literature generally operates with a reciprocity of instruction, so that obligations appropriate to their respective stations in life are outlined for both masters and slaves. Peter speaks of masters (v. 18), but does not address them at all. This could be because Peter's audience includes slaves but no (or few) masters, or it might be that Peter's directives are not narrowly focused on household slaves after all. If the former is the case, then Peter envisions a context where households included Christian slaves in the households of non-Christian masters — a microcosm of the wider situation Peter envisions, with Christians a minority, marginal group within the wider world. Second, Peter has already addressed his audience as "free persons" and as "slaves of God," raising the question how we are to read "household slaves" in v. 18. οἰκέτης *(oiketēs)* is the more specific term for domestic slaves as opposed to slaves assigned to the fields,[39] but it is also a generic term overlapping with δοῦλος *(doulos),* the term for "slave" used in v. 16. Given the nature of slavery as an institutionalized form of marginality

37. The best witnesses (e.g., p⁷² ℵ) are elliptical and so invite the addition of other modifiers clarifying that commendation is "from God" : παρὰ τῷ θεῷ *(para tō̧ theō̧,* C Ψ etc.), θεῷ *(theō̧,* 2464 *pc),* θεοῦ *(theou,* 623 *pc);* cf. v. 20.

38. This unusual phrase has attracted emendation: the substitution of ἀγαθήν *(agathēn,* "good") for θεοῦ *(theou,* "God") (C Ψ etc.) and the addition of ἀγαθήν before θεοῦ (including p⁷²). Elsewhere, Peter writes of a "good conscience" (3:16, 21), but this could suggest either that an original "good" in v. 19 would reflect Petrine style or that "good" has been added under the influence of usage elsewhere in the letter. Undoubtedly, the harder reading is the shorter (i.e., θεοῦ), and it is well-attested (ℵ Aᶜ B P 049 𝔐 lat co).

39. It is therefore difficult to accept the relevance of "agricultural handbooks," to which Harrill draws attention, as providing the background for making sense of Christian household codes *(Slaves in the NT);* Harrill, however, does not deal with 1 Peter.

and Peter's characterization of his audience as people who, because of their loyalty to Jesus, inhabit the outer perimeters of honorable society, it is easy to find in vv. 18-20 an address to all Christians rather than to a subset. The presence of "slave" and "household slave" side-by-side would signal that Peter's instruction applies to all who comprise the "household of God."

This emphasis meshes well with one of Peter's theological foci. Since troublesome relations with those outside the community press for enhanced cohesion within the community, we are not surprised that he epitomizes Christians with familial and household language: "children" (1:14; 3:6), "infant" (2:2), "son" (5:13), "family" (literally "brotherhood," 2:17; 5:9), "house/household" (2:5; 4:17), "servant/slave/household servant" (2:16, 18; 4:10), "beloved" (2:11; 4:12), and "Father" (in relation to God; 1:2, 3, 17). In the context of the ancient Mediterranean, we might expect metaphors of household and family to signal relations of status and power, but this is not the case here where all are children together and all are slaves in the household of Father God.[40]

Third, the christological material in vv. 21-25, which provides in the exemplary and redemptive work of Jesus a warrant for Peter's perspective on unjust suffering, is tied to Peter's instruction to household slaves but betrays no hint that the example of Jesus applies to slaves alone. Indeed, the proverbial character of vv. 19-20 points already in the direction of the more general reach of Peter's instruction. "Household slaves" then refers not only to Christian household slaves but, indeed, to all of Peter's addressees, drawing attention to the practical denial of status concerns within the household of God and, then, to the vulnerability and alienation of all Christians vis-à-vis the wider world.[41]

In this context, the attitude of early Christian theologians like Peter toward slavery invites scrutiny, not least on account of historical appeals to NT households as providing God's own imprimatur for the American practice of slavery.[42] Two conclusions are inescapable. (1) Neither Peter nor other NT writers explicitly condemn slavery as a

---

40. Generally, cf. Lassen, "Roman Family."

41. So also many interpreters — e.g., Achtemeier, pp. 192-95; Bechtler, *Following in His Steps*, pp. 151-54; Brox, p. 128; Elliott, "Backward and Forward," pp. 188-89; Thurén, *Argument and Theology*, p. 140. Combes's study of the metaphor of slavery in the NT highlights the importance of the NT's lack of bias against slaves and its egalitarian approach to issues of status within the Christian community (*Metaphor of Slavery*, pp. 68-94). Harrill's work on defining "slavery" underscores the basic identity of the slave as "other" (*Manumission of Slaves*, pp. 13-17).

42. See the summary comments in C. J. Martin, "Haustafeln"; Harrill, *Slaves in the NT*, pp. 165-92.

social institution. (2) Nevertheless, when one considers the warrants for slavery in the Roman world (particularly the alleged distinction between slave and free with regard to inherent capacities and status), it is obvious that Peter's theological perspective (particularly his identification of his Christian audience, including slaves, as "free persons" [v. 16], his emphasis on "honoring all persons," including slaves [v. 17], and his specific address to slaves as moral agents [v. 18]) must trigger the unraveling of the institution of slavery — at least insofar as this institution rested on arguments from inherent nature and incarnate status in the Greco-Roman world.[43]

As in v. 13, "to subordinate" is best understood as the negative of "to withdraw" rather than as an alternative to the exercise of power or defiance. Finding and occupying responsibly one's place in society, and not passive or unreflective subjection, is more to the point. That subordination, even for slaves, is qualified is demonstrable, first, from the limitations outlined in vv. 13-17, and now through the modifier "in all fear." As is already apparent in 1:17 and 2:17, "fear" (or "reverent fear" or "godly fear") characterizes the regard one has for God; fear of what others think, even in a society wrapped around concerns with public standing, must never become a motivating factor for Christian behavior (3:14). Additionally, the unusual phrase "because of one's consciousness of God" (v. 19) identifies the impetus and muscle behind the courageous steadfastness Peter counsels. Ordinarily, συνείδησις *(syneidēsis)* refers to "conscience," but in this setting it connotes that communal understanding of God and his will that both allows and encourages behavior that, to those outside the faith, would seem nonsensical.[44] This is the nature of the Christian imagination, however — this way of seeing and situating oneself in relation to the world, a patterning of life around the will of God (see 2:15; 3:17; 4:2, 19), which is shared by those of like-minded faith and which empowers and guides characteristic practices (see above on 1:3-12).

---

43. Thébert summarizes these warrants, but also notes their beginning to wane in the imperial period ("Slave"); hence, we should not exaggerate the uniqueness of Christianity in this respect, especially given the ease with which its canonical texts could be used to make the situation of slaves even worse (cf., e.g., Bradley, *Slavery*, pp. 150-53). My perspective on "practice" borrows heavily from the work of Bourdieu (e.g., *Logic of Practice;* Bourdieu and Wacquant, *Reflexive Sociology*), though without the relative fatalism of *habitus* we read in his work. Accordingly, transformation of one's life-world necessarily gives rise to alternative practices. For this reason, I cannot agree with Harrill (*Slaves in the NT*, p. 85) that the argument that the subversion of pagan ethical norms undermined the practice of slavery is without merit; of course, whether one can trace historically a causal relationship from one to the other is an altogether different question.

44. Cf. Selwyn, pp. 176-78; Pierce, *Conscience*, pp. 105-08; Brox, p. 133: "moral subordination ("Bindung an") to the will of God"; Elliott, p. 519: "mindful of God's will."

Subordination is not predicated on the relative goodness of those in authority. Just as honor is due "all people" (v. 17), so subordination applies to masters whether "harsh" (σκολιός, *skolios,* literally, "crooked") or "good and considerate." Engaging society entails discernment regarding the will of God, how best to put into practice one's primary allegiance to God, and judgments regarding the moral goodness of the one exercising authority provide no basis for retreat from participation. Because in some circles in antiquity slaves were regarded as persons devoid of critical facilities, that Peter addresses slaves at all is significant; that he calls upon them to exercise discernment and moral agency in relation to the will of God is especially suggestive.[45]

Vv. 19 and 20 each begin with the causal conjunction "for" (γάρ, *gar*), and proceed with aphoristic utterances providing warrant for the directive about subordination. The structure of these verses, an inverted parallelism, places special emphasis on the logic on which these proverbs are grounded: "because of one's consciousness of God." This is important because, apart from this insight into God's dispositions, these axioms would be hard to swallow.

> v. 19a   For this is commendable, if someone endures pain, suffering unjustly
> v. 19b   on account of one's consciousness of God.
> v. 20   For what credit is it if you endure when you sin and are beaten? Rather, if you endure when you do good and suffer, this is commendable before God.

V. 19a finds its parallel in v. 20, with the latter restating v. 19a both negatively and positively. Different language is used, but the similarities are inescapable. Thus, "commendable" ("grace") is affiliated with "credit," both connoting divine approval;[46] "endure" actually translates two different Greek verbs, but with the same connotation of "courageous steadfastness in the midst of ad-

---

45. "For the slave has no deliberative faculty at all" (Aristotle *Politics* 1.5.6; see 1.5.9; 1.13.7; Thébert, "Slave," pp. 138-40, 164-66; Combes, *Metaphor of Slavery,* pp. 29-33). This perspective was hardly universal, however, particularly in the Roman world where "nature"-based arguments for slavery persisted but were mitigated by arguments based in "law" and not "nature" and by arguments for the essential humanity of both slave and free (see Combes, *Metaphor of Slavery,* pp. 34-37; Harrill, *Manumission of Slaves,* pp. 25-27; idem, *Slaves in the NT,* pp. 19-21, 38-40). At the same time, Harrill points out that the humanization of slaves belonged to discourse among philosophers and moralists, who addressed themselves not to slaves but their own social peers (p. 139); the significance of Peter's addressing his theological criticism of status-based practices to slaves themselves should not be downplayed.

46. For a similar sentiment and parallel language, see Luke 6:32-35. See Michaels, p. 142 (with reference to Exod 33:12, 16; Prov 12:2, etc.).

versity"; and "suffering" is akin to "pain" and "beating." "Beating" (the verb is κολαφίζω, *kolaphizō*) is at home in the world of master-slave relations, but in the NT is found elsewhere only in references to Jesus' suffering (Matt 26:67; Mark 14:65) and in texts wherein Paul identifies with the passion of Christ (1 Cor 4:11; 2 Cor 12:7); its usage here as a cipher for "suffering" anticipates the focus on Jesus' passion and death in 2:21-25. Between these proverbial sayings we find only one contrast — behavior that puts "sin" (in the general sense of "committing a wrong") on display and behavior that constitutes "doing good" (v. 20). The latter signals "suffering unjustly," senseless in normal human evaluation, but honorable in God's perspective.

"Suffering for doing good" is thematic in 1 Peter (see the repetition of the idea in 3:17; 4:15; 5:10), but this does not mean that Peter advises his Christian audience to call for opportunities to suffer. He is not supporting the equation: the more suffering, the more commendation from God. This will become more clear as we turn to vv. 21-25, but it is already obvious that Peter's concern is with "doing good." Obedience to God and the gospel is the issue. What of the suffering that accrues to persons whose lives are thus out of step with the world around them? Peter's response is twofold: (1) rejection by humans is not a barometer of God's perspective, since "the very stone that the builders rejected has become the head of the corner" (2:7), and (2) such suffering will be undeserved. With 2:21-25, Peter will add a third response: innocent suffering as a following in the footsteps of Christ.

2:21-25

21 For to this you have been called, since Christ also suffered[47] on your[48] behalf, leaving you a pattern in order that you might follow in his footsteps —
    22 who committed no sin, nor was deceit found in his mouth;
    23 who, when he was insulted, did not insult in return; while suffering did not threaten, but handed himself over to the one who judges justly;

47. Some witnesses substitute ἀπέθανεν (*apethanen*, "died") (p⁸¹ ℵ Ψ etc.) for ἔπαθεν (*epathen*, "suffered") (read by p⁷² A B C O etc.). "Suffering" better fits the context (see πάσχω [*paschō*, "to suffer"] in vv. 19, 20, 23), and the substitution was likely motivated by the more pervasive dying formula tradition: "Christ died for our sins" or "Christ died for us" (e.g., 1 Cor 15:3; 1 Thess 5:10).

48. Here and elsewhere in this passage, the textual evidence is complicated by competing readings of the second person plural ("you [all]") and the first person plural ("we," "us"). This is due in part to problems of the ear (ἡ- and ὑ- [*hē-* and *hy-*] were practically indistinguishable) and to the appearance of both in the formulaic tradition.

24 who, himself, bore our sins in his body on the tree, in order that, once
    we have died to sins, we might live to righteousness;
  by whose wounds you were healed —
25 for you were straying like sheep, but now have been turned to the shepherd and
guardian of your lives.

What is the "this" to which "you have been called," and to whom does "you"
refer? In terms of local context, Peter's address is to household slaves and
concerns their endurance in the face of unjust suffering. The structure of
2:13–3:12 identifies this passage as its pivot point, however, compelling us to
apply this christological argument in support of responses of courageous
steadfastness in the face of unjust suffering to everyone addressed in the various subunits of Peter's household code — that is, to all Christians. The
wider reach of 2:21-25 is also supported by our earlier recognition that the
referent of Peter's "household slaves" extends more broadly to include Peter's Christian audience by the shift in pronouns — from second person in
v. 21 to first person in v. 24b and back to second person in vv. 24c-25, and by
the proverbial nature of the parallel instruction, addressed to all, in 3:14; 4:1,
19. Accordingly, not only household slaves but Peter's Christian audience of
aliens and strangers is informed of their vocation to remain steadfast in the
context of wrongful suffering.

One of our most pervasive and stubborn views of reality, a kind of
philosophical expression of the physical law that for every effect there is a cor-
responding cause, is that our lot in life is the consequence of our deeds,
whether good or evil, and the experience of suffering is directly traceable to
prior sin.[49] This chain of cause and effect, it is widely believed, is ensured by
God. As a necessary corollary, those who suffer cannot be righteous. This
common view of reality is confronted by Israel's tradition of the suffering
righteous, in which the righteous suffer because they are righteous. This is especially true as Israel nurtures its belief that God will rescue the righteous
through (rather than *from*) suffering. Working with what is perhaps the pre-
eminent expression of this tradition in Israel's Scriptures — Isaiah's Servant
of the Lord, the righteous one whose suffering is the consequence of others'
sins rather than his own — Peter restructures the life-world of his Christian
audience. He can do so only because he can claim as a given that Jesus is Lord
(1:3), that Christ stands in the place of God as the object of faith (cf. 1:8, 21;
2:6-7), and thus that his suffering cannot be attributed to his sin (2:22). If this
is true of Christ, then his suffering for us opens for us the possibility that the

49. See Janowski, "He Bore Our Sins," pp. 49-54.

power and consequences of sin might be wiped out. If this is true of Christ, then suffering need not be the outcome of wrongdoing; in fact, as with Christ, so with his followers, suffering can be the result of righteousness.

Scholars debate whether Peter is drawing on traditional material in vv. 22-25, as opposed to engaging in his own appropriation of Isaiah 53 to the circumstances before him.[50] At one level, this debate is unimportant; so tightly bound to its context is the christological material in vv. 22-25 that our primary concern must be how it serves the letter's argument. How does Peter put christological reflection into play so as to shape the identity and behavior of his audience? On the other hand, if, as seems likely, Peter is drawing on widely recognized Christian tradition, this would ground his instruction in authoritative tradition. Even if this were not the case, however, his christological reflections and their appropriation to his audience's lives would already have been sanctioned by his own apostolic status (1:1), by the definitive authority of Jesus' example, and by their basis in Israel's Scriptures.[51] Multiple sources of legitimation are important, given the topsy-turvy nature of Peter's counsel, this instruction that so fully cuts against the grain of commonly held views of suffering and our sensibilities of fairness and self-protection.

The elegance of Peter's reflections on Christ may blind us to the primary concerns of this text. He is really not about christological reflection here but deploys christology in the service of his instruction about Christian life and witness in the world. This is christology in the service of ecclesiology. Opening with a conjunction of reason, γάρ (*gar,* "for"), Peter ties vv. 21-25 into the foregoing by way of indicating why his audience are to respond to unjust suffering with courageous determination. The expected rationale is given in vv. 21 and 24c-25: you have been called to lives patterned on the obedience of Christ (v. 21) and, indeed, have been transformed through the work of Christ from a past life of sin so that you may live today as Christ lived (vv. 24c-25). The four relative clauses comprising vv. 21-24b ("who," "who," "who," "by whom") provide the warrant for Peter's instructions on discipleship, rooting them in the character and significance of Jesus' suffering. "If badly treated slaves symbolize the suffering of Christian existence amid a hostile society, the suffering Christ functions both as the pattern to be followed in living out that suffering existence and as the means by which the readers were

---

50. Favoring the traditional nature of 2:21-25, see, e.g., Lohse, *Märtyrer und Gottesknecht,* pp. 184-87; and more recently, Pearson, *Christological and Rhetorical Properties,* pp. 116-34; Aitken, *Jesus' Death,* pp. 62-64. Alternatively, see Schlosser, "Guide Lines," pp. 387-89; Achtemeier, "Suffering Servant," pp. 178-79; and the mediating view of Schutter, *Hermeneutic and Composition,* pp. 138-44.

51. Cf. Campbell, *Honor,* p. 133; Aitken, *Jesus' Death,* p. 56.

initiated into the relationship with God and with Christ that empowers them to fulfill their calling."[52]

Peter's vision of response in the midst of adversity is assisted by three affirmations in vv. 21 and 25. (1) First, he welds Christlike response in the face of unjust suffering to the vocation of his audience. The importance of the divine calling on his readers has already been developed in 1 Peter where the verb καλέω (*kaleō,* "call") and its cognate adjective ἐκλεκτός (*eklektos,* "chosen") appear: with regard to holiness (1:15) and the movement from darkness to light (2:1), and more generally to divine election (1:1; 2:4, 6, 9). Consequently, we understand that suffering is not an aberration in the lives of Christians but grows out of the transformation of their lives stemming from new birth. Suffering in this setting is the result of living for, not against, God. Moreover, courageous determination in the face of suffering is an expression of "doing good," of holiness.

(2) Second, he uses picturesque language for discipleship. ὑπογραμμός (*hypogrammos,* "pattern") is found only here in the NT and was used otherwise of lines on a page to assist children learning to write or letters of the alphabet set out for children to copy.[53] Mixing his metaphors, Peter adds the image of "following in his footsteps." This phrase is not found elsewhere in the Bible, but is reminiscent of the call to discipleship as following Jesus (e.g., Mark 8:34). Both word-pictures underline the importance of Christlike performance, putting into play in one's own life and circumstances the dispositions on display in the obedience of Christ.

The metaphor of "performance" would in this case designate the obedience of Christ, as this is interpreted by Peter in 2:21-25, as "script." Performance should not be confused with play-acting, since it assumes all of the seriousness of embodying and giving expression to the character of Christ in one's own life. Whether one is thinking of an analogy with musical or theatrical performance, a script is complete on its own, but also invites greater fulfillment, or activation, in the event of performance. Performance speaks to creative fidelity: "fidelity" in the sense that the notes on the score or words in the script predetermine the parameters of performance, "creative" in the sense that life is too particular and unruly to be carefully scripted, but Christians can nonetheless be persons who are shaped by this script and understand the plotlines of life by it. (Some therefore prefer the metaphor of "improvisation" to "performance.")

---

52. Bechtler, *Following in His Steps,* pp. 193-94; cf. Lohse, "Parenesis and Kerygma," pp. 56-59; Elliott, "Backward and Forward"; Matera, *NT Christology,* pp. 178-80.

53. I have summarized these uses of ὑπογραμμός (*hypogrammos*) and its cognate ὑπογράφω (*hypographō*) from Plato, *Protagoras* 326d and Clement, *Stromateis* 5.8.49; see Schrenk, "ὑπογραμμός."

In this case, even when Christian performance involves no tree of execution, for example, we may still judge that the pattern of Christ's obedience has been followed.[54]

(3) Finally, in v. 25 Peter underscores what has become an ongoing refrain regarding his audience — namely, the contrast between their past and current lives. Drawing on the imagery of Isa 53:6, he portrays the former lives of his audience as "straying like sheep." This is life without a proper sense of direction (characterized by ignorance and futility — 1:14, 18), the antidote for which is Jesus, shepherd and guardian (see Ezekiel 34), the agent of their conversion.[55]

By way of supporting this quality of life, Peter interprets the suffering of Jesus in two ways, as exemplary (and thus to be modeled in the lives of Christians) and as atoning (and thus unique in providing the basis for Christian life). Central to his argument is his appropriation of material related to the Servant of Yahweh in Isaiah 53:

Peter's Claims	1 Peter	Isaiah
Christ committed no sin, nor was deceit found in his mouth.	2:22	53:9
Christ, when he was insulted, did not insult in return; while suffering did not threaten.	2:23	53:7
Christ bore our sins (on the tree).	2:23-24	53:4, 12
By Christ's wounds you were healed.	2:24	53:5
You were straying like sheep.	2:25	53:6

Peter's use of Isaiah 53 brings into focus three observations regarding his presentation of Christ. First, note that the sequence of Peter's affirmations does not replicate the order of the source material in Isaiah 53. Instead, his order follows that of the passion accounts, moving from Jesus' trials (during which he remained silent while he was mocked and beaten) to the cross and its significance. Apparently, Peter found in Isaiah 53 a commentary on Jesus' passion which he then organized in relation to the events of Jesus' suffering and death.[56]

---

54. See, e.g., Barton, "NT Interpretation"; Craigo-Snell, "Command Performance."

55. Hence, I am taking ἐπεστράφητε (*epestraphēte*, "turn") as passive (rather than middle) and identifying the images of shepherd and guardian with Jesus rather than with God. Though God (or his designates) can be symbolized as a shepherd in the OT (e.g., Num 27:17; 1 Kgs 22:17), Jesus (or his designates) has this role in other NT texts (e.g., John 10:1-16; Heb 13:20; cf. 1 Pet 5:4).

56. Peter's exegetical move is consistent with Jewish interpretive procedures more

Second, this raises the question of Peter's theological approach to the Scriptures. Put simply, why did Peter do what no other NT writer did by explicitly claiming that the Suffering Servant of Yahweh was none other than the crucified Christ?[57] To be sure, other NT texts hint at this connection, the most important being the words of Jesus at the Last Supper (e.g., Mark 14:22-24) and the Ransom Saying (Mark 10:45),[58] and Luke records how Philip interpreted Isaiah 53 with respect to the good news of Jesus (though without reference to his crucifixion or its significance: Acts 8:32-33). But this is a far cry from the presentation of a fourth-century church father like Athanasius, who insisted that Isaiah 53 referred to Jesus' death "exceeding clearly" (*De Incarnatione* §34), a perspective that seems more at home with 1 Peter than other parts of the NT. Peter's innovation is found in his earlier comments regarding how the Scriptures must be read. In 1:10-12, Peter observed that the Scriptures must be read as advance testimony "to the sufferings coming to Christ and his subsequent glories" and could be read in this way because it was, in fact, the Spirit of Christ himself who inspired the ancient words.

Heretofore we have not known to which prophetic words Peter was drawing attention. Nor would we have been helped by trolling the Scriptures of Israel in the hope of finding among the prophets plain and direct precedent for messianic suffering. Although it may seem "exceedingly clear" that Isaiah 53 anticipates the suffering of Christ, we cannot escape the reality that Isaiah speaks of the suffering *servant,* not the suffering *Christ;* nor that we cannot find in Second Temple Judaism more broadly (i.e., apart from Christian writings) an expectation of a suffering Messiah.

In 2:21-25, Peter clarifies things. If the Scriptures provide already the fabula (or story behind the story) of rejection leading to glory, then it is the career of Christ, who suffered unjustly while commending himself to the just Judge, that demonstrates that this is the pattern by which to construe the whole of God's purpose as this is revealed in Scripture. The suffering of Christ thus serves Peter as a theological assumption from which to read the Scriptures and make sense of them for Christians in the world. To put it differently, it is not merely that Peter found in Isaiah 53 a "prophecy" that was

broadly in the first century, according to which scriptural texts were shaped in light of later events (rather than events being manufactured in order to "prove" ancient prophecies).

57. Achtemeier addresses this question helpfully ("Suffering Servant"), even if his suggestion that Peter's innovation was the prerequisite for early Christian exploration of the relation of the passion of Christ to Isaiah's suffering servant goes beyond the evidence; it is easier to show how Peter achieved this identification than to argue why others did not.

58. Classically argued in Jeremias, *Eucharistic Words;* cf. Pesch, *Abendmahl;* and, recently, Stuhlmacher, "Isaiah 53." See also, e.g., the citation of Isa 53:12 in Luke 22:37.

"fulfilled" in Christ, but rather that the suffering of Christ and the suffering of Isaiah's servant point to the same reality in God's purpose: God's saving purpose on behalf of a sinful people accomplished in the suffering of Yahweh's sinless servant.[59]

Third, we should observe how the details concerning Christ's suffering are woven tightly into the fabric of 1 Peter.

> Peter refers his audience to Christ's "suffering" (rather than "death") in order to underscore the commonality of their suffering with his (2:19, 20, 21, 23; 3:14, 17, 18; 4:1 [2x], 15, 19; 5:10).[60]
>
> Peter draws attention to Jesus' non-retaliation in the face of suffering, a model for Jesus' followers, reformulating the silence of the sheep before its shearers in Isa 53:9 so that it applies directly to the situation of Christians facing hostility (e.g., 2:19-20, 22-23). Jesus' non-retaliation in the face of undeserved hostility demonstrates his sinlessness (2:22-23).
>
> Earlier, Peter described God as the Father who judges impartially (1:17). Now he declares that Jesus entrusted himself to the just Judge, and he will go on to urge his audience to entrust themselves to a faithful Creator (2:23; 4:19) — all of this in spite of present unjust suffering (2:19, 22-23).
>
> Peter refers to Jesus' having been executed "on the tree" rather than "on the cross" (v. 24). He thus unnecessarily, and all the more purposefully, draws attention to the presumed ignominy of Jesus' death, since this terminology evidences the formative influence of Deuteronomy 21 on early Christian reflection on the death of Jesus: "When someone is convicted of a crime punishable by death and is executed, and you hang him on a tree, his corpse must not remain all night upon the tree; you shall bury him that same day, for anyone hung on a tree is under God's curse . . ." (21:22-23; cf. Acts 5:30; 10:39; Gal 3:13).[61] Using the same interpretive move we find in 2:4-10, however, rather than deny the shame attending Jesus' execution, Peter seems actually to embrace it. Rather than evidence of Jesus' rejection, the cross is actually the signature of the God whose purpose is realized in the atoning death of his Anointed One.

59. Cf. Childs, *Isaiah*, 420-23.

60. The use of πάσχω (*paschō*, "suffer") in the absolute sense to mean "suffer death" is also found elsewhere in the NT — e.g., Luke 24:46; Acts 1:3; 3:18; 17:3.

61. What is more, crucifixion was in the Roman world a form of execution reserved for dissidents and slaves, persons at the bottom of the ladder status-wise.

Just as Peter directs his audience to "do good" rather than "sin" (e.g., 2:15, 20), so he informs us that Jesus was without sin (2:22). Moreover, because he "bore our sins in his body on the tree," we, having died to sins, can live to righteousness (2:24; see 4:1).

The upshot of these points is that we see how fully Peter's christological remarks are embedded in his instructions to Christians — not so that they can share his christological perspective (though this is not ruled out) but so that his christological perspective will shape them. Said differently, if it is true that the suffering of Jesus informs how we read the Scriptures of Israel, particularly Isaiah 53, it is also true that the ensuing narrative of Jesus ought to inform how we read the church. The story of Christians experiencing adversity in the diaspora is nothing less than their participation in the story of Jesus, itself deeply rooted in Scripture. These three — Scripture, Jesus, the church — are woven together as one narrative recounting the outworking of God's plan. As a result, Peter's audience is able to draw strength as well as direction from his interpretation of Jesus' career.

Jesus modeled innocent suffering in two respects. He suffered even though he did not deserve it, and, in the midst of abuse, he did not retaliate. At another level, however, Jesus' suffering was not exemplary but unrepeatable, unique. This concerns its atoning significance. Even if, for Peter, the suffering of Christians is effective (2:12, 15; 3:1-2), their suffering is not effective in the way that Christ's is. It alone is redemptive; as Peter will write in 3:18, Christ's suffering is singular and decisive, "once for all."

How is Christ's death atoning? In the phrase "suffering for you" in v. 21, ὑπέρ (*hyper,* "for the sake of" or "for the benefit of") marks the saving significance of Jesus' death, but does not indicate how it saves. The imagery that Peter draws from Isaiah 53 is more helpful, drawn as it is from the constellation of sacrificial practices in Israel, particularly the purification offering (see Leviticus 4–6; 16).[62] These texts portray atonement as redemption through the

---

62. This is not to say that the practice of sacrifice can simply be mapped onto Isaiah 53 or, for that matter, onto Peter's representation of Christ's death. (For the unease of reading Isaiah 53 against the backdrop of the sacrificial system, see Janowski, "He Bore Our Sins"; followed, e.g., by Childs, *Isaiah,* pp. 417-18. On the other hand, in his discussion of the Servant, Goldingay finds evidence of borrowing from the religious laws in Leviticus and Numbers (*God's Prophet, God's Servant,* pp. 146-47). While explicitly denying the notion that Peter portrays the cross as an altar of sacrifice (an old opinion, argued most recently in Schelkle, p. 85), V. Taylor helpfully observes that 1 Pet 2:21-25 does not tie the meaning of Christ's death to any one sacrifice but uses phraseology reminiscent of the purification offering and the scapegoat narrative of Leviticus 16 (for the thesis that Peter is dependent on the scapegoat ritual, see Windisch, p. 65). He con-

substitution of an animal for a human being and as purification of the sanctuary and, by extension, of the community of God's people. For Leviticus sin pollutes, stains, and spoils, whereas sacrifice cleanses the effect of sin, cultic impurity. Sin has resulted in an estranged relationship between the sinner and God, and it is this separation that sacrifice addresses. "Thus the priest shall make atonement on your behalf for the sin that you have committed, and you shall be forgiven" (Lev 4:35; see 4:31; 5:10, 13, 16, 18; 6:7).

For Peter, two ingredients of the sacrifice are especially developed. In this system, the life of an unblemished animal substitutes for blemished human life. Accordingly, Peter affirms that Jesus "committed no sin, nor was deceit found in his mouth" (v. 22; see 1:19: "a lamb without blemish or defect"). Moreover, in the rite of sacrifice, the laying of hands on the beast's head signals the importance of "identification" or "representation" — with sinners identifying themselves with the beast and the beast now representing sinners in their sin. Accordingly, Jesus "bore our sins . . . on the tree" (v. 24). Peter speaks to the efficacy of sacrifice in terms of exchange and representation: sin and death transferred to the sacrificial victim, Jesus, and his purity and life to those who receive the benefits of the sacrifice.

Peter represents the effect of Jesus' atoning death with two images. First, through Jesus' death, "we have died to sins," so we "live to righteousness" (v. 24), a movement paralleled in imagery taken from Isaiah: "you were straying like sheep, but now have been turned to the shepherd and guardian of your lives" (v. 25). This way of putting things emphasizes again that Christ's suffering was not deserved (see already vv. 22-23); rather, the sin (and straying) was symptomatic of the situation of those for whom he died. What is more, atonement is not something that happens outside a person, but is his or her proceeding through death into life, a cleansing from sin that opens up new life. Thus, Jesus' suffering can rightly be described as an event of "sanctifying atonement," since Christ's death takes the place of others in such a way that affects their very being, that opens to them "a new life-reality."[63] Second,

---

cludes of our text, "In order to express the meaning of Christ's death, it draws upon underlying ideas of the sacrificial system, rather than the special associations of any one rite, and combines them with other ideas, such as those of imitation and of sin-bearing, which have no place in that system" (*Atonement*, p. 30; see pp. 29-30). On sacrifice more broadly, see Milgrom, *Leviticus;* idem, *Cultic Theology;* G. A. Anderson, "Sacrifice."

63. Hofius, "Fourth Servant Song," p. 186: "Christ's death is seen in these sentences not as the substitutionary bearing of the penal consequences of our sin, but as an event of sanctifying atonement." Alternatively, Breytenbach thinks in terms of Christ's taking upon himself the punishment for sin ("Christus litt euretwegen"), but the notion of punishment derives less from 1 Peter and more from the atonement model with which Breytenbach introduces his essay.

drawing on the words of Isaiah, Peter announces that atonement effects healing. Were we to adopt a view of disease at home in the world of 1 Peter, we would recognize that the two images — from death to life, and healing — speak to the same reality: cleansing for holiness. This is because, both in antiquity and in much of the non-Western world today, healing refers to human recovery, to the restoration of health in all its respects, and, then, to patterns of health in which we are fully alive.[64] Peter's concern, then, is with the conformation of his audience into Christlikeness. "The calling of God is to suffer the way Christ did — without reviling — and to live the way he did — without sin."[65] This is made possible by Jesus' suffering.

3:1-7

1 In the same way, wives, subordinate yourselves[66] to your own husbands, so that, even if some disbelieve the word, they might[67] be gained without a word by means of their wives' manner of life, 2 having observed[68] the reverent and holy manner of your lives. 3 Your adornment must not be of the outward sort — the fashionable braiding of hair and the accessorizing with gold or wearing of fine clothes — 4 but rather the inner person, the heart — with the enduring disposition[69] of a gentle, peaceful spirit, which is greatly valued before God. 5 For in this way also in times past holy women who placed their hope in God would adorn themselves, subordinating themselves to their own husbands, 6 as Sarah obeyed Abraham when she called him "lord," whose children you became when you did what is good and feared nothing that causes fear. 7 In the same way, husbands, live knowledgeably with the women,[70] as you would with a weaker vessel, according honor to her as also to fellow heirs of the grace of life, so that your prayers are not hindered.

---

64. J. B. Green, "Healing."

65. McCartney, "Atonement," p. 183.

66. Following Snyder ("Participles and Imperatives," pp. 197-98), I am reading ὑποτασσόμεναι *(hypotassomenai)* as imperatival.

67. The future indicative (here: κερδηθήσονται, *kerdēthēsontai*, "to gain") can be used in a purpose clause where the subjunctive + ἵνα *(hina)* would be expected (BDF §369[2]).

68. Some witnesses read the present participle (-ευοντες [-*euontas*], including p⁷² ℵ* etc.) rather than the aorist (-ευσαντες, -*eusantes*). The aorist matches better the theology of the letter (with its emphasis on the effective witness), and is widely supported (ℵᶜ A B C P Ψ etc.).

69. I am reading ἐν τῷ ἀφθάρτῳ *(en tō aphthartō)* as a dative of means answering the question How might your adornment be that of the inner person?

70. Following Snyder ("Participles and Imperatives," pp. 197-98), I am reading συνοικοῦντες *(synoikountes)* as imperatival.

With 3:1, Peter returns to the sort of instruction expected in a household code, addressing wives, then husbands, in a way that is parallel to his directives to household slaves in 2:18-20. His opening phrase, "in the same way," is rich with possible antecedents: "Follow the pattern of Christ . . ." (2:21-25), "As with household slaves, so with you . . ." (2:18), "Subordinate yourselves as an expression of subordination to all . . ." (2:13), and, especially, "Regard subordination to your husbands as an expression of the directive regarding honoring all" (2:17). This is a reminder that wives (3:1) and husbands (3:7) are not singled out for special instruction as much as they represent additional subgroups for whom Peter works out the nature of Christlike life as "aliens and strangers in the world" (2:11-12). The effect is a particularization of the more general directives in 2:13-17 — that is, 3:1-7 show how the admonition to "honor" everyone is to be worked out in the particular cases of wives and husbands.[71]

As in 2:13, "subordinate" is best understood as the negative of "withdraw" rather than as an alternative to the exercise of power or defiance. The term refers to finding and occupying responsibly one's place in society rather than to passive or unreflective subjection. We may also recall from 2:13-17 that it is "as free people" who are "slaves of God" that Christians, including Christian wives, are able to subordinate themselves. Subordination is thus an expression of freedom, not of coercion. The connection of 3:1-6 with 2:13-17 should also remind us that subordination to any human or human institution is derivative of one's obedience to God. This insight is often taken to mean that subordination to human authorities, such as an individual to the state or, in this case, of a wife to her husband, is an expression of obedience to God. The result is too often the easy equation: "to obey the state or to obey one's husband is to obey God." Although it is true that, for Peter, the subordination of a wife to her husband can be an expression of "doing good" (2:15) and "honoring God" (2:17), this could never be "blind submission." That subordination is not ultimate has been ensured already by the apostle's use of another term, "obedience" (ὑπακοή, *hypakoē*), in relation to God and the gospel (1:2, 14, 22), so that subordination to any human institution is conditioned by obedience to God and the gospel. Moreover, in its barest form the imperative to "be subordinate" is further qualified in 2:13-17 by three phrases: "on account of the Lord," "as free people," and "as God's slaves" (see above on 2:13-17). In 3:1-6, more specific mitigating factors will be identified; by way of introduction to this passage, though, it is important to recall that the claims of humans and human institutions, including those of husbands, do not supplant the claims of the Lord.

---

71. Similarly Spencer, "1 Peter 3:6," pp. 110-11; T. W. Martin, *Metaphor and Composition*, pp. 204-6; *contra* Balch, *Let Wives Be Submissive*, p. 98.

The context Peter envisions is not easily summarized. Biblical scholarship has tended to view the place of women and wives in the Roman world in monochromatic terms, supinely relegated to the domestic sphere. Though the emerging portrait of the "new" Roman woman in classical studies has yet to come into sharp focus, some things have become clear. First, we can no longer speak of "the role of women" in Roman antiquity, but only of a broadening range of "roles." This is because, second, the first decades of the Roman Empire saw significant expansion in cultural roles for women, particularly in the public sphere. Nevertheless, third, the presumed weakness and light-mindedness of women was an underlying principle of Roman law and practice, just as it was true that, however liberated Roman women might have become, they were not so liberated as men. Expanding roles for women, including public benefaction and other forms of influence, were tied to the heightened fortunes of men.[72] This means that Peter's counsel regarding women and men in 3:1-7 can be regarded as a cultural product of the Roman Mediterranean which both reflects (or broadcasts) Roman "family values" and reflects on (or engages critically with) those values; in doing so, however, Peter was not so much blazing an altogether new trail for women or men, but participating, albeit for his own theological reasons, in an ongoing process of painting and repainting the mural of expectations of wives and husbands.

By way of setting the stage for our reading of 3:1-6, of special importance are the widespread expectations of wives with regard to the religion of the household. "A family's religion was transmitted through males, and the *paterfamilias* [the ranking male in a Roman household] was the chief priest. Upon marriage, a girl renounced her father's religion and worshiped instead at her husband's hearth."[73] In his "Advice to Bride and Groom," Plutarch wrote:

> A woman ought not to make friends of her own, but to enjoy her husband's friends in common with him. The gods are the first and most important friends. Hence, it is becoming for a wife to worship and to know only the gods that her husband believes in, and to shut the door tight upon all strange rituals and outlandish superstitions. For with no god do stealthy and secret rites performed by a woman find any favor. (19 [*Moralia* 140D])

72. See Pomeroy, *Women in Classical Antiquity,* pp. 149-226; Rawson, "Roman Family"; Dixon, *Roman Women;* Bauman, *Women and Politics.* Winter has surveyed relevant material with an eye to its importance for Pauline communities *(Roman Wives).*

73. Pomeroy, *Women in Classical Antiquity,* p. 152. See further, Balch, *Let Wives Be Submissive,* pp. 83-86.

Yet the situation Peter envisions is one in which the wife is a Christian, and the husband is not (though this is not to suggest that there are no Christian husbands — cf. v. 7), and, significantly, his directive does not countermand her faith in Christ. That is, the very fact that Peter addresses how to live in this situation, rather than instructing the woman "to worship and know only the gods that her husband believes in," is itself a nonconformist position; that Peter identifies the wife as a covert evangelist within her marriage even more so. From one perspective, this state of affairs merely reflects the teaching of Jesus, who had promised division within families (e.g., Luke 8:19-21; 12:51-53). From another, this is a potentially volatile situation, since the center of the Roman world was, first, the home, from whence the world took shape, and only then, by extension, did Rome order life and set boundaries: everyone with a place, everyone in their place. Rome (the city) defined the life-world of even the far reaches of Roman rule (the empire), and yet the basic unit of the household ordered life within the empire. As a result, disturbance in the one generated disturbance in the other. A mixed household, religiously speaking, entailed competing allegiances having potentially far-reaching consequences. Thus, Origen cites the words of Celsus, one of Christianity's second-century opponents, who complains that followers of Jesus "get hold of the children privately, and any women who are as ignorant as themselves," urging them to rebellion (*Contra Celsus* 3.55).

With regard to his instruction for household slaves in 2:18-20, we saw that Peter's directives expanded beyond his narrow address to slaves to include the whole of his Christian audience. In this way, "household slaves" referred also to persons with the marginal status of household slaves, to Peter's audience of "aliens and strangers in the world." The same can be said of his address to wives in the present passage. This is supported by the overt parallelism between instructions aimed at wives in 3:1-6 and instructions to all in 3:13-16:[74]

	to wives	to all
effectiveness of one's "manner of life" in witness	3:1-2	3:16
reverence toward God in the midst of disbelievers	3:2	3:16
virtue of holiness	3:2, 5	3:15
priority of the heart	3:4	3:15
the virtue of gentleness	3:4	3:16
the importance of hope	3:5	3:15
prohibition of fear of human intimidation	3:6	3:14
the importance of "doing good/righteousness"	3:6	3:13, 14, 16

74. J. K. Brown, "Silent Wives," pp. 396-97. Brown draws attention to a key point of discontinuity, concerning speech (vv. 1, 15); I will return to this issue below.

Of course, it is also true that what is said of all Christians in 3:13-16 applies as well to wives, more specifically addressed in 3:1-6. As with household slaves (2:18-20), so now Peter draws particular attention to wives because they are parade examples of the lives of all Christians in a world of hostility and abuse. What is said to believing wives in relation to their disbelieving husbands is applicable to all believers in relation to a disbelieving world.

Peter's instruction to wives (vv. 1-6) is cast in the form of an inverted parallelism:

> command to wives, particularly for those with disbelieving husbands
> (vv. 1-2)
>> command to wives more generally (vv. 3-4)
>> general exemplar of wifely dispositions (v. 5)
> Exemplar of wifely disposition, particularly for those with disobedient
> husbands (v. 6)

In the more general command to wives (vv. 3-4), with its concern for inward virtue over outward adornment, Peter gives voice to a typical line of thought in Roman antiquity. It has been "baptized," of course, through Peter's provision of more particularly Christian motivations for this focus on "the heart" and his appeal to holy women of the past, but vv. 3-5 nonetheless retain their broad applicability. Accordingly, vv. 1-2, 6 comprise instruction more immediately tied to the particulars of the social situation Peter envisions, in which Christian women are married to non-Christian husbands.

First, with respect to vv. 1-2, 6, Peter's address is specifically to wives with husbands who disbelieve. Peter uses the same expression in 2:8 (cf. 3:20; 4:17), where those who disbelieve are portrayed as persons who reject the Messiah. This suggests not simply "unbeliever," but persons who have actively rejected the gospel and, in the context of 1 Peter, would likely be numbered among those casting aspersions on followers of Jesus. The instruction here provides a welcome hopefulness, since Peter assumes that disbelief need not be a hardened response; rather, disbelievers can be won over to faith. "To gain" or "to win over" is a missionary term,[75] with conversion in this instance a consequence of the husband's witnessing (the term Peter uses [ἐποπτεύω, *epopteuō*] suggests "monitoring") his wife's manner of life. Though it appears in this setting, this instruction is not restricted to wives. Earlier, Peter expresses a similar sentiment, even using the same vocabulary, in his directive to "aliens and strangers in the world": maintain "your honorable way of life

---

75. See Matt 18:15; 1 Cor 9:9-12; Daube, "κερδαίνω."

among the Gentiles, so that, whereas they slander you as evildoers, from observing your honorable deeds, they might glorify God on the day of visitation" (2:12).

Interestingly, the "manner of life" advised by Peter represents Christian dispositions, not Roman. "Reverent" refers to reverent fear before God, and holiness to a conformation to God's own holiness, both expected of all Christians (1:15, 17).[76] That is, borrowing from the imagery of 1:12-21, Peter advises resistance realized in the rejection of ancestral and worldly conventions of behavior and in allegiance to God (rather than the gods of the households in which Christian wives find their home). Peter paints a lifestyle sculpted in the image of the holiness of God as opposed to one shaped by the desires and futile ways expressive of their lives prior to rebirth. Although one might argue that "reverence" and "purity" would be attractive in the Roman world, and that the exercise of these virtues might have made the Christian faith at least innocuous if not also attractive to pagan husbands, the understanding of these qualities in 1 Peter actually takes us in a different direction. These Christian wives are not being told "to fit in," but rather called to the sort of integrity of life that is realized in the maintenance of courageous steadfastness in the midst of adversity. Almost a century later, Justin Martyr would testify to the evangelistic appeal of such behavior:

> It is evident that no one can terrify or subdue us. For, throughout all the world, we have believed in Jesus! It is clear that, although beheaded, and crucified, and thrown to wild beasts . . . and fire, and all other kinds of torture, we do not give up our confession. But the more such things happen, the more do other persons and in larger numbers become faithful believers and worshipers of God through the name of Jesus. (*Dialogue* 110)

The priority of lifestyle over words is puzzling, and all the more when we notice that in v. 16 Peter tells his audience to maintain readiness so that, when asked for a "word" (λόγος, *logos*), they will be able to give a "verbal de-

---

76. φόβος (*phobos*) and φοβέω (*phobeō*) appear, respectively, in 1:17; 2:18; 3:2, 14, 16; and 2:17; 3:6, 14. The term I have translated as "holy" in v. 2 is ἁγνός (*hagnos*) rather than the more usual ἅγιος (*hagios*), found in 1:15. However, the verbal form ἁγνίζω (*hagnizō*) is used with the sense of "be holy" already in 1:22, and ἁγνός (*hagnos*) is juxtaposed with ἅγιος (*hagios*) in the present textual unit (v. 5). See L & N, 1:745-76. I. H. Marshall unnecessarily limits its sense to "sexual morality" (p. 101); though this is included and the relevance in a Roman context of a reference to sexual purity may even have suggested the term (see Michaels, p. 158), the sense in 1 Peter is broader. Among German commentators, Brox's "heiligmäßiges" (pp. 141, 143) is more suggestive than "reinen" (Schweizer, p. 62; Feldmeier, p. 118).

fense" (ἀπολογία, *apologia*). This stands in obvious contrast to his disallowing a "spoken word" (λόγος) here. This discontinuity is not as troublesome as it might at first appear. (1) The emphasis on "manner of life" in vv. 1-2 brings to expression a key emphasis of the letter (1:15, 17, 18; 2:12; 3:1, 2, 16) and so hardly betrays a diminished role for women. (2) The instruction in 3:16 is given to all, including the wives addressed in vv. 1-2. (3) Even in 3:16, words are not volunteered, but are given upon request. This is undoubtedly a function of the oppressive situation within which these Christians lived, and we have no reason not to assume that, as with Christians more generally so with Christian wives of disbelieving husbands in particular, an invitation to speak opened the door to sharing "the word."[77] (4) Echoing the language of Isa 53:7, Peter has it that Jesus was silent in the face of insults (2:22-23). In their silence, Christian women follow the model of Jesus as a strategy of nonviolence, a kind of familial disobedience giving expression to Peter's call for courageous perseverance as a minority group. (5) Given the inversion of social categories signaled already in 2:4-10 and especially 2:21-25, it really was possible to declare victory (before God) in the face of apparent defeat (before humans), for this was a central means by which to undermine the Roman ethos of power and status. In short, "If the injunction to be subject," explained here as the prohibition of speech, "appears at first to function as a religious legitimation of oppression, it turns out, in fact, to be *a call to struggle against the politics of violence in the name of the politics of the crucified Messiah.*"[78]

How does the anecdote regarding Sarah assist Peter's argument? Since Abraham is usually regarded as a model of faith (e.g., Romans 4), in what way might Sarah's situation prove significant to Peter's instruction to Christian wives of disbelieving husbands? The initial problem is to determine to what Peter is referring. Only in Gen 18:12 does Sarah refer to her husband as "lord," but there she is more disrespectful of him than obedient to him. Moreover, in the relevant material in Genesis, it is easier to find evidence that Abraham obeyed Sarah than the other way around.[79] Help comes from two directions. First, we find in Gen 12:11-20 (see also Genesis 20) a text of interest, which

---

77. λόγος (*logos*, "word") is used twice in v. 1 — first with reference to the gospel, second with reference to speech.

78. Volf, "Soft Difference," p. 22 (emphasis original). On the problematic of this prohibition of speech, I have learned from Vouga, "La christologie," especially pp. 316-20; Bauman-Martin, "Women on the Edge," pp. 274-76; J. K. Brown, "Silent Wives"; Michaels, "Going to Heaven," pp. 230-3).

79. Thus, e.g., ὑπακούω (*hypakouō*, "obey") is used of Abraham in Gen 16:2, but never of Sarah in the LXX; and in Gen 21:12, God tells Abraham to do whatever Sarah tells him to do (using the related term, ἀκούω, *akouō*, "to heed").

presents Abraham and Sarah as "aliens," Abraham as a disobedient husband who treats his wife unjustly (compare disbelieving husbands in 1 Pet 3:1), and Sarah's obedience. Second, Jewish interpretation of Sarah provides more points of contact, suggesting an interpretive milieu in which Peter's casual rendering of the relationship between Sarah and Abraham had currency.[80] In any case, Genesis 12 and 20 both recount the status of Abraham and Sarah as aliens, how Abraham's duplicity placed Sarah in harm's way, no response from Sarah of any kind other than acceptance of her husband's scheme, and God's intervention. From these episodes, read within the context of contemporary rehearsals of the Abraham-and-Sarah stories, Peter seems to extrapolate Sarah's entrusting herself to the God who oversees human history and intervenes on behalf of his people, rather than Sarah's fearing what might befall her, either from her husband or on account of her husband's machinations.[81] In this way, she illustrates the very behavior that Christ provided as a pattern for his followers: "while suffering did not threaten, but handed himself over to the one who judges justly" (2:23).

Vv. 3-5 take a more general focus, with vv. 3-4 centered around the nature of appropriate "adornment" and v. 5 providing illustrative testimony.[82] Peter sets up a contrast, "not [outer] . . . but [inner]" (οὐχ . . . ἀλλά, *ouch . . . alla*), playing on a dualism between inner and outer adornment.[83] External

80. Kiley argues that Peter draws on Genesis 18 for "lord," Genesis 20 for the emphasis on prayer in 1 Pet 3:7, and Genesis 12 for the heart of his reference ("Like Sara"); his thesis regarding Genesis 12 is carried further by Spencer ("1 Peter 3:6"), though her alleged list of parallels with 1 Peter 3 presses the evidence further than it will allow. Without disagreeing with Kiley, Sly goes on to suggest that, embarrassed by the portrayal of Abraham vis-à-vis Sarah in the canonical text, later Jewish authors (Philo and Josephus, but also Peter) retold the story selectively to portray Sarah in terms more acceptable in the Roman world ("1 Pet 3:6b"). T. W. Martin draws attention to suggestive analogies for Peter's anecdote in material related to Sarah in the *Testament of Abraham* ("1 Pet 3,6"). Davids ("Second Temple Traditions") borrows from both Sly and Martin to urge that Peter was influenced by Second Temple Jewish amplifications of the Genesis narrative.

81. Here and in 3:14 we find "fear" used negatively. Fear in this instance would signal capitulation to conventional human expectations or values, allowing society to exercise control on one's behavior. This is clearly out of bounds for 1 Peter, where the divine perspective trumps all else.

82. The conjunctive that opens v. 5 is γάρ (*gar*, "for"), by which "the general is confirmed by the specific" (BDAG, p. 189); v. 5 provides neither a warrant for the command in vv. 3-4 nor a model to emulate.

83. Contra Schulz (*Neutestamentliche Ethik*, pp. 628-29), this is not an expression of a dualistic anthropology, but trades on the inner-outer distinction. For a similar thought, see 2 Cor 4:16; regarding Pauline usage, even if Betz ("Inner Human Being") and Heckel (*Innere Mensch*) cannot agree as to the source of Paul's language, both nonetheless distance Paul's usage from Platonic categories of anthropological dualism.

ornamentation is set over against the inner person, a reminder that, in the ancient world, clothing expressed not only status and wealth but *who one is*. To a degree difficult to fathom today, a person *was* her clothing,[84] so it is no surprise that a variety of literary forms (and, as instruments of propaganda, images on coins), including legal documents and philosophical treatises, concerned themselves with appropriate dress. Writing in the 40s, Seneca admires his mother with these words:

> Unchastity, the greatest evil of our time, has never classed you with the great majority of women. Jewels have not moved you, nor pearls. . . . You have never defiled your face with paints and cosmetics. Never have you fancied the kind of dress that exposed no greater nakedness by being removed. Your only ornament, the kind of beauty that time does not tarnish, is the great honor of modesty. (*Ad Helviam* 16.3-5)[85]

Items in Peter's catalog — braiding of hair, gold, and fine clothing — would accordingly be interpreted as windows into a woman's essential being, displaying lack of self-control, immodesty, pompousness, even lewdness. Recall that Peter has already used the related metaphor of disrobing in 2:1: "Take off (ἀποτίθημι, *apotithēmi*, literally 'remove [clothing]') every evil and every deceit, and pretenses and jealousies and all slander."

Set over against eye-catching fashion is a "hidden" heart that pleases God. The identification of God as "the one who alone knows the heart" is axiomatic in biblical literature,[86] and the contrast Peter constructs could not be more plain. Over against eye-catching fashion, the purpose of which was to enhance one's standing in the community, he presents dispositions that are hidden from view, observable only to God, and so oriented toward pleasing him alone. Peter is well aware that concern with the inner person need not shield persons from present abuse. After all, in 2:4-10 he has urged his audience to recognize that the stone chosen by God had been rejected by humans; in doing so, however, he prioritized God's valuation over that of humans. Peter's perspective is eschatological, with the adjective "enduring," the same that he used to describe the inheritance of those who have been born anew (1:4, 23: ἄφθαρτος, *aphthartos*).

---

84. See Berger, *Identity*, pp. 40-43; and, especially on related concerns of wealth and status, Hamel, *Poverty and Charity*, pp. 57-93.

85. Et in Winter, *Roman Wives*, p. 90. More broadly, see Winter, *Roman Wives* pp. 98-122; Balch, *Let Wives Be Submissive*, pp. 99-102.

86. See Acts 1:24; 15:8; 1 Sam 16:7; Deut 8:2; 1 Kgs 8:39; Pss 7:9; 43:21; 64:6; Jer 11:20; 17:9-10, etc.

The dispositions to which Peter draws attention are gentleness and peacefulness. The quality of inner life Peter recommends is not particularly "feminine," as 3:16 makes clear. Although these are virtues prized in the Greco-Roman world, this is unimportant for Peter, whose emphasis falls instead on what God values. This is clear not only from the final phrase of v. 4 ("which is greatly valued before God") but also from v. 5, where placing hope in God results in inward adornment of this kind (see 1:13). Indeed, these dispositions were on display among holy women of long ago, and did not come into view as a result of the interests of Greek and Roman society. If the Greco-Roman world shares God's perspective on this point, this is evidence only of God's grace at work in the world, not of Peter's capitulation to the values of his world.[87] "Hope" in 1 Peter is oriented toward the end-time, evidencing yet again this emphasis on taking the long view. Again we hear in the background Peter's christological affirmation from 2:23: "while suffering [Christ] did not threaten, but handed himself over to the one who judges justly."

With v. 7, Peter turns his attention to husbands — particularly how, in the context of their households, they might live out the command to "honor all" (2:17). The brevity of this instruction, especially when compared to the attention accorded wives in vv. 1-6, may be an indication that Christian husbands in Peter's audience were numerically few. More likely, though, is that, *within his own household*, the lot of the Roman man did not serve well as a metaphor for the oppressed, marginal Christian community within the vast sea of the Roman Empire. Although we have evidence from the early empire of the husband's compassion for his wife, children, and slaves, as well as evidence of the expanding roles of both wife and household slaves in the affairs of the household, both within and beyond the home, it remains true that, within the context of his extended family, the husband's position was one of authority and status.[88] For this reason, we may be wise to notice that, in v. 7, Peter does not repeat the term referring to "wife" in v. 1 (γυνή, *gynē*), but rather a more general term for "female" (γυναικεῖος, *gynaikeios*), thus addressing the husband with regard to the various women comprising his extended family. Not least given typical expectations in the Roman world regarding those of the household following the father in his religious choices,[89]

---

87. Cf. Bede, p. 96: "It is astonishing that even in [the philosophy of] Pythagoras [sixth century BC], with only the law of natural knowledge as guide, this thought is found, that the real adornments of ladies [*sic!*] are modesty, not clothing."

88. See, e.g., Rawson, "Adult-Child Relationships"; idem, "Roman Family"; Eyben, "Fathers and Sons."

89. See above on vv. 1-6. In Acts, see, e.g., the baptisms of Cornelius and his household (Acts 10:2, 24, 27, 33, 44-48), Lydia and her household (16:14-15), and the Philippian jailor and his

in the absence of evidence in 1 Peter to the contrary, there is no reason to expect that Peter is addressing "mixed" marriages at this point.⁹⁰

How are husbands to live with the women? Peter qualifies "live with" in two ways. First, they are to do so "knowledgeably" (κατὰ γνῶσιν, *kata gnōsin*), an enigmatic modifier, made all the more so by the absence of any further reference to "knowledge" (γνῶσις, *gnōsis*) in the letter. For interpretive assistance we may turn, first, to the use of a near-equivalent term in 1:18; 5:9 (οἶδα, *oida*, "know" or "understand") in reference to redemption, and, second, to the use of analogous adverbial phrases in 2:19 ("because of one's consciousness of God") and 1:17; 3:2 ("in reverent fear"). If we take our cues from these other passages, we might achieve a paraphrase like "informed by the character of Christ who redeemed you and the overarching purpose of God." This paraphrase is supported by the second way that Peter modifies his directive to husbands: as the weaker vessel,⁹¹ the woman must receive greater honor. That is, people whose identity is formed in relation to Christ and thus whose life-world has been turned upside down realize that those with lower social status are actually the more to be honored. Following conventional wisdom in Rome, an assessment of women as weak and light-minded⁹² would relegate women to the margins in relation to men. Indeed, for Aristotle, the relation of man to woman was, by nature, that of ruler and subject (*Politics* 1.2). In the topsy-turvy world projected by Peter's christology, however, what is dishonored is to be honored (see above on 2:4-10).

Living "knowledgeably," then, refers to living as persons whose patterns of thought and judgment have been transformed so as to reflect more faithfully the thoughts and judgments of God. Not surprisingly, then, failure to "accord honor to her" results in the failure of a man's prayers. Peter is not voicing a superstitious threat, as though a hex, even a divine one, might be placed on those who behave wrongly toward women. His warning is far more serious than this, for failure to communicate with God is tied to a compre-

---

household (16:31-34). More broadly, cf. Matson, *Household Conversion Narratives;* Sandnes, "Equality within Patriarchal Structures," pp. 153-56.

90. My point is that v. 1 leaves no doubt about the presence of disbelieving husbands, but v. 7 provides no hint of unbelieving (much less, disbelieving) wives; moreover, it is hard to escape the conclusion that "fellow heirs" refers to women who have been born anew (see "inheritance" in 1:4). Similarly, Achtemeier, p. 217. On circumstantial grounds, Gross ("1 Pet 3.7") argues to the contrary; Jobes leaves open the possibility that unbelieving wives are included (p. 208).

91. The term "vessel" (σκεῦος, *skeuos*) is neither particularly feminine nor derogatory (e.g., 2 Cor 4:7; 1 Thess 4:4). In fact, that the woman is "the weaker" means that Peter refers to both men and women as "vessels."

92. Pomeroy, *Women in Classical Antiquity,* p. 150.

hensive misunderstanding of God and God's ways, a error that could not but find expression in the way the husband comports himself with respect to the weaker members of his own household. As we have seen, the impartiality of God in judgment does not mean that God's justice is blind; rather, divine justice is tilted in the direction of society's marginal (see above on 1:17). Now we see that the heads of households are to take their cues from the head of the household of God, the Father himself. Failure to do so distances the husband so far from God's thoughts and ways that his attempts to communicate with God can only falter.

3:8-12

8 Finally, all of you, being of one mind, sympathetic, lovers of the Christian family, compassionate, humble-minded,[93] 9 must not repay evil for evil or insult for insult,[94] but confer blessing instead, because to this you have been called, so that you might inherit a blessing. 10 For
> whoever desires to love life
>> and to see good days
> must keep the[95] tongue from evil
>> and the lips from speaking deceit.
11 Such persons must steer clear of evil and do good,
>> seek peace and pursue it,
12 for the eyes of the Lord are turned toward the righteous
>> and his ears to their prayers,
> and the face of the Lord is set against those who do evil.

With this textual unit, Peter draws to a close the instruction begun in 2:13, his version of a code of conduct for those who dwell in Roman households and

93. Some witnesses (P 049 𝔐) read φιλόφρονες (*philophrones*, "hospitable") rather than ταπεινόφρονες (*tapeinophrones*, "humble-minded") (p72 ℵ A B C Ψ etc.), and some conflate the two (L *pc*). External support for ταπεινόφρονες (*tapeinophrones*) is far superior, and the substitution is likely due to confusion with φιλάδελφοι (*philadelphoi*, "brotherly love"), used earlier in the verse.

94. Following Snyder ("Participles and Imperatives," p. 195), I am reading ἀποδιδόντες (*apodidontes*, "paying") and εὐλογοῦντες (*eulogountes*, "blessing") as "commanding," though not, as Snyder urges, "independent," since the sense of this final section of Peter's household code is still tied to 2:17.

95. Probably under the influence of the LXX (which reads σου at both points in Ps 34:13 LXX), some witnesses add the possessive pronoun αὐτοῦ (*autou*, "his") before "tongue" (ℵ P 𝔐 etc.) and "lips" (P 𝔐 etc.).

the household that was Rome. He addresses "all" — that is, everyone in his Christian audience, returning to the more global instruction with which he began his household code (2:13; cf. 2:18; 3:1, 7). "Finally" marks the beginning of this last unit, building anticipation of a summary of what has gone before. Peter's conclusion does recapitulate some of the major concerns of 2:13–3:12, but it focuses less on instruction around particular relationships and practices and more on the essential dispositions to be cultivated among followers of Jesus. Vv. 8-9a concern themselves with these issues of character, v. 9b identifies the warrant for Peter's instruction, and vv. 10-12 provide confirmation of his directives, grounding them in Scripture (Ps 34[LXX 33]:13-17).

Set side by side in vv. 8-9a are the two staples of Peter's coaching around identity formation for the Christian aliens who comprise his audience: (1) the nature and unity of the group and (2) its stance with respect to persons outside the group.

(1) Within the Christian Family: V. 8 centers on dispositions for life within the Christian community, with Peter describing the ethos of the family of believers. Rather than name particular behaviors, he identifies durable, transposable qualities of character by which people are predisposed to engage with and respond to one another in particular settings. These dispositions generate and organize practices appropriate to particular settings without presuming that all settings (all times and places) are the same. For example, "mutual love" (a possible translation of φιλάδελφος, *philadelphos,* in v. 8) is an essential quality of character for Peter, but he does not (for he cannot) predetermine for all circumstances how that love might be expressed. Remembering that, in a way not always appreciated in the modern world, persons can only *do* what they *are,* Peter prioritizes the formation of Christian character and community while recognizing that persons formed in these ways will bear the fruit of that character in their relations with one another.

He pulls together five terms, all rare in NT usage, each overlapping with and amplifying the others and all demonstrative of the peculiar nature of the Christian community:

> ὁμόφρων, *homophrōn,* refers to "a common pattern of thought" or "shared heart and mind." The term appears only here in the NT, but has semantic partners in Phil 4:2; Rom 15:5 ("harmony") and in a favorite Lukan expression for the church: "one heart and soul." Although useful in characterizing a group set on a common goal, this concept is at home especially in descriptions of ideal friends.[96]

96. Phil 4:2; Rom 15:5: τὸ αὐτὸ φρονεῖν, *to auto phronein.* ὁμοθυμαδόν, *homothymadon,*

συμπαθής, *sympathēs,* refers to a human attitude of proclivity toward acts of mercy, particularly among the weak or distressed; the concept is at home in the household (as in a mother's compassion for her children) but is used in the Greco-Roman world more widely.[97]

φιλάδελφος, *philadelphos,* is the adjectival form of the notion of "brotherly love." I have translated the term with an eye toward "familial love." This is the only appearance of the term in 1 Peter (or in the NT), but related expressions appear in 1:22 (φιλαδελφία, *philadelphia,* "brotherly love"); 2:17; 5:9 (ἀδελφότης, *adelphotēs,* "brotherhood," "family of believers"); and a similar sentiment is found in 5:14: "Greet one another with a kiss of love (φίλημα, *philēma*)." A common image in early Christian discourse (see above on 1:22), familial love would have particular importance for 1 Peter, where a strong sense of "family" identity would mitigate "alien" status in the world.

εὔσπλαγχνος, *eusplanchnos,* employs a physiological diagnosis, "healthy entrails," to communicate a psychosocial orientation of tenderheartedness, affection, or compassion.[98] Modern idiom refers to the "heart" (rather than intestines) as the seat of intimate emotions, especially compassion or tender mercy.

ταπεινόφρων, *tapeinophrōn,* "humble-minded," is that quality of character most out of step in the Roman world. Although modesty or moderation might be regarded as virtuous, outside early Christianity "humility" referred especially to persons of low status, base, ignoble, marginal.[99] In a deft restructuring of "the way the world works," Peter takes a label that might well have been used by unbelievers in a smear campaign against followers of Christ and uses it positively as a characteristic disposition of Christians (see also 5:5-6). He can do this only because of (1) a long record of extolling the virtue of humility in Israel's Scriptures (e.g., Pss 18:27; 25:9; 149:4), including the tradition concerning the humble as the object of divine favor (e.g., Prov

---

appears ten times in Acts, and in Rom 15:6. See *TLNT* 2:580-82; Walton, "ὁμοθυμαδόν in Acts"; O'Neil, "Plutarch on Friendship."

97. This is the only occurrence of the adjective in the NT, though the cognate verb appears in Heb 4:15; 10:34. See *TLNT* 3:319-20.

98. Peter's adjective appears in the NT only here and in Eph 4:32, but the simple terms σπλάγχνα *(splanchna)* and σπλαγχνίζομαι *(splanchnizomai)* occur more widely. See *TLNT* 3:273-75.

99. See *TLNT* 3:369-71. The adjective Peter uses is found only here in the NT, but cognate terms are plentiful.

3:34; cf. 1 Pet 5:5; Jas 4:6, 10; Luke 14:11; 18:14), and (2) the example of Jesus, presented by Peter already as exemplary (2:21-25).

Together, these terms identify circles of Jesus' followers by their characteristic inclinations toward intimacy and orientation-to-the-other — not as strategic behaviors but as embodied qualities. They intermingle various kinds of relationships in Roman antiquity, especially those of the household, the particular ideal of "brothers," "brotherly love," and friendship. Set as it is in formal relationship to Peter's household code, this aggregate of terms and the spheres of relationship from which they are drawn are of real interest because in the Roman Mediterranean "household" language and household codes suggest the structuring of relationships — a place for everyone and everyone in their place — while sibling-oriented language and to a lesser extent the language of friendship generally negate notions of structured hierarchy in favor of mutuality and egalitarianism.[100] Of course, philosophical discussions and social realities in Roman antiquity reveal the inevitable inequities among friends and even siblings such as arise from economic differences, age, or varying skill in public speaking. Thus, we find references to "greater" and "lesser" friends and even to "greater" and lesser" brothers. Nevertheless, the ideal was for "brotherly love" or "friendship" to supersede such distinctions in the service of oneness and symmetry of status. In his work *On Brotherly Love*, Plutarch recognizes inequities that inevitably arise among brothers, then observes:

> One would therefore advise a brother, in the first place, to make his brothers partners in those respects in which he is considered to be superior; . . . in the next place, to make manifest to them neither haughtiness nor disdain, by deferring to them and conforming his character to theirs, to make his superiority secure from envy and to equalize, as far as this is attainable, the disparity of his fortune by his moderation of spirit. (*Moralia* 484D)

Superior brothers ought to share with the inferior, dampening divisions among them (484D-85C), and the inferior ought not degrade themselves in relation to the superior, nor place them too high on a pedestal (485C-86A).

Recognizing that kinship language projects onto relationships a desired outcome but also is powerful to shape relationships in the direction of that

---

100. See Aasgaard, "Brotherhood in Plutarch and Paul"; Horrell, "From ἀδελφοί to οἶκος θεοῦ"; Gehring, *House Church and Mission,* especially pp. 229-87 (though these studies concern themselves with Pauline material).

ideal, we can see how Peter is not so subtly sculpting expectations regarding household order in fresh directions. Here, he does this in the choice of qualities he projects into the communities of Christians to whom he addresses this letter, qualities that place a premium on concord and mutual affection and countermand concerns for self-protection that lead people to ensure that their social inferiors remain in their place. His larger agenda, though, of which the current instruction is one part, is that his audience be conformed to the example of Christ, in whose suffering and death all these qualities of character are on display. The result is a "household of God" the cohesion for which is a cruciform love — that is, a love that takes its content and form from the sacrificial death of Christ on the cross — that both transcends and subverts conventional concerns with status and customary lines of authority.

Although in v. 8 Peter emphasizes patterns of thought and feeling within the Christian family, we should not imagine that he is unbiased with regard to how these dispositions will play themselves out in the lives of his audience. As will become clear in vv. 9-12, he is concerned above all with practices related to speech.

(2) Christians and Those Who Disbelieve: V. 9a, on the other hand, is oriented toward the stance taken by Christians with respect to persons outside the group. Because Peter names particular behaviors ("Do not repay evil for evil . . . confer a blessing"), we might imagine that he has significantly departed from the strategy followed in v. 8. However, his command in v. 9a is based in an unspoken disposition that pervades the ethics of Jesus. I refer to the love command, and particularly to the Christian ethic of enemy-love.[101] In the Sermon on the Plain Jesus introduces similar words: "Love your enemies, do good to those who hate you, bless those who curse you, pray for those who abuse you" (Luke 6:27-28). "Love means forgoing the luxury of spiteful vengeance or calculated retaliation,"[102] and, in the antagonistic world in which 1 Peter was written, this entails opting out of concerns for preserving one's own status and reputation in society and refusing to participate in the give-and-take of challenge-riposte that helped to define conventional social relations. According to Peter, Jesus has already put those words into practice, so it now falls to Jesus' followers to follow in his footsteps (2:21-25).

We begin to grasp the extraordinary character of this appropriation of the love command by noticing two factors. (1) Enemy-love advocates a refusal

---

101. See Piper, *Love Your Enemies,* pp. 122-29. That Peter's instruction reflects the Jesus-tradition of enemy-love is clear even if Peter nowhere uses the term "love" to describe the relationship of Christians to their enemies.

102. Furnish, *Love Command,* p. 56.

to differentiate between friends and enemies, counseling not simply compassion for an enemy in need (a response for which there is ample support, ancient and contemporary) or for humanity in general, but specifically for those who stand in active opposition to Jesus' followers. (2) Enemy-love is realized not by passivity in the face of hostility but by proactive behavior: "conferring a blessing." In this context, "blessing" follows the significance given it in the LXX rather than secular Greek, "to call upon God to bless" rather than "to speak well of."[103] In other words, the response of believers to hostile words goes beyond answering insult with praise and actually involves "prayer for those who abuse" (Luke 6:28) that God might endow them with the benefits of salvation.[104]

Enemy-love comprises behavior modeled after Jesus' response to those hostile toward him (2:21-25) and reflective of the great mercy of God the Father (1:3). In addition to these implicit affirmations, Peter adds in v. 9b an explicit motivation ("to this you were called") and outcome ("so that you might inherit a blessing"). Whether "to this you were called" looks backward (i.e., called to confer a blessing) or forward (i.e., called to inherit a blessing) is grammatically ambiguous, and Petrine usage otherwise does not immediately resolve the issue. A hard choice need not be made, since, in 1 Peter, the call to salvation as an inheritance (1:1-4) includes the call to persist courageously in the midst of adversity (2:21).[105] In fact, it is not too much to say that the tensions of Christian existence in a world hostile to Christian faith, evident already in 1:1 ("chosen, strangers in the world of the diaspora") and pervading the whole letter, come into sharp focus here. Because followers of Jesus anticipate an eschatological blessing, as they encounter hostility in the interim they are to respond with prayers for God's beneficence on behalf of their antagonists.

The character of life advised in vv. 8-9 — and, indeed, the promise that those who live in such a way are those who will inherit salvation — is confirmed in vv. 10-12, with Peter's citation of Ps 34(LXX 33):13-17. This is transparent from vv. 10a, 12, which assure Peter's audience concerning the Lord's faithfulness to the faithful and, therefore, the ultimate demise of hostility. (This continues the thought of 1:17; 2:23; 3:5 concerning God's fidelity in judgment.) The text of the psalm has been altered from its Greek version in the

---

103. See BDAG, pp. 407-8.

104. That this is the content of "blessing" (εὐλογέω) in v. 9a is suggested by the parallel use of "blessing" (εὐλογία, *eulogia*) in v. 9b; the latter clearly refers to eschatological salvation.

105. Similarly, Thurén, *Argument and Theology*, pp. 151-53. The parallel with 2:21 speaks decisively in favor of the view that the "call" embraces *at least* the response sketched in v. 9a; see Campbell, *Honor*, p. 169.

LXX in only minor ways to tie it more closely to vv. 8-9. Its message has been recontextualized, however, so that its reference to "life" and "good days" (v. 10) is set above all in an eschatological framework. This is due to the influence of references to "heirs of life" and the association of inheritance with life in vv. 7, 9-10 (cf. 1:3).

The psalm itself follows the familiar plotline of the rescue or vindication of the suffering righteous. Peter's use of the psalm meshes well with the whole of the psalm, which continues:

> When the righteous cry for help, the LORD hears, and rescues them from all their troubles. The LORD is near to the brokenhearted, and saves the crushed in spirit. Many are the afflictions of the righteous, but the LORD rescues them from them all. He keeps all their bones; not one of them will be broken. Evil brings death to the wicked, and those who hate the righteous will be condemned. The LORD redeems the life of his servants; none of those who take refuge in him will be condemned. (Ps 34:17-22)

This is a reminder that, like other NT theologians, Peter interprets Israel's Scriptures by drawing on their significance within the Scriptures, even while drawing his audience into those Scriptures so as to reappropriate their meaning. The storyline of Psalm 34 is a familiar one, known to us through the story of Joseph, the psalms of the suffering righteous, the stories of Daniel and his friends, Isaiah's Servant Songs, any number of Jewish texts from the Second Temple period, and preeminently in the career of Jesus Christ.[106] This plotline runs throughout 1 Peter, tying together these three narratives — the narrative of Israel, the narrative of Christ (his life, death, and resurrection), and the narrative of Peter's audience. If the storyline really does move from suffering to vindication, then the hostility known to Peter's audience can hardly be the whole story, or even the real story. In an important sense, then, Psalm 34 is woven into the fabric of 1 Peter as a whole.[107]

The psalmic material is apropos for another reason, since it participates in the focus of this whole textual unit on speaking: "(speaking) evil" (vv. 9, 10, 11, 12), "insult" (v. 9), "conferring a blessing" (v. 9), "tongue" (v. 10), "lips"

---

106. Cf., e.g., Genesis 37–41; Psalm 22; Daniel 3, 6; Isa 52:13–53:12; Wisdom 2, 4-5; 2 Maccabees 7.

107. This is not to suggest that Psalm 34 provides the subtext for 1 Peter. Rather, Psalm 34 itself bears witness to or exemplifies the fabula on which Peter builds his own narrative of faithful Christian existence. On the importance of the psalm for 1 Peter, see G. L. Green, "Use of the OT," pp. 280-82, 287; Jobes, 220-23; Snodgrass, "1 Peter II.1-10"; downplayed in Schutter, *Hermeneutic and Composition,* especially pp. 44-49 (though, on this text, pp. 144-46).

(v. 10), "speaking deceit" (v. 10), and "prayer" (v. 12). Speech ethics was an important topic in the Mediterranean world, whether Jewish or Gentile.[108] True, borrowing from Psalm 34 Peter does prioritize "doing good" (v. 11; also being "righteous," v. 12) while shunning harmful words (vv. 9a, 10b). But Peter's emphasis on conduct does not deny the importance of speech, since the relationship between these two is a major concern in literature contemporary with Peter. For example, observing the axiom, "It is character that persuades and not speech," Plutarch goes on to say, "No, rather it is both character and speech, or character by means of speech, just as a horseman uses a bridle, or a helmsman uses a rudder, since virtue has no instrument so humane or so much like itself as speech" (*Moralia* 1.33-34). Similar imagery appears in James 3. And the notion that speech manifests one's true self is affirmed in the Gospel of Matthew, where Jesus warns,

> Either make the tree good, and its fruit good; or make the tree bad, and its fruit bad; for the tree is known by its fruit. You brood of vipers! How can you speak good things, when you are evil? For out of the abundance of the heart the mouth speaks. The good person brings good things out of a good treasure, and the evil person brings evil things out of an evil treasure. I tell you, on the day of judgment you will have to give an account for every careless word you utter; for by your words you will be justified, and by your words you will be condemned. (12:33-37)

Speech is important, then, both because speech *is* action (that is, we do things with words) and because words put on public notice the nature of one's character and commitments.

Speech is a form of world-formation, potent to include and exclude, to build up and to tear down. Indeed, Peter's awareness of the power of words is exhibited in the fact that he has written this letter — or, more to the point, that he uses these epistolary words to create a world and shape an identity. At this juncture in the lives of Peter's audience, destructive words have been directed toward them. Peter's instruction, based in Scripture and the pattern of Christ's own behavior, is that they opt out of the expected contest of words — tit for tat, insult for insult. They are to pursue God's peace, shalom, by involving themselves in the formation of another world through prayer and the pronouncement of blessing.

---

108. See Baker, *Personal Speech-Ethics*, pp. 23-83.

3:13–4:11

This is the final section within the larger unit of 1 Pet 2:11–4:11, which is set off by the direct address with which it opens: "beloved" (2:11). The repetition of the vocative "beloved" in 4:12 marks 4:11 as the end of this unit. In addition to this explicit discourse marker, these boundaries are suggested by parallel references to the glory of God in 2:12 and 4:11, forming an *inclusio*, and especially the presence of the doxological exclamation in 4:11: "To whom be the glory and power forever and ever. Amen" (cf. 5:11). 3:13 begins with an inferential καί (*kai*, "then"),[109] the purpose of which is to ensure Peter's audience that their present suffering (1) does not contradict the divine promise sketched in 3:12 —

> for the eyes of the Lord are turned toward the righteous
> > and his ears to their prayers,
> and the face of the Lord is set against those who do evil

(2) is limited both in its duration and in its capacity to inflict real harm, (3) marks Peter's audience as followers of Christ, and (4) provides the arena in which to put into play the will of God. As with the whole of the larger unit, 2:11–4:11, so here we find a pronounced theocentrism, with God characterized as the one who saves and provides for his people (3:20-21; 4:10-11), whose will is the measure of life lived well (3:17, 18; 4:2, 6), whose judgment vindicates the faithful (3:20, 21; 4:6), and so to whom glory is due (4:11).

Although it includes one of the more interpretively challenging sets of texts in the NT (especially 3:19; 4:6), the significance of this textual unit is straightforward. Its emphasis falls on "good conduct in Christ" (3:16) — an expression that comes into sharper focus when read against the backdrop of several parallel phrases. Thus, with regard to what determines the shape of Christian life, "in Christ" (3:16) is the opposite of "among the Gentiles" (2:12) and "in acts of unrestraint [or 'licentiousness'] . . ." (4:3), a contrast that is furthered by the juxtaposition of life according to the "purpose" or "will" (βούλημα, *boulēma*) of the Gentiles (4:3) rather than in accordance with the "purpose" or "will" (θέλημα, *thelēma*) of God (3:17; 4:2). Whether one is concerned with life in relation to contemptuous outsiders (3:13-17) or in relation to the family of God (4:7-11), the motivation is the same. Peter sets all of life within an eschatological horizon (e.g., 4:5-6, 7) that finds its basis in Christ's redemptive suffering (3:18a) and its pattern in the way of Christ through suffering to vindication and glory (3:18b-22; 4:1, 6). Present suffering is not the

---

109. See BDAG, pp. 494-95.

last word. God's sovereign justice is. Live accordingly — as those who will be brought safely through both the ordeal of the present and judgment at the End.

3:13-17

13 Who, then, will harm you if you become zealous for the good? 14 But even if it should happen that you suffer on account of righteousness, you are blessed. Neither fear them nor be troubled, 15 but sanctify Christ as Lord in your hearts, always ready with regard to a defense for anyone who requests an explanation for the hope that is within you — 16 but with meekness and reverence, maintaining a good conscience, so that when you are slandered those who disparage your good conduct in Christ might be put to shame; 17 for it is better to suffer as those who do good, if it should happen that this is God's will, than as those who do evil.

With this textual unit, Peter more explicitly identifies the agenda served by his brief letter (5:12) — namely, to counsel and encourage his audience in their suffering as Christians.[110] In doing so, he ties his message into the previous instruction to household slaves (2:18-20) and wives (3:1-6), thus validating our earlier decision that those words were only apparently addressed narrowly to specific subgroups, but were actually directed more expansively to a Christian audience whose status in the world at large was analogous to that of slaves and wives in Roman households. As in Peter's instructions to household slaves in 2:18-20, where "doing good" eventuates in "suffering unjustly" — senseless in normal human evaluation, but honorable in God's perspective — so here Peter ensures that, however paradoxical "righteous suffering" might sound to the human ear, it is nonetheless tantamount to a state of blessedness. Similarly, we find an extensive and overt parallelism between instructions aimed at wives in 3:1-6 and instructions to all in 3:13-16, so that every attitude and behavior encouraged among believing wives of unbelieving husbands is now encouraged among followers of Christ in wider pagan society (see above, pp. 93-94). In 3:13-17, Peter provides comfort and sketches the nature of right comportment and conduct in the face of suffering.

The influence of Psalm 34, cited in 3:10-12, continues, both linguistically and, more importantly, thematically.[111] The phrase "those who do evil"

---

110. Similarly, Lohse, "Parenesis and Kerygma," p. 50.

111. See, e.g., Schutter, *Hermeneutic and Composition*, pp. 146-49; Snodgrass, "1 Peter II.1-10"; G. L. Green, "Use of the OT," pp. 278-83.

(ποιοῦντας κακά, *poiountas kaka*) in v. 12 has been recast as "the one who harms" (ὁ κακώσων, *ho kakōsōn*, in v. 13). Those who "desire to love life and to see good days" (v. 10) are now "you" who are "zealous for the good" (v. 13). "Zealous" refers to eager devotion, not simply to "good works" but, as v. 15 will clarify, to the Lord.[112] The "Lord" of Psalm 34 is now identified unmistakably as Christ (vv. 12, 15). Integrity in speech (v. 10) is clarified in terms of meek and reverent witness (vv. 15-16). And the concern with "doing good" and "the righteous" (vv. 11-12) continues unabated (vv. 13, 14, 16, 17). The effect is twofold. First, Peter identifies his audience as the suffering righteous of the psalm, in this way encouraging them to persist in their engagement in the wider world as those who embody goodness in character and practices. Second, identifying his audience with the suffering righteous of the psalm, Peter puts their situation into divine perspective so as to address what must have been a pronounced existential experience of theodicy on their part. If, as the psalmist writes and Peter repeats, "the eyes of the Lord are turned toward the righteous and his ears to their prayers, and the face of the Lord is set against those who do evil" (v. 12), then why do the righteous suffer? Must it not be either that those to whom Peter addresses himself are actually wicked and so the object of the Lord's ire or that the Lord will not or cannot protect his own? In the new reality disclosed in the coming of Christ, Peter writes, there is another option.

Peter's "third way" is spelled out in vv. 13-14a, 17; in order to follow his logic more easily, we would do well to read v. 17 as a follow-on to vv. 13-14a. Accordingly, vv. 14b-16 function not so much to put righteous suffering in perspective as to spell out the nature of faithful life in present onerous circumstances.

Vv. 13-14a, 17 have a proverbial character about them, reminiscent of instruction very much at home in the Jesus tradition and congruent with the interpretive tradition of the suffering righteous in the OT and Second Temple Jewish literature.[113] According to Matt 5:10-11 and Luke 6:22, Jesus redefined "the way things are in the world," using oxymoronic language to declare that those who suffer for the sake of righteousness actually dwell in a state of

---

112. Most scholars think in terms of the wider Greek notion of zeal for a virtue or good cause, as in Hengel, *Zealots*, p. 60. Given the character ethic Peter has been developing, together with his rearticulation of this ethic in vv. 14b-16 (see below), this reading is overly pedestrian. In the NT, compare Acts 21:20; 22:3; 1 Cor 14:12; Tit 2:14. Cf. T. W. Martin, who argues that "the good" is a euphemism for "God" in this context (*Metaphor and Composition*, pp. 285-88).

113. On the former, see, e.g., Harvey, *Strenuous Commands*, pp. 68-115. On the latter, see, e.g., Nickelsburg, *Resurrection*; Ruppert, *Leidende Gerechte*; idem, *Leidende Gerechte und seine Feinde*.

blessedness. This sentiment is clearly echoed in v. 14 (see also 4:14), and is just as jolting in Peter's letter as it must have been (and continues to be) in Jesus' proclamation. This is because proverbial maxims appeal to a kind of enlightened common sense — "what everyone knows" — and draw their force from incontestable observations of the order of the universe — "what goes up must come down," "the rich get richer, the poor get poorer." But Peter's words, and Jesus' before him, turn the observed world and conventional valuations on their head. How can it be that those who "do good" suffer? And who would confuse suffering with a state of blessedness? What seems to be the case is not. This is because the axioms articulated here find their center in a recalibration of the universe — a recalibration for which there is evidence already in the OT in the long tradition of the suffering righteous, and which has now received the divine imprimatur in the life, death, and resurrection of Jesus.

Hence, we should not imagine that Peter's point is that those who "do good" are unlikely to excite the enmity and anger of others.[114] To the contrary, it is precisely by "doing good" that the righteous attract unwanted attention, since their behavior thus portrays them as moving against the traffic in a thoroughfare coopted by those intent on "doing evil." The words of the enemies of the suffering righteous in the Wisdom of Solomon are instructive:

> Let us lie in wait for the righteous man, because he is inconvenient to us and opposes our actions; he reproaches us for sins against the law, and accuses us of sins against our training. He professes to have knowledge of God, and calls himself a child of the Lord. He became to us a reproof of our thoughts; the very sight of him is a burden to us, because his manner of life is unlike that of others, and his ways are strange. We are considered by him as something base, and he avoids our ways as unclean; he calls the last end of the righteous happy, and boasts that God is his father. (Wis 2:12-16)

Because "the good" is calculated in terms of the imitation of Christ and in reference to the holiness of God, those who are eagerly zealous for the good find themselves out of step with the conventions of wider society. Failing to behave according to expected norms, they invite vilification and malice.

A formal analysis of the tradition of the suffering righteous (e.g., in the career of Joseph, the lives of Daniel and his friends, the suffering of the Maccabean martyrs, the psalms of the suffering righteous, and the Servant of Yahweh) underscores what Peter strives to make clear here. This is that con-

---

114. This is claimed by Davids, pp. 129-30.

temporary suffering should not be confused with ultimate harm. When set within the grand story of God's will, the severity of present-day suffering is assuaged. The reality of suffering is not denied nor is this cancerous malice cured, but the crisis of suffering is lessened by its reinterpretation in 1 Peter — by means of assurances that the life-chapter currently being written is not the story's finale and that present suffering effectively serves the overarching, salvific aim of God. We can almost hear in the background the words of Jesus in Luke:

> "I tell you, my friends, do not fear those who kill the body, and after that can do nothing more. But I will warn you whom to fear: fear him who, after he has killed, has authority to cast into hell. Yes, I tell you, fear him!" (Luke 12:4-5)

Indeed, the resurrection and exaltation of Jesus, on which the Christian hope rests according to Peter (e.g., 1:3; 3:21), prompts reflection on the larger theme of resurrection in the OT and Second Temple Judaism. Resurrection is intimately associated with Israel's triumph over its enemies, God's vindication of the righteous who have suffered unjustly, and the decisive establishment of divine justice — all motifs at home in Peter's message. It is only in terms of imaginative structures reformed through this interpretive interplay of the career of Christ and the Scriptures of Israel that Peter's pronouncement of blessing (v. 14a) makes sense and can be heard as encouraging. Moreover, this theological framework helps us to fill in the ellipsis in v. 17, contrasting the "suffering of those who do good" with the "[suffering] of those who do evil." To clarify, Peter urges that suffering in the present and blessedness before God now and in the Day of Judgment are preferable to pleasure or gratification in the present and suffering in the Day of Judgment.[115] At the End, too, those who are antagonistic toward believers — who wish them "harm" and "disparage their good conduct" (vv. 13, 16) — will be put to shame (v. 16; cf. 2:6).

When compared with major strands of the tradition of the suffering righteous, Peter's appropriation of the tradition is peculiar in one important sense. Unlike those psalms that belabor the question of the fate of those who oppose God's faithful, the words of damnation spoken by the Maccabean martyrs against their antagonists, or scenes of judgment like that in Wisdom 5, Peter has very little to say about those who malign believers. In the present text, he observes that they will be "put to shame"

---

115. See Michaels, "Eschatology." This reading is supported by the emphasis on judgment in 3:18–4:6.

(v. 16) and, by means of an ellipsis easily overlooked, that their lot is eschatological judgment (v. 17). If the promise of justice against those who do evil is not altogether lacking in 1 Peter, it remains true that Peter's primary eschatological message concerns the end that the faithful are guaranteed: vindication and honor before God. This emphasis is brought into sharper relief by a comparison with the similarly potent eschatological perspective of 2 Peter. The author of 2 Peter is on the offensive, deploying eschatology as the flashing light of warning, even threat (2 Pet 3:17!), underscoring the certainty that present life has enduring consequences. For 1 Peter, however, eschatology is cast in the role of servant to hope, providing motivation for courageous steadfastness in the face of opposition.[116] Along the same lines, in terms of sketching the nature of contemporary faithfulness, Peter does not engage in invective rhetoric against "the world at large," as though the essence of Christian identity and behavior is to oppose those who reject faith. When Peter adopts a negative stance, he sets himself over against the former lives of his audience rather than against their abusers.

Eschatological horizons are paramount, giving hope to the hopeless who thus find that, even though outside the boundaries of acceptable society, they are at the center of God's salvific intervention.

Peter's rare use of verbs in the optative mood in v. 14 (πάσχοιτε, *paschoite*) and in v. 17 (θέλοι, *theloi*) — which I have translated, "if it should happen that you suffer" and "if it should happen that this is [God's] will," respectively — introduces two important issues. First, ordinarily, the optative expresses potential action and, in a conditional clause like Peter has penned, would introduce a remote possibility. If we were to read Peter's calculation of the situation of his audience in these terms, however, vv. 14, 17 would contravene what we read elsewhere in the letter concerning their condition, where they seem clearly to be the recipients of unwanted, maleficent attention (e.g., 1:6; 2:12; 3:9; 4:12, 14; 5:9). More likely, then, these optative verbs indicate that Peter is writing at a time when one cannot assume a generalized or formal persecution of Christians, during which suffering was more regional, occasional, and unpredictable.[117] Second, the clause concerning what God desires is subject to an erroneous interpretation according to which we would imagine that God might will the suffering of the faithful. "Good conduct" (v. 16) is God's will, rather, even if it results in suffering and even in the midst of suffering (cf. 2:15; 4:19).

In vv. 13-14a, 17, then, Peter claims that suffering in the present does not

---

116. See J. B. Green, "Narrating the Gospel."

117. So Dubis, *Messianic Woes*, pp. 74-75; also Achtemeier, pp. 230-31 ("sporadic"), 238 ("always possible"); Brox, p. 158; Jobes, pp. 227-28.

jeopardize one's status before God. Present suffering produces no ultimate harm. Rather, righteous suffering in the present qualifies one as inhabiting a state of *blessedness* (v. 14a) and is *better* than the eschatological suffering of the wicked (v. 17). Only those who have undergone a conversion of the imagination (see above on 1:3), whose patterns of thought for ordering everyday experiences have begun already to reflect the thoughts and ways of God, could embrace and embody such a message.

Not surprisingly, then, Peter's instructions in vv. 14b-16 build on those patterns of thought, those dispositions, as they set forth faithful Christian response in the face of suffering. Christians are not to fear those who malign them, but rather to "sanctify Christ" — a response that expresses itself in readiness to witness in meekness and reverence of God. Peter draws on Isa 8:12-13 to make his case, but three other considerations help to direct how we interpret the enigmatic directive to "sanctify Christ." First, in the biblical materials, "sanctify" (ἁγιάζω, *hagiazō*) only rarely has humans as the subject and the Lord as object, and then typically with the notion of acknowledging who Yahweh is in himself.[118] Extending the sense of the Isaianic allusion here, Peter considers the "Lord" to be Christ.

Second, in early Christian literature, Peter's phrase finds a remarkable analogy in the Jesus tradition, specifically the beginning of the prayer Jesus taught his disciples, "Father, hallowed be (ἁγιασθήτω, *hagiasthētō*) your name" (Luke 11:2; cf. Matt 6:9). Of special interest is the way in which the logic of Jesus' prayer weaves together the hallowing of God's name with the behavior of God's people ("Your kingdom come. Your will be done, on earth as it is in heaven" [Matt 6:10; cf. Luke 11:2]), a perspective that surfaces instructively in a text like Ezek 36:16-32. There God asserts, "I will sanctify my great name, which has been profaned among the nations, and which you have profaned among them; and the nations shall know that I am the LORD, says the Lord God, when through you I display my holiness before their eyes" (v. 23). Here, we are very close to Peter's call to holiness in 1:15-16: "you yourselves must rather become holy in every aspect of life, just as the one who called you is holy, for it is written, 'You shall be holy, because I am holy.'" We hallow the name of God by embodying his character.

Third, Peter's directive "to sanctify Christ . . . in your hearts" is tied to two further expectations: to maintain a "good conscience" and to practice "good conduct" (v. 16). Here are intertwined a person's center of innermost feelings and loyalties ("heart"), moral awareness ("conscience"), and behavior ("way of life" or "conduct"). Character and commitments are showcased

---

118. Procksch, "ἁγιάζω," p. 111 (with reference to Num 20:12; 27:14; Isa 8:12-13).

in practices.[119] In this case, "sanctifying Christ" determines and compels the integrity of one's moral facilities and cannot but come to expression in one's behavior.

These considerations have the immediate effect of welding together human dispositions with behavior: we can only do what we are, and this we cannot help but do. These considerations also factor into our understanding of the strange clause "sanctify Christ." It is easy enough to see that Peter thinks of Christ as sharing in the identity of God (see above on 1:3-12): Christ is to be "hallowed" as Yahweh is to be hallowed. More to the point, though, is how Peter thus calls for his audience to acknowledge Christ as holy *in the particular way he is being portrayed in this letter.* What is this portrayal? It is the topsy-turvy notion of a suffering servant whom God glorifies, the stone rejected by the builders but honored by God (2:4-10, 21-25). Those who regard as holy the Christ who is characterized in just this way are those who are "in Christ" (v. 16) and whose conduct puts on display the character of God. These are persons whose lives are determined decisively not by their location in the empire, not by their experience of marginal status in the world-at-large, but by their habitation of that space Peter designates as "in Christ" (v. 16).[120] Indeed, reference to an "in" (ἐν, *en,* "boundedness within a container, whether spatial, temporal, or a state or condition") implies an "out," allowing Peter to reverse the conventional order of things. Those regarded as "outsiders" with respect to one's community on account of righteousness are "insiders" with respect to status before God. This is life defined here and throughout the letter in christological terms, with focused reference to the redemptive and exemplary journey of Jesus through suffering and death to his exaltation.

Recognizing the orientation of Peter's thought along these lines, his opening command "Neither fear them nor be troubled" seems almost unnecessary. Of course, this counsel follows easily enough from the promise of God's protection stated in v. 12 and clarified in vv. 13-14a. But it is also important to recognize that, for Peter, "fear" (i.e., reverence, respect, and honor) is due God and God alone. Moreover, those whose lives are defined christologically recognize that they have nothing to fear from those who send malice their way in the present, for they know that the way of vindication and glory is neither blocked by present suffering nor discovered in escape from present suffering. The way of Christ is through suffering to divine honor.

With these considerations in mind, the significance of Peter's use of Isa

119. On this perspective in Scripture, see DiVito, "Old Testament Anthropology"; K. Berger, *Identity,* pp. 70-81.

120. See further, J. B. Green, "Living as Exiles."

8:12-13 comes into sharper focus. In the context of the Syro-Ephraimite war, Isaiah had identified Assyria as a tool of God's power. This means that the reach and power of Assyria were limited (Isa 8:1-22); hence, the arrival of Assyria would not signal the absence of God for, even then, "God is with us" ("Immanuel," vv. 8, 10). Accordingly, the Isaianic text reads: "Do not fear what [they fear],[121] or be in dread. But the LORD of hosts, him you shall regard as holy; let him be your fear, and let him be your dread." In this way, Isaiah opposes two visions of "the way things really are": life secured in strategy sessions and the practice of human power (8:8-9) versus life secured by God and him alone.[122] For Peter, Isaiah's voice is immediate. Two visions of life are juxtaposed, two ways of making sense of the experienced world: following the ways of society at large in what one values and fears and with regard to what intimidates, versus synchronizing life according to the Lord's eschatological aims and thus calibrating one's sense of what really matters by what the ever-present God honors. What God honors, of course, is the faithful suffering of Christ and, by extension, followers who embody Christ's faithfulness in their lives even in the midst of suffering. (Recall that Isa 8:14 made an appearance in 1 Pet 2:8 — in a context taken up with the dismissal of human valuations in favor of divine, with God's valuation regarded as decisive and ultimate.)

This vision of life, centered in the hallowing of a crucified-and-raised Messiah, is to be embodied in "deed" (see Peter's overall heightened concern with "conduct of life"), but also in "word." Within the social context Peter envisions for his audience, verbal witness or defense (ἀπολογία, *apologia*) takes on a particular character. This is not "apologetics" in the modern sense, with its syllogistic reasoning or presentation of indisputable evidence to support the truth of the Christian faith. Nor is it yet the preparation of formal testimony as might be expected in a legal setting (cf., e.g., Acts 22:1; 25:16); though the courtroom is hardly excluded, the language Peter employs invites images of the give-and-take of informal social settings.[123] It is rather the narration of the way of Christ through suffering and death to resurrection and glory, itself none other than a narration of the ways of God from the beginning and on exhibition in the life of Israel as this is recounted in the Scriptures of Israel, all as recapitulated in the lives of Christ's followers.

121. The NRSV has "it fears."

122. Cf. Childs, *Isaiah*, p. 75.

123. "Request" is not technical language for a court proceeding, and Peter's reference to "everyone" or "anyone" (πᾶς) hardly conjures up images of magistrates or governors. Michaels suggests that "Peter sees his readers as being 'on trial' every day as they live for Christ in a pagan society" (p. 188).

Moreover, it is a narration whose articulation should reflect the character of Christ: with meekness and reverence. "Meekness" is "the quality of not being overly impressed by a sense of one's self-importance,"[124] instead committing one's life and sense of justice to God. Hence, it is a close semantic cousin to the unpretentiousness expressed in Christ's passion (2:21-25) and to the humility that Peter will later encourage (5:5-6). "Reverence" (φόβος, *phobos*) speaks to one's basic attitude toward God, not of honor toward one's antagonists; had not Peter just written, following Isaiah, "Do not fear them" (v. 14; Isa 8:12)? In this way, once again Peter underscores that Christian comportment in relation to those who bear malice toward Christians is determined by the fundamental orientation of one's life toward God, by according the highest value to one's relationship with God with the result that it determines all else (see 1:17; 2:17-18; 3:2).

3:18–4:6

18 This is because Christ also suffered for sins,[125] once for all, the Righteous One for the unrighteous ones, in order that he might lead you[126] to God, having been put to death as a human[127] but made alive by the Spirit — 19 by whom he also went and preached to the spirits in prison,[128] 20 since they were disobedient back when the patience of God waited in the days of Noah as the ark was being constructed, in which a few people (that is, eight persons) were saved through water. 21 The counterpart, baptism, now saves you — not as a removal of the stain of the flesh but as a pledge of a good conscience to God — through the resurrection of Jesus Christ, 22 who, having gone into heaven after angels and authorities and powers were

---

124. BDAG, p. 861 (πραΰτης). Cf. πραΰς in 3:4.

125. The manuscript tradition is complex, with this text, read by B P 𝔐, set alongside numerous alternatives, all of which seem to reflect more traditional language regarding Jesus' salvific death — e.g., "Christ died for sins," "Christ died for our [or your] sins," and "Christ died on our [or your] behalf."

126. ὑμᾶς (*hymas*, "you") is read by p⁷² ℵ B P Ψ etc.; ἡμᾶς (*hēmas*, "us") by ℵ² A C K L etc. The two words were virtual homonyms, spelled differently but pronounced the same, so confusion in the scribal process is unsurprising. ὑμᾶς has the better external support and is consistent with the emphasis on the second person in this context. A similar textual problem is found in v. 21.

127. That is, ἐν σαρκί (*en sarki*, "in the flesh" — also in 4:1, 6). I translated this phrase "as a human" in order to avoid unnecessary confusion over Peter's anthropology, as though he held to an anthropological dualism or regarded σάρξ (*sarx*) as evil.

128. Very few minuscules substitute τῷ ᾅδῃ (*tō hadē*, "Hades") for φυλακῇ (*phylakē*), undoubtedly under the influence of the widespread tradition of Christ's "descent into hell."

made subordinate to him, is at the right hand of God. 4:1 Therefore, because[129] Christ suffered[130] as a human, you also must ready yourselves with the same pattern of thought — namely, that the one who has suffered as a human has finished with sin, 2 to the end that you live your remaining time as a human no longer in accordance with human desires but in accordance with the will of God. 3 Enough time has been lost discharging the will of the Gentiles, conducting yourselves in acts of unrestraint, lust, drunkenness, carousing, bawdy partying, and unseemly idolatry. 4 By this they are baffled, blasphemers that they are,[131] that you no longer go along with them in the same flood of unrestrained immorality. 5 Such persons will give an explanation to the one who is ready to judge the living and the dead. 6 For this reason the good news was proclaimed to the dead, that having been judged as humans according to human standards, they might live by the Spirit according to divine[132] standards.

This lengthy unit brings into focus key elements of the message of 1 Peter, intricately interlacing a christology focused on Jesus' death and exaltation, a declaration of God's exercise of sovereign justice, Peter's claim for the certainty of ultimate safety for Christ's followers, and, then, encouragement to live lives congruent with those deepest commitments professed and affirmed in baptism. Harbinger of profound portraits of God (explicitly named in 3:18, 20, 21, 22; 4:2, 6) and Christ (explicitly named in 3:18, 21; 4:1), this text deploys its theological and christological affirmations in the service of assured promise: The faithful are brought safely through the calamity of life in this world as a peculiar people and through divine judgment. This assured promise warrants Peter's admonition to his audience to live (as it were) into their baptism.

Key to our understanding of this section of the letter is our making

129. I am taking the genitive absolute construction (Χριστοῦ . . . παθόντος, *Christou . . . pathontes*) with a causal meaning (on which see Mastronarde, *Attic Greek*, p. 202).

130. The manuscript tradition is complex, with alternatives (e.g., "Christ suffered *on our behalf,*" "Christ suffered *on your behalf,*" and "Christ *died on your behalf*") easily dismissed as later emendations bringing Peter's formulation into line with more pervasive soteriological formulas. This reading is well-attested (p[72] B C Ψ etc.).

131. βλασφημοῦντες *(blasphēmountes)* appears at the end of v. 4, and its function in this sentence is ambiguous (see the discussion in Achtemeier, 283-84; he elects to position it as the introduction to the new sentence encompassing vv. 5-6: "Because they blaspheme . . ."). Some textual witnesses smooth over the problem by substituting καὶ βλασφήμουσιν, "and they blaspheme" (ℵ* C* etc.); βλασφημοῦντες is well-attested (p[72] ℵ[c] A B C[2] P Ψ etc.) and is the more difficult reading.

132. My translation, "according to human standards . . . according to divine standards," reflects the parallelism between κατὰ θεόν *(kata theon)* and κατὰ ἀνθρώπους *(kata anthrōpous)*; for the rendering of θεός *(theos)* as "divine," see BDAG, p. 451.

sense of the complexities of its structure. For example, it is possible to argue that 3:18-22 and 4:1-6 should be interpreted in relative isolation from one another, a case that is especially easy to make with regard to 3:18-22.[133] This is because these verses draw significantly on traditional material,[134] a christological credo tracing the journey of Christ through death to exaltation. The material in vv. 18-19, 22, in particular, has strong affinity with the confession of 1 Tim 3:16: "Without any doubt, the mystery of our religion is great:

> He was revealed in flesh,
>> vindicated in spirit,
> seen by angels,
>> proclaimed among Gentiles,
> believed in throughout the world,
>> taken up in glory.

Moreover, some have found in 3:18-22 a self-contained, chiastic structure:

> A   death of Christ
>   B   spirits in Prison
>   B′   salvation of Noah and Peter's addressees
> A′   resurrection of Christ[135]

At the same time, we should not turn a blind eye to the potential effect of relocating traditional material within a larger argument, transforming it for service to a wider agenda. Even if 3:22 serves well to bring closure to the christological material begun in 3:18, Peter nonetheless moves explicitly in 4:1 to draw out the ramifications of Christ's suffering in ways that continue to intertwine the fate of Christ with that of his followers. Moreover, thoughts of the flood episode, to which 3:20 alludes, are reactivated in 4:4, where Peter refers to Gentile behavior as a "flood (ἀνάχυσις, *anachysis*) of unrestrained immorality."[136] Still further, parallels between 3:18-19 and 4:6, however enigmatic, are easily recognized. Consequently, 3:18–4:6 follows this structure:

---

133. Hartman, e.g., regards 3:18-22 as a "digression," so that 4:1 picks up where 3:17 left off (*Into the Name*, pp. 115-16).

134. For the history of research and the case in favor of finding traditional material in these verses, see Pearson, *Christological and Rhetorical Properties*, pp. 153-202.

135. E.g., Thurén, *Argument and Theology*, pp. 158-59.

136. This is also recognized by Rudman, "1 Pet 3–4." S. E. Johnson ("Preaching") suggests a more complex, though labored, chiasm for 3:18–4:6.

3:18a preamble: Christ's effective death
  3:18b Christ: put to death as a human but made alive by the Spirit
    3:19 he preached to the spirits in prison
      3:20-22 flood and baptism
        4:1-2 live in accordance with the will of God
      4:3-5 flood and judgment
    4:6a good news proclaimed to the dead
  4:6b the dead: judged as humans that they might live by the Spirit

The consequence of this inverted parallelism is to underscore the ramifications of what had already become traditional christology for the nature of Christian hope and Christian life in a world unfriendly to those whose behavior reflects their baptismal commitments. I will examine the message of this textual unit under two headings: (1) The Universal Triumph of Jesus Christ and (2) The Unique and Programmatic Suffering of Jesus.

The Universal Triumph of Jesus Christ. This is the third major christological text in 1 Peter (see also 1:18-21; 2:22-25), and it is worthy of note that it, like the other two, centers on the passion of Jesus Christ. This one, however, advances beyond the former two in its heightened emphasis on the exaltation of Jesus. Moreover, although all three passages bear witness to the sacrificial death of Jesus, this passage moves more pointedly in the direction of another model of the atonement. This is Christus Victor, that classical model of the atonement whereby the suffering and resurrection of Jesus is interpreted in terms of triumph over evil.

One of the puzzles of this text is the character of the spirits in prison to whom Christ preached (3:19), the identity of the dead to whom good news was proclaimed (4:6), and the relation between these two. Scholars have championed a range of possible identities for the imprisoned spirits of 3:19, two of which are primary.[137] (1) These are the disembodied spirits of Noah's contemporaries who perished in the flood and have been kept in prison in Hades. Because rabbinic tradition disallowed such persons a share in the res-

---

137. Actually, at least five views have their champions (see the survey in Grudem, p. 204), but two are primary. For histories of interpretation, see Reicke, *Disobedient Spirits,* pp. 7-51; Dalton, *Christ's Proclamation,* pp. 15-41 (see also Dalton, "1 Pet 3:19"). For a manageable survey of contemporary views, see Bauckham, "Spirits in Prison"; for contemporary analysis of the major positions in the context of a text-linguistic approach to the issues raised by this text, see Westfall, "1 Pet 3:19-22." The difficulties of this text have funded a small cottage industry — see the catalog of articles and books in Casurella, *Bibliography,* pp. 64-71, which covers all of 1 Peter 3 but is almost exclusively concerned with 3:18-22, with the question of the status of women (3:1-6) a distant second place.

urrection ("The generation of the Flood have no share in the world to come" [*Mishnah Sanhedrin* 10.3a]), Peter's declaration that the salvation won by Christ extended even so far as to include them would be all the more remarkable. The evangelistic role of Christ would be further underscored in 4:6.[138] (2) The imprisoned spirits are the fallen angels of Gen 6:1-6 who were responsible for bringing upon the whole earth the Great Flood and were therefore imprisoned — at least, this is how some Jewish literature represents reflection on Gen 6:1-6.[139] The majority view favors this second option. With regard to "the dead" of 4:6, most scholars today tend toward viewing these as believers who have died, though some argue that "the dead" are undifferentiated persons who, in death, are allowed to hear the good news. Accordingly, for most scholars, 3:19 and 4:6 are unrelated.[140]

I will depart from the majority view by claiming both that Peter's message is more integrated into his letter than these options allow and that this text supports more than one potential referent for the "spirits" in 3:19. I will claim:

> that the "spirits" of 3:19 and the "angels, authorities, and powers" of 3:22 are overlapping but not identical categories;
>
> that "the angels, authorities, and powers" include those "powers" of all sorts, extending beyond, but not necessarily ruling out, spiritual realities, whether aligned with or (as in 3:19) against the will of God;
>
> that the "powers" are brought into relationship to Christ not as a matter of "subjugation" but, recalling how "to subordinate" was used in Peter's household code (2:13–3:12), as finding and occupying responsibly their place in the created order;
>
> that, taken as a whole, 3:18–4:6 assures Christians of divine judgment, entailing accountability for the disobedient and vindication of believers;
>
> that "the dead" of 4:6 are dead members of the human family given postmortem opportunity to hear the good news; and
>
> that this textual unit (and especially 3:18-19, 22; 4:6) extends the meaning of Jesus' lordship (from 3:12, 15) by affirming the universal exaltation of Jesus Christ in a way analogous to Phil 2:9-11: "Therefore God

138. So, e.g., Goppelt, pp. 258-59.

139. E.g., *1 Enoch* 10–16; 18; 21; *Jubilees* 5:6; *2 Baruch* 56:13, etc. So, e.g., Brox, pp. 168-76; Achtemeier, pp. 255-58. A related view has it that the fallen angels are not themselves in view, but their progeny are; these would be the evil spirits who descended from the fallen angels.

140. In short, the work of Dalton *(Christ's Proclamation)* has carried the day for most scholars with respect to both the imprisoned spirits of 3:19 and the dead of 4:6.

also highly exalted him and gave him the name that is above every name, so that at the name of Jesus every knee should bend, in heaven and on earth and under the earth, and every tongue should confess that Jesus Christ is Lord, to the glory of God the Father."

Behind the "imprisoned spirits" of 3:19, most scholars find the influence of "The Book of the Watchers," a Jewish work dating from the third or early second century BC, which comprises the first 36 chapters of *1 Enoch*. "Watchers" takes its name from the account of the fallen angels (or Watchers) in *1 Enoch* 6–16 — a story that significantly embellishes the report concerning the "sons of God" in Gen 6:1-6. Enticed by the "handsome and beautiful daughters" of the human family, the angels determined to "choose wives for ourselves from among the daughters of man and beget us children" (*1 Enoch* 6:1-2). Accordingly, "they took wives unto themselves . . . began to go unto them . . . and taught them magical medicine, incantations, the cutting of roots, and taught them (about) plants. And the women became pregnant and gave birth to great giants whose heights were three hundred cubits" (7:1-2). These giants sinned against humanity and against the earth. Though Enoch intercedes on behalf of the Watchers, God pronounces judgment on them: "From now on you will not be able to ascend into heaven unto all eternity, but you shall remain inside the earth, imprisoned all the days of eternity" (14:5).[141] Accordingly, "spirits" in 1 Pet 3:19 refers to those Watchers, or to the giants fathered by those Watchers, and it is to them that Christ addressed himself. The propriety of this interpretation is underscored by 2 Pet 2:4-9, where we find a more highly developed but kindred thought: "For if God did not spare the angels when they sinned, but cast them into hell and committed them to chains of deepest darkness to be kept until the judgment; and if he did not spare the ancient world, even though he saved Noah, a herald of righteousness, with seven others, when he brought a flood on a world of the ungodly; . . . then the Lord knows how to rescue the godly from trial, and to keep the unrighteous under punishment until the day of judgment."[142]

But there is more going on in this text than this interpretation allows. The "spirits" of 3:19 find their counterpart in 3:22 in a reference to "angels," as might be anticipated in a reading that finds Watchers in the background of Peter's claims, but also with reference to "authorities and powers." In this context, ἄγγελος *(angelos)* can refer to evil spirits or to angels; "authorities"

---

141. Translations from Isaac, "1 Enoch."
142. See further, Dalton, "1 Pet 3,19 and 4,6."

(ἐξουσία, *exousia*) to entities, whether human or otherwise, authorized by reason of office to exercise power; and "powers" (δύναμις, *dynamis*) to entities, whether human or supernatural, functioning in extraordinary ways. This is Peter's only reference to what are widely subsumed in NT study under the heading of "powers and principalities" or simply "powers," so it is not immediately obvious how best to understand them. Outside 1 Peter we find comparable lists, for example, in Rom 8:19-22, 38-39; 1 Cor 15:24-26; Eph 1:21; 6:12; Col 1:16; 2:9-15. From these, we can determine that the NT writers had no technical vocabulary for "the powers." As a result, we would be well-advised to think in terms of an array of powerful agents whose particular role or level in a hierarchy of power is impossible to determine. Nor do we find commentary on the identity or essential character of these "powers," though it is clear that with reference to them the NT writers are drawing back the curtain to reveal the spiritual dimension of what might otherwise appear to be the mundane goings-on of the world in which we live. These "powers" appear to operate on a continuum between their enfleshment in human beings and human institutions on the one hand and disembodied heavenly beings (e.g., angels and demons) on the other, suggesting that these are entities of God's creation who animate and influence social structures and organizations with malevolent capacities and aims.[143]

For many, the language of "authorities and power" might as well be glossolalia, so foreign is it to the categories that shape everyday existence in the modern world. As Bultmann quipped long ago, "It is impossible to use electric lights and the wireless and to avail ourselves of modern medical and surgical discoveries and at the same time to believe in the New Testament world of spirits and miracles."[144] That Bultmann's statement was presumably typed on a manual typewriter, that "wireless" meant an AM radio receiver, and that he would never have imagined an MRI only underscores the point. As will become even more clear in 1 Peter 5, however, our unawareness of the forces at work in the background of what we experience does not diminish their reality. Like a fissure in the earth's surface allowing molten lava to escape, so Peter slices through our imagined world of facile reductionism, which attributes "reality" only to the material and sensate, to reveal the inner aspect of social, material, and tactile manifestations of coercive power. Although guilty of his own reductionism, Wink urges modern people to recognize "principalities and powers"

143. See the summary of theological issues related to these entities in Dawn, "Powers and Principalities"; Reid, "Principalities and Powers." In different ways, they strike a helpful balance between the overly demythologized (i.e., de-supernaturalized) view of Wink (e.g., *Naming the Powers*) and the overly spiritualized view of C. E. Arnold (e.g., *Powers of Darkness*).

144. Bultmann, "NT and Mythology," p. 5.

as the spiritual essence of an institution or state or system, "demons" as spiritual power emanated by organizations or individuals bent on overpowering others, "gods" as the archetypal or ideological structures that determine reality, and "Satan" as the power that solidifies around collective idolatry and inhumanity.[145] Wink unhelpfully and inappropriately vacates the "powers" of the diabolic forces that animate human institutions aligned against God and his people, but he rightly avoids the opposite extreme that concerns itself with spiritual forces devoid of their expression in human institutions.

To a degree not always recognized, the NT reflects little concern with the "powers" as personalities, whether individually or collectively, focusing instead on their contribution to the order of things. "Their personalities are obscured in the overall hierarchy, even as people refer to the 'authorities' or 'city hall' without knowing who they are personally."[146] But Peter himself makes clear, the personhood of these "powers" is not altogether a mistaken category since the "spirits" of 3:19 exercised volition in the direction of disobedience, are subject to judgment, and engage the world in a way analogous to that of Christians ("to subordinate" — 2:13, 18; 3:1, 22; 5:5). Changeable, capable of good or evil, appearing in various guises, they are "not quite gods nor quite like us," and "often play a more central role in daily cult than do the proper gods. They are in fact the everyday version of that ambiguous realm of mediation between deity and time. . . ."[147]

The NT relates angels to other figures such as "principalities" and "powers" (3:22; see 1 Cor 15:24; Eph 1:21; Rom 8:38), but without identifying any of these as necessarily "evil" (cf. Col 1:16). In 1 Peter in particular, "to be subordinate" is a verb applied to slaves, women, young people — indeed, to all Christians — quite apart from any indication that these persons have been aligned against God and his purposes; hence, when "angels and authorities and powers" are said to have been subordinated to the exalted Christ (3:22), this carries no requisite implication that these cosmic figures were previously aligned against God. (Of course, this would not be true of the "spirits" in 3:19.) But Peter's language does leave room for the possibility that such forces have asserted themselves as "autonomous centers of power,"[148] thus departing their creaturely purpose (cf. Col 2:15).

Peter introduces images of warfare that are at home not only in Scripture but were long influential in the church and, in some circles at least, are now being recovered.[149] This is important in three ways for this letter. First, Peter is able to sum up the work of Christ in terms of his conquering Hades and the "powers" whose existence is out of step with God's purpose.

145. Wink, *Naming the Powers*, pp. 104-5.
146. Noll, *Angels of Light*, p. 147 (see more fully, pp. 124-53).
147. Jenson, *Systematic Theology*, 2:117.
148. The language is Pannenberg's (*Systematic Theology*, 2:105).
149. Cf. Boyd, *Problem of Evil.*

Second, the paradox of Christian existence comes into focus here. Daily life for Peter's audience is realized in a marginal status in the world that, by conventional standards, contravenes Peter's assessment that they are God's elect. Similarly, though Christ has triumphed over the "powers" and is enthroned as God's co-regent, Peter can nonetheless claim that "your adversary, the devil, like a roaring lion is on the prowl, seeking someone to devour" (5:8). Though liberated, believers must continue to "resist" (5:9). This gives fresh meaning to the struggles of the present, since it locates them in the messianic age, which is characterized by a struggle whose outcome has already been determined. It sharpens Peter's emphasis on the Christian life as a peripatetic, nomadic life, an amphibian movement on the borders of two worlds — one world in which the distinguishing icon is the cross of Christ, that scandalous consequence of God's choosing as the cornerstone what the builders rejected (2:4-8), the other for which a pyramidal hierarchy determines the distribution of power, privilege, and honor. And it insures that evidences of destructive power do not tell the whole story, since God is at work to redeem and restore even in the midst of those maleficent displays. As Thielicke realized, "The cunning devices of the devil become an act in salvation history — no less! Everything, literally everything, happens very differently from what we imagine. Everything, literally everything, happens exactly as we dare to hope in those moments when we show the greatest abandon in our faith in Jesus Christ."[150]

Third, it identifies believers as recruits rather than victims. They may experience life as persons under the oppressive thumb of social maltreatment, but the character of this battle is not so mundane. Cosmic alignments, good versus evil, Christ versus the powers, come to expression in the seemingly unremarkable responses Christians make to the evil directed at them in the guise of corrosive, damning speech. The children's rhyme — "Sticks and stones may hurt my bones but words will never hurt me" — fails to account for both the world-forming power of speech and the malevolent "powers" whose aims stand behind vitriolic words, and thus also for the significance of Christlike response to those words (2:21-25).

Still further, although πνεῦμα (*pneuma*, "spirit"), the term Peter uses in 3:19 of those in prison, can refer to angelic beings, it can also refer to a human person.[151] By this I mean not a disembodied person or "soul," since in the NT "spirit" can refer to one's "inner life" without thereby naming a "part" of a person and in the science of Greco-Roman antiquity "spirit" need not refer to human non-corporeality or non-physicality — whether in ancient medicine or

---

150. Thielicke, "Out of the Depths," p. 242.

151. Indeed, had Peter wanted to limit the concern of 3:18-19 to "angels," he could easily have used the term ἄγγελος (*angelos*, "angel"), which he does use in 3:22, rather than πνεῦμα.

in speculation concerning the afterlife.[152] In Acts 17:16, for example, Paul is "vexed in his spirit,"[153] with "spirit" used in a way analogous to "heart." With regard to the nature of post-resurrection corporeality, consider the testimonies of Luke and Paul. Although the disciples in Luke regard Jesus as a πνεῦμα (*pneuma*, 24:37) — by which they probably mean a ghostly apparition or the disembodied residue of a dead person — such an analysis of things is flatly contradicted by Jesus, who immediately demonstrates that he is no ghost. Jesus grounds the continuity of his identity ("It is really me!"), first, in his materiality, his physicality, in the constitution of flesh and density of bones: "Look at my hands and my feet; see that it is I myself. Touch me and see . . ." (24:39). Jesus presses further, requesting something to eat, then consuming broiled fish in the presence of his disciples (24:41-43), thus demonstrating that he is no angelic being.[154] In fact, within the categories of natural science in Paul's day, πνεῦμα (*pneuma*) is a kind of "stuff," and, working within those categories, the apostle can speak of the afterlife using the cognate πνευματικός (*pneumatikos*, "pertaining to the spirit," 1 Cor 15:44, 46) to identify the substance of the resurrection body. Reflecting a prominent interpretive tradition, Paul thinks of the afterlife in astral terms, with the resurrection body made up of the same matter of which the stars are made — that is, quintessence, that fifth and highest element of the universe, beyond air, earth, fire, and water. The reference to "the spirits of the righteous" in Heb 12:23 functions similarly — namely, to designate the godly dead (and not just a part of them).[155]

For this reason, we should not be surprised to find in 1 Pet 4:6 a parallel activity to that recorded in 3:19, though this time with manifestly human recipients of the good news. Although many interpreters hold that Peter refers to Christians who have already died, this argument presumes what is not in evidence in 1 Peter — namely, a context of anxiety over the fate of Christians who have died prior to Christ's return as in 1 Thessalonians. Moreover, the idea of postmortem proclamation and even conversion is not as rare in early Christianity as is often postulated.[156] In the *Shepherd* of Hermas, written in

152. See, e.g., von Staden, "Body, Soul, and Nerves"; Padgett, "Body in Resurrection"; D. B. Martin, *Corinthian Body*, pp. 21-25, 117-20.

153. My translation; NRSV: "deeply distressed."

154. E.g., Tob 12:15, 19: "Raphael, one of the seven angels who stand ready and enter before the glory of the Lord," observes, "Although you were watching me, I really did not eat or drink anything — but what you saw was a vision."

155. Cf. Lane, *Hebrews*, 2:470-71; Ellingworth, *Hebrews*, pp. 680-81.

156. See Klumbies, "Verkündigung unter Geistern und Toten"; Horrell, "1 Pet 4.6," pp. 85-87. Derrett has gathered evidence for parallel views in Judaism ("He Descended into Hell," pp. 238-40). Horrell's theological, literary, and grammatical arguments ("1 Pet 4.6") speak decisively

the first half of the second century and enormously popular in the second and third centuries, we read: "When these apostles and teachers who proclaimed the name of the Son of God died in the power and faith of the Son of God, they delivered their proclamation even to those who had died previously and gave them the seal of the proclamation. So they went down with them into the water and again rose up from it. And these went down living and rose up living. But those who died before went down dead, and rose up living" (*Similitudes* 9.16.5-6, LCL). Also from the early second century, the *Gospel of Peter* has it that in the immediate aftermath of the resurrection Jesus and the two assisting him out of the grave "heard a voice out of the heavens crying, 'Hast thou preached to them that sleep?' and from the cross there was heard the answer, 'Yea'" (10:41-42).[157] 1 Cor 15:29, that notorious passage regarding "baptism on behalf of the dead," is susceptible to a similar reading.

All of this means that we need not jettison early Christian interpretation of Peter's work and the tradition it represents. From the early second century on,[158] Peter was widely regarded as referring to Christ's descent into Hades in order that he might (1) share fully the fate of humanity, (2) conquer Death or Hades (or both), (3) rescue the righteous dead, and/or (4) proclaim salvation to the dead.[159] Although literary testimony to this tradition is wide-

---

against the popular identification of "the dead" (following Dalton, *Christ's Proclamation*) of 4:6 with Christians who had already died.

157. ET in Maurer and Schneemelcher, "Gospel of Peter," p. 225.

158. Strangely, Dalton (*Christ's Proclamation*, pp. 16-17) thinks it significant that 1 Pet 3:19 was used to defend the notion of "Christ's descent" no earlier than Clement, wondering in particular why this text was not used by Irenaeus. Apparently following him, Jobes (p. 241) writes, "In fact, this passage in 1 Peter was only much later brought in to provide some biblical defense for the *descensus* view." Apart from recognizing that this is largely an argument from silence (since the literary remains for the post-apostolic age are not as full as we might wish and since in some cases, such as the *Gospel of Peter*, we simply do not know whether 1 Peter might have been an influence), Clement of Alexandria and Irenaeus were contemporaries, roughly speaking, so the importance of Clement's obvious dependence on 1 Peter can hardly be dismissed as "late." Similarly, Jobes's suggestion (p. 247) that the traditional interpretation of 3:19-20 as a reference to "Christ's descent" arose as a consequence of the loss of *1 Enoch* after the second century does not take seriously enough the evidence that this interpretation antedates the close of the second century.

159. This is not to suggest that the only basis for belief that "Christ descended into Hades" was 1 Pet 3:19-22, however. Buchan's study of Christ's descent to the dead in the theology of Ephrem Syrus locates Ephrem's canonical influences elsewhere, especially in Matt 27:45-54; Mark 15:33-39; Luke 23:44-49; John 19:28-37; Rom 8:28-30; 1 Corinthians 15; Col 1:15-19, etc. ("Christ's Descent to the Dead"). Among other texts susceptible to this reading, see especially Eph 4:9. A lengthy, narrative description is found in *Christ's Descent into Hell* (usually dated to the fifth or sixth centuries), known to us as chs. 17-27 of the *Gospel of Nicodemus*. See, e.g., *Gos-*

spread, I will mention only three early examples. From the turn of the second century, the *Odes of Solomon* refers in several passages to Christ's descent into Hades, among which one of the more prominent is from *Ode* 42:

> Sheol saw me and was shattered,
>> And death ejected me and many with me.
> I have been vinegar and bitterness to it,
>> And I went down with it as far as its depth.
> Then the feet and the head it released,
>> Because it was not able to endure my face.
> And I made a congregation of living among his dead;
>> And I spoke with them by living lips;
>> In order that my word may not be unprofitable.
> And those who had died ran towards me;
>> And they cried out and said, "Son of God, have pity on us.
> And deal with us according to Thy kindness,
>> And bring us out from the bonds of darkness.
> And open for us the door
>> by which we may go forth to you,
>> for we perceive that our death does not touch Thee.
> May we also be saved with you,
>> because you are our Savior." (42:11-18)[160]

Was the *Odes of Solomon* dependent on 1 Peter for this interpretation? Apart from naming 1 Peter or directly quoting its text, this is not easy to discern. What is clear is that *Ode* 42 and 1 Peter share such common motifs as imprisonment and proclamation to the dead.

Around 167 AD, Melito wrote, "Who is my opponent? I, he says, am the Christ. I am the one who destroyed death, and triumphed over the enemy, and trampled Hades under foot, and bound the strong one, and carried off man to the heights of heaven, I, he says, am the Christ" (*On the Passion* 102). Again, without claiming any certainty about dependence on 1 Peter, we can nonetheless recognize that this text shares its emphasis on the triumph of Christ.

Among his several theological concerns relative to Christ's descent to Hades, Clement of Alexandria writes of the fate of those who died apart from knowledge of the gospel:

---

pel of Peter 10:41-42; Ignatius, *Magnesians* 9; *Odes of Solomon* 15:9; 17:10-16; 24:5; 29; 42:11-20; *Acts of Thomas* 10, 156, etc. For a useful assembling of the evidence, see Bauckham, *Fate of the Dead,* pp. 38-44; and for a convenient index to selected witnesses, see Bray, pp. 107-8, 113-14.

160. ET in Charlesworth, "Odes," p. 771.

What then? Did not the same dispensation obtain in Hades, so that even there, all the souls, on hearing the proclamation, might either exhibit repentance, or confess that their punishment was just, because they believed not? And it were the exercise of no ordinary arbitrariness, for those who had departed before the advent of the Lord (not having the Gospel preached to them, and having afforded no ground from themselves, in consequence of believing or not) to obtain either salvation or punishment. For it is not right that these should be condemned without trial, and that those alone who lived after the advent should have the advantage of the divine righteousness. (*Stromateis* 6.6)

There is no doubt that, in his several references to Christ's descent, Clement has drawn on 1 Peter.

In addition to literary evidence, numerous Byzantine and late medieval paintings depict Jesus' descent into hell, taking 3:19 as a reference to the righteous dead.[161]

More recent is the narrative portrait in C. S. Lewis' *The Chronicles of Narnia,* and specifically the final pages of *The Lion, the Witch and the Wardrobe.* Aslan, we may recall, has been slain on the Stone Table by the witch and her minions. Proclaiming victory over Aslan, the witch gathers her legions to conquer those loyal to Aslan. But, the next day, the Stone Table is broken into two pieces and Aslan stands before two of his friends alive. Aslan explains that, "when a willing victim who had committed no treachery was killed in a traitor's stead, the Table would crack and Death itself would start working backwards." Following this, Aslan runs quickly to the witch's stronghold with its courtyard full of statues — dwarves, giants, centaurs, Dryads, and talking animals whom the witch has turned into stone. Breathing on them, Aslan restores them to life, then moves into the house itself, searching in every nook and cranny, since "you never know where some poor prisoner may be concealed." This, Lewis explains, was "the ransacking of the witch's fortress," followed by the march to the scene of battle where they joined the struggle and overcame the witch and her army.[162] Throughout Lewis's *Chronicles* we find congruence but not a one-to-one parallel with the Christian story; likewise, in the series of scenes concerned with Aslan's death and its aftermath, the details of Lewis' narrative imaginatively record close analogies with the tradi-

---

161. See Hornik and Parsons, "Harrowing of Hell"; also Farrar, *Life of Christ,* pp. 433-37. It might be objected that the phrase in 3:19, "he also went," means that Christ's proclamation to the imprisoned spirits postdates his resurrection, but this is not grammatically necessary.

162. Lewis, *The Lion, the Witch and the Wardrobe,* pp. 142-74 (quotations from pp. 160, 167, 168).

tion of "Christ's descent into hell" at some points more than others. It is nonetheless clear that Lewis is reflecting on the traditional idea of "the harrowing of hell," with its defeat of Death and the Devil as well as the release of those imprisoned, all set within an atonement theology that centers on Christ the Conqueror of evil.

There is no single tradition of interpretation regarding "Christ's descent into hell." When I urge that we take this interpretive tradition seriously, then, I do not mean to embrace all the variations on the theme of "Christ's descent" but rather to encourage an openness to the christological pattern by which the tradition renders this Petrine text meaningful. How the ancients might address the interpretive issues that concern twenty-first-century students of Peter is not always clear, in the same way that their interpretive engagement with the Petrine text can leave us scratching our heads. What is clear is that, to a degree that has little contemporary analogy, learned Christians like Clement gauged their exegesis theologically, in terms of the church's kerygmatic confessions (and not in ways decisively determined by philological or historical considerations, as in recent centuries).

An arresting illustration of this is found in Theophylact's *Commentary on 1 Peter* from the eleventh century:

> It was the habit of the Fathers to take this verse completely out of context. They therefore said that the word *dead* has two different meanings in Scripture, referring either to those who are dead in their sins and who never lived at all or to those who have been made conformable to the dead of Christ. . . . But if they had paid the slightest attention to context, they would have seen that here the "dead" are those who have been shut up in hell, to whom Christ went to preach after his death on the cross.[163]

Modern commentators appeal *to context* generally in order to disassociate 3:19; 4:6 from any reference to Christ's descent, but Theophylact argues *from context* for Christ's preaching in Hades.

For persons whose tendency is to think of Scripture providing the *foundation* for theological claims, an interpretive approach of the sort we have outlined will seem problematic. This is because most of us imagine that, in order to take at face value a theological datum, it must be witnessed in Scripture. We should recall that, well into the second century, a number of Christian books circulated just as widely, or more so, than those that would eventually be collected to form the NT Scriptures — that is, there were no generally accepted authoritative texts that could serve this foundational

---

163. Cited in Bray, p. 114.

role. More to the point, in the theological hermeneutic of the early church, the witness of 1 Peter need not provide a foundation for belief in Christ's descent into hell; rather, belief in Christ's descent into hell might provide the lens by which to make sense of texts like 1 Pet 3:19; 4:6. For those interpreters, faithful reading of Scripture followed the divine economy by which God had assembled the mosaic of Scripture. Interestingly, a similar hermeneutic is now championed, for example, by N. T. Wright; claiming to have discerned an overarching drama in the divine story, he now interprets biblical texts within that drama. Without prejudging the authoritative status of the historical drama that Wright articulates, we can nonetheless observe with Wright that this narrative structure orders his exegetical moves as he turns to examine particular texts.[164]

That Peter is himself friendly to such interpretive maneuvers is clear from 3:21, where he labels the Flood as an antitype of baptism; there, as in early Christian typology more generally, interpretive interest moves beyond the analysis of particular words and grammatical relationships in deference to the larger, overarching patterns of the biblical narrative, the architecture of the Scriptures themselves.

Two additional brief notes require attention. First, "prison" (3:19), though not a typical term for hell in the NT, is used in this way in Rev 20:7 (cf. 20:1-3: "bottomless pit," "great chain," "locked").[165] Second, although we do not read in Peter the terminology of "hell" or "Hades," in the cosmology of Second Temple Judaism (as well as the mythology of the Greco-Roman world), a reference to "the dead" necessarily conjures images of the underworld. This is because Sheol (in the Hebrew OT) or Hades (in Greek) is the place of the dead. In Israel's Scriptures Sheol is that "place where the dead are dead."[166] In the Second Temple period, the concept of Hades was in a state of flux, sometimes regarded as a place of detention, where the dead await their punishment at the judgment, but sometimes, as in Luke's parable of the rich man and Lazarus (Luke 16:19-31), as a realm where the outcome of pending judgment is already observed, with the righteous already participating in rewards, the wicked already suffering punishment.[167] In fact, evidence from the world of Peter would allow for readings of Hades as the general abode of the dead; the intermediate abode for all of the dead prior to the final judgment;

---

164. See, e.g., N. T. Wright, *People of God*, pp. 216-19.

165. See Reicke, *Disobedient Spirits*, pp. 116-17.

166. Mendenhall, "From Witchcraft to Justice," p. 68. Jarick pushes further, urging that Sheol is that "post-mortem realm devoid of all that pertains to life and hope" ("Questioning Sheol," p. 30). More fully, see now Johnston, *Shades of Sheol*.

167. See Bauckham, *Fate of the Dead*, pp. 86-90.

the intermediate abode of the wicked and the righteous prior to the final judgment, during which time punishments and rewards are already being assessed; and exclusively the place of punishment for the wicked.[168] This means that Christ having died entails his descent into the realm of the dead, Sheol or Hades, just as Peter's Pentecost speech affirms: "For you will not abandon my soul to Hades, or let your Holy One experience corruption" (Acts 2:27). How much more this descent might entail is suggested by the references to proclamation in 1 Pet 3:19; 4:6.

The net effect of these considerations is that, in a particularly graphic form, Peter makes strong affirmations regarding the meaning of Christ's death, resurrection, and exaltation. Though cast in a different form, his confession parallels that of Paul in Phil 2:10-11, where "in heaven and on earth and under the earth" refers to all heavenly beings, all who are living on earth at Christ's return, and all the dead.[169] In making this claim, Peter draws on one of the most important OT texts in early Christianity, Ps 110:1, to refer to Jesus' ascension and enthronement at the right hand of God (3:22). This reaffirms a common motif in Petrine christology — namely, exaltation through suffering (rather than instead of or in spite of suffering). Peter's point expands further, however, to include the subordination of all "powers" to Christ. On the basis of the usage of this same verb, ὑποτάσσω *(hypotassō)*, in 2:13, 18; 3:1, 5 ("Be subordinate to every human institution . . . household slaves to your masters . . . wives to your own husbands . . ."), we can only assume that (1) Peter uses it in the same way as before, so that, at the exaltation of Christ, the "powers" were positioned in their proper place in the created order, and (2) Peter thus reaffirms that human subordination to human institutions is derivative of, and so superseded by, subordination of all to Christ. With this powerful image, Peter thus asserts the sovereignty of God over human and, indeed, cosmic affairs, reiterating the message of 3:13-17: present suffering cannot generate ultimate harm.

Other motifs come into play as well. That proclamation is made to "the spirits in prison" and good news is proclaimed to "the dead" are expressions both of God's comprehensive judgment and impartiality (cf. 1:17; 2:23; 3:5; 4:17-18) and of the comprehensive work of Christ in redeeming all who will respond to the word proclaimed. Thus, "God can judge all people, both the living and the dead, since the gospel has been announced to all, the dead as

---

168. See the summary in Bauckham, "Hades, Hell"; and especially, idem, *Fate of the Dead*, pp. 9-80.

169. So Hofius, *Christushymnus*, pp. 53-54; et al. Kreitzer likewise sees a connection between the affirmation of Christ's descent into hell and the Philippians hymn ("Phil 2:9-11," pp. 120-21).

well as the living."[170] This perspective is represented in the Apostles' Creed, in a clause no longer repeated in all Christian traditions: "he descended into hell." As Luke Johnson recognizes,

> The descent of Jesus into hell is, in this view, an expression of God's universal will for salvation and a part of his cosmic victory, so that every tongue, even those "under the earth," should proclaim that Jesus is Lord (Phil 2:10-11). In terms of the movement of the creed, the burial represents the nadir of downward descent, the ultimate expression of Jesus' sharing the human condition, even to the depositing of the flesh in the soil like a seed (John 12:24; see 1 Cor 15:35-41).[171]

As Paul put it, "For to this end Christ died and lived again, so that he might be Lord of both the dead and the living" (Rom 14:9).

The Unique and Programmatic Suffering of Jesus. Central to Peter's argument in this textual unit (and more generally in the letter as a whole) is the efficacy of Christ's death. His focus on Christ's suffering is tied into the immediately prior material in two interrelated ways. First, having just credited his audience with "righteous suffering" (3:14), in 3:18 Peter refers to Jesus Christ as the Righteous Sufferer *par excellence*. Second, the journey of Jesus from suffering to exaltation, together with the efficacy of his death, warrants Peter's claim in 3:17 that "it is better to suffer as those who do good." These two are related precisely in Christ's actualization of the career of the Righteous Sufferer so that his suffering has salvific meaning and leads to his exaltation. Early Christian passion theology identified Jesus' death in these terms, and Peter's dependence on the tradition reflects especially its indebtedness to Isa 52:13 ("See, my servant shall prosper; he shall be exalted and lifted up, and shall be very high") and 53:11 ("The righteous one, my servant, shall make many righteous, and he shall bear their iniquities").[172] Earlier, Peter had drawn on the Isaianic material above all to interpret Jesus' suffering as prototypical for Christians, though the atoning significance of Jesus' suffering was not overlooked (2:21-25). In the present text, this admonition is reaffirmed, but the emphasis falls first on his suffer-

---

170. Horrell, "1 Pet 4.6," p. 78; cf. S. E. Johnson, "Preaching to the Dead," p. 51.

171. L. T. Johnson, *Creed*, p. 175.

172. On the importance of the tradition of the Righteous Sufferer in early Christian reflection on Jesus' death and resurrection, see, e.g., Ruppert, *Jesus als der leidende Gerechte?* On allusions to Isa 52:13–53:12 in this pericope, see especially Pearson, *Christological and Rhetorical Properties,* pp. 153-202. Pearson also finds Isa 54:9 in the background of 1 Pet 3:20, but this is less convincing.

ing as an unrepeatable (ἄπαξ, *hapax*) salvific act the end of which is "to lead you to God" (3:18).

In 2:21 Peter portrayed the suffering of Jesus as programmatic for Christian life ("leaving you a pattern in order that you might follow in his footsteps"). He reprises this emphasis in the present text, though in a more subtle way, when in 4:1 he directs his audience to "ready" themselves "with the same pattern of thought." The analogy between Christ and his followers is not exact, since Christ's behavior provides not only the blueprint for his followers but also its basis. Hence, whereas the saying in 4:1, "the one who has suffered as a human has finished with sin," is general enough to apply both to Christ and his followers, it does so in different ways. Christ's once-for-all suffering does away with sin (3:18) so that, in their suffering, his followers might be finished with sin. Having resolved the problem of sin through his death, Christ is "finished with sin." Having departed their former lives of lust, lewdness, and idolatry (4:2-3), a withdrawal that has won for them suffering at the hands of those who continue thus to live, those of Peter's audience have "finished with sin."

Christ's suffering and death were "as a human" just as their suffering is "as humans" (3:18; 4:1). "Human" translates σάρξ *(sarx)*, which for Peter has to do with "life as it reflects and/or pertains to this world" (1:24; 3:18, 21; 4:1, 2, 6). What of Christian suffering? In 4:2-3, Peter draws attention to contrasting times: "your remaining time as a human" and "time lost." The past was marked by living "in accordance with human desires" and "discharging the will of the Gentiles," whereas the present is characterized by living "in accordance with the will of God." This recalls similar language in 1:14, where the previous time was one of "being shaped by the desires that marked your former time of ignorance," and 1:17-19, in which the present time is to be lived "with reverent fear during the time of your dwelling in a strange land, knowing that you were liberated from the emptiness of your inherited way of life . . . by the precious blood of Christ." As there, so here, the atoning death of Jesus funds new life. As there, so here, present life is marginal existence, inhabiting the shadows of imperial ways of thinking and acting, suffering as a people not really at home.

A further parallel is suggested by the analogous language in 3:18 ("made alive by the Spirit") and 4:6 ("live by the Spirit"). Whether either refers to the Holy Spirit is debated. Speaking against this reading is the parallel, σαρκί *(sarki)*–πνεύματι *(pneumati)*, "in [or by] the flesh–in [or by] the spirit," which appears in both. How can Jesus be raised to life *by* the Spirit if he is put to death *in* the flesh (3:18)? (The same question can be asked of 4:6, where "the dead" are in view.) Does not the balance of these two terms in the dative

135

require symmetry in grammatical function?[173] One might answer in the affirmative but construe the death-giving agent as human beings and the life-giving agent as the Spirit.[174] Alternatively, we might take our cue, as I have, from 4:1-2, where Peter juxtaposes suffering "in the flesh" with living "by the will of God" (σαρκί — θελήματι, *sarki — thelēmati*), which counters the need for simple grammatical balance. The primary import of the juxtaposition of these two texts is how they cement the motif of continuity between Christ and Christians: so in suffering and death, so in life and vindication. And this contributes to the larger motif in the letter, whereby Peter clothes his readers in the robes of the suffering and glory of Jesus Christ. Although Paul and Peter use different terms (Paul: φρονέω, *phroneō*, with reference to a pattern of thinking, feeling, and acting;[175] Peter: ἔννοια, *ennoia*, "pattern of thought"), the parallel with Phil 2:5-11 is nonetheless instructive.

Phil 2:1-8	1 Pet 4:1-2
An appeal to live in a way that reflects the mind of Christ ("Let the same mind be in you that was in Christ Jesus . . ."), who "emptied himself, taking the form of a slave, being born in human likeness. And being found in human form, he humbled himself and became obedient to the point of death — even death on a cross."	"Therefore, because Christ suffered as a human, you also must ready yourselves with the same pattern of thought — namely, that the one who has suffering as a human has finished with sin, to the end that you live your remaining time as a human no longer in accordance with human desires but in accordance with the will of God."

In both instances, Christians are urged to adopt for themselves and put on display in their lives the pattern of thinking demonstrated in Christ's suffering. Recalling our earlier comments regarding the triumph of Christ in Phil 2:10-11 and 1 Pet 3:18, 22, we now see that the parallel extends further to include the notion of Christian participation in the "way" of Jesus Christ through suffering to vindication and exaltation. In 1 Peter 4, the note of vindication is sounded in a peculiar way, in Peter's guarantee of judgment in 4:5. As elsewhere in 1 Peter, the exercise of impartial, sovereign justice belongs to God (1:17; 2:23). Believers and unbelievers are thus set in an ironic contrast: Whereas believers are to ready themselves (ἕτοιμος, *hetoimos*) to give an ex-

173. So, e.g., Elliott, p. 645.
174. As in Achtemeier, p. 250.
175. Thus Fowl, *Philippians*, p. 28.

planation (λόγος, *logos*) for the character of their lives (3:15), those who live according to human desires (4:2), following the will of the Gentiles (4:3), will be required to given an explanation (λόγος, *logos*) to the God who stands ready (ἑτοίμως, *hetoimōs*) to judge.

Peter also connects Christ's suffering (which "leads you to God"), the days of Noah and the water that "saves" (διασῴζω, *diasōzō*), and the baptism that "saves" (σῴζω, *sōzō*). Peter himself refers to baptism as the antitype (ἀντίτυπος, *antitypos*) of the Flood, which is therefore a significant but incomplete foreshadowing of baptism. This connection is furthered by Peter's side comment noting that only "a few people" were saved — anticipating the minority status of Peter's Christian audience. With respect to the days of Noah, Peter's reference is to God's bringing Noah and his kin safely through the calamity of divine judgment as they passed from the old, sin-filled world into the new world. Baptism serves similarly, though perhaps not in the expected way. In Peter's hands, baptism signifies new birth: a genuine turning from old life to new, realized in finding one's identity in a new web of relationships, a transformation of one's values and allegiances within the new community, and the embodiment of a new life-world evidenced in altered dispositions and attitudes (see above on 1:3). But this "genuine turning," far from a once-and-for-all event, is realized in ongoing commitment. This is the importance of the difficult term in 3:21, ἐπερώτημα *(eperōtēma)*, which usually has the sense of "making an appeal" but here refers to the power of baptism to signify a "pledge" or "acceptance of new duties," the goal of which is a good conscience.[176] Baptism must give way to a life that reflects baptism, a life in which the believer grows into the commitment made at baptism. This is related to the means of salvation in Peter's writing. In the shorthand phrase of 3:18, Christ's suffering "for sins" is presented as a purification offering, a sacrificial act that prioritizes the offering of the lives of those for whom the sacrifice is made. At the same time, Peter identifies the resurrection of Jesus Christ as the salvific event (3:21; compare 1:3, 21).[177]

If the Flood is an antitype of baptism, might we also imagine that the pagans of 4:3-4 find their antitype in the disobedient spirits of 3:19-20?[178] Peter regards their lives as overwhelmed by a veritable "flood" of lewdness and idolatry, a reminder that in the biblical tradition "water" is sometimes metonymic for evil and chaos (e.g., Pss 74:13-14; 89:9; Isa 27:1; 51:9-10; Hab

176. See Brox, 178-79; Hartman, *Into the Name*, pp. 116-17.

177. Indeed, this is a primary emphasis of Peter's theology of resurrection, an emphasis that highlights the active role of God in the provision of salvation (Schlosser, "Résurrection de Jésus").

178. See Rudman, "1 Pet 3-4," pp. 401-2.

3:15; Rev. 21:1). Likewise, then, baptism is the movement from the deluge of sensual pleasure ("profligacy," "unrestrained immorality") to new life in accordance with the will of God.

So radical is the transformation of new birth that those with whom these Christians shared their former manner of life are baffled by their failure to do so any longer. This emphasizes, yet again, the distinction between believers and unbelievers and indicates the basic stance of courageous resistance Christians are to maintain vis-à-vis the wider world. The categories are transformed. What is celebrated as customary living among the Gentiles is dismissed among Christians as a waste of time. Following the will of God implicates the Christian in a baffling failure to conform to conventional expectations. So sharp are these lines drawn that Peter is able to refer to those completely lacking in self-control and engaging in idolatry, the very ones who situate themselves over against Christ's followers, as "Gentiles" and "blasphemers." As we have seen in 2:9-10, Peter applies Israel's own self-descriptors to Christians (e.g., "a royal priesthood, a holy nation") so fully that he is able to use the collective term "the Gentiles" to refer to all who do not follow Jesus (see 2:12). "To blaspheme" could have the more pedestrian sense of "to slander" or "to defame" in social relations, but in this context its significance is more likely tied to the religious notion of "impugning God's honor." This is not only because of the reference to idolatry, but also because insults directed at persons so fully identified with the will of God are thereby directed at God himself. In a setting characterized in this way, suffering, when evaluated according to divine standards, is a badge of honor.

Finally, we cannot overlook those portraits of Sheol or Hades, the abode of the dead, which draw on the imagery of water (e.g., 2 Sam 22:5-6; Job 26:5; Ps 69:15; Jonah 2; Rev. 20:13).[179] Those saved by the water in the days of Noah and those saved through baptism follow the way of Christ — his suffering, death, and journey into the abode of the dead, as well as his vindication. The water that endangered Noah and his kin actually served to rescue them, the death of Jesus that was to have silenced him and countermanded his message was actually the means by which he triumphed, and so the suffering of Peter's Christian audience, far from destroying them, marks them as those who have pledged themselves to Christ and who will share in his resurrection. Here is the decisive demonstration that whatever the source of calamity — divine judgment, the machinations of "powers" at work in the world, or abuse from those with whom Christians shared their former life — the righteous are brought safely through it.

179. See Johnston, *Shades of Sheol*, pp. 114-24.

4:7-11

7 The end of all things has come, so keep a disciplined mind and exercise vigilance for the purpose of prayer, 8 before all else maintaining unceasing love for one another, for love covers a multitude of sins, 9 practicing hospitality toward one another without grumbling, 10 and serving one another as good stewards of the varied grace of God, just as each person has received a gift. 11 If someone speaks, let it be as though declaring the pronouncements of God; if anyone serves, let it be from the strength that God supplies, so that in all things God may be glorified through Jesus Christ — to whom be the glory and the power forever and ever. Amen.

Drawing inspiration from Peter's earlier references to the "remaining time" (v. 2) and God's readiness "to judge the living and the dead" (v. 5), this textual unit casts an eschatological shadow over the whole of life within the family of believers.[180] In fact, together with its emphasis on the generosity of the God who empowers the Christianity community for service and who is to be glorified in all things (vv. 10-11), these two motifs, eschatology and the household of faith, frame Peter's instruction.

More or less constantly throughout 3:13–4:6, Peter has focused on the relation of his Christian audience to contemptuous unbelievers.[181] His portrayal of the situation reached its apex in 4:1-4, which interpreted the suffering of believers in relation to the suffering of Christ, thus emphasizing the unwarranted nature of the malice directed toward them (see 3:14, 18: suffering of the righteous), and detailed the wide chasm separating Christians and their opponents in terms of life-orientation (human desires versus God's will, v. 2) and characteristic behavior. Although hardly countenancing withdrawal from society, Peter's perspective nonetheless points to the tensions inherent in living in and engaging with the wider world. Distinctions in essential alle-

---

180. T. W. Martin insists that v. 7a is the close of the previous textual unit, that οὖν (*oun*, "therefore") in v. 7b marks this clause as the beginning of a new section (*Metaphor and Composition*, pp. 235-36). To the contrary, just as οὖν in 4:1 identifies the suffering of Christ (3:18-22) as the warrant for the directives of 4:1-6, so οὖν in v. 7b identifies the pending eschaton (v. 7a) as the warrant for the directives of vv. 7b-11.

181. In 2:11-12, Peter drew out the ramifications of his work in identify formation (e.g., 2:9-10) in terms of a basic stance vis-à-vis the world. In that context Peter's thought was that, through the "honorable way of life among the Gentiles" practiced by his audience, those outside the Christian community "might glorify God on the day of visitation." Peter's message there finds its counterpart in our present unit. Here, however, attention is turned to the inner life of the community, and it is believers who are to glorify God in all things, now and forever.

giances and social behavior are naturally foregrounded in the context of pressure from outsiders. This pressure prioritizes the need for cohesiveness among insiders and urges renewed attention to community solidarity. Accordingly, Peter's choices of language index a strong semantics of partnership — including such familial terms as "love," "hospitality," and "service/household steward"; and an orientation to "the other" or "one another" (εἰς, *eis,* "for" + the reflexive pronouns ἑαυτούς, *heautous,* and ἀλλήλους, *allēlous,* in vv. 8, 9, and 10). That each phrase of this textual unit is tradition-laden, drawing on forms of instruction characteristic of (even peculiar to) the Christian community, highlights Peter's emphasis on communality:

> v. 7a reproduces a standard formula for eschatological pronouncement
>
> v. 7b depends on a catechetical pattern
>
> v. 8a reprises the love command
>
> v. 8b is proverbial, deriving from Prov 10:12
>
> v. 9 draws on the familiar motif of hospitality
>
> vv. 10-11a recalls the motif of "spiritual gifts" (e.g., Rom 12:6-8; 1 Corinthians 12), and may borrow from the Jesus tradition represented in Luke 12:42
>
> v. 11b is a doxological closing[182]

Turning his attention thus to the internal life of Christian communities and doing so with imagery borrowed from household relations, Peter addresses his concern for harmony among believers. In doing so, however, he also voices a telling strategy for engaging the wider world of Roman antiquity. This is because, in Greco-Roman political philosophy, the household was a microcosm of the body politic. Here was focused the range of social relationships and obligations, including the distribution and deployment of power, the proper observation of honor-based status strata, and boundary-making and boundary-keeping with respect to those outside the household. That is, the household provided the arena in which were inculcated an awareness of one's place in the world in relation to others and how appropriately to defer or to command respect. Consequently, relations within the household had a ripple effect outside the household. If among Christians mutuality should become a defining practice, if Christians should embrace the ideal of other-oriented service without reference to status honor, and if Christians should exercise among themselves unwavering love, then this cannot help but score a blow against a world distinguished by status-based distribution of power and

---

182. For this compositional analysis, see Schutter, *Hermeneutic and Composition,* p. 72.

privilege. That Peter counsels a relational ethic focused on the mutuality of "one another" statements while at the same time celebrating Christ (and not one's social betters) as the rightful recipient of "glory" (or "honor" — δόξα, *doxa*) and ruling power, is thus an intensely political statement. Remembering that the primary image of Christ in 1 Peter is "the one who suffers" — that is, one whose marginal status in the world not only was documented by his maltreatment at the hands of his contemporaries but also is recognized and, indeed, esteemed by Peter — it is difficult to avoid the conclusion that Peter's household ethic is purposely dissident, dramatically so.

We should not be surprised that Peter's theology has so marked a political edge. This is true more generally for those who follow Jesus — who proclaimed the advent of an alternative dominion, the kingdom of God, who was executed as a threat to the state, and who, in an empire ruled by Lord Caesar, was proclaimed by his disciples as Lord. More particularly for 1 Peter, we need only remind ourselves that Peter's audience is a dispersion people, strangers in the world, persons whose commitments to the lordship of Jesus Christ have led to transformed dispositions and behaviors that place them on the margins of respectable society (1:1-2). More to the present point, they are a people for whom "an imperishable, uncorrupted, and unfading inheritance" is "reserved in heaven" (1:4). Inhabiting this eschatological landscape, Peter sketches the shape of intramural behavior expected of his audience.

Although τέλος *(telos)* can refer to "end" in the sense of a termination or conclusion, it is also used in the NT with the sense of "the goal to which a process is being directed." "Goal" is the sense in which the term is used in 1:9 ("salvation" is the "goal [τέλος] of faith") and 4:17 (in reference to the "end" of unbelievers), and this is its sense, too, in v. 7. For Peter, the goal to which the saving purpose of God is directed is "at hand." This assertion echoes a clause in Mark's summary of Jesus' message: "the kingdom of God is at hand" (1:15), where the perfect form of the verb "approach" (ἐγγίζω, *engizō*) is also found (see Rom 13:12; Jas 5:8). How best to translate this verb (ἤγγικεν, *ēngiken*) is the locus of controversy.[183] Has the End "arrived" or is it (only) "imminent"? Either reading is possible, grammatically speaking, so context must be determinative. For 1 Peter, two observations are pertinent. First, clearly, "the end" has already come; this is evident in 1:20 where Peter observes a reference to Jesus' advent that Jesus was "revealed at the end of the ages." Second, and just as clearly, his reference to "all things" in v. 7 connotes a cosmic transformation that has not yet been realized (4:2, 6). This means that Peter's statement registers the present as "the end," but clarifies "the end" as

---

183. See the short summary in G. B. Caird and L. D. Hurst, *NT Theology*, pp. 32-34.

itself a process yet to reach its completion in the final judgment. The same tension appears earlier in the letter: Christ, having been revealed at the end of the ages (1:20), yet to be (finally) revealed (1:13). Hence, the advent of Jesus Christ marks the midpoint in a history that spans the period from creation to the final revelation of Jesus Christ, with the "present" of Peter's Christian audience assessed as "the last days."

The implications of this are several. First, when set against the backdrop of contemporary Jewish apocalyptic thought, Peter's marking of the times interprets the suffering of believers as nothing less than a participation in the Messiah's own suffering, by which God actualizes his salvific purpose. This perspective is already meaningful in 3:18-22, but will become especially important in 4:12-19.[184] Second, a theology that emphasizes the End deprives present institutions — by which I refer both to patterns of expected behavior reinforced by social sanctions and to organizational structures that legitimate and propagate such behavior[185] — of their authoritative and/or conventional status. "By declaring that all that is taken for granted will end, eschatological scenarios undermine the cultural system that masquerades as common sense."[186] If by introducing an eschatological compass for navigating life in this world Peter relativizes the claims to ultimacy voiced by present institutions and encourages social behaviors almost guaranteed to attract unwanted attention, then, third, it is incumbent on him that he lay out the character of the community and its practices that are faithful to that eschatological vision. This is precisely what he does.

Patterns of behavior reflect patterns of thought, just as they help to form them. That is, the repetition of distinctive patterns of behavior forms in us a sense of identity, which is itself exhibited in our behaviors. In this respect, the eschatological note Peter has sounded functions as a basic image/schematic for making sense of and ordering Christian experience. Eschatology is a cornerstone of the Christian imagination: a lens through which to view day-to-day life and the whole of time *(conceptual)*, comprised of beliefs and values to which the Christian community, individually and collectively, is deeply attached *(conative)*, whose terms give rise to certain behaviors *(action-guiding)*.[187] This is

---

184. So Dubis, *Messianic Woes;* Dubis, however, does not struggle with the interpretation of v. 7a.

185. I am following Wuthnow, *Communities of Discourse,* pp. 5-17; Bellah, et al., *Good Society,* pp. 10-11.

186. Meeks, *Christian Morality,* p. 180.

187. See above on 1:3-9; I have borrowed this formulation of human "imagination" from Flanagan, *Problem of the Soul,* pp. 27-55.

the significance of Peter's opening salvo, with its emphasis on discipline of mind. Compare:

> 1:13: "having readied your mind for action, practicing vigilance (νήφοντες, *nēphontes*)"

> 4:7: "The end of all things has come, so keep a disciplined mind and exercise vigilance (νήψατε, *nēpsate*)."

> 5:8: "Remain vigilant (νήψατε, *nēpsate*)! Stay alert!"

The first verb ("keep a disciplined mind") is the relatively rare σωφρονέω *(sōphroneō)*, used only six times in the NT, which might refer to the exercise of reason or sensibility. Together, the two verbs comprising the directives of v. 7 amplify one another; one is tempted to say "double seriousness,"[188] though the primary emphasis would be on a sober awareness of the way things really are, and thus the exercise of a wisdom measured in terms of the eschatological life-world Peter has projected. Literally, the second verb, νήφω *(nēphō)*, refers to the opposite of drunkenness. We quickly discern, then, a deliberate contrast with the lewdness and general want of self-restraint on display among "the Gentiles" (4:3-4). Lacking formation in the Christian faith ("living hope," 1:3), they structure their lives around lusts and expend their energies in living under the mastery of their own wills; the result is a deluge of unrestrained immorality. Not so with Peter's Christian audience, whose thought patterns have been sculpted through reflection on the redemptive suffering of Jesus (4:1), who structure their lives around the will of God (4:2), and who understand the nature of the times and so align themselves around the actualization of God's saving purpose (4:7).

This (re-)formation of thoughts and feelings is for the purpose of prayer. Together with Peter's doxological interests in v. 11, this is a reminder that the community of the faithful is not an end unto itself but is an expression of the will of the God who has called it into being and gives it life. This is the third reference to prayer in the letter and it, like the other two, has nothing to say about *how* one ought to pray (i.e., Peter provides no "technology of prayer"), but concerns itself instead with (1) readiness to pray through alignment with God's character and God's way (see especially 3:7) and (2) an awareness of the gracious character of the One to whom prayers are directed (see especially 3:12).

With three parallel phrases — "maintaining love," "practicing hospital-

---

188. So Lohse, "Parenesis and Kerygma," p. 59.

ity," and "serving" — vv. 8-11a map out in broad but meaningful terms what practices flow out of the sort of Christian formation in which Peter engages in his letter.[189] (1) The love Peter countenances is mutual ("for one another") and unceasing, just as he has already articulated in 1:22. Love entails a group ethos of solidarity and loyalty, an essential disposition favoring others in the community and so a refusal to harm them, and a commitment to harmony within the group. It is closely related to the familial language Peter uses to define the community of believers. Unlike the parallel in 1:22, though, here Peter expands on the qualifier "unceasing" with the added maxim that "love covers a multitude of sins."[190] Concerning this proverb, Clement writes, "Love hides a multitude of sins. Love puts up with everything and is always patient" (*1 Clement* 49:5). Paul wrote similarly, "Love endures all things," before going on to urge in a claim that parallels Peter's reference to "unceasing" love: "Love never ends" (1 Cor 13:7-8).[191]

(2) In the Mediterranean generally, and particularly in the early Christian movement, hospitality was a valued practice (e.g., Heb 13:2).[192] By "practice," I refer to those behaviors generated by — but, in a positive feedback loop, also formative of — one's deepest commitments, without recourse to self-conscious coordination or rule-following. Christians practice hospitality, then, without necessarily setting out to do so, since practices of hospitality emerge from hospitable character. This is suggested in three ways in v. 9: (a) by Peter's use of the adjective φιλόξενος *(philoxenos)*, "hospitable," rather than a verb (describing who we are rather than what we do since, after all, we can only do what we are), (b) his qualification of hospitableness as "without grumbling" — suggesting practices of hospitality that are uncalculated and therefore unbegrudging,[193] and (c) the reminder in vv. 10-11 of the uncalculated grace of God, whose gracious initiative empowers and inspires gracious

---

189. Vv. 8 and 10 employ participial constructions, v. 9 adjectival, each, then, filling out the lines of behavior that have their source in the mindset that Peter prescribes in v. 7. Contra, e.g., Campbell (*Honor*, p. 195 n. 83) and Jobes (p. 276, though see the apparently contrary view on p. 281), there is no reason to morph them into imperatives.

190. Cf. Jas 5:20; *1 Clement* 49:5; *2 Clement* 16:4. Peter's rendition is closer to the Hebrew of Prov. 10:12 ("but love covers all offenses") than the Greek ("love [φιλία, rather than Peter's ἀγάπη] covers all who do not love dissension"), making it almost certain that Peter deploys this clause as an axiom rather than consciously as a scriptural citation.

191. This interpretation is more probable than the suggestion that Peter is speaking of divine forgiveness at the eschaton. See the discussion in Achtemeier, pp. 295-96; Jobes, pp. 278-79.

192. See Koenig, *NT Hospitality*; Pohl, "Hospitality"; more generally, idem, *Making Room*.

193. Inhospitality could be a weapon in the arsenal of disputes over orthodoxy and orthopraxis, as in 2 and 3 John.

human response. In this sense, then, hospitality is inherently generous, participating in and reflecting the divine hospitality.

One of the premier expressions of hospitality in early Christianity was the need to make room for itinerant servants of the gospel (e.g., Matt 10:9-14; Acts 18:1-3; Phlm 22), giving rise to challenging questions regarding who were authentic representatives of Jesus (e.g., *Didache* 11); related to this is the use of the home as a locus for missionary activity. Peter seems not to be concerned with this manifestation of hospitality, however. His use of the phrase "to one another" and the overall force of vv. 7-11 suggests instead that he is concerned with the practice of hospitality within the Christian community. Three scenarios come to mind. First, as in the larger Christian movement of the period, the question arises where Christians will gather when they meet.[194] Christians generally met at least weekly, with those with larger houses hosting as many as 50, but more usually 30 or 40, persons (see Rom 16:23). In the absence of such patrons, Christians would have gathered for communal worship in smaller groups and in spaces less well-appointed, such as small flats or the back rooms of shops. Not least because of Peter's assumptions regarding the social pressures under which his audience lived, we should also imagine, second, the need for sanctuary and, third, more generally, for shared meals. Sharing meals, of course, includes the not insignificant need for the satiation of hunger. They also bear importance as social events. To welcome people at the table was tantamount to extending familial ties to them; table fellowship encoded messages about inclusion and exclusion, boundary-keeping and -crossing, and status.

(3) Finally, Peter presents God as both the source and the model of how those of his audience ought to comport themselves within the Christian community. In Scripture, the vocabulary of grace connotes spontaneous kindness and acts of generosity — in the case of God, welling up from his own character, and in the case of humanity, resourced through the reception and embodiment of the ungrudging initiative of God.[195] Eight times in 1 Peter (1:2, 10, 13; 3:7; 4:10; 5:5, 10, 12), χάρις *(charis)* refers to the benevolence of God. Here, the varied grace of God is expressed more specifically in gifts — which are freely and graciously given, yet gifts which, in the giving, include both the capacity for and the call to service. Importantly, gifts are (a) given to (b) each person, and the exercise of all gifts belongs in the general category of (c) "service." This means that (a) gifts have their origin in God's initiative and are therefore useless to those who might want to use them to index levels of sta-

---

194. Cf. Gehring, *House Church and Mission*; Schnabel, *Early Christian Mission*, 2:1301-6.
195. See *TLNT* 3:500-506; J. B. Green, "Grace."

tus,[196] (b) no believer is overlooked in the distribution of gifts, implying a kind of democratization of divine beneficence, and (c) the status assigned to every Christian is, as it were, lower than the others in the community of believers, so that every single believer is cast as the servant of the rest. It is hard to imagine a set of claims more damaging to the highly stratified world of Roman antiquity, a world in which, from an early age, persons were schooled in locating themselves in a hierarchy of status and gauging their behavior toward others — whether in acts of obeisance or domination.

Although "in all things" (v. 11) undoubtedly refers to the patterns of thought, prayer, and hospitality mentioned in vv. 7-9, as well as to every other aspect of life in and outside the community of believers, the presence of this phrase in the lengthy sentence of v. 11 encourages a conclusion either that the two gifts Peter does mention, speaking and serving, are metonymic for all possible gifts, or that these two gifts are intended as comprehensive tags for the whole of life. A case can be made either way, and it is not clear that a decision on this question is important. Luke can refer to the whole of Jesus' ministry with the phrase "all that Jesus did and taught" (Acts 1:1), suggesting the breadth of a reference to "word and deed" or, in this case, "said and served." On the other hand, parallel references in Rom 12:6-8 and 1 Cor 12 prompt the view that Peter's "speaking" and "serving" stand in for all sorts of gifts that might give expression to the "varied grace of God." Either way the conclusion is the same: the capacity to serve within the community of believers is a gift and a call which owes itself to God's generous initiative.

The close of v. 11, which serves as the conclusion of this textual unit as well as the fitting end of this major section of Peter's letter (2:11–4:11), is a doxology. In 2:11-12, Peter had expressed the anticipated outcome that, through the good conduct of his Christian audience, unbelievers might glorify God. In 3:22, he extended this idea to include angels, authorities, and powers, in recognition of Jesus' exaltation to the right hand of God. Here, he reiterates those earlier thoughts and expands them. Now God is to be glorified, but it is expressly stated that this is *through* Jesus Christ, to whom also belong glory/ honor and power.[197] On the one hand, this evidences what Peter is otherwise at pains to argue — namely, that righteous suffering, far from disqualifying someone from honor, is actually highly esteemed in the divine economy, and

---

196. Peter provides no hint that "gifts" are anything other than ordinary human capacities that nonetheless owe their origins to God and through God's grace are enhanced for ministry within the Christian community.

197. The referent of ᾧ (*hō*, "to whom") in v. 11d is ambiguous. It could refer back to God or to Jesus Christ. Given the location of "Jesus Christ" in the sentence, immediately prior to ᾧ (*hō*), however, Jesus is the more likely choice (see further, Michaels, pp. 252-53).

that Jesus, the prototypical Righteous Sufferer, and not the human institutions comprising the empire, is the one who holds ultimate power and to whom honor is due. In a world where the distribution of power and privilege are determined in relation to social status, this is a remarkable claim indeed. On the other hand, Peter's doxology evidences how Jesus is reverenced in reference to God, with whom, then, Jesus shares Christian adoration and devotion. Praise to God is *through* Jesus Christ — that is, the occasion and content of praise is God's mighty acts of salvation in Christ, and praise to Jesus Christ is set within (and not over against) praise to God.[198] If, as in 1:3-12, the revelation of Jesus Christ at the end of the ages is nothing less than a disclosure of God's character and purpose, then so, too, praise to Jesus Christ is encompassed in praise to God. Here again in 1 Peter, then, we find ourselves in the company of an affirmation of Jesus' divinity — not in ontological or functional terms (since these categories would be anachronistic), but in terms of Jesus' sharing in the identity of God.[199]

4:12–5:11

This final section of the body of 1 Peter is clearly demarcated — at the outset by the use of the vocative "Beloved" as the apostle addresses his audience directly (see 2:11) and at the close by the presence of a doxological statement (5:11). The dual emphasis on suffering and glory in 4:12-13 and 5:9-10 also forms an *inclusio* around this segment of the letter, providing clarity around the focus of the section as a whole. Finally, 5:12-14 has the form of a letter closing, and this is another indication, this time from considerations of genre, that 5:11 marks the conclusion of the body of the letter.

Structurally, this segment comprises three textual units, set off by the appearance of οὖν (*oun,* "therefore") in 5:1, 6. The result is an ABA′ pattern:

A suffering in eschatological perspective (4:12-19)
   B proper conduct within the community of the faithful (5:1-5)
A′ suffering in eschatological perspective (5:6-11)

The question is how the material directed toward relations within the community (5:1-5) is linked to the surrounding instruction on suffering (4:12-19;

---

198. Hurtado, *Lord Jesus Christ,* especially pp. 151-52 (though in reference to Pauline theology).

199. See p. 25 n. 37 above.

5:7-11). To readers of 1 Peter, the answer is anything but unexpected; as we shall see, it is of a piece with the identity reformation to which Peter has devoted himself from the opening verses of his letter.

Three motifs weave their way throughout this major segment of the letter. Perhaps the most noticeable is that of suffering. This motif is lexicalized with πάθημα (*pathēma*, "suffering," 4:13; 5:9) and πάσχω (*paschō*, "suffer," 4:15, 19; 5:10), as would be expected in this letter.[1] Peter's term for the content of that suffering, ὀνειδίζω (*oneidizō*, "revile" or "vilify," 4:14), is used only here in the letter, but is nonetheless reminiscent of earlier characterizations of Christian suffering in this letter (e.g., 2:12; 3:9, 16). As important as these might be for setting the tone of 4:12–5:11, of greater interest are those terms that, for the first time in this letter, place suffering on a grander cosmic scale and demonstrate irrefutably both the cause of that suffering and the place of suffering in God's eschatological purpose. These terms include πύρωσις (*pyrōsis*, "fiery ordeal," 4:12) and πειρασμός (*peirasmos*, "test" or "temptation," sometimes in the service of diabolic aims, 4:12), together with the identification of the ultimate adversary, the figure who stands behind all Christian suffering, as "the devil" (5:8). Though not unique within 1 Peter as a whole, four related emphases help to fill out Peter's perspective on suffering in this section of his letter: the temporal limitations on present suffering versus the ageless glory to come (4:13, 17; 5:10), the importance of suffering for the right reasons (4:15, 19), intimations that the suffering of Christians is a participation in the suffering of Christ (4:13, 14, 16; 5:1), and the placement of the experience of suffering in an interpretive matrix of joy and glory (4:13-14; 5:1, 4, 10).

The second of the three motifs is easy to overlook for those of us who tend to take the *theo*logy of this and other NT books for granted. This is the focus of this letter segment on God, remarkable even in a letter otherwise known for its theocentricism. θεός (*theos*, "God") is used explicitly 39 times in 1 Peter, 10 times in these 18 verses. "God" appears especially in phrases denoting divine origin, ownership, or identity: Spirit of God (4:14), household of God (4:17), gospel of God (4:17), will of God (4:19; similarly 5:2), flock of God (5:2), mighty hand of God (5:6), and God of all grace (5:10). "God" is the object of glory in 4:16, and again, implicitly, in 5:10-11. God's actions, in clauses where the word "God" is explicit, include opposing the proud and giving grace to the humble (5:5), calling the faithful to share in his eternal glory (5:10), and restoring, supporting, strengthening, and establishing Peter's Christian audience (5:10). In clauses that mention God with a personal pronoun, "he" anoints his people (4:14), judges all people (4:17), exalts the faith-

---

1. See 1:11; 2:19, 20, 21, 23; 3:14, 17, 18; 4:1, 12, 15; 5:10.

ful (5:6), and cares for the faithful (5:7). Additionally, for the first time in 1 Peter, God is named as "Creator," and further characterized as "faithful" (4:19). For those with ears to hear, the redoubled theocentrism of this final section of the letter preserves an important emphasis on the great mural of God's initiative, provision, and unrivaled sovereignty — a perspective which, if genuinely embodied, would militate against human tendencies to myopia in the face of opposition, console those caught up in the torment of ostracism and malice, generate fresh motivation for living in accordance with the will of God, and endow a full-bodied Christian hope.

Third, this section of Peter's letter has an unusual aggregate of verbs in the imperative:

> Do not be surprised at the fiery ordeal (4:12).
> Rejoice insofar as you share in Christ's sufferings (4:13).
> Let none of you suffer as a wrongdoer (4:15).
> When suffering as a Christian, do not be ashamed (4:16).
> When suffering as a Christian, glorify God (4:16).
> Let sufferers entrust themselves to a faithful Creator (4:19).
> Elders, tend the flock (5:2).
> Young people, subordinate yourselves (5:5).
> All of you, clothe yourselves with humility (5:5).
> Humble yourselves (5:6).
> Remain vigilant (5:8).
> Stay alert (5:8).
> Resist the devil (5:9).

Alongside these, Peter indexes additional attitudes and conditions that either already are or ought to be characteristic of Christians in the midst of their suffering: bliss (4:13), joy (4:13), blessedness (4:14), and continuing in well-doing (4:19). It almost goes without saying, then, that in this last section of the body of his letter, Peter is majoring on responsive, Christian behavior in circumstances populated by insult, abuse, suffering.

Behavior is only the tip of the iceberg, however. Peter's concerns run beneath the surface to identify, promulgate, and celebrate patterns of thinking and feeling that reflect the transformation of dispositions, modes of valuation, and volition characteristic of those who have been given "new birth into a living hope through the resurrection of Jesus Christ from the dead" (1:3). *If God*, whose glory Peter celebrates and whose power he proclaims, exercises his peerless status in faithfulness — exalting, caring, restoring, supporting, strengthening, and establishing his people, and *if Christ*, whose suffering and disgrace, leading to his resurrection, vindication, and glory, mark him as the Righteous Sufferer par excellence, *then how much more should Christians* see the honor they have before God not as a fulcrum for the leveraging of power, pride, or privilege, but as vocation, empowerment, and declaration of freedom for performing the will of God, providing shepherd-care, subordinating themselves, comporting themselves in humility, maintaining alertness, and resisting evil, as well as rejoicing and praising God?

4:12-19

12 Beloved, do not be surprised at the fiery ordeal taking place among you so as to test you, as though something strange were happening to you; 13 rather, to the degree that you are participating in the sufferings of Christ, you must rejoice, in order that you may also rejoice with great joy at the revelation of his glory. 14 When you are vilified because of the name of Christ, you are blessed, for the Spirit of glory[2] — indeed, the Spirit of God — rests on you.[3] 15 Now let none of you suffer as a murderer, thief, or evildoer, or as a mischief-maker;[4] 16 but when you suffer as a Christian, do not be ashamed, but glorify God because of this name, 17 for it is time for judgment to begin with the household of God — but, if first for us, what will be the end of those who disbelieve the good news of God? 18 And if the righteous person is saved only with difficulty, where will the godless and the sinner appear? 19 Accordingly, those who suffer according to the will of God must entrust their lives to a faithful Creator by doing good.

---

2. Some witnesses (including $\aleph^*$ A P) insert καὶ δυναμέως — thus, "the spirit of glory and power"; it is difficult to explain why, if original, these words would have been dropped and easy to imagine an expansion based on the conjunction of "glory" and "power," e.g., in some version of the Lord's Prayer (e.g., *Didache* 8:2). The shorter text is well-attested (including p[72] B K L Ψ) and preferred.

3. P Ψ 𝔐 (and others) add "blasphemed according to them, but glorified according to you." The originality of the longer reading is defended by Rodgers ("Longer Ending"; cf. Michaels, pp. 265-66), but its absence in the earliest and best manuscripts (p[72] $\aleph$ A B etc.), together with the theological gravity it introduces, leads to its being categorized as a later gloss (also Achtemeier, p. 303).

4. The textual tradition is complex, reflecting the difficulty presented by the obscure, but for this reason likely original, term ἀλλοτριεπίσκοπος *(allotriepiskopos)* How best to translate this term remains disputed. In a lengthy excursus on the problem, Achtemeier prefers "one who defrauds others" (pp. 311-13; cf. Brox, p. 220: "embezzler"). Others prefer "busybody" (Michaels, p. 268) or the more generic "meddler" (Jobes, p. 289; similarly, Elliott, pp. 785-88). With the NRSV, I have opted for the catch-all "mischief-maker."

Suffering is paramount in this textual unit, with Peter drawing together and extending the relevant threads of this letter. The gravity of the subject is both recognized and somewhat mitigated by the kinship and affection Peter claims with his audience, referring to them as "beloved" (v. 12; cf. 2:11) and using the first person plural "us" to register a strong sense of solidarity between himself and these persons experiencing distress. The nature of Christian (i.e., "honorable" versus "shameful") suffering, the etiology of suffering, the presence of God in suffering, the meaning of suffering within the divine plan, and responses to suffering befitting the faithful — these are the angles from which Peter invites his audience to view their clear and present, noxious reality. Peter's message reaches its climax in v. 19, where he synthesizes the immediate consequence of the perspective he has developed in terms of Christian response: They must "entrust their lives to a faithful Creator by doing good." This is a fitting summary of much of the letter, with its stress on God's goodness, sovereignty, and purpose; on the imitation of Christ, who "when he was insulted, did not insult in return; while suffering did not threaten, but handed himself over to the one who judges justly" (2:23); and on well-doing. Consolation and encouragement are Peter's agenda here, and he presses his agenda by means of a theological hermeneutics of Christian experience in a hostile world.

If "hermeneutics" refers broadly to reflection on and the practice of human understanding, theological hermeneutics has to do with how the gospel impinges on and resources the enterprise of human understanding, and thus on the formation of persons and ecclesial communities. In primarily subtle ways, Peter locates the injurious day-to-day lives of his audience within the sphere of the scriptural tradition, read in ways that reflect apocalyptic streams of thought in the Second Temple period and in relation to the Jesus tradition. Overall, Peter's scriptural interpretation displays commitments to the authority, verity, and immediacy of the Scriptures and to their embodiment in the community of the faithful. Two uses of the Scriptures invite our consideration.

First, in v. 14, Peter borrows the language of Isa 11:2 (LXX) to insist that suffering for Christ is the occasion of the anointing of the Spirit. Isa 11:1-2 reads:

> And a staff will come out of the root of Jesse,
>   and a blossom will come up from his root.
> And the spirit of God will rest on him,
>   the spirit of wisdom and understanding,
>   the spirit of counsel and strength,
>   the spirit of knowledge and godliness.[5]

---

5. My translation from the LXX.

Having already claimed that the Spirit of Christ spoke through the prophets, revealing the Messiah's suffering and glory (1:10-12), Peter would not surprise us were he to interpret the "root of Jesse" on whom the "spirit of God" rests as the Messiah; in fact the first century already knew a tradition of a messianic interpretation of Isa 11:2. Peter, however, appropriates the Isaianic text more broadly with reference to the messianic community. Whereas Isaiah has it that the "spirit of God will rest on him," Peter writes that "the Spirit of God . . . rests on you (plural)." At one level, this too is unsurprising, given Peter's having already conjoined the messiahship of Jesus with the suffering Servant of Yahweh and patterned Christian discipleship in relation to Isaiah's Servant of Yahweh (2:21-25). Of greater consequence, however, is the interpretive move already within Isa 11 to broaden the sense of "root of Jesse" to include the holy remnant of Israel:

> And he will raise a sign to the Gentiles,
>> and gather those of Israel who have experienced loss,
> and he will gather the exiles of Judah
>> from the four corners of the earth. (Isa 11:12)[6]

In this way, Isaiah identifies a community that will participate in the messianic age of the Spirit.[7] Taking his cues from the prophet, Peter interprets present hostility and suffering through an exegesis that confirms the status of his audience as the messianic community within the grand purpose of God. Suffering for the sake of Christ finds its meaning in Isaiah's messianic ruler.

Peter further interprets the Isaianic pronouncement through an inelegant combination of words which we might render literally "for the [. . .] of glory and (καί, *kai*) the Spirit of God rests on you." I have taken καί as epexegetic, identifying the Spirit of glory as the Spirit of God. This certifies in the strongest possible terms that those who suffer because of Christ would be mistaken to read their suffering as symptomatic either of God's displeasure or of God's absence. To the contrary, those who suffer because of Christ bear the honorable recognition that comes from the God who sustains them for continued witness through the active presence of the Spirit. Rather than allowing the more conventional view that suffering and dishonor contravene the status of the elect before God, this exegesis appropriates the promise of the Spirit to rest on the believer precisely in the midst of distress.

Insofar as Isaiah both associates the work and power of the Spirit with a reconstituted people (e.g., Isa 32:1-17; 44:1) and links "glory" with return

---

6. My translation from the LXX.
7. See further, e.g., Isa 2:1-4; 4:2-6; 32:14-15; 44:2-3; 59:21.

from exile (e.g., Isa 4:2; 35:1-2; 40:5; 60:1-2), we are justified in seeing, further, that Peter paints the suffering of Christians onto the larger canvas of the restoration of God's people. This draws together the twin notions of exile and election found in the letter's opening verses, invests experiences of hostility with meaning within God's redemptive plan, and anticipates the dissolution of suffering in the coming eschaton.

Additionally, we may recall from 1:1-2 that the Spirit is the agent of God's power for the work of "making holy" — a motif of significance elsewhere in the letter (1:15, 16, 19, 22; 2:5, 9; 3:15). Evidently, the antidote to the threats of exilic life is the sanctifying work of the Spirit, who enables God's people not only to survive as a distinct people, but to embody the call to holiness as a sign to the Gentiles. This is true even when holiness so distinguishes God's people from their neighbors (see 4:3-4!) that it results in their becoming the objects of derision. Continued faithfulness is possible because "the Spirit of glory — indeed, the Spirit of God, rests on you."[8]

Other texts stand in the background of Peter's message in vv. 12-19. In v. 17, Peter may draw on Ezek 9:6 for his claim that God judges others only after he has judged his own people.[9] V. 18 cites Prov. 11:31, recontextualizing the eschatological judgment of God more specifically in reference to Peter's theology of messianic woes.[10] And in v. 19 we may have in Peter's reference to "doing good" a further development of his interest in Psalm 34 (see 3:10-12). Such citations and allusions add to the overall picture of Peter's dependence on the Scriptures of Israel by suggesting the importance of scriptural idiom as a means of inviting reflection on how these texts were selected and recontextualized, as well as how this interpretive work serves to invite Peter's audience further into Israel's story so as to make it their home. Of more immediate significance for our reflection on Peter's use of the Scriptures, though, is his dependence on the messianic woe tradition, traceable within Israel's sacred texts and extending beyond them into other literature, including works that would be included in the NT.

Second, then, Peter's greatest dependence on Scripture and its interpretation is realized in his interpretation of Christian suffering as a participation in the messianic woes of the end time. Although no biblical text is cited, Pe-

---

8. On the Spirit in 1 Peter, see J. B. Green, "Faithful Witness in the Diaspora."

9. See Schutter, *Hermeneutics and Composition,* pp. 37-38, 75. D. E. Johnson's argument that Mal 3:1-3 and Zech 13:9 stand in the background of v. 17 ("Fire in God's House") has been effectively countered by Jobes (pp. 291-92).

10. See Dubis, *Messianic Woes,* pp. 163-67; Dubis, however, leaves open the possibility that divine judgment expresses "God's punitive recompense" and "God's retribution" (p. 166), motifs that are lacking in 1 Peter.

ter's thesis nevertheless represents a rather developed exegesis along christological lines of the scriptural expectation of the calamities that would accompany the advent of the age of salvation. Indeed, vv. 12-19 represent a veritable echo chamber of voices from this tradition. Dubis has demonstrated that virtually every clause in vv. 12-19 is susceptible to a reading that locates it within the Jewish and early Christian traditions of the messianic woes[11] — those trials and tribulations that (among other things) (1) are temporally proximate to the advent of the Messiah, (2) are characterized in formulaic ways as famine, war, disease, apostasy, strife within kin groups, betrayal, and so on, (3) exhibit a crescendo in instances and expression of unrestrained immorality, (4) may find expression in persecution of the righteous, (5) may provide the basis for an eschatological sieving, distinguishing the righteous from the wicked, leading to the deliverance of the righteous and the punishment of the wicked, (6) constitute an arena for highlighting the sovereignty of God and his support for his people, and (7) urge continued trust in God, together with continued practices consistent with that faith.[12] Numerous texts in the OT and the literature of Second Temple Judaism not only consent to but expand, sometimes dramatically, on the perspective we read in Dan 12:1: "There shall be a time of anguish, such as has never occurred since nations first came into existence. But at that time your people shall be delivered. . . ." The tradition itself was pliable, so it was easy for early Christians to mold it in light of their claim, first, that the suffering and death of Christ are integral to the cosmic battle preceding the End, by which the age of salvation was given birth, and, second, that the suffering and martyrdom of Christ's followers participate in these "birth pangs." Clearly, this is a perspective that Peter shares.

This means, first, that suffering is not (or, at least, should not be) unexpected (v. 12). Peter's play on words is noteworthy. The Gentiles are surprised (ξενίζω, *xenizō*) that Christians no longer participate in a flood of immorality (4:4), but Christians should not be surprised (ξενίζω, *xenizō*) when (and not if)[13] they suffer, as if something strange (ξένος, *xenos*) were happening. The two are related, since it is because they no longer participate with the Gentiles in immorality that Christians now participate with Christ in suffering.

Second, however, to participate with Christ in suffering is to place one-

11. Dubis, *Messianic Woes*.

12. For this list, I am dependent on Dubis *(Messianic Woes)*, but also the older study by Russell, *Jewish Apocalyptic,* pp. 263-84; Pobee, *Persecution and Martyrdom;* and especially Allison, *End of the Ages.* Allison in particular points out the elasticity of the tradition.

13. In vv. 14 and 16, Peter's conditional clauses assume the reality (and not simply the possibility) of hostility.

self in the pattern of Christ's career as Peter portrays it. Drinking deeply from the scriptural wells of the Righteous Sufferer, Peter has plotted a path from suffering to glory for Jesus. He now does the same for Christ's followers, from suffering to glory. Indeed, he makes the capacity "to rejoice with great joy" when Christ's glory is finally revealed dependent on participation with Christ in his suffering.

Third, the present "fiery ordeal" (note the use of the present tense verb "take place," v. 12) may originate in diabolic chicanery (5:8), but it is not happening outside God's awareness or purpose; rather, this is a fire of refinement (1:6-7)[14] and present suffering is the means through which God inaugurates eschatological salvation. I do not intend thus to attribute to either God or Peter macabre interests, as though God requires that people suffer so that final deliverance might come or as if God were holding back final deliverance so that people might suffer. Rather, "new birth" repositions persons in the world in ways that may well invite hostility (see 4:3-4), and it is this faithfulness that brings near the salvific reign of God. Peter's use of the term "trial" (πειρασμός, *peirasmos*, v. 12; see 1:6) refers to diabolic temptation just as easily as divine test, and this introduces the paradox that the process of refinement can develop and deepen human life (testing) but also impede and corrupt human life (temptation).[15]

Fourth among the many ramifications of Peter's use of the messianic woes tradition is his presentation of the nature of judgment (vv. 17-18). The suffering of the faithful itself signals the onset of eschatological judgment, both in the sense of purgation for the faithful (v. 12) and in the sense that the sifting taking place in the present will carry forward into the eschaton. Judgment, then, is inescapably for all, though in saying this it is important also to remember that "to judge" means "to evaluate," "to discern," or "to distinguish," and not necessarily "to condemn." Judgment will result in salvation for the righteous, but only barely. This demonstrates the seriousness with which Peter (borrowing from Prov. 11:31) takes the situation of his audience. Their situation is dire, and apart from God's protection hopeless. Peter may seem less forthcoming with regard to the fate of the rest of humankind. However, by querying where they will "appear," he is again borrowing from the messianic woe tradition, which promises destruction. As 3:17 has already proclaimed, it is better to suffer in the present (for doing good) than to suffer in the eschaton (for doing evil). In the generic description in 4:17-18, those outside the Christian community are disbelievers, godless, and sinners. As we

---

14. Cf. Campbell, *Honor*, pp. 201-3.
15. So Moberly, *Bible, Theology, and Faith*, p. 240.

saw in 2:8, "to disbelieve" is not simply a matter of lacking faith; there, as here, it refers to the more active rejection of God's good news, the announcement of God's liberation and restoration in Christ (see on 1:12, 25). This is tantamount to rejecting God himself.

Thus far, I have noted something of the range of ways in which Peter has exercised his theological hermeneutic by way of grappling with Christian suffering — its etiology, its relation to God's presence and empowerment, and its significance within the divine plan. My focus thus far has been on the way Peter demonstrates the capacity of the Scriptures to speak of and into the lives of his contemporaries. More briefly, now, I will draw attention to how Peter draws on the Jesus tradition and its interpretation within early Christianity, for these also figure centrally in his theological approach to these difficult circumstances.

Although this text is dense with interpretive perspective on suffering, little of what Peter has to say is unique to this letter. Let me document some of the more noticeable parallels:

> suffering accrues to those who follow Christ (e.g., Matt 10:25; Mark 8:34; Acts 14:22; 1 Thess 3:3; 1 John 3:13)
>
> the presence of the Spirit is with those undergoing persecution (Luke 12:11-12; Acts 4:1-6; 7:51)
>
> the necessity and/or nobility of suffering because of the name of Christ (Mark 13:13; Acts 5:41; 9:16; 21:13)
>
> "blessed (μακάριος, *makarios*, also in 1 Pet 4:14) are those who are persecuted for righteousness' sake (δικαιοσύνη, *dikaiosynē*; δίκαιος, *dikaios*, "righteous one" in 4:18), for theirs is the kingdom of heaven. Blessed are you when people revile (ὀνειδίζω, *oneidizō*, also in 4:14) you and persecute you and utter all kinds of evil against you falsely on my account. Rejoice and be glad (χαίρω + ἀγαλλιάω, *chairō* + *agalliaō*, also in 4:13) for your reward is great in heaven . . ." (Matt 5:10-12; cf. Luke 6:22)
>
> the prohibition against shame in the context of suffering, with "shame" sometimes referring to the denial of one's faith or apostasy (Mark 8:34-38; 2 Tim 1:8, 12, 16)
>
> tying participation in Christ's glory into participation in the suffering of Christ (Rom 8:17; Phil 3:10-11; Heb 10:32-36)

This level of commonality may reflect the universality of the experience of suffering among followers of Christ, a reality that Peter will acknowledge in 5:9: "The same kind of sufferings are being accomplished in the case of your family of believers throughout the world." Undoubtedly, this is an important aspect of the word of consolation Peter here mounts.[16] Similarly, tying his discourse into widespread Christian tradition prompts a strong sense of identity, even unity (with respect to purpose and sympathies), with the wider Christian movement. More locally, as in the letter as a whole, Peter's lack of stark originality accords privilege to solidarity within the Christian community rather than to possible variations of belief among Christ's followers; in less hostile times, potential lines of fissure within the larger Christian community might be explored. This is not the case in the setting Peter envisions, which includes not only the church's minority and embattled presence in the larger world, but also a theology with close family ties to later formulations of orthodoxy within the Great Church (from the Rule of Faith/Truth in Irenaeus to the Nicene Creed) and a strong commitment to the embodiment of allegiances and beliefs in faithful, Christlike practices.

What happens to these snippets of oral and written "texts" from the Jesus tradition and early Christian theological formulation when they are woven into Peter's letter? They are "entextualized" — that is, they are set in a fresh context, a new discourse that provides for them a preferred reading.[17] Of course, on the one hand, Peter's discourse benefits from its association with the message of the one, Jesus Christ, whose righteous suffering comprises the charter for Christian faith and faithfulness. For Peter, Christ both authorizes and exemplifies this message. On the other, the apostle locates Jesus' teaching and early Christian reflection on Jesus' teaching within his own theological narrative.[18] This entails the claim that the time in which his audience lives is "the end of the ages," so as a matter of natural course is characterized by suffering in the name of Christ; additionally, this is a time that anticipates the End, with final judgment based on decisions made and behaviors practiced in the present.

Peter's theological engagement in this section serves the related purposes of consolation and encouragement. As Holloway has reminded us, consolation as a kind of moral instruction was widely practiced in the ancient world, though Greco-Roman philosophy handled it in different ways. Cicero summarizes:

> Some, like Cleanthes, believe that the consoler's only task is to convince the person afflicted with grief that the alleged "evil" is not an evil at all. Others, like the Peripatetics, argue that the evil in question is not great. Others, like the Epicureans, try to avert our attention away from evil

16. So Holloway, *"Nihil inopinati accidisse,"* p. 447.
17. See Blommaert, *Discourse,* pp. 47-48.
18. See J. B. Green, *"Narrating the Gospel."*

things to good things. Others, like the Cyrenaics, think that it is sufficient to show that nothing unexpected has happened. (*Tusculan Disputations* 3.31.76)

Comparison of such approaches as these with 1 Peter is helpful in part for setting in sharper relief what Peter is not saying. We find with Peter no denial or diminishing of evil, for example. Suffering is not idealized. He does not blame his audience for their suffering nor in any way suggest that their suffering is merely their just deserts. Moreover, his directive to rejoice (v. 13) reminds us that joy is not integral to suffering. Of the strategies Cicero reviews, Peter's is closest to that of the Cyrenaics, whose perspective is that grief results from unexpected misfortune, pain that catches us off-guard. The prophylactic to grief, then, is the contemplation of future evil in anticipation of its eventuality; its antidote is the reminder that "nothing unexpected has happened." This is similar to Peter's counsel, "Do not be surprised at the fiery ordeal . . . , as though something strange were happening to you" (v. 12). As warrants for this counsel, Peter reminds his audience of the suffering of Christ and the will of God regarding suffering (vv. 13-16; cf. 5:6, 10), as well as of the suffering attendant to the end of the ages (vv. 12-19) and the suffering of others (5:1, 3, 9).[19] It would be a mistake to emphasize overmuch the connection of Peter's message with the Cyrenaics, however. This school of philosophers was influential in the later fourth and early third centuries BC and took an approach to life decidedly different from that of this letter. Whereas the Cyrenaics counted as wisdom the orientation of one's life in and for the present, 1 Peter — both in the letter as a whole, but also in this present word of consolation — is manifestly future-oriented. The Cyrenaic emphasis on the pleasure of the moment stands in stark contrast with the eschatological edge of Peter's theology. Moreover, the theological endorsements for relating suffering and joy, both present and future, are simply lacking in the larger Greco-Roman world apart from the resources specific to the Jewish tradition.

Consequently, our focus should fall less on the potential influence of a Greco-Roman philosophical school and more on the script that comes to light in these verses. After all, it is precisely in times of crisis and conflict that hidden transcripts, dissident ways of construing the world, surface and, perhaps, begin, however hesitantly, to undermine conventional ways of thinking and judging. Peter recognizes the price to be paid for positioning oneself outside the mainstream of dominant Roman values and practices — historically,

19. So Holloway, *"Nihil inopinati accidisse"*; he finds parallels, e.g., in Philo *De specialibus legibus* 2.8.7; 1 Thess 3:1-10; Phil 1:28-30; and John 16:1-4a.

both then and now, a price related to any number of shunning responses: misunderstanding, loss of voice, loss of recognition, ostracism, exile, threats to life and family, incarceration, declarations of insanity, even loss of life.[20] But he interprets this price in ways not at all at home within Roman ideology, by setting it on the path of those who in their righteous suffering thus participate in the distress and vindication of the Christ, the Righteous Sufferer. Theirs are the tribulations by which the messianic age is given birth into the world and the beginning of eschatological judgment. Whatever consolation we find in Peter's message comes through a transformation of category, of life-world, by which to render present experience meaningful.

Given Peter's message, his audience, then and now, might find themselves inquiring, How should we then live? In vv. 12-19, he develops his answer along three lines. First, in a sentence that pivots on the conjunction ἀλλά (*alla,* "but," "rather"), "surprise" at suffering should give way to joy (vv. 12-13). Similarly, in v. 16, "shame" in suffering, which may have the extended sense of denying Christ in the midst of suffering (see above), is contrasted with "glorifying God." In the first instance, rejoicing finds its basis in the completion of the suffering/glory pattern: those who suffer with Christ now will share in his glory in the eschaton. In the second, the praise of God is motivated by impending judgment: those who suffer now will not suffer damnation in the eschaton. The warrant for these two words is different in each case, but the effect is the same.

Second, Peter takes pains to define the sort of suffering he invests with such heightened significance. It is "participating in the sufferings of Christ" (v. 13), "because of the name of Christ" (v. 14), "as a Christian" (v. 16), "because of this name" (v. 16), and "according to the will of God." As I noted with reference to 3:17, this suffering in the service of God's will ought not be read as a claim by the apostle that God wills suffering, but rather that serving the will of God in a disbelieving world has suffering as its potential (sometimes probable) outcome. This is one of three occasions in the NT where the term "Christian" is found (see also Acts 11:26; 26:28), and its sense can be determined from three observations. (1) It was common practice to extend a leader's name with the suffix -ιανός *(-ianos)* to denote a follower.[21] (2) In Acts, "Christian" is applied to Jesus' followers in contexts of hostility, a practice that continued into the second century. This, then, was no term of endearment but of slander — and why not, given the historical memory that the one whom his followers wor-

---

20. See Scott, *Hidden Transcripts;* Bourdieu, *Language and Symbolic Power.*

21. Greek thus follows the Latin practice of adding *-anus.* Cf., e.g., "Herodians" (Mark 3:6; 12:13), "followers of Herod." See MHT 2:359-60.

shiped experienced the ultimate humiliation of execution on a Roman cross? Speaking of the fire of Rome, Tacitus reports that

> Nero fastened the guilt and inflicted the most exquisite tortures on a class hated for their abominations, called Christians by the populace. Christus, from whom the name had its origin, suffered the extreme penalty during the reign of Tiberius at the hands of one of our procurators, Pontius Pilatus, and a most mischievous superstition, thus checked for the moment, again broke out not only in Judaea, the first source of the evil, but even in Rome, where all things hideous and shameful from every part of the world find their center and become popular. (*Annals* 15.44)

Although in 1 Peter the term comes from Peter's own pen, so to speak, it is nonetheless used in the context of hostility against Christ's followers.[22] (3) Finally, in the present context, the term "Christian" keeps company with the related phrases "because of the name of Christ" and "because of this name." "Christian" may be the language of outsiders and "because of the name of Christ" of insiders, but they both identify Christ's followers as those who so identify with Christ that they are marked out in the world as he was and so share in his suffering. It requires no analysis of potentially shared sources to recognize that Peter's words focus the terms of discipleship in ways similar to what we find in the Gospel of Mark: "If any want to become my followers, let them deny themselves and take up their cross and follow me. For those who want to save their life will lose it, and those who lose their life for my sake, and for the sake of the gospel, will save it" (8:34-35).

Peter also clarifies the nature of Christian suffering by stating the negative: not "as a murderer, thief, or evildoer, or as a mischief-maker" (v. 15). Whether addressing the realm of what is legal or what is moral, these terms represent long lists of possible behaviors that lie outside the circle of behavior consistent with identification with Christ. The suffering Peter honors is the consequence of holiness that finds expression in difference from one's former life, not in the ongoing expression of those futile ways (see 1:14-16, 18; 4:3).

Peter's third response to the imagined question, How shall we then live? encapsulates the rest: entrust yourselves to a faithful Creator by doing good (v. 19). The opening word of v. 19, ὥστε (*hōste*, "therefore," "accordingly") identifies this as the conclusion to which Peter's argument has been moving. The notion of "doing good" is prevalent in this letter (e.g., 2:15, 20; 3:6, 17), where it refers to putting into play, or performing, the good news (see above, pp. 84-85). It would include those practices of love, hospitality, and service

22. For an index of relevant texts, see BDAG, p. 1090.

Peter enumerates in vv. 7-11, as well as those behaviors he will develop in 5:1-5, but his attention in vv. 12-19 is especially on Christian behavior in the wider world. This would be a form of engagement expressed in courageous resistance that Peter has championed throughout the letter, as well as a way of life patterned after Christ, who, when suffering, did not threaten or insult (2:22-23). For Peter, "entrusting" oneself to God ought not be relegated to the status of an "inner commitment"; rather it is an embodiment of one's faith enacted precisely "by doing good." Given Peter's viewpoint on the integrity of human life, "inner" and "outer" are aligned with one another this completely. Analogous (though not strictly parallel) references are found with reference to Jesus, who "handed himself over to the one who judges justly" (2:23), and with reference to holy women "who placed their hope in God" (3:5).

In the context of marginality and distress Peter envisions, the "correct" response would be to reclaim the old ways of life, unrestrained immorality springing up from human lusts (1:14-16, 18; 4:3). Who would not judge as too demanding the cost of deviance from imperial conventions? In such a setting, a response of surrender to what must have seemed herculean pressures in favor of conformity to societal expectations would have strong support. Rejoicing, glorifying, entrusting, and continuing in well-doing, all in the midst of suffering — these are behaviors of courageous resistance.

In v. 19, we find the only reference to God as "Creator" in 1 Peter (and the only use of κτίστης, *ktistēs,* "Creator" in the NT). Whatever else it is, this is an affirmation of the unmatchable power and gracious initiative of God, expressed in his creative work. Pressing further, though, Peter may be engaging in a soft polemic against Roman hegemony, embodied in Rome's rulers, who were acclaimed with the title of "founder" or "creator."[23] Imperial accomplishments measured in the founding of a city or extension of an empire are puny in comparison with the awesome work of God. Faced with this comparison, who could kowtow before Roman ideology and social sanctions, imagining that these might possibly be of ultimate consequence? In this case, Peter would be calling on Christians to entrust themselves to the initiative, protection, and judgment of the God of the universe rather than the initiative, protection, and judgment of Rome. In addition, the eschatological setting of vv. 12-19 may also support a reading that acknowledges the capacity of God to create anew; in this case, the apostle's encouragement has its basis in the expectation of God's new creation.[24]

---

23. Foerster, "κτίζω κτλ.," pp. 1025-26.

24. So Dubis, *Messianic Woes,* pp. 174-75. See, too, Peter's reference to "the end of all things" in v. 7.

5:1-5

5:1 Therefore, I, a fellow elder and witness of the sufferings of Christ as well as one who shares in the glory about to be revealed, exhort the elders[25] among you: 2 Like shepherds, tend the flock of God among you, exercising oversight not under coercion but voluntarily, in a godly way, not greedily but freely, 3 not as those who lord it over those assigned to you but as examples for the flock, 4 and at the revelation of the Chief Shepherd you will receive an unfading crown of glory. 5 In the same way, younger people, subordinate yourselves to the elders. And all of you, clothe yourselves in humility toward one another, for God opposes the arrogant but gives grace to the humble.

The shift from 4:19 is marked, first, by the presence of οὖν (*oun,* "therefore"), in 5:1, but also by Peter's unprecedented shift to first person address ("I, a fellow elder . . .") and the unmistakably in-house character of his instruction in 5:1-5. Given Peter's reference to "the household of God" (4:17), we might think of this short textual unit as patterned after the household duty code prevalent in Peter's world (see above on 2:11–4:11). Although it is possible to connect vv. 6-7 to vv. 1-5 on thematic grounds, with admonitions regarding humility ranging from v. 5b through v. 7, the repetition of οὖν (*oun,* "therefore") in v. 6 suggests, instead, that v. 5b completes the "household code" material of vv. 1-5 and serves as a bridge into the final unit of the letter body, vv. 6-11.

One of the puzzles of this textual unit is the inferential conjunctive with which it begins. What is the relation of 5:1-5 to 4:12-19?[26] From what in 4:12-19 are we to infer 5:1-5? Some interpreters have assumed that the movement is from eschatological joy and glory (4:13) to the notion of partners in glory (5:1, 4).[27] Although helpful, this would not account for the whole of vv. 1-5, and particularly not for the added instruction to elders (vv. 2-3) and Peter's address to the younger people and to all in v. 5. We might also imagine that 5:1-5 draws out the implications of "doing good" in 4:19. Two observations push us

---

25. Some witnesses add τούς (*tous,* "the," e.g., ℵ Ψ), suggesting the possibility of a defined set of "elders." My translation uses the definite article, but not because I regard τούς (*tous*) as original. Rather, given the role assumed of these persons in vv. 2-3, I am assuming that "elders" refers not simply to "the older people among you" but to leaders who are likely to be drawn from among those who are older. τούς (*tous*) is missing in p[72] A B etc.

26. Brox refers to οὖν (*oun*) in v. 1 as "an extremely loose connection" ("ein höchst lockerer Anschluß," p. 225).

27. E.g., T. W. Martin, *Metaphor and Composition,* p. 257; cf. Bechtler, *Following in His Steps,* p. 201.

in the direction of a more integrated solution. First, and most obvious, Peter addresses himself to three groups with a verb cast in the imperative appropriate to each:

vv. 1-2   elders   like shepherds, tend the flock of God
v. 5a   younger people   subordinate yourselves to the elders
v. 5b   everyone   clothe yourselves in humility

Second, much of the terminology Peter employs in these verses divides itself into two (spacious) semantic domains — words associated with honor/glory and terms that mitigate an inflated view of one's importance.

Honor/Glory	Mutuality/Humility
elder	fellow elder
partner in the glory to be revealed	suffering of Christ
exercising oversight	shepherd/tend the Flock
coercion	voluntary, like God
greedily	freely
lording it over	serve as an example
crown of glory	Christ is the Chief Shepherd (cf. 2:21-25!)
arrogance	subordinate yourselves
	clothe yourselves in humility

It is as if one set of terms, by underscoring the privileged position of those composing the household of faith, surfaces the question, How should our privileged position express itself? The second set of terms provides an answer to this question. Honor before God is not an excuse for the exercise of privileged status over others. We who buy into the system of valuation exemplified by Christ and advocated by Peter, with its emphasis on the path from suffering to glory (4:12-19), must see that this has direct bearing not only on how we comport ourselves in a hostile world but also in our common life as believers. We do not embody one set of standards outside the community (so that we can make sense of our marginal status in a world set against us) only to adopt a different set of standards inside the community (so that we can marginalize other believers). Yet again we have evidence that Peter is calling for a transformation of heart and life, a conversion of the imagination, that reforms biases and disposition at such a basic level that it cannot but reform ways of relating to others — all others, unbelievers and believers alike. In short, 5:1-5 particularizes 4:12-19 for relationships within the community of believers, drawing out inferences (οὖν, *oun*, "therefore") from the change of life-world *(Lebenswelt)* documented in 4:12-19 for the particular sets of persons named in 5:1-5: elders, younger persons, and everyone.

Even the order of the "household code" in vv. 1-5 supports this interpretation of things. Typically, the household code begins with those who are to occupy a subservient role, first putting them in their place. Peter, however, begins with those in positions of leadership, and spends the majority of the words he has allotted to his household instruction to guiding their behavior.[28] What is more, his instruction reaches its pinnacle in his address to "all" in v. 5b — an "all" that would manifestly include the leadership. "Humility" is to characterize everyone, including leaders. Whatever hierarchical mode of thinking might be discernible in Peter's self-representation or in his talk of "elders" is vacated by (1) Peter's refusal of special privilege by locating himself as an elder alongside other elders (συν-, *syn-*, "with" or "co-"), (2) Peter's recognition that the glory in which he will participate is nothing more or less than others will enjoy at the Last Day (v. 1b: "who shares in the glory about to be revealed"; v. 4b: "you will receive an unfading crown of glory"), (3) Peter's recognition that elders function as shepherds under the umbrella of the Chief Shepherd, whose suffering and humility he has already identified as paradigmatic (2:21-25), and, then, (4) the adjectives and verbs Peter uses to constrain (e.g., "not lording it over") or to arouse (e.g., "clothe yourselves in humility") behavior within the community of believers.

Additional evidence that, in instructing his audience, Peter is not exercising conventional authority is his apparent refusal to distribute directives simply on the basis of his apostolic office. He provides warrants for his exhortation. (1) He is a "fellow elder." This could be nothing more than a statement about Peter's advanced age, but the role and attitudes outlined in vv. 2-3 lead us to conclude that he is describing himself, together with the elders among his audience, as persons involved in leadership within Christian communities.[29] Because it is set in close proximity to Peter's instruction regarding gifted service in 4:7-11, talk of "elders" in this context should not lead us immediately to thoughts of institutionalized leadership and offices. The text presents less formalized roles and practices of leadership. (2) Peter is a "witness of the sufferings of Christ and partner in the glory about to be revealed." According to the passion accounts of the NT Gospels, the twelve apostles were nowhere to be found at the scene of the crucifixion, but this does not

---

28. Cf. Michaels, "Going to Heaven," p. 266.

29. The model for leadership by elders probably derives from synagogal practices; see, e.g., Patzia, *Emergence of the Church*, pp. 171-74.

disqualify Peter's self-description. In Luke 22:28, for example, Jesus addresses his companions as those who have stood by him in his "trials" (using the term πειρασμός, *peirasmos,* used of the suffering of Christians in 1 Pet 4:12). So Peter could be representing himself simply as one who witnessed the suffering characteristic of the whole of Jesus' ministry, culminating in his execution. Other referents are possible, however. A "witness" (μάρτυς, *martys*) is not only one who "observes" but also one who "advocates" — not, then, a dispassionate commentator but a biased participant in the role of providing testimony.[30] Peter speaks as one who commends the suffering of Christ, most probably as one whose life displays that suffering. How else could Peter — who has just written that suffering is only to be expected, and that only those who find joy in participation in the sufferings of Christ now will rejoice at the revelation of his glory (4:12-13) — claim to be one who shares in the glory about to be revealed? In other words, Peter not only talks about the way of suffering–glory exemplified by Jesus, but also walks that path. And this assures the reliability of his counsel at the same time that it qualifies him for the pulpit from which to declare it.

It is easy enough to imagine that "leadership" is first and foremost a question of office or station, and that we might sift the data in 1 Peter and elsewhere in the NT for a technology of leadership, as though these texts were concerned with leadership structures and styles.[31] Peter's perspective is quite different. For him, the character of the leader is paramount. Using language reminiscent of Luke's portrayal of Paul's final address to the Ephesian elders (Acts 20:17-36), he identifies elders as shepherds, then qualifies the exercise of oversight through three antitheses (vv. 2-3):

> not under coercion but voluntarily, in a godly way,
> not greedily but freely,
> not as those who lord it over those assigned to you but as examples
>   for the flock

The imagery of shepherding and sheep (literally, "shepherd the sheep," v. 2) runs deeply into Israel's Scriptures and is significant for at least three reasons. First, Israel is God's flock and he is their shepherd (e.g., Pss 23:1-4; 28:9). Peter's reference to the Chief Shepherd in v. 4 identifies Jesus as the true shepherd by whom God's scattered people have been regathered and restored. It also relativizes the role of elders. Their "authorization" as shepherds may call

---

30. See Marincola, *Authority and Tradition,* p. 104.

31. See the much-needed corrective in the work of Clarke — e.g., *Serve the Community;* idem, "Embodying Leadership."

for them to exercise authority, but it is an authority with defined limits, circumscribed by God's purpose exemplified in Christ.[32] Second, Israel's leaders, identified as shepherds, have been unfaithful, resulting in the need for faithful leadership (e.g., Jer 23:1-4; Ezekiel 34), a role now taken up by these elders. Third, the Fourth Gospel witnesses to a tradition whereby Jesus calls upon Peter to "tend my sheep" (John 21:13-17), a vocation now mediated through Peter to these elders.[33] "Peter," says Hilary of Arles, "is telling the leaders of the church exactly what the Lord told him: 'Feed my sheep.'"[34] All of this is to say that the role of elder is deeply rooted in Israel's Scriptures and takes its essential character from the nature of God, known in relation to believers in 1 Peter for his gracious beneficence.

Indeed, the first antithesis directs elders to act in conformity with God's own exercise of leadership: not as one who is obligated to act but as one within whom the exercise of beneficent care is natural. This is the essence of divine grace.[35]

The second antithesis turns on a traditional critique of avarice. The term Peter uses is rare, a compound of αἰσχρός (*aischros*, "morally unacceptable, shamefully immoral") and κέρδος (*kerdos*, "that which is gained, a profit"), but a close semantic kin of other words denoting "love of money." The opposite is πρόθυμος (*prothymos*), an eagerness to contribute to the needs of others without calculation.[36] The significance of money in this context becomes more clear when we recall that the exchange of money (or other form of material exchange) is a profoundly relational practice, assuming and propagating well-established social scripts. Ordinarily, to give was to initiate a relationship of indebtedness so that who gives to whom serves as an index for the power of one person over another. Ordinarily, to give "freely" in such a context would be an oxymoron, since any gift bears within itself the cycle and obligation of repayment.[37] Like the term "hospitality" in 4:9, then, this seem-

---

32. In other words, the issue of legitimacy of leadership is tied not only to the identification of a particular person or persons to wield authority but also to the limits within which that authority can appropriately be exercised (see Seymour-Smith, *Anthropology*, p. 166).

33. Cf. Michaels, pp. 282-83; Achtemeier, p. 325.

34. Hilary of Arles, *Introductory Commentary on 1 Peter;* cited in Bray, p. 122.

35. See J. B. Green, "Grace," following, especially, Andersen, "Yahweh, the Kind and Sensitive God." I have translated κατὰ θεόν *(kata theon)* as "in a godly way" in an attempt to suggest the idea of "as God would do it" and not simply "as God would will it." See Jobes, pp. 304-5.

36. See *TLNT,* 3:180-84; the term can be used of benefactors who give willingly, freely, without expectation of return.

37. For my understanding of the relationship between economic exchange and social relations, I am dependent on Sahlins, *Stone Age Economics*. For the problem of "gift," see Derrida, *Counterfeit Money.*

ingly innocuous reference to financial gain is shorthand for deeply embedded, formalized social systems, whose significance is out of proportion to what the use of a word or two might suggest.

Jesus warned that service of God was incompatible with service of Mammon (Matt 6:24; Luke 16:13), and the need to be free of the love of money is a requisite of both leaders (e.g., Acts 20:33; 1 Tim 3:3, 8) and others of the Christian community (e.g., 1 Tim 6:10; Heb 13:5). The absence of avarice was also a prized virtue within the larger Roman world.[38] Leaders in particular are warned about attachment to money for a number of reasons. To receive money would be to place oneself in obligation to those who provided it, placing a leader in a position of potential compromise in the service of one's patrons. To receive money for providing leadership might communicate erroneously that the gospel was something other than God's gracious gift.[39] In Luke's recounting of Paul's farewell address to the Ephesian elders, then, we should not be surprised to find Paul's declaration "of the whole counsel of God" correlated with his claim, "I coveted no one's silver or gold or clothing" (Acts 20:27-33). The *Didache* puts it most succinctly, calling the Christian leader who lives off of the work of others a "Christ-merchandiser" (12:5).[40]

The *Didache* is here concerned with itinerants who remain with a Christian community for a lengthy time. "If he wants to remain with you, and is a tradesman, let him work and eat. If he does not have a trade, use your foresight to determine how he as a Christian may live among you without being idle" (12:3-4, LCL). In other places, however, we find that material support, whether in the form of hospitality or some other sort of payment, is not out of the question (e.g., Luke 10:7; 1 Corinthians 9). Rather than offering a blanket rejection of the notion that Christian leaders might somehow be compensated, then, Paul's own typical practice of self-support and the directives we read in the *Didache* are attempts to undercut the allure of compensation, the abuse of the hospitality (and other forms of material support) of others, and the possibility of endangering the spread of the gospel through relationships of obligation to wealthy patrons.[41] Evidently it is virtually impossible to overstate the attraction of money (hence, its characterization by Jesus as Mammon — that is, as a kind of "divinity" or "power"), a reality that opens the way to sharp, seemingly absolutist directives.

---

38. See *TLNT*, 1:245-46.
39. Cf. 1 Corinthians 9; 2 Cor 2:17; 6:10.
40. χριστέμπορος *(christemporos)*; my translation.
41. See, e.g., Bassler, *God and Mammon*.

More than perhaps anything else, practices with respect to money index relationships and register allegiances.[42] More than perhaps anything else, money serves as a barometer of one's deepest motivations and predispositions. For Peter, there is no middle way and the choice is clear: greed or beneficence.

The final antithesis contrasts "high-handed authoritarianism"[43] with "leading by example." This is a colorful conjunction of terms, since for Peter Jesus is "Lord" (κυριος, *kyrios;* 1:3; 3:15), but the exercise of his lordship is realized in his serving as the "pattern" for Christian behavior, a pattern realized in his suffering (2:21-25). Elders exercise oversight not by "lording it over" (κατακυριεύω, *katakyrieuō*), but by serving as "examples." As Jesus is the Chief Shepherd and elders are shepherds, so Jesus provides the "pattern" and elders a "model." Their leadership is realized in their embodiment of the character of Christ, which Peter describes in these terms:

> who committed no sin, nor was deceit found in his mouth;
> who, when he was insulted, did not insult in return; while suffering did not threaten, but handed himself over to the one who judges justly;
> who, himself, bore our sins in his body on the tree, in order that, once we have died to sins, we might live to righteousness;
> by whose wounds you were healed. . . . (2:22-24)

Their practices of leadership are thus measured by their conformity to the courageous endurance of Christ, his humility and selflessness, and are accountable to him as the Chief Shepherd.[44]

One of the uncertainties of v. 3 is the question, For whom are elders to serve as examples? Peter uses a term, "allotment" or "portion" (κλῆρος, *klēros*), that would later be used of "clerics" or clergy. The Venerable Bede, for example, writes, "Not as lording it over the [lesser] clerics," apparently taking "elder" as a "[superior] cleric."[45] Peter opens no room for a clergy-lay distinction, however, and his use of "allotment" likely refers to the grouping of Christian communities into small units for purposes of oversight.[46]

"Doing good" (4:19) in the case of elders takes the form of exercising the

---

42. In spite of the more recent publication of a number of significant studies related to possessions and wealth in Scripture, for theological engagement L. T. Johnson's study of *Sharing Possessions* remains the place to start.

43. Achtemeier, p. 328.

44. That Christ (and not God) is the Chief Shepherd is suggested by 2:25; and by references to the impending revelation of Christ's glory in 1:7, 13; 4:13.

45. Bede, p. 115.

46. Cf. Schweizer, *Church Order*, pp. 111-12.

sort of shepherd-care and oversight summarized in vv. 2-3 and has as its consequence both the patterning of one's life and leadership after Christ in the present and participation in Christ's glory at the End. Having set out on the way of Christ from suffering to glory, elders will indeed find at the end of that path "an unfading crown of glory." "To receive" (κομίζω, *komizō*) connotes eschatological compensation elsewhere in the NT, whether negative (Col 3:25) or, as here and in 1 Pet 1:9, positive (e.g., Eph 6:8; Heb 10:36). Similarly, "revelation," though referring to the advent of Christ in 1:20, is used eschatologically here (and, e.g., in 1 John 2:28). The "crown" was a widely used symbol of honor in the Greco-Roman world, awarded in such spheres of life as in sports, the military, and political life, but is used in the NT also of eschatological accolades (e.g., 1 Cor 9:25; 2 Tim 4:8).[47] With a figure the meaning of which would have been unmistakable, then, Peter underscores his claim that rejection and vilification among humans (2:4-8; 4:12-19) is rendered inconsequential by God's recognition of and reward for faithful service.[48]

In v. 5 Peter presses his household instructions further — first, to another subgroup, "younger people"; second, to the community as a whole, "all of you." Although capable of a range of interpretations, "younger" probably means nothing more than those members of the Christian communities who were not elders.[49] If the responsibilities of the elders are summed up in "Shepherd the sheep," those of the "younger people" are summed up in Peter's imperative, "Subordinate yourselves to the elders." As before, "to subordinate" does not entail a repudiation of the exercise of power or rebelliousness, but rather finding and occupying responsibly one's place (see above on 2:13). Subordination in this context would require that the "younger" recognize the role to which the elders are called: oversight as examples for the flock. But even this is not blind submission, since the "younger" are privy to the instruction received by the elders and know that their oversight is to be a reflection of the care of Christ on their behalf.

---

47. See Grundmann, "στέφανος, στεφανόω."

48. Given the topsy-turvy system of valuation at work here, together with Peter's hyperinterest in Jesus' suffering, it is difficult not to see in the background the portrait of Jesus who, in his passion, received a crown of thorns (Matt 27:29; Mark 15:17; John 19:2, 5). For the characters within the passion accounts, this was a form of mockery and humiliation, but for the Christian audiences of the Gospels it was an ironic acclamation of Jesus' true status.

49. This reading makes sense of the division of "all of you" (v. 5b) into two subgroups: "elders" (vv. 1-4) and younger ones (v. 5a). See Goppelt, pp. 350-51; Feldmeier, pp. 158-59. The best case for a more limited group has been made by Elliott, who argues that "younger" refers to "younger in the faith" — i.e., neophytes (cf. 1 Tim 3:6: not a "recent convert") ("Ministry and Church Order").

Peter's directive to everyone counters the possibility of blind submission to authority just as it sabotages all attempts to exercise authority on the basis of status: "Clothe yourselves with humility." In antiquity, what one wore was an index of one's social position. "One's garment announces what one is for another, not what one is in and for oneself."[50] That Peter would instruct *everyone* to wear the *same garment*, irrespective of its color or quality or texture, is itself already a startling negation of the social distinctions that among people in Roman antiquity would have been worn like uniforms in a parade.

But Peter goes much further, identifying the one garment to be worn by all as "humility" — or, better, given the relative rarity of the term he uses, as "that way of thinking, feeling, and acting associated with the lowly." In his citation of Prov. 3:34 ("God opposes the arrogant but gives grace to the humble"), Peter will use a term more at home in the Greek Bible: ταπεινός (*tapeinos*, "humble, lowly," used 77 times in the Greek Bible), but here he uses ταπεινοφροσύνη (*tapeinophrosynē*, used 7 times in the Greek Bible). Conscripting a word built on the root of one of his favored terms (φρονέω, *phroneō*, "think"), Peter thus concerns himself, and his audience, with a frame of mind or pattern of thinking that belongs to persons who have done with positioning themselves in the world's social hierarchy in order to ensure that they are treated with appropriate esteem by their social underlings. When so much of life is directed by the compass of social stratification, with honor and shame the north and south poles, the consequences of this metamorphosis are practically infinite. The form of one's greeting, such gestures as the averting of the eyes and the raising of the chin, the range of one's information-sharing, the material and color of one's clothing, the nature of economic exchange with others, one's treatment before the courts, possibilities for friendship and matchmaking, invitations to share a meal and the quality of food to place before others, the obligation to truth-telling, assumptions about seating arrangements, who can speak to whom and under what conditions — the list of affected expectations and interactions is practically endless. All these forms of behavior are set aside in favor of a single disposition within the family of believers: to comport oneself in ways that esteem others.

In today's world, care must be taken lest we assume that the opposite of humility is or can only be self-promotion or self-assertion. In the world of Peter, believers may have chafed at their marginal status out of a concern to claim the status that would have been theirs by heredity, and in the Christian communities to which Peter addresses himself some may well have (erroneously) positioned themselves above the rest. In

50. K. Berger, *Identity*, p. 41.

such contexts, pride or arrogance is indeed sinful. Not least on account of Peter's assumptions regarding the marginal status of most if not all of his audience, however, it is worth inquiring into how sin of this nature might manifest itself in marginalized persons and communities. In fact, among some, sin can take the form of a numbing of the self just as easily as, among others, it is displayed as self-assertion — as a failure to embrace one's personhood rather than as a predisposition toward extending it at the expense of others. "To subordinate oneself," we cannot forget, is the opposite of "withdrawal," and is not a form of resignation. It is active engagement. A world build around social stratification works only if those who are of high status exhibit disrespect toward those of lower status *and* if those of low status esteem those of higher status. Manipulation of others and other forms of coercive behavior, moreover, can be performed by those who seem to be powerless as well as by those whose power is more visible and muscular. Seen in this way, "pride" is more pervasive than its popular identification with *machismo* or conceit might suggest. Although sin related to the honor-shame continuum might be expressed as *machismo*, it also has its shadowy sides, as persons at all points of the continuum of power and privilege refuse to embrace either *only* or *fully* their places as equals within the household of God.

Peter's citation of Prov 3:34 provides further warrant ("for" or "because") for his admonition to humility of thought and life. It does so by allowing the antithesis of God's behavior toward the arrogant and the humble to demonstrate Peter's desired outcome. "Arrogance" is a widely denounced vice — e.g., Sir 10:7: "Arrogance is hateful to the Lord and to humans."[51] In a Greco-Roman setting, at least, not the denouncing of "arrogance" but the opposition of "arrogance" to "humility," as if these were the only available options, would have been troubling. It is one thing to urge against arrogance and ludicrous presumption but quite another to encourage among all persons slavish ways of thinking and acting in the world; "humble" describes the enslaved, after all, not the free.[52] Favor (or "grace") is due the esteemed, not the lowly. The lowly are the objects of antagonism, not the esteemed. But Christians are slaves, "slaves of God" (2:16), so "lowly" is an appropriate descriptor. What is more, if the apportioning of honor is God's prerogative, then worldly conventions are neutralized; new canons are in place; the social order has been rewritten.

---

51. My translation. In the Greco-Roman world, the arrogant is "the one who with pride, arrogance and foolish presumption brags of his [*sic*] position, power and wealth and despises others" (Bertram, "ὑπερήφανος, ὑπερηφανία," p. 525).

52. See Grundmann, "ταπεινός κτλ," pp. 1-3, 11-12.

5:6-11

6 Accept your humble status, therefore, under the mighty hand of God, so that he may exalt you at the proper time, 7 casting on him your every distress, for he cares for you. 8 Remain vigilant! Stay alert! Your adversary, the devil, like a roaring lion is on the prowl, seeking someone to devour. 9 Resist him, standing firm in the faith, recognizing that the same kind of sufferings are being accomplished in the case of your family of believers throughout the world. 10 But the God of all grace, who called you into his eternal glory in Christ, after you have suffered a short while, will himself restore, strengthen, empower, and secure. 11 To him be the power forever. Amen.

At the close of v. 5, Peter prepares for the opening emphasis of this textual unit on humility, and we might be tempted to outline the structure of ch. 5 so as to draw these two verses together. Three observations favor the outline as I have presented it. First, as in v. 1, the shift from the preceding material is marked by the presence of οὖν (*oun*, "therefore"). As will become clear, vv. 6-11 function in much the same way as vv. 1-5, drawing out the implications of 4:12-19; whereas vv. 1-5 center on life within the household of faith, however, vv. 6-11 concern the place of the Christian family in the wider world. Second, "humility" is understood in two different ways in vv. 5 and 6. In v. 5, "clothe yourselves in humility" is an active decision on the part of Christians, who thus locate and conduct themselves in ways that extend honor to others of the household of faith. In v. 6, however, the verb "to humble" is cast in the passive voice; humility in this case is not a quality of character one embraces, then, but a position in the world assigned by others. As Peter begins this textual unit, then, the issue is not whether Christians will humble themselves since, in the world at large, they are already suffering dishonor. The question, rather, is how they will respond to, or interpret, their abasement. Peter urges them to accept their humble status,[53] not simply as a consequence of human rejection but as the outcome of their tracing through their lives the pattern of Jesus Christ (2:21-25) and thus performing the will of God. Third, with their shared eschatological horizons and their mutual emphases on the great power of God and the exaltation of the faithful, vv. 6 and 10-11 form an inclusio around this textual unit.

---

53. See Achtemeier, p. 338 (with reference to Gen 16:9; Jer 13:18). Achtemeier, however, thinks that v. 6 draws an inference from v. 5, rather than seeing vv. 1-5 and vv. 6-11 as drawing out in tandem the ramifications of 4:12-19.

Peter interweaves three primary motifs: the situation of his audience, the character of God, and the nature of expected, Christian response.

(1) The Situation of Peter's Audience: The apostle rehearses the situation of Christians in ways now familiar to us, while also extending his description in unexpected ways. Unexpected, first, is the way he traces the origin of Christian suffering beyond the usual suspects, those worldly blasphemers who cast aspersions on Christ's followers because they conform their lives to the will of God rather than to human desires. Behind them, Peter now makes abundantly clear, stands the devil. We found hints of this deeper reality in 4:12, with its reference to their "fiery ordeal" and "testing," but the identification of suffering with the devil in 4:12 is made sure in 1 Peter only by the explicit naming of the devil as their adversary in 5:8. The basic sense of διάβολος *(diabolos)* is "slanderer,"[54] a term particularly apt in a letter where the primary attack on Christians has been the slow-working malignancy of verbal abuse. Here, as elsewhere in the NT (e.g., Acts 10:38; Eph 6:11; 1 Tim 3:6-7; 2 Tim 2:26), διάβολος *(diabolos)* refers to the embodiment of evil, a transcendent figure set in opposition to God, God's purposes, and God's people. The effect is that those who oppose God are cast as agents of the devil, and, for 1 Peter, the work of the devil is not enacted by the devil personally but through those institutions (that is, as in 4:7-11, both those patterns of expected behavior reinforced by social sanctions and those organizational structures that legitimate and propagate such behavior) that are set against God and God's people. How does the devil accomplish this? The Venerable Bede, whose commentaries often serve as compendia for the interpretive work of his forbears, quotes in length "the words of the blessed Cyprian":

> He goes around us individually, and like an enemy besieging those shut up, he examines the walls and explores whether there might be some part of our members less firm and less trustworthy, by entrance through which a way inside may be effected. He offers to the eyes unlawful appearances and seductive pleasures, that he may destroy purity through sight; he tempts the ears by harmonious music, that he may get rid of and weaken christian [*sic*] strength by the hearing of a pleasant sound; he arouses the tongue to reviling, he urges the hand to capricious murder when it is excited by injuries; he provides unjust gains, that he may make a cheat; he piles up dangerous profits, that he may ensnare the soul by money; he promises earthly honors, that he may take away heavenly ones;

54. BDAG, p. 226.

he manifests false values, that he may steal away the true. And when he is not able to deceive secretly, he threatens clearly and openly, bringing forward the fear of violent persecution in order to overcome the servants of God; always restless and always hostile; [he is] cunning in peace, violent in persecution.[55]

Though originally penned in the third century and recited in the eighth, Cyprian's exegesis is a case study in the simultaneity of Scripture — that is, its capacity to speak pointedly into multiple contexts. Cyprian's reading is helpful for its reminder that the purposes of the transcendent enemy are put into effect through mundane social relations, the use of the five senses, and the affairs of daily business; for his awareness of the struggle in 1 Peter over one's "manner of life" — whether it will incarnate the holiness of God and follow the pattern of Christ's example or revert to the ways of former futility (1:18); and for his recognition that the diabolic agenda is not the destruction of Christian persons but their apostasy. This is the significance of the devil's seeking someone "to devour."[56]

In the Scriptures of Israel, the roar of the lion (that aspect of leonine behavior to which Peter draws particular attention) is associated with two primary features — both of which are actualized in this word of warning. The lion roars in search of prey (e.g., Ps 104:21; Amos 3:4) and to evoke fear (e.g., Amos 3:8; Isa 30:6).[57] Having just observed the significance of the lion's predation, we should also recall that "fear" is, for Peter, to be directed toward God alone, as reverent allegiance. Intimidation, whether from the lion/devil or from those persons or institutions that, however unwittingly, serve his agenda, is ruled out (see 1:17; 2:17; 3:14-15).

Peter also departs from previous descriptions of the experience of distress among Christians by extending his précis beyond that subset of the faithful community to whom he addresses this letter to include also Christians throughout the world. On one level, Peter uses different language to communicate his earlier claim that suffering is hardly unanticipated but is rather inevitable for those who live in accordance with the will of God and thus against the grain of society at large (4:12). Additionally, he articulates a theology of suffering that denies the popular notion that distress can be explained autobiographically. According to this misguided view, my lot in life is the product of my decisions; my experiences are nothing more than what I deserve, my reward or punishment as appropriate. If the whole family of be-

---

55. Bede, pp. 117-18; citing Cyprian *De Zelo et Livore* 10.2-3.
56. Cf. Michaels, "Going to Heaven," p. 263.
57. Strawn, *What Is Stronger Than a Lion?* p. 35.

lievers throughout the world is undergoing suffering, however, a less individualistic and more systemic, cosmological explanation is required. This, of course, is what Peter has given in v. 8. The apostle fills out his view of suffering further with his use of the verb ἐπιτελέω (*epiteleō*, "complete") to describe the suffering of the Christian family. Here the verb seems to connote "cause something to happen as fulfillment of an objective or purpose."[58] In other words, while rejecting any possible interpretation of suffering as capricious or meaningless, Peter also rejects the idea that the devil can create havoc in a way that would threaten God's sovereignty. Even the execution of the devil's plans takes place within the orbit of God's care. As in Job 1–2 (where Satan, like the lion in 1 Pet 5:8, is "on the prowl"),[59] trials come from the devil as temptation but serve God's purpose of testing.[60]

It should not escape us that v. 9, which attributes the situation faced by Peter's audience to Christians universally, has the effect of broadening the application and appeal of Peter's letter to the whole of the Christian family. In an important sense, even from this more narrowly historical perspective, if Christians outside of the Anatolian peninsula (1:1) were to read Peter's letter, they would not be reading someone else's mail but would find what for them too would be a word on target. Locating 1 Peter within the Christian canon thus preserves and promulgates impulses toward a more catholic audience already resident in the letter itself.

Summarizing, the apostle envisions indignity in the social sphere (v. 6), affective responses of anxiety or worry (v. 7), recognition of an enemy of cosmic magnitude, the devil (v. 8), and the suffering of Christians locally (v. 10) and throughout the world (v. 9). Within an otherwise dire portrayal of these realities, Peter provides some relief by locating the present within eschatological horizons (vv. 6, 10-11), especially contrasting the temporal limitations of present suffering ("a short while," v. 10) with limitless, future glory ("eternal," vv. 10-11). It is within these parameters of existential distress that the other two major emphases of this paragraph gain their significance.

(2) The Character of God: Peter fills in the mural of his portrait of God, presenting God's character and activity along the lines of two classic representations of the God of Israel: God the Mighty Warrior and God the Merciful.

---

58. BDAG, p. 383.

59. 1 Pet 5:8: περιπατέω (*peripateō*); Job 1:7: περιέρχομαι (*perierchomai*); 2:2: διαπορεύομαι (*diaporeuomai*).

60. See Goppelt, pp. 359-62.

God the Mighty Warrior	**God the Merciful**
the mighty hand of God (v. 6)	he cares for you (v. 7)
he will lift you up (v. 6)	God of all grace (v. 10)
God will restore, support,	God, who called you . . .
strengthen, and secure (v. 10)	(v. 10; cf. 1:1-2; 2:9-10)
to him be the power forever (v. 11)	

My drawing attention to these two domains of God's character and action is not meant to separate one set of divine dispositions from the other. Rather, it is to draw attention to God's capacity, even in the face of an adversarial roaring lion, to consummate his purpose and to protect and restore his people.

In his explication of the OT motif of the Divine Warrior, Longman has identified a threefold pattern. First, Yahweh reveals to Israel that war is pending, and thus when and whom they were to engage in battle. Israel is to enter war not on its own initiative, but according to God's direction. Second, pains are taken to ensure the presence of God in the midst of battle; if Yahweh is present, then Israel need not (and must not) depend on more potent weapons, more stalwart defenses, or superior numbers. According to the psalmist, "A king is not saved by his great army; a warrior is not delivered by his great strength. The war horse is a vain hope for victory, and by its great might it cannot save" (Ps 33:16-17). In the face of battle, says Israel, "Our pride is in the name of the Lord," not in chariots or horses (Ps 20:7). Third, after the battle has been engaged, praise is given to Yahweh. Israel, when obedient, wins the war because of the power of Yahweh.[61] Peter's presentation serves the same interests: identifying the presence of battle and the nature of the enemy, as well as how best to engage in the struggle. The adversary is the devil, and the weapons of warfare are summarized as "resistance" (see further below). The present resources of God are promised: his mighty hand, his care, and his call. V. 10 is more detailed, providing an accumulation of terms whose meanings overlap significantly: "restore or supply," "support, strengthen, or establish," "strengthen or empower," and "secure or establish." These verbs document the inability of suffering or the devil to do ultimate damage as well as God's intent and capacity to restore and vindicate his people. Although these verbs are future in orientation, their actualization is not held back until the eschaton; God is already equipping his people for faithful resistance in anticipation of final restoration.[62] Finally, Peter brings this textual unit to a close with a confession and celebration of God's dominion. Within the message of the letter, God's

---

61. Longman, "Warfare," pp. 836-37; see Longman and Reid, *God Is a Warrior.*
62. See Jobes, pp. 316-17; Goppelt, pp. 365-66.

dominion would have to entail his overpowering of the devil; hence, whatever strength the adversary is able to muster, that power is overshadowed by power of God. Within Peter's world, ultimate power might seem to have been the property of the Roman Empire, with its extravagant claims to importance; again, however, Peter draws the body of his letter to its finale with this acclamation of God's peerless dominion.

Rather than imagining that Peter is slavishly following a set form for speaking of God the Warrior, we should recognize that both the pattern of the Divine Warrior and Peter are reflecting on that premier expression of God's power: exodus. Indeed, what he is working out before our eyes is nothing less than the pattern prototypically on display in the liberation of God's people from Egypt: the people are in distress, God hears their cries, and God acts decisively to deliver. Consider Israel's ancient "credo":

> A wandering Aramean was my ancestor; he went down into Egypt and lived there as an alien, few in number, and there he became a great nation, mighty and populous. When the Egyptians treated us harshly and afflicted us, by imposing hard labor on us, we cried to the LORD, the God of our ancestors; the LORD heard our voice and saw our affliction, our toil, and our oppression. The LORD brought us out of Egypt with a mighty hand and an outstretched arm, with a terrifying display of power, and with signs and wonders; and he brought us into this place and gave us this land, a land flowing with milk and honey. (Deut 26:5-9)

The points of contact between Peter's presentation and Israel's confession are numerous — including the alien status of God's people, the affliction visited on them as a minority people by the majority, God's care for his people in distress, God's intervention on their behalf, declaration of God's power (including the parallel reference to God's "mighty hand"), and the divine provision of an inheritance.

Let me pursue two further ways that Peter builds on this pattern of God's liberation. First, reference to the "mighty hand" of God is a well-known example of metonymy in Israel's Scriptures, used especially in references to God's liberation of Israel from Egypt (e.g., Exod 32:11; Deut 4:34; 5:15; 7:19; Dan 9:15) — that definitive act of liberation in Scripture recalled in this (the only) reference to God's mighty hand in the NT.[63] In a suggestive play on words, Peter speaks in v. 6 of God's "mighty (κραταιός, *krataios*) hand" and in

---

63. For parallels without the adjective "mighty," see, e.g., Luke 1:66; Acts 4:30; 11:21; 13:11. In the NT, the "hand of God" is more usually mentioned in references to Jesus' exaltation to the "right hand of God," as in 3:22.

v. 11 of God's "might" (κράτος, *kratos*). Second, note how Peter presents Christ as the means of God's intervention. This is the significance of the phrase "in Christ" in the description of the God "who called you into his glory in Christ" (v. 10). In Greek, "in" is a pliable preposition, capable of at least two senses in this context. "In" may denote agency, suggesting, then, that Christ is the means by which God works salvation; Peter has worked this out in detail in 1:18-19; 2:21-25. "In" may denote "container," suggesting "in the sphere of Christ," or, better, participation with Christ in suffering and glory. This would mean, of course, that sharing in the "eternal glory in Christ" is contingent on standing firm, even when to do so is to invite harassment motivated by nothing more than the gulf that separates "doing good" as a believer, and "doing evil." The correlation of "suffering a short while" with "eternal glory" in the case of believers has its ground and guarantee in the journey of Christ from suffering to glory.

It is not too much to say that, here in vv. 6-11, Peter puts before his audience two views of the world — the same reality understood in quite different ways. The question is, What do you see? What do you know? One is a world of distress and suffering and humiliation. The other neither denies nor downplays these experiences, nor does it exempt believers from future struggle. Instead, it limits the duration of suffering, and locates all harsh treatment and misery on the map of God's character, God's power, and God's purpose. From this perspective, the canvas of life belongs neither to the empire nor to the devil; it is God who is at work with care and grace; it is God who will restore, strengthen, empower, and secure; and it is God who will vindicate, exalt, and gather his people into his unending glory.

(3) Expected Response: Only those who have embraced this way of seeing, this pattern of knowing, can respond in the way Peter directs. Adopting a staccato style unusual in this letter, the apostle promotes this clipped catalog of imperatives: accept your humble status (v. 6), remain vigilant (v. 8), stay alert (v. 8), and resist the devil (v. 9).

In the honor-shame game, identity is formed relationally and one's status is not so much assumed by oneself as allocated by others. Pivotal in determining the game's outcome are answers to such questions as, Who adjudicates status? On what basis? Status in relation to which set of peers? With his inelegant use of the passive form of the verb "to humble" in v. 6, Peter provides one set of answers to these questions. With respect to the wider Roman world, with status based on conformity to conventional practices and adjudicated in the court of public opinion, the jury is already in. Christians are disgraced as social deviants. Theirs is an ignominious life. With respect to the world of the empire, Christians do not choose honor or shame; social status is chosen for them, attributed to them by others. Humility in this case is not a quality of character one embraces, then, but a position in the world assigned by others. Social humiliation follows naturally in the footsteps of the decision to embrace the way of Christ. The choice left to Peter's audience of believers, then, is how to respond, how to render ignominy meaningful. By urging them to accept their humble status, Peter transforms the honor-shame game by substituting new answers to those pivotal questions. With his reference to humility "under the mighty hand of God," Peter identifies God as the arbiter of status, thus redefining the basis on which high status might be granted.

What is more, with v. 7 Peter explains *how* to accept one's humble status: by "casting on him your every distress." As Christ "handed himself over to the one who judges justly" (2:23), as holy women had "placed their hope in God" (3:5), and as Peter has already encouraged his audience to "entrust their lives to a faithful creator" (4:19), so now Christians allow God to be God by laying their cares on him. Casting one's cares on God is a recognition of God's monopoly on justice as well as a deep-seated confession of God's power to accomplish his purposes. It is an enacted credo.

Peter's instruction says in abbreviated form what we find more fully developed in Luke 12 (see Matt 6:25-34), demonstrating yet again his familiarity with and dependence on the Jesus tradition. In Luke 12 center stage belongs to Jesus' teaching about anxiety and God's gracious provision for his people, both set within an eschatological context that invokes faithful service and watchfulness. One of Jesus' sayings is of immediate interest in the context of Peter's message:

> I tell you, my friends, do not fear those who kill the body, and after that can do nothing more. But I will warn you whom to fear: fear him who, after he has killed, has authority to cast into hell. Yes, I tell you, fear him! Are not five sparrows sold for two pennies? Yet not one of them is forgotten in God's sight. But even the hairs of your head are all counted. Do not be afraid; you are of more value than many sparrows. And I tell you, everyone who acknowledges me before others, the Son of Man also will acknowledge before the angels of God; but whoever denies me before others will be denied before the angels of God. (Luke 12:4-9)

Linguistic parallels are practically nonexistent, but conceptually there are numerous points of contact. Among these could be named the promise in Luke and Peter that the malicious work of the devil is incapable of doing ultimate harm as well as a warning against apostasy. It is Jesus' sparrow analogy that invites special reflection in this context, however. Sparrows may be of little value in the marketplace, but are nonetheless remembered by God. Note, however, that in Jesus' analogy, God's care for them does not keep sparrows from being sold in the marketplace nor from being eaten. In the same way, God's care for his people is not voided when he does not rescue his people *from* danger. Just as sparrows can be bought and sold, humans can suffer calamity at the hands of their oppressors, but not apart from God's attentiveness, not outside of his care, and certainly not in a way that circumvents God's redemptive purpose. Indeed, for Peter, God's restoration comes *through* suffering, not *from* it.

Peter has used the admonition to vigilance twice before, in 1:13 and 4:7, but the call to alertness is new to the letter. "Stay awake!" (γρηγορέω, *grēgoreō*) is often used in appeals for eschatological readiness (e.g., Matt 24:42; 25:13; Mark 13:35, 37; Luke 12:37) — a usage that fits well the current context. It underscores the importance of adopting God's view of things and patterning life in ways that account for both the threat of present evil and the certainty of eschatological judgment.

The imperative most rich in significance is found in v. 9: "Resist the devil!" Similar directives are found in Jas 4:7; Eph 6:11-13. Its importance in 1 Peter is twofold. First, the devil's desired outcome in the case of believers is apostasy, and, indeed, among the threats of exilic life two stand out especially: assimilation and defection. As weapons of engagement, Peter offers two responses, the first an adjectival phrase ("firm in the faith"), the second a participial phrase ("recognizing that the same kind of sufferings are being accomplished in the case of your family of believers throughout the world"). "Faith" in this instance pinpoints those commitments common to believers by which they order their lives. The whole of Peter's letter gives expression to this "faith," with the result that "standing firm" would be parsed as a refusal to revert to the former ways of life that continue to characterize the Gentiles (e.g., 4:3) and as a resolve to practice holiness in all of life (e.g., 1:13-16), to live in obedience to the truth (see 1:22). In the second phrase, Peter engages in theological formation around the experience of suffering by denying that interpretation that identifies suffering with an individual's just deserts and by intimating the divine purpose at work in suffering (see above). Resistance is standing firm on the basis of what one knows to be true, and this makes the shaping of what one "knows" all the more crucial.

Second, by naming the devil as adversary, Peter attributes the source of suffering to the devil rather than to those flesh and blood persons who participate in harassment and vilification. Though previously we might have imagined that responsibility for the suffering of believers could be laid at the feet of those "Gentiles" (2:12; 4:3) whom Peter variously describes as disbelievers (2:6-7; 3:1) and disobedient (2:8; 4:17), now we learn that the battle is much more involved, being played out in the context of the cosmic struggle between good and evil. This puts the church's human oppressors in a different light — not because they lack moral responsibility, since impartial judgment is assured (1:17; 2:12; 4:5, 18), but because they are implicated in a malevolent plan the dimensions of which transcend what even they might have imagined. From a human vantage point, the agenda might appear to be the shaming and maltreatment of those who fail to live up to the standards set by respectable Roman society; this is bad enough, but those aims are frighteningly overshadowed by the active presence of an even darker intent. From a diabolical perspective, the agenda is to provoke defection from the faith, apostasy. Far more is at stake than social standing.

5:12-14

12 With Silvanus, whom I regard as a faithful brother, I have written to you briefly, encouraging and bearing witness that this is the true grace of God — on which you must stand. 13 She who is the fellow elect in Babylon[1] greets you, as does Mark my son. 14 Greet one another with a kiss of love. Peace to you all who are in Christ.

Peter's letter closing includes a number of features typical of early Christian letters,[2] though in terms of its function here two observations stand out. First, 5:12-14 forms an inclusio with 1:1-2. In the letter opening, Peter identified his audience, paradoxically, as both "strangers in the world of the diaspora" and God's elect. In the letter closing, he repeats these identity markers through references to his own location in Babylon and to the "fellow elect" who joins him in his greeting. Likewise, in the letter closing, Peter pronounces "peace" on his audience, echoing his greeting in 1:2. In a parody of the letter opening, however, Peter no longer locates his audience "in the world of the diaspora in Pontus, Galatia, Cappadocia, Asia, and Bithynia" (1:1). They are, rather, "in Christ" (5:14; cf. 3:16; 5:10). Between these two references, in the letter body, Peter places a premium on the status of believers in relation to God, on their liberation in Christ, and on the manner of life that flows from these. They are to distance themselves from their own pasts, but are never

---

1. Unveiling the meaning of Peter's reference to Babylon, a few minuscules read Ῥώμη (*Rōmē*). The potentially ambiguous "fellow elect" is clarified in ℵ *pc* vg^{mss} sy^p by the addition of ἐκκλησία (*ekklēsia*).

2. These are of particular concern to Achtemeier, pp. 348-56.

urged to withdraw from their disbelieving peers. Peter concerns himself less with constructing boundaries and more with defining the center and pattern for God's people. True, his audience comprises "a stateless minority in the context of a massive empire,"[3] but, for Peter, the lives of these followers of Christ are determined decisively not by their location in the empire but by their habitation of a space he designates as "in Christ."

Second, in vv. 12, 14, Peter sums up the message of this letter: with regard to persons outside the family of faith, the crucial response is to stand on the true grace of God; with regard to persons within the household of faith, the essence of Peter's teaching is summed up in his directive, "Greet one another with a kiss of love."

Peter is joined in his letter closing by three personages. He identifies Silvanus as the person tasked with carrying the letter to Peter's addressees on the Anatolian peninsula (1:1).[4] This means that Silvanus would have been intimate enough with the author and production of this letter that, carrying it from one place to the next (where we might expect copies to be kept), he could properly serve as a personal link between Peter and his audience and appropriately "perform" the letter — reading it aloud, modulating his voice and gesticulating for emphasis.[5] (Literacy, defined in terms of ability to read and write, characterized no more than 10 to 15 percent of early Christians,[6] so access to Peter's writing for most was necessarily through oral performance. Additionally, those who could read did so orally [cf. Acts 8:30].) By way of inviting for Silvanus a favorable hearing on his circuit, Peter provides for him a character reference, staking his own reputation on his opinion that Silvanus is a "faithful brother." Given the emphases of this letter, this is a far-reaching commendation, since it identifies Silvanus as one whose manner of life is congruent with the gospel as Peter has explicated it; moreover, in a letter oriented so fully around images of household and kin, Peter's authoritative reference to Silvanus as "brother" locates him immediately and conclusively "within the family." Silvanus could have served as Peter's secretary in the production of this letter — a common practice in the first-century world, including the world of early Christianity[7] — but this is not suggested by the phrasing of v. 12.[8]

---

3. So Smith-Christopher characterizes the Hebrews in exile (*Exile,* p. 144).

4. Peter's Silvanus is often identified with the Silvanus/Silas of Acts 15:22-35; 15:40–18:5; 1 Thess 1:1; 2 Thess 1:1; 2 Cor 1:19, but we have little basis for a judgment either way.

5. On letter carrying, see Richards, *First-Century Letter Writing,* pp. 171-87.

6. Gamble, *Books and Readers,* pp. 1-10.

7. This is ably discussed in Richards, *First-Century Letter Writing;* with a more extensive account of the evidence regarding secretaries in Richards, *Secretary.*

8. This has been demonstrated by Richards, "Silvanus Was Not Peter's Secretary"; irre-

The particular identity of "Mark" is uncontroversial precisely because Peter gives us so little on which to base an opinion. *Markus* was a common name in the Roman world. "My son" could be taken literally (we know Peter was married — cf. Mark 1:30; 1 Cor 9:5) or figuratively, referring to someone for whose entry into the faith Peter was responsible (as in, e.g., 1 Tim 1:2; Tit 1:4; Phlm 10). Eusebius, quoting Papias, who himself credits "the Elder," names the Mark who wrote the Gospel of Mark as Peter's interpreter (*Historia Ecclesiastica* 3.39.15). This tradition dates back at least to the beginning of the second century. However, this does not take us much further toward a resolution to our identity problem, since we do not learn from Eusebius whether the "Mark" to which the tradition refers is actually the "John Mark" of Acts 12:12, 25; 13:13, etc.[9]

Also challenging is Peter's reference to "the fellow elect in Babylon." "Fellow elect" is gender specific, feminine, and could refer either to a particular woman, perhaps Peter's wife or a coworker, or to the Christian community of Rome. It would be strange for Peter to mention Silvanus and Mark by name, but not his wife or coworker,[10] and we have evidence otherwise of the feminine personification of the church (e.g., 2 John 13). Peter is thus probably highlighting the kinship of the Christian community in Rome with those of the Anatolian peninsula, whose solidarity in suffering Peter has already observed (5:9). Why Rome? Used similarly in the book of Revelation (e.g., Rev. 17-18), "Babylon" has become a cipher for a world-power hostile to God — in this case, "Rome," though "Babylon" is not so much identified with Rome as used as a brand to characterize what Rome has become.[11] This recapitulates

---

spective of the title of his article, however, Richards is aware that evidence against finding in Peter's phrase διὰ Σιλουανοῦ . . . ἔγραψα *(dia Silouanou . . . egrapsa)* a reference to Silvanus' secretarial role is not evidence against Silvanus' actually having served in that role.

9. Cf. Horrell, "Petrine Circle," pp. 48-50.

10. Applegate argues that Peter refers to a woman who has been a missionary and church leader and does so for a rhetorical aim — namely, to sanction the household code, and especially 3:1-6, since Peter anticipated that it would find resistance from women leaders in Asia Minor ("Co-Elect Woman"). Again, however, it is unclear why Peter would refer to her in this veiled way while naming Silvanus and Mark. Moreover, given both what we know of the social situation for women in Asia Minor and my reading of 3:1-6 (above), my sense is that Peter is already engaged in a hermeneutic of resistance and would not have anticipated the reception of his letter in the terms Applegate imagines. It would also be useful for Applegate to provide evidence from Peter's first-century world that a female voice would carry the sort of authority, beyond that of an apostle, that her argument requires.

11. Referring to the biblical critique of Babylonian ideology, specifically its religion and imperialism, B. T. Arnold notes that Babylon comes to symbolize an evil power and oppression (*Babylonians*, p. 11).

for us the perspective on suffering we find elsewhere in the letter, for it draws attention to the systemic character of harassment and the institutionalization of evil in patterns of sanctioned behavior and organizational structures that legitimate and propagate such behavior. The association of the name "Babylon" with the historical exile of Israel in the sixth century BC, a dispersion from which Israel never fully recovered, also reminds us that 1 Peter is a circular letter written to exiles of the dispersion, bringing us back full-circle to the beginning of the letter (1:1-2).

This letter closing gives Peter the opportunity to set out his purpose in writing. His reference to his letter as "brief" follows letter-writing convention and should not be taken too literally. With over 1800 words, 1 Peter is well beyond the average of 87 words for letters of Greco-Roman antiquity.[12] He has used the word "encourage" on two other occasions in his letter (2:11; 5:1), and his reference to his own testimony recalls 5:1 as well. With this language, Peter places his own reputation as "an apostle of Jesus Christ" (1:1) — as one who has commended the passion of Christ by a life that exhibits Christlike suffering and as one who is Christ's partner in the glory to come (5:1) — to back his claim that "this is the true grace of God." Grace, throughout the letter, refers to God's favor and honor and to the substance of salvation.[13] As such, it serves as a disarmingly terse resume of the liberating work of God in Christ on behalf of believers, including, not incidentally, the honorable status believers now have before God and the ensuing promise of vindication — all this in spite of the way things must seem for persons living the marginal, sometimes tortuous lives of "aliens and strangers in the world" (2:11).[14] *This* is true — that is, *this* (and not some other interpretation) represents the way things really are (ἀληθής, *alēthēs*, "true"). "Take your stand" would then represent all of Peter's directives to believers concerning their lives in the world. In this way, the text of 1 Peter validates our earlier insistence that Peter did not counsel believers to assimilate themselves in order to "get along," and similarly our finding that Peter did not encourage believers to adopt servile ("submissive") dispositions and behaviors toward those in authority. To be sure, "standing on the true grace of God" conjures up no images of retaliation or violence; such categories of behavior are expressly proscribed in Peter's letter. But "standing" is consistent with Peter's encouragement of a basic posture of courageous resistance.

---

12. Having reviewed approximately 14,000 letters from the period, Richards finds that the average length was 87 words, with a range of 18 to 209 words. Cicero's letters were somewhat longer, averaging 295; Seneca's even longer, averaging 995; and Paul's longer still, averaging 2,495 (*First-Century Letter Writing*, pp. 163-64).

13. See 1:2, 10, 13; 2:19, 20; 3:7; 4:10; 5:5, 10, 12.

14. See Campbell, *Honor*, pp. 228-29.

Many reasons might be given for the kiss of greeting in the Roman world (reunion of friends, for example), but public kissing was a restricted practice that helped to demarcate lines of social interaction.[15] Kissing was demonstrative of inclusion, kinship, and honor (cf., e.g., Luke 7:45; 15:20; Acts 20:37). Peter qualifies this greeting as a "kiss *of love*," bringing to the fore in summary form the whole of his teaching around the intramural relations of the household of faith. Throughout the letter, "love" has been promoted as a defining characteristic of dispositions and behaviors within the community of believers — signifying a group ethos of solidarity and loyalty, an essential pattern of mind favoring others in the community, and a commitment to oneness within the group. This emphasis on the community of believers is triggered by the familial terms that dot the landscape of Peter's letter, together with metaphors of new birth, newborn babies, and the converted as children comprising a family whose Father is God. Familial love denotes a strong sense of identity as a kin group (see 1:22; 2:17; 3:8; 5:9) that would stand in sharp contrast to the more pervasive experience of "strangerhood." Such sentiments are concentrated in this, the final appeal of the letter: "Greet one another with a kiss of love."

From the perspective of religious studies, the "kiss of love" has the quality of ritual, a communication system prompting the use and construction of the sacred world. Rituals are socializing structures the performance of which generates identity and relationships. For our thinking about the "kiss of love," two basic features of ritual are especially telling: the power of ritual to focus the attention of people on specific relations or networks of relations sharing a common center in the life of God and the physicality of ritual (tactile, visible, somatic), nesting the community's essential commitments within physical demonstration. As a greeting, the "kiss of love" serves as a threshold into a time and space determined by familial relations made possible through new birth, pressing to memory's margins the damage of life in a world hostile to the faith. As ritual, the "kiss of love" renews, strengthens, and recreates those patterns of thinking and feeling, that quality of life, determined by the merciful initiative of God who brings liberation in Christ and creates a household structured around his grace. Paradigmatic practices like the "kiss of love" are rituals, then, that bring into focus the defining values of the community of practice.[16]

---

15. Klassen's survey of the evidence ("Sacred Kiss") reveals what little precedent there was in ancient Judaism or the Roman world for the practice of the "sacred kiss." He underscores its role in group formation and as a display of one's faith.

16. On ritual, I am following Paden, *Religious Worlds.*

The "kiss of love" thus concentrates Peter's theology of love and redemptive images of household life, as it helps to construct the very reality it intends to represent. Here is Peter's understanding of the Spirit's sanctifying work within the community and the character of the believing community in bodily form. The "kiss of love" is embodied theology.

Theological Horizons of 1 Peter

The Theology of 1 Peter

As Brevard Childs tells the story, "biblical theology," as a discrete discipline, is a post-Reformation phenomenon.[1] The Reformation's appeal to the Bible as sole authority in matters of faith signaled a change in emphasis away from a dogmatic ecclesiastical framework toward the delineation of the theology of the Bible sans the earlier presumption that the message of the Bible and the content of church dogma were coterminous.[2] Medieval Christianity had presumed no necessary historical gap between the Bible and contemporary faith.[3] This may not at first blush seem much different from the hermeneutics of the Reformation, in which the Bible functioned as "a compendium of divine doctrine";[4] to be sure, in either case, the relationship between the Bible and theology is regarded as immediate. However, the Reformation noted with seriousness the theological development that had occurred in the church subsequent to the generation of the books comprising the OT and NT, asserting over against that theological heritage the priority of Scripture. Hence, although he has his antecedents, we may find a helpful point of beginning in Johann Philipp Gabler, writing at the end of the eighteenth century, who proffered a methodological distinction between dogmatic theology and biblical theology which, in many of its basic points, would win widespread support.[5]

---

1. Portions of this introduction are adapted from J. B. Green, "Scripture and Theology"; idem, "Theological Interpretation."

2. Childs, *Biblical Theology,* pp. 3-4.

3. Cf. Boers, *NT Theology,* pp. 16-18.

4. Baird, *History of NT Research,* 1:184.

5. For a translation of Gabler's famous lecture and discussion of its significance, see Sandys-Wunsch and Eldredge, "J. P. Gabler."

Gabler sketched a three-stage process by which one might move from historical analysis of the biblical texts to a biblical theology: (1) careful linguistic and historical analysis, (2) engagement in a synthetic task, the purpose of which was to identify those ideas common among the biblical writers, and (3) arrival at the transcendent (timeless and universal) principles of the Bible. If one were to engage in dogmatic theology, one would begin here, with these transcendent ideas, so as to adapt them to particular contexts. In this way, the Bible (and, for Gabler, this meant especially the NT) was positioned as the basis or fountainhead of all theology. Although the second step might be dropped by some interpreters, and although additional steps might be proposed, this essential process carried the day for many interpreters over the next two centuries and continues to have its champions today. Thus, for example, in the mid-1800s, the Princeton theologian Charles Hodge would claim that "the Bible is to the theologian what nature is to the man of science. It is his storehouse of facts." Two tasks are thus identified: to ascertain and state the facts contained in the Bible (the work of the exegete) and to discern their inner relation and arrange them harmoniously (the work of the systematic theologian).[6]

Although the approach outlined in Krister Stendahl's celebrated essay in the *Interpreter's Dictionary of the Bible* cannot simply be identified with Gabler's work,[7] it is via Stendahl's distinction between "what it meant" and "what it means" that the relationship between biblical studies and theology is now popularly conceived. And such distinctions are ubiquitous in contemporary discussion. Heikki Räisänen insists that Gabler was right in his programmatic distinction between the historical and theological tasks of the exegete, for example, just as Peter Balla affirms in his reassessment of the field that the task of NT theology is distinct from systematic theology; for Balla, the NT is viewed as "source" for theology and is not itself "faith seeking understanding."[8] Contributions to the genre "a theology of the NT" in the past three decades further signify the ascendency of this way of construing the theological mission of biblical scholars, for almost invariably they point to the important, inaugural step of engagement in the "descriptive task" — which Stendahl presented thus: "[O]ur only concern is to find out what these words meant when uttered or written by the prophet, the priest, the evangelist, or the apostle — and regardless of their meaning in later stages of religious history, our own included."[9] To cite one further, contem-

6. Baird, *History of NT Research*, 2:32.

7. For a comparison of the two, see Stuckenbruck, "Johann Philipp Gabler," pp. 154-57.

8. Räisänen, *Beyond NT Theology*; Balla, *Challenges to NT Theology*.

9. Stendahl, "Biblical Theology, Contemporary," p. 422.

porary example, in his introduction to a "biblical theology of the New Testament," Peter Stuhlmacher outlines his own three-stage hermeneutic: (1) historical analysis of the biblical texts, (2) historical reconstruction of the relationship among these elements, and (3) interpretation of this reconstruction for its relevance to the present.[10]

The *format* of the Two Horizons Commentary may appear to perpetuate Gabler's program, since it moves from commentary to theological horizons, with reflection on the theology of the book preceding theological conversations of a more constructive sort. Appearances can deceive, of course. In fact, the format of the series is more a bow in the direction of the current state of play in theological studies than a principled display of the "what it meant/what it means" dichotomy. It is a simple truism that, over the last two centuries, systematic theology and biblical studies have come to have increasingly poor relations. Today, however mysterious it might seem to those outside formal theological studies, we have "theologies" with little discernible interest in the Christian Scriptures on the one hand, and, on the other, numerous examples of and strong arguments for the extrication of biblical exegesis from theological interests and commitments. In spite of countervoices,[11] in theological schools, departments of theological and biblical studies typically exist in relationships of antipathy. They may share a relationship of mutual respect and even support, but the disciplines they represent are each constitutive of a stable epistemic community regulated by standards of excellence and aims that are generally mutually exclusive. Only rarely does one find mutual respect giving way to the sort of interdisciplinarity where fresh epistemic trails are blazed, where the concerns of systematic theology actually shape the ways in which biblical studies is conducted, and vice versa. More pervasive has been the suggestion that it is the task of the student to search for paths of integration among the thickets of a curriculum whose presuppositions hinder and sometimes deny the possibility of discovery of the fountain of integration. More pervasive are those scholars who are trained according to accredited standards that guard the one discipline from what are typically regarded as the naive or colonizing efforts of the other.[12]

---

10. Stuhlmacher, *Biblische Theologie*, p. 12.

11. From the side of theological studies — e.g., O'Collins and Kendall, *Bible for Theology*; Scalise, *From Scripture to Theology*. From the side of biblical studies — e.g., Francis Watson, *Text, Church and World*; idem, *Text and Truth*; Seitz, *Word without End*; Fowl, *Engaging Scripture*.

12. A consequence of such developments has been the ghettoizing of biblical studies and an identity crisis for practitioners of this discipline. Jeanrond queries, "What can the study of

So the format of the Two Horizons series accounts for the state of play but in varying ways also works to overcome those dichotomies by promoting a stronger sense of partnership and necessary integration. This, after all, is where most of us live — without a moment's hesitation or second thought, we voice our theological *and* biblical formation in prayer, for example, as in the rest of life.

By way of countering the program put forward by Gabler and widely embraced in the years that would follow, I begin with a counterclaim: Peter's letter is neither raw material for the building of a theological house nor does it provide raw material for the theological enterprise. Along with the rest of the Christian Bible, 1 Peter is not itself "the gospel." It is, rather, witness to the gospel, and that in a particular world within the ancient Roman Mediterranean. Hence, it is not transcultural *per se,* even if — for theological, historical, and literary reasons — it has the capacity to speak beyond its context of origin. First Peter is neither simply nor primarily a "source" for theological data, but is already an exemplar of the theological task, that is, already respresents the working out of the ramifications of the gospel. We may learn "theology" from 1 Peter, but more significantly we learn "doing theology" from 1 Peter, how it models the instantiation of the good news in its particularities. In 1 Peter already we find "theology" both in its critical task of reflection on the practices and affirmations of the people of God to determine their credibility and faithfulness, and in its constructive task of reiteration, restatement, and interpretation of the good news vis-à-vis its horizons and challenges.

My task, then, in this section is to sketch how Peter has engaged in theological work. I will do so by addressing some of the expected theological loci — God, Christ, Spirit, Church, and so on — though in doing so I will also suggest why he portrays (for example) God the way he does. Of the various ways open to him through God's self-disclosure, especially in Israel's Scriptures and in the advent of Christ, why these emphases? In the following two sections, I will attempt to bring 1 Peter into conversation with other voices in the Christian canon, and with regard to selected theological concerns of contemporary importance.

---

the Bible offer to the diverse interests of students late in the twentieth century? What is the contribution of biblical studies to the academy, to society at large and to the different Jewish and Christian communities? In other words, what is the discipline of biblical studies good for these days?" ("After Hermeneutics," p. 85). Cf. Bockmuehl, "Possible Futures."

"Aliens and Strangers in the World": A Contextual Theology

Like other NT books, 1 Peter is implicated in a paradox. In order to serve pastorally and prophetically those in the first-century "world of the diaspora in Pontus, Galatia, Cappadocia, Asia, and Bithynia" (1:1), it must incarnate its encouragement and testimony within the cultural confines of that locality. It must become indigenous theology. But if 1 Peter is to have significance beyond the historical world it envisions it cannot sit so comfortably within the setting of the Anatolian peninsula that its message is reduced to its cultural and geographical boundaries.

As Robert Wuthnow has observed, "Great works of art and literature, philosophy and social criticism, like great sermons, always relate in an enigmatic fashion to their social environments." This is because "they draw resources, insights, and inspiration from that environment: they reflect it, speak to it, and make themselves relevant to it"; but "they also remain autonomous enough from their social environment to acquire a broader, even universal and timeless appeal."[13] Stephen Greenblatt speaks similarly of the twin concepts of "constraint" and "mobility": the ways in which cultural moorings constrain or control behavior, including the production of cultural products like letters and ideas, versus the capacity of those cultural products to transform the social energies and practices out of which they were formed.[14] That this is precisely what 1 Peter intends is easily demonstrated — most explicitly by the universalizing of its audience in 5:9; more pervasively by its unrelenting assault on the values and practices by which the wider world of 1 Peter would have been constructed. If Peter addresses his message to those living in Anatolia who suffer as Christians, then asserts that "the same kind of sufferings are being accomplished in the case of your family of believers throughout the world," then his message can hardly be constrained by Anatolian borders. And if he militates against the socioreligious conventions that govern everyday life among his audience, then, again, his message overflows the banks of a life determined by Roman order.

Wuthnow refers to the paradox before us as "the problem of articulation":

> If cultural products do not articulate closely enough with their social settings, they are likely to be regarded by the potential audiences of which these settings are composed as irrelevant, unrealistic, artificial, and overly

---

13. Wuthnow, *Communities of Discourse*, p. 3.
14. Greenblatt, "Culture."

abstract . . . ; but if cultural products articulate too closely with the specific social environment in which they are produced, they are likely to be thought of as esoteric, parochial, time bound, and fail to attract a wider and more lasting audience.[15]

The problem is particularly acute with regard to a letter like 1 Peter, which is self-evidently bent on challenging the status quo. How can Peter situate himself within the very world he is calling into question? How can Peter attract a hearing among those whose identities have been shaped by and whose fortunes are tied to the very world he seeks to undermine? Undoubtedly, this paradox lies at the root of different readings of 1 Peter since the 1970s, with some interpreters urging that Peter's message has not really escaped the constraints of Roman respectability, nor intended to do so, and others finding in 1 Peter a higher degree of disengagement from Roman ideals. Our interest in Peter's "local theology,"[16] then, centers not simply in querying the social conditions that shaped Peter's message but also, and critically, why those conditions did not shape that message further.

Mapping Peter's audience on the broad scale, we find them on the Anatolian peninsula, sometimes called "Asia Minor," sometimes simply "Asia," known today as western Turkey. Home to civilizations of impressive antiquity and fountainhead of Indo-European languages, by the time of Peter's letter, this area had been more thoroughly Romanized than many other regions of the Greco-Roman world. From the time of Alexander, Anatolia had served as a land bridge connecting the eastern and western reaches of Greek and then Roman rule. Although its central plateau supported agriculture, the area is known to us especially for its cities — including those mentioned in Revelation 2–3, and others noted in Acts as venues of the Pauline mission.

Hidden within these few seemingly innocuous observations about the geography of the area to which Peter addresses himself are a number of key considerations:[17]

On account of its role as a thoroughfare for east-west travel across the empire, the peninsula had long served as the homeland for migrant groups and increasingly became the home of cosmopolitan populations whose common denominator was Roman influence. Archaeological remains are extensively Roman, with the expected register of

15. Wuthnow, *Communities of Discourse*, p. 3

16. I have borrowed the term and some principles of analysis from Schreiter, *Local Theologies;* more broadly, see Flemming, *Contextualization in the NT.*

17. See, e.g., Trebilco, "Asia"; Jeffers, *Greco-Roman World,* pp. 259-92.

public arenas: baths, theaters, stadia, and fora. Evidence of heightened Roman influence in these material remains urges our taking seriously the prospect of heightened pressure toward social integration into Roman ways. By the time of Peter's letter, the older Greek notion of the city-state had long receded in favor of a politics governed by a primary commitment: allegiance to Rome and propagation of Roman unity and Roman superiority. It was, after all, Rome's imperial destiny to "form one body under the name of Romans" (Tacitus, *Annals* 11.24).

Urban areas encountered more traffic and were thus open to greater degrees of cultural exchange. Whether motivated by intellectual hunger, the quest for acceptance and honor in the changing world, or some other reason, urbanites would have been more intimate than their rural counterparts with pressures to conform in the face of cultural mores and innovations. Moreover, cities were centers of wealth, resourced especially by old native aristocracies or Roman colonizers from Italy, including some of the equestrian and senatorial orders. Indeed, the "peace of Rome" that characterized the early empire occasioned an unprecedented era of prosperity for Anatolia, with public buildings constructed with the support of private benefaction and, to a lesser degree, municipal funds. Provincial elites were the feet and hands of imperial Rome, extending its structures locally and thus inviting imperial recognition and advancement for their cities. Cities also concentrated the population, making it easier to exercise widespread and calculated resistance to persons who failed to conform to societal expectations or otherwise disturbed the status quo. Cities thus functioned powerfully as mediators of Roman values and Roman ways.

As a region of ancient traditions and interurban competition, Anatolia bred multiple religious expressions, including the old gods and the new. According to the account of Paul and Barnabas's entry into the Anatolian city of Lystra in Acts 14:8-20, these would have included Zeus and Hermes. Long-established local deities would also have been the objects of worship, even if they were renamed, as was probably the case with Artemis (Acts 19:23-41). Chief among these, of course, was the worship of the emperor: Lord Caesar, Savior of the World. Failure to participate in the imperial cult and worship of the traditional gods was to call upon oneself the charge of "atheism," inviting unwanted attention in the form of social shunning, censure, or worse. Remembering that daily religious practices were typically explicit and public, involving whole communities, it is easy to see how easily nonparticipation would have been recognized.

What dispositions and practices would have been accorded privilege in such an environment? Among the range of possibilities that might attract our attention are the following:

"Doing good" was defined as public benefaction — charitable giving for the advancement of the city, never for the marginal; and for the honor that would accrue to the "cheerful giver," not as an expression of altruism.[18] It almost goes without saying, then, that "doing good" would not have connoted selfless activity on the part of one's associates or those in need or performance conforming to such external standards as the character of Yahweh.

Honor and shame qualified as decisive values, emphasizing (1) how status was allocated — via ascription (factors over which we have no control, such as family lineage or gender) or performance (factors over which we do have control, such as education or expressions of piety or bravery), (2) an elevated concern with one's public face, (3) the use of shaming techniques, such as name-calling or public ostracism or malice, as forms of social control, (4) the reality that honor accrued to those whose behavior conformed to accepted norms, and, therefore, (5) the importance of determining accurately the canons by which honor was to be measured.

The gods pervaded everyday life, with "fitting in" measured by participation in the imperial cult and other forms of worship that would be from a Jewish and Christian perspective nothing less than idolatry, and with "atheism" (failure to participate in the sacrifices and meals associated with local and imperial gods) regarded not only as a social imbroglio but a violation of the sacral order that beckoned the often-unpredictable rancor of the gods.

Identity, corporate and personal, was formed in terms of the cultural narrative provided by Rome, with its twin emphases on imperialism and colonization on the one hand, "peace" through "order" on the other. The narrative provided by Rome was totalizing: it absorbed all other cultural narratives, placed itself as the pinnacle of all histories, and harbored no competitors. Edward Said has noted, "neither imperialism nor colonialism is a simple act of accumulation and acqui-

18. P. Brown, *Poverty and Leadership*, pp. 1-9.

sition. Both are supported and perhaps even impelled by impressive ideological formations that include notions that certain territories and people *require* and beseech domination, as well as forms of knowledge affiliated with domination."[19] There is no escaping the central role of Rome (the city) in defining the life-world of even the far reaches of Roman rule (the empire).[20] Here is the center, the navel of the universe. "As a rock creates radiating waves when thrown into a still pond, so the Roman world had circles of radiating spiritual energy."[21]

What happens in the household (that "seed-bed of the state")[22] merits special attention. This is because the orderliness of household relations was both a model for and the basis of order within the empire (with persons "assigned a precise place in a vast system of orders, classes, tribes, and centuries").[23] Moreover, Rome regarded itself as a household with the emperor as reigning male "head of the family."

Given the breadth and depth of Roman influence in Anatolia, together with the enthusiasm with which things Roman were propagated, the presence of Christian communities in the region cannot be understood merely or even primarily in spatial terms. To the contrary, in 1 Peter we have opportunity to take the measure of the encounter of the gospel with a symbolic universe at the center of which stood Rome. Rome ordered life, set boundaries: everyone with a place, everyone in their place. The question is how, with Peter's encouragement, that order might be disestablished and a new order instigated.

It is within this cultural space that Peter names his audience as "strangers in the world of the diaspora" (1:1), persons "dwelling in a strange land" (1:17), and "aliens and strangers in the world" (2:11). In varying ways each of these descriptions points to an essential characteristic of Peter's audience: they are not at home. As Peter develops this metaphor, several features come to the fore:

Life in present circumstances is short-term.

"Citizenship," a category useful for indexing both "status within a community" and "criteria of good conduct," is associated with a heavenly inheritance and not with a Roman province.

19. Said, *Culture and Imperialism*, p. 9.
20. Cf. Griffin, *"Urbs Roma."*
21. Helgeland, "Time and Space," p. 1299.
22. Cicero *On Duties* 1.53-55; cited in Gardner and Wiedemann, eds., *Roman Household,* p. 2.
23. Nicolet, "Citizen," p. 26.

> Diasporic status is the consequence of believers having declared their
> allegiances to a homeland not of Roman creation; they are strangers
> because they refuse any longer to embrace the manner of life into
> which they were born and in which they were reared. They are mis-
> fits.
>
> Refusing the norms of Roman life, they suffer the consequences. They
> suffer *as Christians*.

In order to grasp the significance of the situation Peter envisions, it is important to reflect momentarily on issues of social stratification. In the post-
industrial era, our tendency is to characterize people in economic terms,
using terms like "class" or categories like "annual income" or "relation to
the means of production." With respect to Roman antiquity, M. I. Finley
has observed the relative uselessness of such thinking, not only because relative wealth did not, on its own, define people in these ways, but also because of the virtual absence of what we today might call a "middle class."[24]
For purposes of evaluation of Roman antiquity, "status" is a more useful
category, as it accounts for the determination of social boundaries by
means of positive and negative assessments of honor. Status situation is reflected in the style of life expected of those who "belong," the restrictions
applied to the "inner group" with respect to social interchange with those
within and outside the status circle. Status honor is a register that accounts
for wealth, particularly esteeming landed wealth over earned riches, but
also other factors, such as family heritage, ethnicity, and gender. In the present case, the pivotal factor is none of these. Rather, these are people whose
commitments to the lordship of Jesus Christ have led to transformed dispositions and behaviors that place them on the margins of respectable society.
Their allegiance to Christ has won for them animosity, scorn, and vilification. Their lack of acculturation to prevailing social values marked them as
misfits worthy of contempt. With respect to the portrait Peter painted,
Miroslav Volf clarifies helpfully:

> Christians do not come into their own social world from the outside
> seeking either to accommodate to their new home (like second genera-
> tion immigrants would), shape it in the image of the one they have left
> behind (like colonizers would), or establish a little haven in the strange
> new world reminiscent of the old (as resident aliens would). They are not
> outsiders who either seek to become insiders or maintain strenuously the

---

24. See Finley, *Ancient Economy*.

status of outsiders. Christians are the insiders who have diverted from their culture by being born again.[25]

The consequence is that believers, whether male or female, slave or free, rich or poor, eke out their lives on the margins of respectable society. If they were honorable males, they are dishonored. If they were free, they now have all the access to power and privilege of a slave. If they had wealth, it does them little good in the marketplace of prestige and is likely short-lived, since, although the right kind of wealth might buy status in Roman antiquity, carrying the label of an atheist or other socioreligious deviant is an easy ticket to downward mobility, economically speaking.

People living in this reality face certain challenges and temptations. Identity and boundary maintenance are pivotal: Who are we in relation to them? What is the basis of our constitution as a community? What are our characteristic practices? By what strategies are these maintained? If not to the dispositions and practices of the surrounding populace, then where might believers turn to evaluate attitudes and behavior? If not to the Roman narrative of conquest, colonization, and subjugation, all in the name of peaceful beneficence, then by what hermeneutic might believers make sense of daily life and the passing of years? Equally pressing is the socioreligious challenge confronting diasporic people: the perennial possibility and threat of assimilation and defection. And the stakes are raised for Christians whose commitments and manner of life serve to transform them into social deviants who have contracted the slow-working, malignant cancer of social opposition and maltreatment.

At the end of his letter, Peter announces that he has written for the purpose of "encouraging and bearing witness that this is the true grace of God" (5:12). What is this "true grace of God"? What are the theological resources Peter brings to the table? How has he engaged in the theological task of bearing witness and speaking encouragement within these sociohistorical horizons?

"New Birth into a Living Hope": Peter's "Narrative"

Obviously, 1 Peter is a letter. It does not "tell a story." In what sense, then, can I refer to Peter's "narrative"? "Narrative theology" refers to a constellation of approaches to the theological task typically joined by their antipathy toward forms of theology concerned with the systematic organization of proposi-

---

25. Volf, "Soft Difference," p. 18.

tions and grounded in ahistorical principles, and by their attempt to discern an overall aim and ongoing plot in the ways of God as these are revealed in Scripture and continue to express themselves in history.[26] Hence, even though the form of Peter's discourse is not "narrative," it participates in one — or, better, it presumes and grapples with the grand story of God's engagement with the world and his people for theological purposes. Speaking broadly, this is the story of God's purpose coming to fruition in the whole of God's history with us, from the creation of the world and humanity's falling away from God, through God's repeated attempts to restore his people, culminating in the coming of Jesus of Nazareth and reaching its full crescendo in the final revelation of Christ and the new creation. More pointedly, the question is, What is the narrative Peter recounts?

My interest in narrative centers in large part on the importance of narrative in identity formation. Recent work in neurobiology emphasizes the peculiarly human capacity for and drive toward making *storied sense* of our world and lives. Memory formation is narratively determined, so we naturally explain our behaviors through the historical narratives by which we collaborate to create a sense of ourselves as persons and as a people. Patients who have experienced selected lesions to the brain demonstrate the inability to see what they cannot believe to be true,[27] just as those of us with unaffected brains operate normally with a strong hermeneutical bias on the basis of prior beliefs, so that we actually perceive stimuli when none are physically presented.[28] We humans experience a general deficit of incoming sensory data necessary for an unambiguous interpretation of the object of our perception. This is true from the seemingly more mundane activity of our visual systems to larger-scale hermeneutical concerns, our reflection on and the practices of human understanding. These sensory limitations notwithstanding, our "cortical networks *fill in*. They make their best guess, given the incomplete information. . . . This general principle, expressed colloquially as 'jumping to conclusions,' guides much of human behavior."[29] Various terms name the structures by which we "fill in" — "imagination" ("a basic image-schematic capacity for ordering our experience"[30] or ". . . the power of taking something as something by means of meaningful forms, which are rooted in our history and have the power to disclose truths about life in the

26. See Yandell, ed., *Faith and Narrative*.

27. E.g., Ramachandran, *Human Consciousness*, ch. 2.

28. The importance of "belief" has only begun to be studied empirically; see Schacter and Scarry, eds., *Memory, Brain, and Belief.*

29. Koch, *Quest for Consciousness*, p. 23.

30. M. Johnson, *Body in the Mind*, p. xx.

world"[31]), for example, or "conceptual schemes." To put it differently, life-events do not come with self-contained and immediately obvious interpretations; we have to conceptualize them and we do so in terms of imaginative structures or conceptual patterns that take the form of narrative. Hence, the narratives we tell and embody regulate how we construe the world.

From this perspective, attending to narrative theology, even in our engagement with an epistolary text like 1 Peter, is attending to the power of theology to shape a people's way of making sense of what they experience day-by-day. This does not mean that "ideas" are ruled out of court, but rather that ideas gather meaning within a particular narrative by which imaginative structures are (trans)formed. In this context, narrative representation is identity formation through theological intervention.

That Peter's presentation invites this kind of theological analysis is evident at the most basic level by the way he peppers his discourse with chronological markers, the most explicit being the terms καιρός (*kairos,* "a definite or favorable time," "an opportune time," 1:5, 11; 4:17; 5:6) and χρόνος (*chronos,* "a season," "a period of time during which some activity occurs," 1:17, 20; 4:2, 3).[32] Less obvious but nonetheless important markers of time include the generous use of participles and temporal adverbs. From the outset of Peter's letter, both in 1:3-12 and 1:13-21, the apostle demonstrates an interest in plotting the course of history and locating his audience within it, so as to press home a number of critical theological affirmations: (1) irrespective of present evidence to the contrary, the course of history serves God's aims; (2) God is in fact the sovereign whose purpose will be actualized; (3) present struggles have meaning within the plotline of God's agenda; (4) present struggles are temporary while impending glory is endless; and (5) the present is the arena for Spirit-empowered faithfulness toward God and courageous resistance in the world.

Peter's introductory blessing (1:3-12) is littered with time-oriented terms: "time" (vv. 5, 11), "in the last time" (v. 5), "for a short time" (v. 6), "at the present time" (v. 8), "testify in advance" (v. 11), and "now" (v. 12) — on the basis of which a timeline is easily constructed, thus couching the whole of Peter's message in a particular understanding of "the times." In *the past,* God gave Peter's audience new birth — that is, a reconfigured relationship to himself as their Father and a transformation of life-world that refocused their lives around a future inheritance. *The future,* when Jesus Christ is revealed, signals the cessa-

---

31. Bryant, *Faith and the Play of Imagination,* p. 5.

32. For a similarly historical approach to the question of the propriety of this kind of analysis, see Bauckham, "Reading Scripture."

tion of "various trials" and marks the time when God will reveal salvation, will reveal Jesus Christ in final glory, and will give believers their inheritance. Between past and future, *the present* is known for its onerous trials. At the same time, God's power is *presently* guarding those under duress who, in spite of appearances, are "receiving the goal of faith": salvation.

Similarly, in his presentation of believers as children of a holy God (1:13-21), Peter sketches a temporal map, locating events (or conditions) that figure centrally within the narrative pattern by which Peter orders the lives of his audience.[33] These include:

> *Primordial Time (1:20).* Inscribing the sacrificial death of Jesus into the timeless plan of God, Peter urges that God's own agenda stands behind Jesus' redemptive work, so that the sacrificial death of Jesus provides insight into the very nature of God.
>
> *Time of Ignorance/Futility (1:14, 18).* Misconceiving the nature of God and life before God, they were blinded to what God was doing, so that they were shaped by the coercive power of desires rooted in ignorance.
>
> *Revelation of Jesus at the End of the Ages (1:20).* As the midpoint in a history that spans the period from creation to the final revelation of Jesus Christ, the advent of Jesus Christ and particularly Jesus' suffering and resurrection give meaning to the whole of history.
>
> *Time of Liberation (1:18-19).* Drawing deeply from the well of Israel's life and moving effortlessly among Israel's images of reconciliation and rescue, Peter forges an atonement theology the focus of which is liberation from slavery, not to Egypt, but to an inherited way of life that is empty and characterized by insatiable cravings and idolatry.
>
> *Period of Life as Aliens (1:17).* For those who have been born anew, this can only be a time of living as strangers subject to day-to-day, cancerous slander and bedevilment, an exilic life for persons called to courageous resistance centered on an alternative structuring of time and formative narrative, a rejection of ancestral and contemporary conventions for behavior, and allegiance to a competing god/God.
>
> *Final Revelation of Jesus Christ (1:13).* Peter exposes the eschatological horizons of life for those who have been born anew, providing a reminder that vindication is the certain successor to the suffering of the faithful and directing his audience to live their lives in ways determined by that future.

33. See Green, "Narrating the Gospel."

If we readjust our lens to a wider angle, we can visualize on a larger scale the narrative by which Peter orients the lives of his audience:

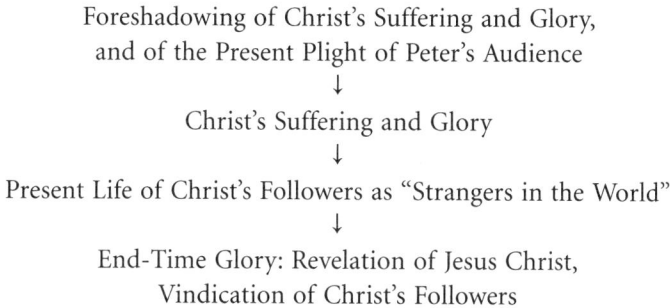

Foreshadowing of Christ's Suffering and Glory,
and of the Present Plight of Peter's Audience
↓
Christ's Suffering and Glory
↓
Present Life of Christ's Followers as "Strangers in the World"
↓
End-Time Glory: Revelation of Jesus Christ,
Vindication of Christ's Followers

From the narrative elements sketched in 1:3-21, the plotline of Peter's narrative theology is obviously capable of more nuance and complexity. But this simplified representation has the advantage of focusing our attention on three affirmations that are clearly central to Peter's work: (1) present circumstances make sense only on the expansive canvas of the whole of God's purpose and activity, from the very foundations of the world to the eschaton; (2) God's aims come into focus in the suffering-glory pattern preeminently disclosed in Christ; and (3) the lives of Christ's followers take their meaning and find their hope in God's purpose — which was realized in the suffering-glory pattern of Christ and is now being recapitulated in his followers. Clearly, the axis of Peter's message is Jesus Christ, whose career discloses the way God gets things done.

What agenda is served by this concern with "the times," this attention to the emplotment of God's story? First, recalling that Peter's audience is primarily Gentile, and so unskilled in rehearsing the story of God's dealings with Israel, Peter works to form them through a particular way of construing their history that is deeply rooted in the eternal plan of God and that takes seriously the formation and nurture of God's people, Israel, through Passover, exodus, and the pattern of reconciliation through sacrifice. For Peter, the only true categories for making sense of daily existence are determined by a particular narrative, the scriptural story. Second, remembering that we tell stories not only to make sense of the world, but to form identity and community, we see that in selecting these particular events and in ordering them in this particular way Peter is set on constructing the identity of the communities to which he has addressed himself. Although we would never confuse Peter's letter with a narrative text, his concern with marking the times suggests an agenda like that of those who use narrative to represent history.[34] In this way, he orients his audience toward the future consumma-tion of God's plan at the same time that he grounds their identity in a divine strategy that predates creation itself. He is already working to collapse the self-evident historical distinctives between Israel of old and these communi-ties of Jesus-followers in the service of a theological unity that conjoins old and new. On account of the initiative of God, manifest in the passion and resurrection of Jesus, these communities stem from the same roots. They are one. The result is a strong sense of continuity with the past, a secure place within the arc of God's gracious purpose, and a firm basis for projecting oneself into a future made certain in Jesus' resurrection from the dead. Third, this concern with future and past has present significance. Peter's at-tention to "the times" carefully articulates the nature of present-day exis-tence — not as an anomaly in God's story nor a challenge to God's faithful-ness, but as an opportunity for identification with Christ and for putting into play the human vocation to imitate the holiness of God.

"To Him Be the Power Forever": God in 1 Peter

The claim that 1 Peter is a thoroughly theocentric letter is often advanced,[35] and rightly so, given Peter's certainty that every creative, providential, and salvific act is God's doing and the way the apostle defines faithful living under the canopy of God's election, God's call to holiness, and in relation to the per-formance of God's will. This is not to shortchange the importance of christol-ogy to the letter, since Christ is the mediator of God's salvation and ongoing beneficence, since in Peter's suggestive formulations of a trinitarian theology Christ shares in God's identity, and since God is known as "the God and Fa-ther of our Lord Jesus Christ" (1:3). Nevertheless, the high status Peter allo-cates to Christ is set within the supremacy of God.[36]

The situation of Peter's audience presses hard on two concerns that be-come central to the image of God he presents. On the one hand, for the most part, they are Gentile in origin, their religious ideas and practices having cut deep ruts in their collective consciousness. Before they received new birth from God, they were firmly shaped by the passions of their inherited way of life (1:14, 18). Some of their cities would have had lively Jewish populations,

---

34. Lowenthal, for example, argues that historiography serves the functions of identity-formation, legitimization, pedagogy, and continuity *(Foreign Country)*.

35. E.g., Elliott, pp. 109-10.

36. So Hurtado, "Christology," p. 173.

with the result that we can assume that the ways of Yahweh and allusions to and citations of Israel's Scriptures in 1 Peter would have been understood and explained within largely Gentile Christian communities. However, Jews were generally not esteemed in these cities, and there is every reason to believe that, prior to their new birth, many in Peter's audience would themselves have been mobilized in opposition to Jews on account of their bizarre religious (including strange eating) habits and their failure to participate in the daily worship practices of the Romans.[37] Having been formed according to deeply ingrained ancestral traditions and living in a world in which those traditions continue to hold sway, what roots will give these followers of Christ the stability they need, both in terms of an identity embedded in antiquity and in terms of dispositions and practices appropriate to their new faith? As van Unnik rightly observed, "Transition from paganism to Judaism meant a transition from one system of ancestral traditions to another. Here it proclaimed a completely new life in Christ."[38] What I want to urge is that Peter addresses this need theologically — that is, by his portrait of God.

On the other hand, we cannot escape the ubiquity of suffering (trials, testings, oppressive speech) in Peter's letter and so in the situation of his audience as he envisions it. As the scriptural tradition admits, experiences of suffering surface questions about the character of God, the meaning of history, and the nature of faithfulness (e.g., Psalms 6, 13, 35, and 74). Peter's presentation of God is concerned with these concerns as well.

God the Lord of History. Peter never refers to God in these terms, but nonetheless affirms God's sovereignty over all, from the creation of the world to the final revelation of Christ and eternal glory. Without engaging in the construction of detailed timelines found among the apocalypticists, Peter is like them with regard to the grand scale with which he paints God's work. God chose Christ the liberator before the creation of the world (1:20; cf. 2:4), is the faithful Creator (4:19), instigated the end of the ages through the liberating work of Christ (1:19-20), raised Jesus from the dead and gave him glory (1:3, 21; 3:21-22), foreknew the status of Peter's audience as elect strangers in the world (1:1-2). Having sent the Spirit (1:12) and liberated them from past futility (1:14, 18), he gave them new birth (1:3, 23) and formed them into his own people (2:5, 9-10). He has reserved a heavenly inheritance for them (1:4) and is present powerfully to guard them through his faithfulness for a salvation ready to be revealed (1:5; cf. 1:9-10); he will restore, strengthen, empower, and secure those who suffer on account of their faith (5:10); he ushers in the

---

37. See, e.g., Levinskaya, *Diaspora Setting,* pp. 137-52.
38. Van Unnik, "Critique of Paganism," p. 141.

eschaton (4:7, 17), will reveal Christ in his glory (1:7, 13; 5:1, 4) and share his incomparable glory with the faithful (1:7; 5:10-11), and is the final arbiter of human performance, the impartial judge to whom believers may entrust themselves (1:17; 2:23; 3:5; 4:5-6; 5:5). Narratives are identified through their beginning, middle, and end, and in the grand narrative of God's work, according to 1 Peter, God is the primary actor at each point: at creation (beginning), redemption (middle, including the formation of Israel as God's people and, through the work of Christ, the extension of Israel's identity to followers of Christ), and final glory (end). "To him be the power forever. Amen" (5:11).

The effects of this theological perspective are several: (1) History is not the arena for the outworking of the capricious gods of the Roman world, but the canvas on which God is actualizing his purpose. (2) The God whose aims and activity span the beginning and end can be trusted not only to fulfill his saving purpose but also to bring justice. This includes the vindication of his own people. God's people, therefore, can entrust themselves to his powerful goodness. This includes resisting the temptations to take upon themselves the role of judge and retaliate against those hostile toward them. "Because God is sovereign, there is not need to seek retaliation or vengeance; their vindication, and consequently the punishment of the unjust, is in God's hands, not theirs."[39] (3) The pain of present trials is not dismissed or minimalized, but is put in perspective. Peter assures his audience that, for those who suffer because of their stubborn, courageous commitment to the will of God, present harm is neither permanent nor ultimate in its effects. "Who, then, will harm you if you become zealous for the good?" (3:13). (4) Even though present trials can be traced to the work of "your adversary, the devil" (5:8), diabolic purpose and activity are circumscribed by a deeper purpose. Suffering is not the whole story, but must be understood within the grand mural of God's aims. Though without reference to 1 Peter, Wolfhart Pannenberg identifies the reality to which Peter points when he writes that "no destructive power is the only determinative ground of the creaturely reality in which it holds sway. Through all other powers and fields of force may be seen also the working of the divine Spirit as the origin of life in the creatures."[40]

God the Father. God is first introduced as "Father" in relation to Peter's audience (1:2), and then as "Father of our Lord Jesus Christ" (1:3). This portrait is continued with reference to the "Father who judges impartially" (1:17) and in the identification of believers as God's children (1:14) through rebirth (1:3, 23). Accordingly, God's actions are consistent with his wisdom and intention and

---

39. Michaels, p. lxvii.
40. Pannenberg, *Systematic Theology,* 2:109.

are the outworking of his great mercy. These three affirmations of God — his redemptive purpose, his compassion toward those in need, and his impartial justice — serve both hermeneutical and promissory functions. Divine choice and alien status are deeply rooted in God's purpose as this comes to expression in the Scriptures, so the dissonance of present life, chosen by God but held in contempt in society, is neither a contradiction of God's plan nor a sign of God's callousness or incapacity to rescue his people, and it will not go unanswered by God. Peter demonstrates that the way of Jesus Christ was the path of suffering leading to vindication and glory (e.g., 2:20; 4:13-14; 5:1, 10). Moreover, he urges that the model of Jesus Christ interprets and is interpreted by the Scriptures of Israel (cf. 1:10-12, 19 [Isa 52:13–53:12]; 2:4-10 [Ps 118:22; Isa 8:14]; 2:21-25 [Isa 52:13–53:12]; 4:1-2, 17) and thus discloses the nature of God's overarching salvific plan. Hence, it is not surprising that this same pattern — suffering leading to vindication and glory — is descriptive of those who follow in Christ's footsteps (e.g., 4:12-14; 5:10). As a promissory note, Peter's theology assures his audience of God's impending intervention to vindicate his people and usher them into his eternal glory. As a theological hermeneutic, his portrait of God the Father provides the pattern by which to render present existence meaningful within the framework of God's past work of liberation and promise of an incomparable and inviolable inheritance.

The identification of God as "Father of our Lord Jesus Christ" reflects the gospel traditions that bear witness to Jesus' filial relationship with God (e.g., Matt 7:21; 10:32-33; Mark 1:9-11; 9:7; 14:36; Luke 2:49; 10:21-22). By means of this father-son predication, the god to whom Peter refers is thus identified as the God known to us in Jesus Christ. To speak of God as "Father" directs attention to God's faithfulness to his promises and to the beneficence of God available in Jesus. According to Peter, both Jesus and believers find their identity in relationship to God, but they do so in different ways. Whereas Jesus' relationship to God is immediate, the fatherhood of God in relation to believers is mediated through Jesus Christ. Peter's affirmation of the fatherhood of God is implicated in a teleological trajectory, tied as it is to God's work in the past, present, and future. God's fatherhood is evident in the past in God's raising Jesus from the dead, is on exhibition in the present through his guarding believers for salvation and the evangelistic offer of grace, and is the basis of future hope with respect to the salvation that will be revealed at the last time.

God the Arbiter of Honor. Again, we have introduced language foreign to 1 Peter in order to summarize several key affirmations. These center on divine election (1:1; 2:4, 9-10; 5:13), the holiness of God (1:15-16), the fear of God (1:17; 2:17-18; 3:2, 6, 16; cf. 3:14), and the will of God (2:15; 3:17; 4:2, 19; cf. 4:3). Of these phrases, only one centers explicitly on God's character — the holiness of God — but all speak to a transformed pattern of thinking and behavior centered on God. In Peter's agonistic world, where one's identity is so comprehensively determined in relation to public opinion, the construction of life around God's character and purpose is the site of real metamorphosis.

Holiness ". . . refers to the radical otherness of Yahweh, who may not be easily approached, who may not be confused with anyone or anything else, and who lives alone in a prohibitive zone where Israel can enter only guardedly, intentionally, and at great risk."[41] In Israel's Scriptures, God's holiness is the basis for divinely initiated election and covenant, rescue and advocacy, but also Yahweh's call to Israel that their relationship with him must be on his terms: "You shall be holy, for I the LORD your God am holy" (Lev 19:2).[42] Israel must be a different people because their god is a different God.

The consequence is a topsy-turvy way of finding significance in the world. In the community defined by faithfulness to Christ, what is honored and valued contrasts with Roman norms. The dispositions and practices to be cultivated, together with the canons for esteem and identification within the community, find little parallel in the universe of Rome. Christ himself is the supreme example of this transformed perspective on reality: "rejected by humans but in God's perspective elect, honored" (2:4).

Taking their cue from God's otherness, these other phrases — reverence for God, election, and God's will — refer to a divinely determined status set in opposition to the values embodied in Roman practices. As such, they constitute a response of resistance centered on an alternative structuring of "the way things are," and provoke a rejection of ancestral and contemporary conventions for behavior. They bear witness to Christian allegiance to a competing god/God embodied in a manner of life inspired by his own character and made possible by a liberation that reverberates with echoes of the story of Israel's exodus from Egypt. Reverent fear of God, then, is rooted in images of God's gracious response to cries for help rather than those of threatening judgment, allowing Peter to raise the specter of divine judgment in order to counter concerns with social standing in his world. Pronouncements from the court of public opinion or the valuation of the holy God: Which will shape the daily life of Christ's followers? "Fear of God" has to do with the fundamental orientation of one's life toward God and according the highest value to one's relationship with God so that it determines all else, and not with intimidation, anxious dread, or terror.

41. Brueggemann, *Theology of the OT*, p. 288.
42. See Brueggemann, *Theology of the OT*, pp. 288-93.

God, Who Abhors Idolatry. In the Scriptures of Israel, alongside God's holiness, his "otherness," stands his jealousy; he allows no rivals. "You shall worship no other god, because the Lord, whose name is Jealous, is a jealous God" (Exod 34:14). This quality of God's character is recognized in the unrelenting critique of idolatry in Peter's letter. True, the term "idolatry" appears only once, in the vice list of 4:3, but it stands in the background and foreground of the letter in a number of ways. In Peter's world, much of cultic life was public and inclusive, involving everyone in the view of the whole community. This includes practices of the imperial cult in the Anatolian peninsula, celebrated in temples, but also in the open, center squares of cities, for example, and in theaters and in stadia. Householders performed sacrifices on altars set outside their houses during parades. Even foreigners and non-citizens might be included. Living in cramped quarters and on a subsistence diet, many found in banquets held in relation to sacrifices and religious festivals their only real opportunities for significant social interaction and ample meat and wine. It was practically impossible that persons could fail to participate without their absence being noted and public judgment passed accordingly. Opting out of cultic practices, then, was not an easy decision either to make or to maintain.[43] Within Jewish and Christian discourse, idolatry is often associated with sexual impropriety and greed,[44] so it is not immaterial that Peter distances his audience from their past sexual misdeeds (4:3) and insists that ecclesial leaders must exercise shepherd care without greed (5:2). Idolatry can also be labeled as "blasphemy" (4:4; see Isa 66:3 LXX).

The Triune God. Though it would be a mistake to suggest that, writing in the first century, Peter embraced the trinitarian formulations to be generated in subsequent centuries, we can nevertheless see both how Peter anticipates those formulations and how Peter's theology is hospitable to a reading that takes its point of departure from the ecumenical creeds. That is, far from obscuring our understanding of 1 Peter, the classical theological tradition helps us to identify the relation of Father, Christ, and Spirit, which otherwise might have escaped our attention.[45]

Thus, in 1:1-2, the existence and status of the Christian community is the outgrowth of the Father's purpose, the Spirit's sanctifying work, and the redemption of Christ. In 1:3-12, Peter identifies God the Father as the primary actor who has given new birth, raised Jesus from the dead, reserved an inheritance, guarded his people, and sent the Holy Spirit; portrays Christ as the me-

---

43. Borgen, *Early Christianity,* pp. 40-43; J. Marcus, "Idolatry," pp. 153-54.
44. See, e.g., Rosner, "Idolatry," pp. 571-72, 574; J. Marcus, "Idolatry," pp. 154-57.
45. See Moltmann's "trinitarian hermeneutics" (*Trinity,* pp. 61-65).

diator who, through his journey through suffering to glory, mediates God's salvific work; and identifies the Holy Spirit as "the Spirit of Christ," thus affirming both Christ's preexistence (cf. 1:20) and the intimate association of both the Father and Christ with the Spirit. In this way, Peter speaks of Christ as the one whose activity was manifest long ago through the Holy Spirit, speaking of Jesus at the very point at which we might have anticipated that he would speak of God (cf. 4:14). Similarly, in Peter's exegetical work in 1:23–2:3, Peter identifies Christ as the "Lord" named in the Scriptures (cf. Ps 34:8; Isa 40:8); the "word" is the good news concerning the Lord Jesus (1:25), who is the Lord whose goodness has been tasted (2:3). Here again Jesus stands in the place of God. By means of his resurrection from the dead and "having gone into heaven," Christ is at the right hand of God with all angels, powers, and authorities subordinate to him and is installed as co-regent with God (3:21-22). 1 Peter 4:11 and 5:11 witness parallel expressions of praise, the one to Christ and the other to God. Rounding out this portrait, we find in 1 Peter that the Spirit guides the appropriation of the Scriptures, with the result that one embraces a christological hermeneutic that finds in its pages the suffering, death, and glorious vindication of Christ (1:10-12; 4:12-14); and enables faithful living in the present (1:1-2; 4:12-14). Given the pressures of exilic living, holiness — engagement in the world of nations as the people belonging uniquely to Yahweh and therefore representing his character and ways — is possible though the liberating work of Christ and the agency of the Spirit.

What does this mean for our understanding of God in 1 Peter? First, working within the monotheism of Second Temple Judaism, Peter joins other first-century Christian theologians in identifying Christ as the object of worship[46] — not in opposition to Yahweh nor as a deity alongside Yahweh. Hurtado refers to this as a "'binitarian mutation' in Roman-era Jewish monotheism" that, nonetheless, had a home within contemporary Judaism; he urges, "These devotees to Jesus . . . proclaimed his supreme status as God's unique 'Son' and their 'Lord' entirely in terms of the actions and will of the one God."[47]

Second, the God who is known on account of his revelatory activity in relation to his creatures — that is, in the narrative (or drama) of his engagement with his people — is the God disclosed in the divine drama as "persons" and not only "person." The faith of Israel, so central to Peter's message, is cen-

46. Wainwright urges that "worship constituted the primary locus of Christ's recognition as Lord by Christian believers" (*Doxology*, p. 47), relating this to the development of the doctrine of Christ's divinity (pp. 45-86).

47. Hurtado, *Historical Questions*, p. 53; more fully, see idem, *Lord Jesus Christ.*

tered in its affirmation of the oneness of God (Deut 6:4), but this is not contrary to Peter's theology. Rather, this faith is explicated through God's resurrection of Jesus from the dead and his enthronement of Jesus at his right hand.[48] Moreover, though hidden to people of old, this same Christ was present by means of the Spirit to inspire the writings that would be actualized in his suffering and resurrection, demonstrating that the prophets of Israel and Peter bore witness to the same divine reality. The actors in the divine drama, then, are three: Yahweh, Christ, and the Spirit — proclaimed narratively in relationship to one another, with the Father sending Christ and the Spirit, Christ identified with the Father, and the Spirit identified with Christ.

What does it mean that Christ is "identified" with the Father, and the Spirit with Christ? On the negative side, I am resisting both essentialist and ontological categories of personal identity and refusing the category of "function" that allows for what one "does" to be segregated from who one "is." On the positive side, I am embracing notions of personhood that depend on categories of relationality and narrative continuity. In addition, I am embracing a definition of agency that refuses any dichotomy between performance and sentiment (or character).[49] God discloses his identity in relation to his creatures, but the identity he discloses is one in which Father, Christ, and Spirit share divine agency in the service of the one purpose of God in relation to his creation.

Clearly, Peter is not engaged in speculative theology or in an *apologia* for a trinitarian doctrine of God. Comments relative to our interest work more at the level of assumption than explicit affirmation, a feature of Peter's discourse fully congruent with his largely working from within widespread Christian thought. Peter gives no indication that he thinks he has departed from "what everyone believes" when he writes offhandedly of the preexistence of Christ or when he composes a doxology in praise of Christ (as to God). What purpose is served, then, by these trinitarian ruminations? They serve Peter's theological agenda in many ways. In his references to Father, Son and Holy Spirit, the apostle articulates the single aim of God, the certain identity of the path from suffering to glory as the "true grace of God" (5:12), the way of Christ as the hermeneutical perspective by which to render meaningful the paradoxical lives of "chosen strangers in the world," the mediation

---

48. See Jenson, *Systematic Theology*, 1:63-89.

49. Beginning with observations made by Bauckham *(God Crucified)* and Thompson *(God,* pp. 17-55), my understanding of identity has been shaped on the negative side by C. Taylor, *Sources of the Self,* and on the positive side by Di Vito, "Old Testament Anthropology"; R. Martin and Barresi, "Personal Identity"; Rorty, ed., *Identities;* K. Berger, *Identity;* Bynum, *Metamorphosis.*

of God's salvation (past, present, and future) through Christ and the Spirit, the unbroken narrative of God's redemptive work, and the enormity of the divine resources brought to bear on behalf of persons suffering on account of their allegiance to Christ.

"The Sufferings Coming to Christ and His Subsequent Glories": Peter's Christology

In 1 Peter, all roads lead to and through Christ. For the apostle, God's character is known through Christ and God's purpose is effected by Christ; the end time is inaugurated by Christ, Christ is veiled but active as mediator of God's benef- icence in the present, and the End will be fully actualized in the final revelation of Christ; the Christian community finds in Christ its basis, model, and end; and Christ, not the emperor, is the Lord to whom allegiance and honor are due. In its three major christological passages (1:18-21; 2:21-25; 3:18-22), the let- ter documents its key christological declarations: the liberating death of Christ, the paradigmatic suffering of Christ, and the character of Christ's jour- ney through suffering to glory — all for our salvation.[50] Peter's christological affirmations recognize the supremacy of God the Father, but locate Christ at the center of the letter's rhetoric; indeed, at crucial points, Christ stands in the place of God (1:11, 25; 2:3). In its main outlines, Peter's christology is very much at home in the NT: though righteous, Christ suffered and died on a cross; he was raised up by God and enthroned at God's right hand; his death, resurrec- tion, and ascension are for our salvation; the manner of his life is exemplary for Christian life; there can be no better epitaph than that of participation in his suffering and glory; his revelation in glory will mark the End; and all of this is the outworking of God's overarching plan.[51]

Given the varieties of messianic ideas in Second Temple Judaism,[52] it is worth inquiring into the particular understanding of "Christ" we find in 1 Pe- ter. An outline would include the following:

> the function of the word "Christ" as a virtual name or second name for Jesus, with a titular sense urged only with reference to the sufferings of "the Christ" in 4:13; 5:1 and to scriptural anticipations regarding Christ in 1:11; 3:15 (alluding to Isa 8:13);

---

50. Cf. Goppelt, *Theology*, pp. 176-78.
51. Similarly, Achtemeier, "Christology," pp. 140-41.
52. Cf., e.g., Charlesworth, ed., *Messiah;* Neusner et al., eds., *Judaisms and Their Messiahs.*

the status of Christ as the Lord (1:3, 25; 2:3; 3:15) worthy of praise (4:11) and as one with authority to "send" Peter as his representative (1:1);

the innocence or righteousness of Christ and his obedience to his Father (1:2, 3);

Christ's inauguration of the end of the ages, the promise of his revelation at the End, and his veiled presence in the interim (1:7, 13; 4:13; 5:1, 4);

Christ's preexistence (1:11, 20);

Christ's exemplary and effective death (1:2, 19; 2:21-25; 3:18-22; 4:1; 5:1), including the interpretation of Christ's sufferings as "woes" that inaugurate the End (4:12-19);

Christ's vindication by God and the salvific ramifications of his resurrection and ascension (1:3, 11; 2:4; 3:18-22; 5:1); and

Christ as mediator (especially 2:5; 3:16; 4:11; 5:10, 14).

Set against the backdrop of messianic ideas in first-century Judaism, four motifs come into sharper focus. First, at the most general level, "Christ" or "Messiah" would have been used in Jewish tradition and thought to designate a divinely appointed mediator of eschatological salvation. Although never sundered from this basic Jewish sense, "Christ" for 1 Peter is the focus of devotion in a way unparalleled in previous and contemporary Jewish literature. Among contemporary Jews whose expectations for God's intervention to restore Israel included a messianic figure (or figures), such hopes were invariably set within a larger network of expectation regarding God's eschatological intervention to vindicate his people. Among his followers, however, the person of Christ himself was central. This was true to such a degree that, irrespective of how they might have spoken of themselves, they quickly became known as "Christians" (4:16; Acts 11:26; 26:28). Speaking of the fire of Rome, Tacitus reports that

> Nero fastened the guilt and inflicted the most exquisite tortures on a class hated for their abominations, called Christians by the populace. Christus, from whom the name had its origin, suffered the extreme penalty during the reign of Tiberius at the hands of one of our procurators, Pontius Pilatus, and a most mischievous superstition, thus checked for the moment, again broke out not only in Judaea, the first source of the evil, but even in Rome, where all things hideous and shameful from every part of the world find their center and become popular. (*Annals* 15.44)

Coined by persons hostile to Jesus' followers by way of denigrating them for their worship of one who experienced the ultimate humiliation of execution as a criminal on a Roman cross, among his followers the label "Christian" would come to be embraced as an honorable way to identify and to be identified with Christ. This is a perspective shared by Peter's christology.

Second, however, the means by which that salvation is mediated would have been surprising. Peter speaks of the journey of Christ through suffering to glory so often that our ears might become habituated to it. The combination of these words "Christ" and "suffering," a commonplace in 1 Peter, is nonetheless jarring. This is because, for both Jew and Gentile, Jesus' crucifixion would have branded him in the most ignoble terms (e.g., 1 Cor 1:23). In their depiction of the ordeal Jesus endured in his suffering and death, the Gospel records make this clear by focusing on the myriad attempts to dishonor Jesus: spitting on him (Matt 26:67; 27:30; Mark 14:65; 15:19), striking him in the face and head (Matt 26:67; Mark 14:65; Luke 22:63), ridiculing him (Matt 27:29, 31, 41; Mark 15:20, 31), insulting him (Matt 27:44; Mark 15:32; Luke 22:65), and derisively mocking him (Mark 15:16-20, 29-32; Luke 22:65; 23:11, 35-37); he even suffers the humiliation of having been abandoned by his closest friends. Executed publicly at a major crossroads or on a well-trafficked artery, devoid of clothing, denied burial, and left to be eaten by birds and beasts, victims of crucifixion were subject to optimal, unmitigated, vicious ridicule. Whereas the word "christ" had the basic sense of "anointed one," and whereas in traditions that had developed from the Scriptures of Israel, the term would have signified the most honorable status for God's envoy, for Peter "christ" is unmistakably enmeshed in conventional notions of dishonor and rejection. Nevertheless, it is precisely this ignominious suffering and death that is effective for liberating God's people. And it is this humiliated, spurned Christ whom God vindicates, raises up, and enthrones.[53]

Third, in the development of Jewish messianism in the two centuries before the advent of Christ, God's people learned to identify transcendent figures as eschatological agents of salvation, typically borrowing from some of the more enigmatic passages in Israel's Scriptures. These include Melchizedek, "priest of God Most High" (Gen 14:18-19), about whom almost nothing is known, but who reappears in Second Temple Jewish literature as a messianic figure; and "One Like a Son of Man," apparently Yahweh's authorized vice-

---

53. This is not to say that Peter's portrait of Christ is without precedent in Israel's Scriptures and interpretive traditions. The pattern of the Persecuted and Vindicated Righteous has deep roots in Israel's Scriptures (e.g., Genesis 37, and the Suffering Righteous One of the Psalms, Isa 52:13–53:12; Daniel 3, 6), and in Second Temple literature (e.g., Wisdom 2, 4-5; see Nickelsburg, *Resurrection*). The innovation we find in 1 Peter and in early Christian texts more generally is the attribution of this pattern specifically to "the Messiah."

regent (Dan 7:13-14).[54] Without betraying any direct dependence on those texts, 1 Peter nonetheless portrays Christ as more-than-human, especially in its references to his preexistence (1:11, 20), his conquering of Death and Hades, his status vis-à-vis "the powers," and his enthronement (3:18-22). It almost goes without saying that this emphasis on Christ's transcendence in no way undermines his humanity in 1 Peter; indeed, if anything, it is the latter that is most on display, with the apostle's stubborn emphasis on Christ's exemplary suffering.

Fourth, as in Jewish tradition, so in 1 Peter, the Scriptures of Israel provide many of the predicates for God's agent of deliverance. However, the usual accretions are lacking. Identification of Christ as Son of God or with other, related language, such as Son of David, is lacking. That is, we find little to suggest an identification of Christ with expectations of a royal messianic figure; neither does Christ fulfill the prophetic or priestly roles we sometimes find among descriptions of the Messiah. Although Christ is presented as an alternative "lord" to that of the urban elites of Peter's world or to the conventional notion of Caesar's supremacy, and although following Christ entails engagement in courageous resistance against Roman values and practices, we find nothing in 1 Peter with which to compare the portraits of Christ in military garb, slaying Israel's enemies, evident in *Psalms of Solomon* 17–18 or *2 Baruch*.[55] Instead, Peter interprets the "stone" of Isa 8:14 in messianic terms (2:6; cf. Ps 118:22); and Christ is the "righteous one" (3:18; cf. Isa 53:11), Yahweh's Suffering Servant (2:21-25; e.g., Isa 53:4, 6, 7, 9, 12), whose sacrificial death brings liberation (1:2, 18-19; 2:24; e.g., Exod 12:5-7; 24:8; Lev 16:15-16).

This accent on Christ's suffering is crucial for Peter's message to a Christian audience whose faithfulness to God has as its immediate consequence marginal existence in the world. Peter develops the suffering of Christ in three ways that have immediate ramifications for the situation he addresses:

> *Christ, Model of Innocent Suffering (2:19-20; 3:16-17; 4:1-2, 13-16).* Though righteous, Christ suffered at the hands of those whose disbelief sets them in opposition to the will and ways of God. He exemplifies faithfulness in suffering both in his refusal to retaliate and on account of the undeserved character of his suffering.
>
> *Christ, Model of Effective Suffering: Christ's suffering was effective as the basis of liberation (1:2, 19; 3:18).* Analogously, the suffering of Christ's followers is a form of witness with the potential of turning unbeliev-

---

54. See Nickelsburg, *Ancient Judaism*, pp. 97-106.
55. See *2 Baruch* 29:3; 30:1; 39:7; 40:1; 72:2.

ers to God (2:12, 15; 3:1-2). Moreover, the suffering of Christ's followers is a participation in the suffering of Christ — that is, in the messianic woes by which the age of salvation is actualized (4:12-19).

*Christ, Model of the Vindication of the Suffering Righteous (1:11; 2:20; 4:13-
14; 5:1, 10)*. The journey of Christ is proof that suffering on account of
one's faithfulness to God is neither the whole nor the end of the
story. Rather, suffering is a precursor to glory. Vindication is neither
rescue from suffering nor does it come in spite of suffering; rather,
the path to vindication and glory is through suffering.

As central as Christ's suffering is to Peter's christology, it is only one
node in the narrative Peter sketches. Of the various elements of the story of
Christ from which Peter might have drawn, he documents the following:

the preexistence of Christ (1:11, 20),
the advent of Christ (1:13) and his "faithfulness" in his earthly sojourn
(1:2; this includes various allusions to the teaching of Christ — e.g.,
the love command [3:8-9]),
the suffering of Christ (1:2, 11, 19; 2:4, 7, 21-25; 3:18-19; 4:1, 13; 5:1),
Christ's proclamation to the spirits/deceased (3:19-20; 4:6),
the resurrection of Christ (1:3, 13, 21; 3:21),
the ascension and enthronement of Christ (3:22), and
the (final) revelation of Christ in glory (1:7, 13; 5:1).

Significantly, Peter's is a christological narrative that reaches from "before the
creation of the world" (1:20) to "the last time" (1:5), and which therefore plots
a metanarrative by which the whole of reality is measured. Accordingly, Peter's christology calls for a reevaluation of all human systems of judgment
and valuation, highlighting instead God's choice of the marginal and rejected.
It militates against the totalizing metanarratives plotted by such human institutions as the empire, bent on ordering the whole of human life in subjugation to the dispositions and practices it sanctions. It universalizes the story of
Israel so as to render it the tale of God's people, now christologically determined; accordingly, Israel's "difference" from "the Gentiles" is not dismissed,
but reoriented in relation not only to the holiness of God (1:14-16) but also to
dispositions and behaviors that "sanctify Christ" (3:15). In this way, christology orders both the nature of the new reality God has inaugurated in the advent of Christ and the character of behavior of those who follow Christ.[56]

56. See Acthemeier, p. 66.

Moreover, the christological narrative Peter plots is both open and closed — closed with respect to what God's purpose is and the certainty of its actualization at the End, open with respect to the twists and turns the narrative will take on account of human agency and particularly with respect to who will demonstrate themselves to be faithful (or not) to the will and ways of God. This means that, at its most basic, Peter's narrative is an invitation whose entry is new birth through Christ's resurrection, whose journey is exilic life and a share in the sufferings of Christ, and whose end is a share in the glory revealed in Christ. It is a narrative, then, that invites habitation in this sense, that the divinely determined story of Christ, which both interprets and is interpreted by Israel's scriptural story, is the narrative that most decisively shaped and gives meaning to the life of the Christian community and its members.[57]

"Spirit of Christ, Spirit of Glory": The Holy Spirit in 1 Peter

Two major challenges of diasporic living are the threat of assimilation and the concomitant need to pursue a holy life, and the need to give meaning to the struggles of life in the diaspora. Although 1 Peter does not refer to the Holy Spirit often, its understanding of the Spirit nonetheless tracks with these two concerns.[58] As the divine agent of sanctification and the enabler of scriptural interpretation, the work of the Holy Spirit is, in 1 Peter, intimately tied to faithful life as strangers in a strange land.

"Making holy" is an important feature of Peter's instruction (1:15-16, 19, 22; 2:5, 9; 3:15), and Peter makes clear that the agent of sanctification is the Spirit (1:1-2). The apostle, in fact, maps his readers by locating them "in the sanctification of the Spirit" or "in the realm of holiness engendered by the Holy Spirit" (1:2). That the Spirit is powerful to effect this metamorphosis is underscored by the past work of the Spirit in the evangelization of Peter's audience (1:12) and by the agency of the Spirit in raising Jesus from the dead (3:18). Indeed, one of Peter's most unambiguous descriptions of the Spirit is in terms of the divine power at work in people — an emphasis that underscores the status of both new birth and "making holy" as divine gift.[59]

---

57. On this notion of "habitation," see Wolterstorff, "Living within a Text."

58. For bibliography on the pneumatology of 1 Peter and for more detail see Green, "Living as Exiles."

59. This concern is picked up as a key emphasis of Wesleyan-Methodist theology — cf., e.g., Klaiber and Marquardt, *Living Grace*, pp. 194-96, 285-309. See also Moltmann, *Spirit of Life*, pp. 174-75.

In two texts, Peter conjoins the work of the Spirit with the appropriation of the Scriptures: 1:10-12; 4:12-14. In 1:10-12, Peter sets out how the Scriptures of Israel must be read — namely, as "testifying in advance to the sufferings coming to Christ and his subsequent glories" and in continuity with the faith communities comprising Peter's audience, a continuity guaranteed by the Holy Spirit. What Peter's readers require is a way to locate their present, difficult circumstances within a web of meaning that will encourage persistent fidelity. Ready to hand were ways of construing the world that undermined any notion of their status as God's elect: How could they attract hostility and rejection if they were blessed with divine honor? Required is an alternative narrative, which Peter provides in terms of a particular reading of the biblical story. The story of salvation is this: the prophets who prophesied in advance, testified to the sufferings destined for Christ and the subsequent glory. How do we know that this reading of the Israel story is true? The Spirit validates it. They prophesied through the Spirit, and the gospel message, which embodies this story, was brought by means of the Spirit. What is more, the same Spirit at work long ago is currently at work in the community of believers, and so provides for a consistent witness to the same reality. The result is not a collection of prophecies in search of fulfillment, nor are Israel's Scriptures categorized as "sources of information" for Peter's theological work. Instead, Israel's Scriptures themselves are identified as kerygmatic witness, with congruence over time in testimony to God's aim guaranteed by the Holy Spirit, that enabler of authentic exegesis of Israel's story, Israel's Scriptures.

In 4:12-14, then, the apostle presents a case study in scriptural interpretation whereby he shapes the theological imagination of his readers. First, he interprets their suffering as a participation in the messianic woes of the end time. Although no biblical text is cited, Peter's thesis represents an exegesis of the scriptural expectation of the calamities that would accompany the inauguration of the age of salvation. Second, Peter borrows the language of Isa 11:2 to insist that suffering for Christ is the occasion of the anointing of the Spirit. There was already a tradition of interpreting Isa 11:2 with reference to a messianic figure, and here Peter appropriates the Isaianic text with reference to the suffering messianic community. This is unsurprising since he has already joined the messiahship of Jesus with the Isaianic suffering Servant of Yahweh and his interpretation of the character of Christian discipleship with the pattern of the Servant (2:22-25). Hostility and suffering ("the fiery ordeal") are set within a narrative determined by an exegesis that writes the way of suffering for the sake of Christ into the way of Isaiah's messianic ruler. Rather than allowing the perhaps more probable view that suffering and dishonor contravened the status of the elect before God, this exegesis appropriates the promise of the Spirit to rest on the believer precisely in their distress.

Beyond these two major concerns, a few summary remarks are possible. In an unusual juxtaposition of predicates, the Spirit who is "sent from heaven" (1:12) is the "Spirit of Christ" (1:11) and the "Spirit of God" (4:14). Peter thus demonstrates clearly that the Spirit must be understood intimately in relation to the Father and Christ within Peter's portrait of the triune God. At the same time, though the Spirit acts as a person within the divine drama, Peter devotes little energy toward developing the Spirit's distinct identity. Nevertheless, it is clear that, if salvation is the gift of the Father, then it is grounded in the redemptive work of Christ and is both mediated to persons and effected in the lives of believers and the believing community by the Spirit. The power of the Spirit to bless believers in their suffering is a guarantee of the glory to come: the God who anoints with the Spirit in troubling circumstances in the present is the same God who invites his people to share in his glory in the End. But the anointing of the Spirit cannot be considered either a prophylactic against or a medicament for suffering. This, after all, is the Spirit of Christ — that is, the Spirit whose character and activity conforms to that of Christ, who entered into glory by means of the *Via Dolorosa*.

"Love One Another Deeply and Unceasingly":
1 Peter and the Community of Believers

The word "church" (ἐκκλησία, *ekklēsia*) appears 114 times in the NT, but never in 1 Peter. Nevertheless, the message of 1 Peter is ecclesially oriented and ecclesially determined, more so than most other NT documents. The language Peter uses to identify and define the community of Christ's followers aggregates around two poles: appellatives typical of God's people in Israel's Scriptures and the familial metaphor. Regarding the first, the most impressive constellation of images is found in 2:9-10:

> You, on the other hand, are an elect clan, a royal priesthood, a holy nation, a people for God's possession, so that you might announce the wondrous acts of the one who called you out of darkness into his marvelous light — you who once were not a people but are now the people of God, who once were not shown mercy but now have been shown mercy.

Additionally, Peter's audience is comprised of God's elect (1:1, 16; 3:9; 5:10; cf. 5:13), strangers in the diaspora (1:1), those who have entered a covenant initiated by God (1:2) and await their inheritance (1:3; 3:9). They constitute "a spiritual house" and "are being built to be a holy priesthood, in order to offer spiritual sacrifices" (2:5). Christian women are "children of Sarah" (3:6). By means of baptism, believers are typologically related to Noah and his family, rescued from the flood (3:20-21). Those outside the community of believers are "Gentiles" (2:12; 4:3). As Achtemeier has observed, for Peter, "the language and hence the reality of Israel pass without remainder into the language and hence the reality of the new people of God."[60]

1 Peter is also the home of numerous images of family and household. These include:

> expressions making use of the term οἶκος (*oikos*, "household") or one of its cognates: "household of God" (4:17), "household slaves" (2:18), "sharing a home with" (3:7), "(household) stewards" (4:10; see also 2:5, where "spiritual house" more likely refers to the temple);
>
> deployment of the form of the "household code" (2:13–3:12) to instruct the audience regarding the character of their engagement in the world;
>
> images of "new birth" (1:3, 23) and growth (2:2), together with the identification of God as "Father" (1:2, 3, 17); and
>
> familial language and terms of endearment: "children" (1:14), "brotherly love" (1:22; 3:8), "born anew" (1:23), "parentage" (or "seed," 1:23), "newborn babies" (2:2), "mature as children" (2:2), "brotherhood" (2:17; 5:9), "hospitality" (4:9), "brother" (5:12), "son" (5:13), and the "kiss of love" (5:14).

While reserving for later discussion questions related to the status of the faithful community within larger society and Peter's vision of the community's comportment within the world, here I want to draw attention to other aspects of the nature of ecclesial life resident in these descriptors.

First, the apostle leaves no doubt as to the origin of the church. It is a community called into being by God. It owes its existence to the purpose of the Father, realized in the liberating work of Christ and the transforming work of the Spirit. Set in relation to the "associations" and "guilds" of the Greco-Roman world, not the religious character of the church per se but its

---

60. Achtemeier, p. 69. Achtemeier is less helpful, however, in his arguing for Israel as the "controlling metaphor" of 1 Peter (pp. 69-72; similarly, idem, "Newborn Babes"). In this, he seeks to counter the thesis of T. W. Martin that the controlling metaphor of 1 Peter is the diaspora *(Metaphor and Composition)* — a worthy objective, perhaps, but one that works under the faulty assumption that 1 Peter has (or needs) a "controlling metaphor."

manifestly divine origin would have special significance. Given the marginal nature of Peter's audience of believers, the apostle's repeated reminder of the firm mooring of the church to God's gracious initiative would have provided crucial consolation.

Closely related, the identification of Christians with the building of a "spiritual house" (2:5) is reminiscent of God's promise of a new community, a promise to be realized in God's restoration of his people and institution of his righteous rule. And related to this is the expectation — found in Israel's Scriptures but developed more expansively in the Second Temple period — of a new temple, replacing the old, to be built by the Messiah.[61] In 2:4-6, we find parallel, matching christological and ecclesiological predications, not so much to emphasize the church as "construction project" (which, in any case, is not otherwise developed in the letter) but to underscore the identification of Christ with the community of his followers, with Christ as its cornerstone.[62]

Second, we may remind ourselves of the importance of identity and boundary maintenance in exilic life: Who are *we* in relation to *them?* What is the basis of *our* constitution as a community? The world within which Peter's audience dwells is qualified by the socioreligious threat confronting a people challenged with the recurrent threat of assimilation and defection. Under such circumstances, a heightened sense of community identity is not only natural but critical. Peter thus anchors his audience in the solid granite of Israel's ancient story, inscribing them into the story of Israel, including the liberation associated with exodus as well as the hope of New Exodus; providing them with a strong sense of identity in unbroken connection to the ancient past; and nurturing in them a sure hope in a faithful God. Moreover, as exilic identity is a matter of disciplined life oriented toward survival as a distinct people, so, in the present, Peter urges his audience to embody the call to Israel in exodus and exile to be holy in the midst of Gentiles.

The wealth of Peter's descriptors takes seriously the need for clear identity markers among a people whose experiences of opposition among the general Anatolian population would have undermined any conventional claim to status before God and could have splintered their experience of oneness. Characterizing them with the language of election and of kinship urges the identification of a family of believers called to faithful testimony in the face of hostility.

Third, these descriptors establish, assert, and uphold relationships between Peter and his audience, promoting solidarity and kinship within the

---

61. See above on 2:4-10.
62. See Strecker, *Theology of the NT,* pp. 637-38.

communities of the letter's destination. Such language projects onto relationships a desired outcome but also is powerful to shape relationships in the direction of that ideal, so we can see how Peter is sculpting expectations regarding household order in fresh directions. He does this in the choice of qualities he projects into the communities of Christians to whom he addresses this letter, qualities that place a premium on concord and mutual affection while countermanding concerns for self-protection that lead people to ensure that their social inferiors remain in their place. Peter's interest in unceasing love is focused in part on the practice of hospitality within the Christian community. The house is a place of gathering for communal worship, for sanctuary, and for shared meals — the latter of significance both for meeting the needs of the hungry within the exilic community and for cultivating familial ties. Antagonism is the experience of believers in the world and is not to characterize life within the Christian family.

Peter's larger agenda is that his audience be conformed into the example of Christ, in whose suffering and death all of these qualities of character were on display. The result is a "household of God" the cohesion for which is a cruciform love — that is, a love that takes its content and form from the sacrificial death of Christ on the cross.

Fourth, given the importance of honor and status distinctions in Greco-Roman society, and especially in such institutions as the household, the city, and the voluntary association,[63] we might expect Peter's metaphors to signal relations of status and power. This is not the case. All are children and servants in the household of Father God. It is true that, in 5:1-5, Peter refers to himself as "elder," potentially suggesting his authority in a hierarchical pattern of relationships, but he immediately relativizes his own position by referring to himself as a "fellow elder," by banking his authority on his participation in the suffering of Christ, by insisting that the work of an elder is aimed at the benefit of others rather than self-aggrandizement,[64] by rejecting lordly behavior while countenancing humility, and by a reminder that the true leader, the Chief Shepherd, will come in judgment.

Fifth, in spite of the popularity of 2:9-10 as a prooftext in support of the Christian doctrine of the "priesthood of all believers," Peter's message actually runs in a different direction. He is concerned not with the priesthood of persons within the church but with the priestly function of the church itself. That is, to embrace the mantle of Israel's identity as God's peo-

---

63. See Clarke, *Serve the Community.*

64. πρόθυμος *(prothymos)*, used only here in the NT: "eager to meet the needs of others rather than seek gain for themselves" (BDAG, p. 870).

ple is inescapably to embrace Israel's vocation to mediate the purpose and blessings of God to the world. Here, then, we come to the question of the mission of the church in the world in 1 Peter, a discussion to which I will return (see pp. 279-88 below).

We have already observed that Peter urges other images of the church, images not directly related to Israel as God's people and to the church as God's "household," and these invite reflection on issues the surface of which we have hardly begun to scratch. Thus, for example, the ecclesial community is comprised of those:

> who follow in the footsteps of Christ (2:21) so fully that they are worthy of the name "Christian" — that is, who so identify with Christ that they are marked out in the world as he was and so share in his suffering (compare Luke's depiction of the apostles as persons who "rejoiced that they were considered worthy to suffer dishonor for the sake of the name" [Acts 5:41; cf. Mark 8:34-38]);
> who on the ground of the resurrection wait for the "salvation ready to be revealed at the last time" (1:5) and whose life is determined by that expectation;[65] and
> for whom the capacity to serve within the community of believers is a gift and a call which owes itself to God's generous initiative (4:11).

Finally, however, we should ask, What of the classic loci of Christian ecclesiology, its confession that the church is one, holy, catholic, and apostolic? As with our earlier ruminations concerning the triune God, we can inquire into how these traditional concerns might order our reading of 1 Peter without thereby assuming either that 1 Peter (or any other biblical book, or the Bible as a whole) must provide the foundation for the church's confession concerning its own nature or that it must address each of these issues at all.

One: To claim the oneness of the church is, first, to proclaim the oneness of God; as the Alexandrian Jew Philo could claim, "Since God is one, there should be also only one temple" (*De specialibus legibus* 1.12.67), so the church has claimed that the one church is an expression of the one God. At this rudimentary level, 1 Peter is very much at home, with its clear, negative appraisal of idolatry in all its forms (e.g., 4:3; cf. 1:14, 18), and with its clarity that it is the one God who has called and formed disparate persons, even Gentiles, into the one people of God. Of course, in making this claim, by "church" we would mean something other than a single edifice, like the Jeru-

---

65. Moltmann, *Theology of Hope*, p. 326.

salem Temple — or, for that matter, any other organizational structure. We refer, rather, to the inherent unity of the church realized and made visible in its mutual love and in the integrity of its stance in the world. This is not to imply that the "true" church is unorganized, since gatherings of people entail the emergence of polity, whether formal or otherwise; it is to say, rather, that the unity of the church undergirds and orders its organizational structure.[66] This is why Peter can move so easily between words of mutuality and egalitarianism on the one hand, and of elders and shepherds on the other. Nor is it to suggest that the "true" church is invisible. However much Peter's audience might have desired invisibility or anonymity in the world, the church that would consider itself heir to Peter's vision of the church cannot but be visible in its courageous and costly engagement in the world.

Holy: The church's holiness moves from the indicative to the imperative. By nature of its existence as the people called out by God, a primary emphasis of 1 Peter, the church is holy, for this is what holiness entails: "set apart by God." Sanctification refers to the "divine act through which God chooses something for himself and makes it his own, thus letting it participate in his nature."[67] This is the very reality to which Peter bears witness when he refers to the church as "a holy nation, a people for God's possession" (2:9). But to be called out by God is as much vocation as status, as much charge as gift, so that "you yourselves must rather become holy in every aspect of life, just as the one who called you is holy" (1:15). Similarly, in words reminiscent of the prayer Jesus taught his disciples, Peter instructs his audience to "sanctify Christ as Lord in your hearts" (3:15) — instruction that cannot be segregated from the call to imitate the Lord so that his name, reputation, and character do not suffer debasement. Küng holds these concerns in tension when he writes that "the Church is holy by being called by God in Christ to be the communion of the faithful, by accepting the call to service, by being separated from the world and at the same time embraced and supported by his grace."[68] However, given the ease with which "being separated from the world" can be read so as to ghettoize the church, we must recall that, for Peter, holiness is realized in engagement in the world, and particularly in confident resistance to its patterns of expected thinking and acting reinforced by social sanctions and to those organizational structures that legitimate and propagate those dispositions and that behavior. To put it differently, for Peter Christian identity and practice are not defined negatively vis-

---

66. Cf. Bloesch, *Church*, 100.
67. Moltmann, *Spirit of Life*, p. 174.
68. Küng, *Church*, p. 419.

à-vis those who reject the ways of Yahweh, but positively in relation to the way of Christ.

Catholic: By its designation as one of the "Catholic Letters" of the NT 1 Peter was alleged to have been intended for a general readership; this designation did not mean that it (or others of the collection) were universally recognized.[69] Without raising the question of the catholicity of 1 Peter in the first centuries of the church, it is noteworthy that, in its introduction, 1 Peter makes no claim to an ecumenical readership. Instead, it designates an audience, geographically located on the Anatolian peninsula, socio-religio-politically located as marginal to mainstream society. In what sense, then, can we speak of Peter's ecclesiology as "catholic" — that is, as universal and inclusive in its essential identity?[70] First, it is worth reflecting on the fact that Peter addresses groups of Christians across an expansive geography, but never differentiates among them. He seems to regard them as a single church or "household," sharing the same gospel, struggling with the same realities. Second, within its own pages, 1 Peter ties the situation of his audience to that of all believers: "the same kind of sufferings are being accomplished in the case of your family of believers throughout the world" (5:9). This has the effect of broadening the application and appeal of Peter's letter to the whole of the Christian family; in the NT, of course, this rhetorical move on the part of Peter is not unique (cf., e.g., 1 Cor 1:2; 2 Cor 1:1; Col 4:16). As a result, the subsequent location of 1 Peter within the Christian canon preserves and promulgates impulses toward catholicity resident already in the letter itself. Third, it is possible to read 1 Peter as an invitation to a kind of catholicity — that is, as an invitation for Christians in all times and everywhere to read it as mail addressed to them. In order to do so, however, Peter's Model Readers[71] would become those who embrace and embody the status of persons whose identity as pilgrims in the world grows out of their experience of the new birth, whose lives are radically marked by their membership in a community defined by its

69. Kümmel, *Introduction,* pp. 387-88. Strangely, Kümmel argues that the geographical markers of 1:1 are not to be taken literally. "What is in view is Christians as members of the true people of God, who live scattered throughout the earth as strangers, since their true home is in heaven (cf. Gal 6:16; Phil 3:20; Heb 13:14; also 1 Pet 1:17; 2:11)" (p. 418).

70. For this definition of "catholic," see Küng, *Church,* pp. 388-92; Bloesch, *Church,* p. 101.

71. I have borrowed the term "Model Reader" from Umberto Eco, who observes that, "to organize a text, its author has to rely upon a series of codes that assign given contents to the expressions he [*sic*] uses. To make his text communicative, the author has to assume that the ensemble of codes he relies upon is the same as that shared by his possible reader. The author has to foresee a model of the possible reader (hereafter Model Reader) supposedly able to deal interpretively with the expressions in the same way as the author deals generatively with them" (*Role of the Reader,* p. 7).

allegiance to Christ, whose lives thus stand in an ambiguous relationship to the mores and values of the world around them, and, accordingly, whose practices attract for them opposition from their neighbors. 1 Peter is addressed to just such people and is read best by those who share its theological assumptions and those who hear its opening as an invitation to embody its world. The question is whether we are ready to be included in a community defined in these terms.

Apostolic: The tradition has understood apostolicity in two primary ways — with reference to apostolic succession and with regard to continuity with the apostles in terms of teaching and mission. The former, troublesome among a number of traditions, especially congregationalists,[72] may seem to find support in a letter like 1 Peter, since it speaks with the authoritative voice not only of an apostle, but of *the* apostle, Peter (1:1). At the same time, it should not escape notice that Peter claims no apostolic relationship to those to whom he addresses this letter and identifies himself as an "elder" among "fellow elders" (1:1; 5:1). Manifestly, the authority behind his letter is not his apostleship, but the purpose of God, the work of Christ, the transformative power of the Spirit, the Scriptures understood christologically, and the developing Christian tradition (including the Jesus tradition). The question whether we could claim that 1 Peter stands in and promotes "the teaching of the apostles" is made complex by repeated attempts (which began in modern times with Walter Bauer in 1934[73] but have recently recruited voices increasingly shrill and brassy) to prioritize diversity among expressions of the Christian faith in the first centuries, with the concomitant denial that one could speak of a generally agreed "teaching of the apostles" so early. Looking backward, of course, it is easy enough to insist that 1 Peter participates in the continuity of apostolic teaching since the letter itself helps to define that continuity. More than this, however, we should mention the high degree to which NT scholars have long insisted that 1 Peter has little to offer by way of a unique theological message, suggesting instead that 1 Peter stands in the mainstream of Christian teaching, even casting Peter in the role of mediator among early Christian theologians;[74] additionally, at numerous points we have seen how dependent Peter has been on the developing christological tradition.[75] Peter further models apostolicity by his appropriation of the kerygma for the world

---

72. See Grenz, *Community of God*, pp. 468-69.

73. Bauer, *Orthodoxy and Heresy* (originally published in German, 1934). I. H. Marshall provided a helpful counterbalance in "Orthodoxy and Heresy."

74. E.g., Dunn, *Unity and Diversity*, pp. 384-85; Bruce, *Peter*, pp. 42-43.

75. Cf. Pearson, *Christological and Rhetorical Properties.*

he envisions, and by his vision of mission — in praise to God, in unceasing love within the church, and in costly, courageous involvement in the world.

"When You Suffer as a Christian": Peter's Perspective on Suffering

Peter has a well-developed registry for the experience of suffering: trials (1:6), testing (1:7; 4:12), suffering (1:11; 2:19, 21, 23; 3:14, 17; 4:1, 13, 15-16, 19; 5:1, 9, 10), being beaten (2:20), the tree as an instrument of execution (2:24), intimidation (3:14), slander (3:16), fiery ordeal (4:12), vilification (4:14), and judgment (4:17).[76] A brief rehearsal of this data supports three immediate observations. First, Peter does not envision a situation within which followers of Christ are the objects of formal persecution.[77] Second, apart from his descriptions of the passion of Christ, the suffering Peter envisions is especially verbal shaming, one of the chief weapons in the arsenal of social ostracism. For all its informality and verbal character, however, the suffering Peter describes is no less real. Luke Johnson observes,

> Persecution and martyrdom, after all, have a certain clarity and comfort. Lines of allegiance are obvious. However painful the choice, it need be made only once. But scorn and contempt are slow-working acids that corrode individual and communal identity. Social alienation is not a trivial form of suffering. Persecution may bring death, but with meaning. Societal scorn can threaten meaning itself, which is a more subtle form of death.[78]

Third, Peter carefully weaves the hostility his audience faces into wider interpretive cloth. Insults and reproach are more than they seem. With incessant references to "suffering," Peter ties the experiences of his audience into the suffering and death of Christ. And he paints both Christ's suffering and theirs within the larger mural of an eschatologically significant cosmic struggle by which God actualizes his salvific purpose.

We can build on these observations by reflecting on the myriad ways Peter works to give perspective to suffering.

Suffering as Refinement. Tearing a page from the widespread view of the "educational value" of suffering in the ancient Mediterranean world,

---

76. Adapted from Skaggs, p. 14.
77. The evidence for state-sanctioned persecution is surveyed in Moule, *Birth*, pp. 152-76.
78. L. T. Johnson, *Writings*, p. 435.

Peter writes of the purgative effect of suffering (1:6-7; 4:1-2, 12).[79] Suffering is the means by which the faith of believers is perfected.

Suffering and Honor. Suffering may be the consequence of society's attempts to clothe followers of Christ in humiliation and shame, but Peter turns this interpretation on its head. To the contrary, suffering is a sign of the genuineness of one's faith, an affirmation of one's identity before God, and a concrete measure of the value in which the believing community is held by God. Peter assigns no blame and nurtures no guilt. Instead, he emphasizes God's valuation of those who suffer on account of their allegiance to God's purpose and identifies suffering as the occasion of blessing and the empowerment of the Spirit (e.g., 2:4-8, 15, 19-21; 3:17; 4:14, 19).[80]

Suffering as an Expression of Trust. Among those who have adopted a new pattern of thinking, who have experienced a conversion of the imagination, suffering rather than retaliation is an expression of trust in the God who judges without reference to one's honorable status in the world (1:17; 2:23; 3:5; 4:15-19). Suffering without retaliation is a refusal to tear away from God his role of determining the standards of and carrying out justice.

Suffering as Solidarity. Innocent suffering is both an imitation of and a participation in the suffering of Christ and an expression of solidarity with believers throughout the world who suffer similarly (2:21-25; 4:1, 5:1, 9).[81]

The Temporality of Suffering. Peter emphasizes the temporal constraints placed on suffering, "a short time," "a short while" (1:6; 5:10; cf. 1:17; 4:2), and contrasts this with the eternal nature of the future inheritance and glory (1:4; 5:10).[82] Suffering characterizes the present time, because the behaviors of Christians bring to expression their transformed dispositions and allegiances in ways that cut against the grain of the ways of larger society (e.g., 1:14, 17-18; 4:2-4), but "the end of all things has come" (4:7).

The Efficacy of Suffering. Just as the suffering of Christ was efficacious for liberation (1:2, 18-19; 2:21-25), so the suffering of believers is effi-

---

79. See especially Talbert, *Learning through Suffering* (on 1 Peter, pp. 42-57). Goppelt erroneously categorizes suffering in 1 Peter as an expression of divine judgment (*Theology*, p. 175). Peter provides no hint that Christians "deserve" their marginal existence, but emphasizes rather their (and Christ's) innocent suffering.

80. See Berger, *Identity*, pp. 180, 184.

81. See Berger, *Identity*, p. 182.

82. See Berger, *Identity*, p. 183.

cacious. Peter develops this along two lines, first, it may be a catalyst for the conversion of unbelievers (2:12); second, the suffering of Christians is a participation in the messianic woes by which God inaugurates the age of salvation (4:12-19).

Suffering and Social Engagement. It is almost unbelievable that Peter never himself vilifies those pagans on account of the hostilities doled out to believers, nor urges his audience to vilify their antagonists. He casts no blame and never allows for an interpretation of pagans as evil on account of their stance over against Christians. (They are, instead, idolaters and slaves to their lusts.) Indeed, suffering is only to be expected for the righteous who live in an idolatrous world. Nor does Peter encourage withdrawal to a more sectarian existence less likely to attract the negative attention that has resulted in alienation and humiliation. Instead, suffering is the occasion for persistent faithfulness and vigilance, imitation of Christ, mutual love within the Christian family, and a stance of courageous resistance in the world.[83]

Suffering and Glory. The pathway on which believers are set is not identified simply or exclusively with suffering, but is part of a larger journey from new birth through (righteous) suffering to vindication and glory. Peter can therefore set the compass of his audience toward the future. In this way, too, suffering takes its meaning from the pattern of the Suffering and Vindicated Righteous that runs like a thread through the fabric of Israel's Scriptures and that comes to decisive expression in the career of Christ.

The significance that Peter allots suffering is not the consequence of his particular interest in theodicy, or even in suffering per se. Rather, he visualizes the experience and threat of suffering on a larger canvas — one not determined by the Roman struggle over power and privilege or by contests for status in Roman society. Social alienation may not be trivial as a form of suffering but, to Peter's way of thinking, the stakes are much higher. This is because "testing" comprises a crisis of decision, of faithfulness, of outcome, since it is at one and the same time the opportunity for the refiner's fire to carry out its work of purifying faith and the opportunity for diabolic forces to wrestle God's people away from their faith through temptation. Israel's own history of journey — especially the meandering from Egypt to the land of promise

---

83. See Berger, *Identity,* pp. 181, 184.

that defined Israel as a people — is a case study for the sort of theological analysis in which Peter is engaged.

What could be more natural, more unaffected, than that those who assign their allegiances to the God and Father of the Lord Jesus Christ would find themselves at odds with those whose allegiances reside in ancestral traditions and the religions of the Roman world? And, given the simple disparity in the numbers of Christ-followers versus those engaged in imperial worship, is it not only to be expected that Christians would find themselves on the margins rather than the center of society? Such mundane expectations notwithstanding, Peter diagnoses social ostracism as a "fiery ordeal," the roaring of that adversary the devil, the opportunity for diabolic temptation. Christians may experience life as persons under the injurious thumb of social humiliation, but the character of the battle is not so mundane. Cosmic alignments, good versus evil, Christ versus the powers, come to expression in the seemingly unremarkable responses Christians make to the evil directed at them in the guise of corrosive, damning speech. Mutual love within the family of believers, the refusal of retaliation, courageous resistance in the form of "doing good" — these dispositions and behaviors strike a heavy blow against unseen but ever-present maleficent forces as they counter the threats that help to define habitation of a strange land: absorption and apostasy. Love within the community of faith, courageous activity in relation to the structures of the world — these are the weapons of warfare in the battle in which Peter's audience finds itself. Hence, Peter brings a virtual phalanx of perspectives on suffering to bear in order to urge believers to stay on the road of faithfulness, and then to assure them that they will be brought safely both through the calamity of life in this world and through divine judgment. The certainty of this promise warrants Peter's admonition to his audience to "do good," to orient themselves continually around the will of God — indeed, to become holy in every aspect of life.

1 Peter and the New Testament

What can be said of the relationship of 1 Peter to the NT? In the twentieth century, a number of studies drew attention to parallels between Peter and Paul, Peter and James, and Peter and the Synoptic Gospels, many attempting to trace Peter's direct dependence on the Jesus tradition and on Paul.[1] Rather

---

1. Most recently, e.g., Herzer, *Petrus oder Paulus* (against dependence of Peter on Paul); Metzner, *Rezeption* (for dependence of Peter on Matthew); for surveys, see Selwyn, pp. 365-466; Elliott, pp. 20-30.

228

than rehearse that discussion, I want to focus on its significance for Peter's rhetorical strategy. Additionally, I want to comment on the relationship between 1 and 2 Peter, the two NT documents that bear the name of this apostle. I am focusing on 1 Peter and the NT, largely excluding from consideration the OT, because I am reserving discussion of Peter's use of Israel's Scriptures for later.

"Your Family of Believers throughout the World":
Peter's Rhetorical Strategy

In his *apologia* for what he terms a "postmodern orthodoxy," Thomas Oden reports,

> I once had a curious dream that rekindled my deepest theological hopes. The only scene I can remember was in the New Haven cemetery, where I accidentally stumbled over my own tombstone only to be confronted by this astonishing epitaph: "He made no new contribution to theology." I was marvelously pleased by the idea and deeply reassured.[2]

The same could be, and often has been, remarked of Peter, or at least of 1 Peter, though typically with less pleasurable reactions than Oden reports of himself. In his introduction to early Christian literature, for example, Helmut Koester turns to 1 Peter as an example of "the legacy of Paul," writing, "Except for the name of the sender (1 Pet 1:1), nothing in this writing points to Peter; everything is Pauline or general Christian tradition." Robert Spivey and Moody Smith allow that the author of 1 Peter could be an original thinker, but focus more on his indebtedness to "a significant body of Christian tradition" and assert that the letter contains numerous Pauline motifs and ideas. And in his survey of NT ethics, Wolfgang Schrage examines the contribution of 1 Peter among the "deutero-Pauline epistles," since the letter espouses largely Pauline and deutero-Pauline views.[3]

Additionally, affinities with the letter of James and with other NT writings are noticeable. Of course, the suggestion that 1 Peter's theology is not really Petrine begs an important question. What do we know of Peter's theology, apart from the correspondence that has come to us in his name?

According to the early tradition, the Gospel of Mark was written by

---

2. Oden, *Agenda for Theology*, p. 11.

3. Koester, *Early Christianity*, pp. 292-93; Spivey and Smith, *Anatomy of the NT*, pp. 421-26; Schrage, *NT Ethics*, pp. 268-78.

"Mark," the interpreter of Peter. Eusebius quotes Papias, who himself credits "the Elder" as the source of this information (Eusebius *Historia Ecclesiastica* 3.39.15):

> This also the elder says: Mark, who was the interpreter of Peter, wrote down carefully, but not in the right order, everything that he remembered, both what had been said by the Lord and also what had been done by him. For he had neither seen nor had he followed the Lord, but later (he followed) . . . Peter, who shaped his teachings to the needs (of the hearers), however, not in such a way that he gave an orderly account of the sayings of the Lord. So Mark did not make a mistake in writing down some things as he remembered them. For he had one concern, not to omit anything that he had heard or to falsify anything in it.

This tradition, which probably dates back to the turn of the second century AD, is picked up and echoed in the latter part of that century by Irenaeus and Clement of Alexandria. Even if taken at face value (its representation of the origin of the Gospel of Mark is debated by scholars), it does not lead us to imagine that the Second Gospel is "Peter's Gospel" — that is, that through it we have direct access to Peter's understanding of the faith. Rather, "the Elder" reports that Peter passed on to his interpreter only anecdotes while Mark has provided a full-blown narrative, a report that opens the way for us to consider Mark's creative contribution. The Evangelist's innovation would have consisted above all in the choice of episodes to recount and in the way he has woven them together to signal causality and purpose. Nor do the speeches attributed to Peter in Acts give us such access, since they have been shaped by their appropriation within the Lukan narrative. Hence, we lack indisputable canons against which to measure how "Petrine" 1 Peter actually is.

What is evident is the remarkable degree to which the thought of 1 Peter belongs within the mainstream of early Christian thought as this is represented in the NT. Several common strands are woven together.[4]

(1) At several points, 1 Peter appears to reflect traditions about Jesus underlying the Gospels. For example,

> 1 Pet 3:9: "Do not repay evil for evil or abuse for abuse; rather, repay with a blessing."
>
> Luke 6:28: "Bless those who curse you."

---

4. I have also documented these parallels in Achtemeier, et al., *Introducing the NT,* pp. 521-26.

1 Pet 3:14: "But even if you do suffer for doing what is right, you are blessed."

Luke 6:22: "Blessed are you when people hate you, and when they exclude you, revile you, and defame you on account of the Son of Man."

Matt 5:10: "Blessed are those who are persecuted for righteousness' sake. . . ."

1 Pet 2:12: "Conduct yourselves honorably among the Gentiles, so that, though they malign you as though you were evildoers, they may see your honorable deeds and glorify God when he comes to judge."

Matt 5:16: "Let your light shine before people in order that they might see your good works and glorify your heavenly Father."

This congruence points to the familiarity of the author of 1 Peter with Jesus material.

(2) 1 Peter also shares affinities with other Christian literature in the NT — with Paul (for example):

1 Pet 1:14: "Like obedient children, do not be conformed to the desires that you formerly had in ignorance."

Rom 12:2: "Do not be conformed to this world. . . ."

1 Pet 4:10-11: "Like good stewards of the manifold grace of God, serve one another with whatever gift each of you has received. Whoever speaks must do so as one speaking the very words of God; whoever serves must do so with the strength that God supplies. . . ."

Rom 12:6-7: "We have gifts that differ according to the grace given to us: prophecy, in proportion to faith; service in serving. . . ."

With Paul and James (for example):

1 Pet 1:6-7: "In this you rejoice, even if now for a little while you have had to suffer various trials, so that the genuineness of your faith . . . may be found to result in praise and glory and honor when Jesus Christ is revealed."

Rom 5:3-5: "We also boast in our sufferings, knowing that suffering produces endurance, endurance produces character, character produces hope, and hope does not disappoint us, because God's love has been poured into our hearts through the Holy Spirit that has been given to us."

Jas 1:2-3: "Consider it all joy when you face all kinds of trials, knowing that the testing of your faith produces endurance; and let endurance have its full effect, so that you may be mature and complete, lacking in nothing."

And other points of correspondence may be noted — for example:

1 Pet 2:6-8	Rom 9:32-33
1 Pet 3:8-9	Rom 12:16-17
1 Pet 2:13-17	Rom 13:1-7
1 Pet 1:3	Eph 1:3
1 Pet 3:22	Eph 1:20-22
1 Pet 1:14	Eph 2:2-3
1 Pet 2:4-6	Eph 2:20-22
1 Pet 1:10-12	Eph 3:5
1 Pet 1:23–2:2	Jas 1:10-11, 18-22
1 Pet 5:5-9	Jas 4:6-10
1 Pet 4:8	Jas 5:20
1 Pet 3:18	Heb 9:28
1 Pet 4:6	Hebrews 11
1 Pet 1:1; 2:11	Heb 11:13
1 Pet 3:9	Heb 12:17
1 Pet 1:2	Heb 12:24
1 Pet 4:14	Heb 13:13
1 Pet 2:25	Heb 13:20

(3) We can also point to the use of kerygmatic traditions in 1 Peter. The letter appears to draw on hymnic or confessional material in 1:18-21; 2:21-25; 3:18-22, for example, and so participates in the process of drawing on and reformulating the developing tradition of the church as it seeks to instruct and encourage Christians in Asia Minor.

The congruity between 1 Peter and other NT texts is plentiful and pervasive, more than enough to indicate the conformity of this letter to the trajectory of Christian tradition and interpretation otherwise present in the NT. However, Peter is doing more than mimicking early tradition. He appears to have his own access to those elements of the tradition also picked up by Matthew and Luke, Paul and James, and others, and like them he embeds those materials within his own constructive thought by way of addressing the needs of his audience. In this way, he indicates the immediate relevance of the gospel to the conditions of his implied readers.

(4) Another form of tradition on which Peter draws is in his use of a "household duty code," known throughout the Greco-Roman world as well as in the NT (e.g., Eph 5:21–6:9; Col 3:18–4:1; 1 Pet 2:13–3:12).

(5) Moving to a wide-angle lens, we observe that 1 Peter teems with citations from and allusions to Israel's Scriptures; in fact, the Scriptures serve as the fountainhead of virtually all of the metaphors employed in the letter. The immediate effect of the use of Israel's Scriptures in 1 Peter is to root fundamentally both the message of this letter and, just as importantly, the identity of its readers in Israel's history and in scriptural authority. Here again, at some points, Peter employs the Scriptures in ways comparable to other NT writers. For example, one can compare the drawing together of OT texts in 2:4-10 with a similar exegetical argument in Rom 9:25-33. This demonstrates in another way how solidly Peter stands in the developing Christian theological consensus.

Parallels between 1 Peter and other NT materials ought not to be exaggerated, however. As far back as the mid-1970s, John Elliott prophesied "the liberation of 1 Peter from its 'Pauline bondage,'" a sentiment echoed more recently in Ralph Martin's assessment of the theology of 1 Peter.[5] In the same way that we can recognize that, say, Matthew and Luke draw on similar traditions about Jesus and yet attribute theological integrity to each of these two Evangelists, we can also recognize that Peter can draw on common Christian tradition while orienting it in ways peculiar to the circumstances he addresses. His unrelenting emphasis on the suffering of Christ, his structuring of the narrative of the outworking of God's purpose from before creation to the eschaton, his emphasis on hope, his articulation of a political ethic oriented toward courageous and costly resistance to conventional patterns of thinking and acting reinforced by social sanctions and to organizational structures that legitimate and propagate those dispositions and that behavior, his pronounced emphasis on God (including his openness to including Christ and the Spirit as actors in the divine drama), his concern with the identity of the church — in these and other ways, we see Petrine emphases coming to the fore.

Claiming that 1 Peter lacks a distinctive theology, some dismiss the letter from serious consideration in a study of biblical theology. Others, as we have had occasion to note, have adopted a more positive perspective, casting Peter in the role of mediator among early Christian theologians.[6] Whether Peter

---

5. Elliott, "Rehabilitation," p. 248; Chester and R. P. Martin, *Theology,* pp. 130-33. See also I. H. Marshall, *NT Theology,* pp. 642-59.

6. E.g., Dunn, *Unity and Diversity,* pp. 384-85; Bruce, *Peter,* pp. 42-43.

played such a role, my own sense is that the essential coherence between the theology of this letter and the work of, say, Paul and James, represents a strategic theological move on the part of Peter. The challenges of pluralism outside the church and the experience of hostility in the larger empire more generally provide for Peter an occasion for reflecting on and articulating what is emerging as common theological ground within the church. Challenges to the church from the outside provide the occasion for solidifying the church's roots in the ancient purpose of God, drawing out the continuity from Israel of old to the contemporary life of God's people, and remembering that the primary orientation of faithful life is the God and Father of our Lord Jesus Christ. Periods of heightened hostility from outsiders provide little by way of the leisure necessary for internecine distinctions over matters less central to the christological center of the community and its faith. Challenges from the outside also press for clarity regarding institutional roots and legitimacy. The rhetoric and message of 1 Peter is thus inscribed deeply into the saga of Israel, grounded in the eternal purpose of God, and participates fully in the emerging Christian consensus, as Peter explores the significance of the great mural of Israel's story — interpreted now through the pivotal events of Jesus' life, death, and resurrection — and emphasizes the common ground of the faithful as they look for places to secure their feet in the struggle for faithful witness.

"This Is Now . . . the Second Letter I Am Writing to You" (2 Pet 3:1): 1 and 2 Peter

My interest in the relation of 1 and 2 Peter will seem obvious to some, strange to others, depending on one's background.[7] To the uninitiated in formal theological studies, it will seem obvious that 1 and 2 Peter are closely related and ought to be read serially, as one might read 1 and 2 Samuel or 1 and 2 Corinthians. After all, both carry the name of Peter, a "pillar" of the early church (Gal 2:9), and the second letter presents itself as a follow-up to the first (2 Pet 3:1). Why not examine these two letters side-by-side in order to ascertain a "Petrine" gospel?

To the theologically trained, on the other hand, the interesting relationship is not between 1 and 2 Peter, but between 2 Peter and Jude. Critical readers will discern in parallels like Jude 17-18/2 Pet 3:1-3 evidence of 2 Peter's dependence on Jude, prompting the conclusion that 2 Peter ought to be read as "2 Jude." Moreover, stylistically, the two letters are sufficiently distinct that it

---

7. I have adapted this section from Green, "Narrating the Gospel."

is hard to imagine that they share a single author. And, whereas 1 Peter calls itself a "brief letter" (5:12) and actually takes the form of a letter, 2 Peter refers to itself as a letter (3:1) but looks more like "testamentary literature," a literary form that allows an honored figure to speak across time and space, even from the grave.[8] In "critical studies," then, the location of 1 and 2 Peter side-by-side and their attribution to a common author are of no interpretive consequence.

From yet a third perspective, however, given their canonical titles and shared attribution, 2 Peter invites theological reflection in relation to 1 Peter. According to this reading, the distinctions between these two books do not detract from but rather enhance our appreciation of their fecundity as a coordinated "Petrine" witness within the biblical canon.[9] Theologically, we are pressured to read 1 and 2 Peter together, in spite of historical differences calibrated in terms of tradition history, authorship, genre, and style. This compulsion comes above all from their shared attribution to the apostle Peter and the interpretively significant remark in 2 Pet 3:1: "This is now, beloved, the second letter I am writing to you. . . ." A narrative-theological approach can help us to see how, when read together, historical differences registered in recent study of these books actually enrich our theological reflection.

How does 2 Peter represent the grand story of God, from creation to new creation? "Peter," as I shall refer to the author of 2 Peter, presents a straightforward, linear narrative:

(1) Israel's past → (2) Christ event → (3) present →
(4) eschatological judgment

Note that a narrative-theological emphasis does not disregard "cognition" or "truth." 2 Peter is obviously interested in "knowledge," an interest that is documented in the range of terms it deploys: *epignōsis* ("knowledge, recognition" — 1:2, 3, 8; 2:20), *gnōsis* ("knowledge" — 1:5, 6; 3:18), *epiginōskō* ("know, recognize" — twice in 2:21), and *ginōskō* ("know" — 1:20; 3:3). But this is not "knowledge" of principles and systems. Rather, Peter refers to the formal aspects of our faith, which cannot be segregated from but actually find their meaning within the narrative content and context of God's revelation of himself to us. To put it differently, this knowledge is "tacit" and "embodied" — that is, what "we just know" on account of personal formation within the community of God's people and is so embedded in our lives that it is not easily codified. "Truth" has

---

8. On these and related matters of introduction, see Achtemeier, et al., *Introducing the NT*, pp. 513-34.

9. So Wall, "Canonical Function."

meaning in relation to the ongoing story. In "Peter's" reckoning, (1) Israel's past provides exemplars of divine judgment and rescue. (2) The Christ event is less the turning point of history and more the guarantee of Christ's ability to do what is promised. Christ's divinity (1:1) and divine power (1:3) ensure that he is able to give his people all that is needed for faithful life in the present. Reflection on the transfiguration (1:16-18) verifies Christ's glory, and "Peter's" barest mention of Jesus' death (in the language of "purchase," 2:1) serves as a critical reminder that his audience has been liberated from one form of slavery in order to exercise their freedom *from* the world (2:20) and *in* faithful living.

It is precisely at the conjunction of (1) and (2) — Israel's past and the Christ event — that 2 Pet 3:1-2 should attract our interest: "This is now, beloved, the second letter I am writing to you; in them I am trying to arouse your sincere intention by reminding you that you should remember the words spoken in the past by the holy prophets, and the commandment of the Lord and Savior spoken through your apostles." "Peter" thus positions 2 Peter as a follow-on to 1 Peter, but, more critically, urges that these two books share a common purpose: "*in them* I am trying to. . . ." The agenda "Peter" lays out for these two letters has to do with putting into play the words of the prophets and the commandment of the Lord, mediated through the prophets. (1) Israel's past and (2) the advent of Christ are set side-by-side, with a view to how (4) eschatological judgment ought to impinge on (3) present faith and life. With these words, "Peter" prompts a theological hermeneutic — that is, a mode of understanding that takes seriously how theological commitments order our reading of Scripture. Developed more fully in 1 Pet 1:10-12, this hermeneutic is one that finds Christ and the Scriptures of Israel as mutually informing.[10] This is because they say the same thing, albeit in different theological idioms; how could they not, since the prophets of old spoke as inspired by the Spirit of Christ (1 Pet 1:11)? The importance of Israel's Scriptures is not worked out in terms of promise and fulfillment, then, but as simultaneity of substance and address. This means that Peter finds an essential unity in the outworking of God's purpose, from the prophets to Christ to the apostles and thus to the community of Christ's followers. In this context, "remembrance" ([1] and [2]) is concerned with (3) a present life marked by creative fidelity: "fidelity" in the sense that the words of the prophets and commandment of the Lord set the parameters of faithful performance, "creative" in the sense that life is too particular and unruly to be carefully scripted, but Christians

---

10. The connection of 2 Pet 3:1-2 to 1 Pet 1:10-12 was noted already by Boobyer, who saw 2 Pet 3:1-2 as the starting point for comprehending how the two letters should be related ("Indebtedness of 2 Peter").

can nonetheless be persons shaped by this script, and who allow their lives to be set within its plot lines.

(3) Present existence is cast within (4) the eschatological horizon of impending judgment. Irrespective of the message of the false teachers, judgment will take place. In this way, "Peter" posits that the pattern of history is revealed, the nature of the end is known, and the present can be evaluated accordingly. This means that "Peter" interprets the present in light of his convictions regarding the future. In short, although the narrative "Peter" shapes is a linear one, it emphasizes Israel's past and God's promised future in order to shape a perspective on the present, and it formulates the Christ event as the ground for Christian life and godliness.

Of the four nodes in "Peter's" narrative, two are especially underdeveloped: Israel's past and the advent of Christ. One receives special attention: eschatological judgment, with the End construed above all in terms of the transformation of creation. From different angles and with varying degrees of intensity, these three shed light on the fourth: the present. Situating 2 Peter theologically in relation to 1 Peter, we might not be surprised that, as 1 Peter sculpts the grand story, two nodes of the narrative receive copious attention: Israel's past and the advent of Christ. (On the "narrative" of 1 Peter, see above, pp. 199-202.) Thus, the christology of 1 Peter fills in the blanks, as it were, for 2 Peter. Similarly, in comparison with 2 Peter, 1 Peter provides a far more robust and theologically engaging interaction with the story of Israel as the story of God's people, including Peter's Christian audience. This paves the way for us to locate the exemplars of Israel's past that are brought into focus in 2 Peter within the larger mural of Israel's life as this is painted in 1 Peter. On the one hand, the difference between these two letters, read from this narrative-theological perspective, can be explained by the "differences in present existence" to which each is addressed: 2 Peter toward false teaching with its concomitant immorality, 1 Peter toward the enigmatic marginal status of believers in the world. On the other, 2 Peter is able to do little more than drop hints about the relationship of the church to Israel's past and point in the general direction of the significance of Christ's advent because it presumes a reading of 1 Peter, where these hermeneutical compass points are prominent.

At one point, 1 and 2 Peter overwhelmingly share a common emphasis, narratively speaking. Both have a well-developed eschatological horizon, even though this horizon is developed in distinctive ways. Both assure their audiences of the certainty of the End and of final judgment. Both draw attention in this way to the fact that the present is not all there is, but points to and serves a future reality that mitigates the present's claims to ultimacy. Both engage in backshadowing, insisting that our sure knowledge of a certain future leads us to see that the future casts its shadow backward on present life, calling for conduct congruent with the way things really are and in the End will be shown to be. For 1 Peter, however, eschatology is cast in the role of servant to hope, providing motivation for courageous steadfastness in the face of opposition. For 2 Peter, eschatology serves as the flashing light of warning (3:17!), underscoring the certainty that present life has enduring consequences. Both insist that the End will reveal what is really valued by God and, then, what ought to be valued in the present by God's people. And both shape a narrative theology within which those values — those dispositions, those ways of thinking and acting — are second nature. Between them, 1 and 2 Peter, we encounter the eschatologically determined pastoral task of afflicting the comfortable (2 Peter) and comforting the afflicted (1 Peter).

When examined from this perspective, 1 and 2 Peter emerge as exercises in imagination- and world-shaping, supported by one of the most potent weapons in the formation and reformation of identity: narrative. Narrative does not imply a dismissal of "reality as it really is," but insists that "reality" is subject to numerous representations; narrative does not declare that facts are constituted by their narration, but that there are multiple ways of construing facts.[11]

To illustrate with reference to 2 Peter, clearly one way "to read" the world as it is would be to deny any claim of ultimate justice. Do we not see all around us evidence that the immorality of others leads to their apparent happiness, to our exploitation, but not to their punishment? For "Peter," however, such a reading is possible only for the nearsighted and blind (1:9), those lacking true understanding (2:12). Such people seem free, but are actually slaves to corruption (2:19). If they would open their eyes to the whole of God's story, they would recognize the certainty of divine judgment — and order their lives accordingly.

To illustrate with reference to 1 Peter, execution on a cross, according to the dominant narrative of Roman antiquity, was an ignominy, and the Christian experience of ostracism and insult likewise shameful and debilitating. Following the adage that the best defense of the marginal and powerless is narrative, Peter spins a different narrative, not by creating "new facts" but by according privilege to some facts over others and in ordering them in a particular way — writing the story of his Christian audience into the story of Christ, itself already understood within the plotline of Israel's story and, indeed, within the story of God's purpose from creation to new creation. As a result, "the stone that the builders rejected has become the

11. See Phelan, *Narrative as Rhetoric,* pp. 1-23.

very head of the corner" (1 Pet 2:7). In other words, given the inversion of categories of valuation within Peter's narrative (e.g., 2:4-10, 21-25), it really was possible to declare victory (before God) in the face of apparent defeat (before humans), for this was a central means by which to maintain courageous steadfastness in the face of adversity and to undermine the Roman ethos of power and status.

Engaging Theology with 1 Peter

We have proceeded thus far under the assumption that 1 Peter is itself witness to the gospel, appropriating the good news in a particular world within the ancient Roman Mediterranean. It does so, however, in universalizing ways. Both in the way it collapses historical distinctions between Israel and the church and in the way it characterizes Christian life throughout the world, its message resists relegation to an audience of Christ-followers on the mid-first-century Anatolian peninsula. These impulses toward ongoing significance are validated, first, theologically, and, derivatively, hermeneutically.

The capacity of 1 Peter to engage Christians directly — Christians around the world and throughout history — is claimed theologically in the church's recognition of 1 Peter as Scripture. To affirm "1 Peter is Scripture" is a theological statement. It draws attention, first, to the origin, role, and aim of this text in God's self-communication.[1] Second, it locates persons and a people, those who read it as Scripture, on a particular textual map, a location possessing its own assumptions, values, and norms for guiding and animating particular beliefs, dispositions, and practices constitutive of that people. Because of its priority in the generation and sustenance of the world it supports, 1 Peter as Scripture also holds the potential for confirming or for reconfiguring the beliefs and commitments that orient our lives in the world.[2]

Our recognizing the status of 1 Peter as "Scripture" opens the door to further validation at a hermeneutical level. By this I mean, first, that, as Scripture, 1 Peter addresses itself to the church — not only to those followers of Christ comprising Peter's "authorial audience" (that is, the reader "*presumed by* rather than marked in the text," whose character can be discovered only by looking at the text in terms of the context within which it arose)[3] — but the

---

1. See Webster, *Holy Scripture,* p. 5.
2. Cf. Kort, *"Take, Read,"* pp. 2-3.
3. Rabinowitz, "Reader-Response Theory," pp. 606-7.

church universal. This claim renders immediately problematic standard approaches to biblical interpretation in modern times, that paradigm of historical criticism which assumes a historical definition of the church. That is, whereas modern biblical interpretation *might* speak of the worldwide church (though even this would stumble over consideration of local instantiations of the church), it can scarcely speak of the one people of God across time. This *historical* judgment is countered by the *theological* affirmation of the oneness of the church that receives 1 Peter *as Scripture.* Thus, for example, Lutheran theologian Robert Jenson has observed, *". . . the initiating error of standard modern exegesis is that it presumes a sectarian ecclesiology"* — one that fails to acknowledge that ". . . the text we call the Bible was put together in the first place by the same community that now needs to interpret it."[4] From what he regards as a "baptist" [*sic*] theological perspective, James McClendon insists similarly on an account of biblical authority that finds its center in "a hermeneutical motto":

> *the present Christian community is the primitive community and the eschatological community.* In other words, the church now is the primitive church and the church on the day of judgment is the church now; the obedience and liberty of the followers of Jesus of Nazareth is *our* liberty, *our* obedience.[5]

McClendon is quick to point out that this "motto" provides no impetus for dismissing the hard work of biblical scholarship, but rather the opposite. Taking seriously Scripture's ongoing theological relevance and authority presses even more the need for the work of interpretation. As early Jewish interpretation of Torah recognized, a commitment to these texts as Scripture requires extending their meaning from the past into the present, with "readers fighting to find what they must in the holy text."[6]

At a second level, derivative of the church's recognition of the status of 1 Peter as Scripture, I am concerned with interpretive theory and specifically the rediscovery of the reader — or, in our case, the church as readerly community — in philosophical hermeneutics. From early in the twentieth century, innovations in hermeneutical theory began to shift the weight of emphasis from interpretation as the discovery of meaning contained within a text toward interpretation as the generation of meaning. Accordingly, emphasis is placed on the process whereby "the right of the reader and the right of

---

4. Jenson, "The Religious Power," 98; italics original.
5. McClendon, *Ethics*, p. 31.
6. Boyarin, *Intertextuality*, p. 16.

the text converge in an important struggle that generates the whole dynamic of interpretation."[7] From this perspective, one's historical and cultural distance from the text erects no barrier to but is a necessary factor in the process of interpretation.

Persons weaned on historical criticism or otherwise concerned about engaging Peter as theologian in the way I have begun to suggest may rightly be anxious about my commitment thus far to a reader-oriented approach to the letter's theology. After all, there are a range of readerly perspectives, and the results of some seem hardly at all to have much relation to the text alleged to have been read.[8] For this reason, I need to declare my interest in a particular kind of reader, the Model Reader, as well as explain briefly what this means.

It is true that other readers might have impressed themselves into this task — implied readers, competent readers, authorial readers, informed readers, and real readers among them.[9] I find these other possibilities less helpful for theological interpretation, however. For example, our access to Peter's *intended* readers or his *first, flesh-and-blood* readers is limited by what we can project from the letter itself; hence, these categories falter for lack of firsthand descriptions or testimony. In any case, specifically theological interpretation of Scripture moves beyond a narrow interest in the voice or intent of the human author to accord privilege to the role of this text in divine self-disclosure.

I have borrowed the concept of the Model Reader from semiologist, novelist, and culture commentator Umberto Eco. He speaks of good reading as the practice of those who are able to deal with texts in the act of interpreting in the same way as the author dealt with them in the act of writing.[10] Such a reader is the precondition for actualizing the potential of a text to engage and transform us, for it is this reader whom the text not only presupposes but also cultivates. This requires that readers enter cooperatively into the discursive dance with the text, while leaving open the possibility that the text is hospitable to other interpretations.

---

7. Ricoeur, *Interpretation Theory*, p. 32. Gadamer moved hermeneutics in this direction by insisting that the scientific quest for truth is not the only path to truth; art, for example, is "known" through a hermeneutic by which we are transformed in relation to it. Gadamer analogously called for a type of hermeneutical consciousness whereby the act of understanding is imagined as a fusion of one's own horizon (i.e., confronting one's own historicality) with the historical horizon embodied in these texts from the past *(Truth and Method)*.

8. For a convenient typology of perspectives in reader-response criticism in NT studies, see Vanhoozer, "Reader."

9. See Rabinowitz, "Reader-Response Theory."

10. E.g., Eco, *Role of the Reader*, pp. 7-11; idem, *Interpretation and Overinterpretation*.

Obviously, this approach eschews an interpretive agenda governed by readerly neutrality, that holy grail of biblical studies in the modern period. Apart from the anthropological reality that each of us reads from a certain place that can only to some degree be transcended but never fully escaped and that what we hear in biblical texts is more or less determined by the wavelengths to which our ears are tuned, "objectivity" in theological interpretation is not even desirable.[11] Writing of "understanding" in her novel *The Telling*, Ursula LeGuin observes, "One of the historians of Darranda said: *To learn a belief without belief is to sing a song without the tune*. A yielding, an obedience, a willingness to accept these notes as the right notes, this pattern as the right pattern, is the essential gesture of performance, translation, and understanding."[12] Accordingly, such dispositions and practices as recognition, acceptance, devotion, attention, and trust characterize the Model Reader.[13] The consequence of this concern with the Model Reader in the context of theological interpretation is a concern with the formation of persons and communities who embody and put into play, who perform, the narrative of Scripture.

Use of the category of Model Reader does not allow apathy concerning historical questions, since Eco's model attends to what he calls "world structures." The text of 1 Peter is present to us as a cultural product, which draws on, actualizes, propagates, and/or undermines the context within which it was generated. The Model Reader generated by this text protects the text from colonization or objectification by the Reader by giving the text its own voice from within its own sociocultural horizons. We are nevertheless able to embrace the role of Model Reader the more easily because (1) so much of our humanity is shared with the world within which this text found its origins and (2) the text itself, when read closely and with respect for its difference, as in intercultural exchange more generally, discloses its primary sociocultural horizons. Far more challenging is our developing the habits of life that make us receptive to the vision of God, God's character and God's project, animating 1 Peter as Scripture and, then, textualized in and emanating from these pages. In this case, the Model Reader must not only learn to recognize the importance of household codes or intertextuality (for example) in 1 Peter, but

---

11. By "objectivity" I refer to dispassionate, uncommited, unaffected exegesis, sometimes described as "scientific" inquiry (i.e., biblical studies as *Wissenschaft*). I am not excluding the much-needed capacities to weigh interpretive options and to engage in self-criticism, even self-overcoming. My thinking on this distinction has been shaped by Haskell, "Objectivity Is Not Neutrality."

12. LeGuin, *Telling*, pp. 97-98; emphasis original.

13. See Webster, *Holy Scripture*, pp. 68-106.

must come to the letter with a disposition of risky openness to a reordering of the world, repentance for attitudes of defiance of the grace of God's self-revelation, a conversion of the imagination. Such readers seek "no longer" to be "shaped by the desires that marked your former time of ignorance," but rather to "become holy in every aspect of life, just as the one who called you is holy, for it is written, 'You shall be holy, because I am holy'" (1:14-16). This is why I have maintained that the primary gulf separating 1 Peter and contemporary readers is more theological than historical.

This perspective is not unlike the kind of theological exegesis championed by Karl Barth and examined by Richard Burnett.[14] Scripture is foremost witness to the Word rather than source or repository of content, whether historical or cultural or theological. The Word creates its hearer, who, then, is invited to participate in its subject, which is God himself. Interpreters are invited to think with the Scriptures, not about them. Context is pivotal, and historical context ought not be overlooked, but this is comparatively insignificant. "The fact that 'the whole Bible authoritatively proclaims that God must be *all in all*' meant that God Himself, that revelation, was the actual context in which the Bible was to be understood."[15]

If theology is critical reflection on the church's practices,[16] then the way is open to ask how Peter the theologian might direct us in our own theological formation. We can express this interest because recognizing 1 Peter as theological discourse (and not merely the raw material for theological discourse) allows us to think of "doing theology" as the exercise of a "craft" rather than as the amassing of encyclopedic knowledge and systematic organization of truth claims comprising theology's content. On this, the perspective of Alasdair MacIntyre is especially helpful. As he puts it, a craft might involve procedures and steps and might build on a history of performance, but it is ultimately defined by complexity and innovation that break out of those procedures and help to constitute evolving rules.

> The authority of a master within a craft is both more and other than a matter of exemplifying the best standards so far. It is also and most importantly a matter of knowing how to go further and especially how to direct others towards going further, using what can be learned from the tradition afforded by the past to move towards the *telos* of full perfected work. It is in thus knowing how to link past and future that those with authority are able to draw upon tradition, to interpret and reinterpret it, so

14. Burnett, *Theological Exegesis.*
15. Burnett, *Theological Exegesis*, p. 101.
16. See Wood, *Formation of Christian Understanding.*

that its directedness towards the *telos* of that particular craft becomes apparent in new and characteristically unexpected ways.[17]

Mastering a craft thus entails standing in a tradition and engagement with the present, but it is especially about developing particular intuitions, forming particular dispositions, becoming a particular kind of person whose commitments and predilections have been shaped in relation to the activity in question. To learn the craft of theological interpretation from Peter, then, would be at least to stand within his tradition of a christological reading of both Scripture and the lives of his audience (indeed, of the whole of time spanning from before the creation of the world to the eschaton), and to do so from a self-conscious location within the theological narrative he has both identified and helped to weave.

I have urged, then, that, although we may learn "theology" from 1 Peter, more significantly we learn "doing theology" from 1 Peter. In 1 Peter already we find "theology" both in its critical task of reflection on the practices and affirmations of the people of God to determine their credibility and faithfulness, and in its constructive task of reiteration, restatement, and interpretation of the good news vis-à-vis its horizons and challenges. And this includes inquiring into how 1 Peter might engage us in theological discourse on matters of contemporary concern. What, then, does Peter contribute to theological formation? In this final section, I want to focus on three particular theological loci — namely, theological hermeneutics, the nature of humanity and the concomitant character of salvation, and theological engagement with culture.

"The Spirit of Christ Which Was in Them":
Peter and Theological Hermeneutics

"Theological interpretation," according to Kevin Vanhoozer, "is biblical interpretation oriented to the knowledge of God."[18] By way of filling this out somewhat, we can say that, if *hermeneutics* refers to reflection on and the practice of human understanding, and if *theological hermeneutics* refers broadly to how doctrine impinges on the enterprise of human understanding, then a *theological hermeneutics of Christian Scripture,* with which we are interested here, concerns the theological role of Scripture in the formation of persons and ecclesial communities. As such, we are concerned with the po-

17. MacIntyre, *Three Rival Versions of Moral Inquiry,* 65-66.
18. Vanhoozer, "Theological Interpretation," p. 24.

tentially mutual influence of Scripture and doctrine in theological discourse and, then, with the role of Scripture in the self-understanding of the church, and in critical reflection on the church's practices.

Issues of this sort do not come naturally for biblical scholars or for theologians. Perhaps in services of worship we hear the exchange:

> This is the Word of the Lord.
> Thanks be to God.

However, biblical scholarship in the modern period has not oriented itself toward approaches or development of means that would enable us to tune our ears to the voice of God. How do we read 1 Peter as Christian Scripture so as to hear God's address? The methods of choice have generally focused elsewhere: the voice of the reconstructed historical Jesus, the voice of the redactors of the Gospels, or the voice of the "community" behind the text, for example. Reading biblical texts as Christian Scripture so as to hear God's address, however, has not been a priority. Maybe, then, it is not surprising that Wesley Kort can offer this commentary, "At one time people knew what it meant to read a text as scripture, but we no longer do, because this way of reading has, since the late medieval and reformation periods, been dislocated and obscured."[19]

Karl Barth is famously remembered for his programmatic expression of the task of theology: "dogmatics does not ask what the apostles and prophets said but what we must say on the basis of the apostles and prophets."[20] However, as pastors and theologians have often complained, the passing of two centuries of biblical studies has left both the church and those engaged in constructive theology with little access to "what the apostles and prophets said." Tom Wright, himself no mean biblical scholar, admits that "many systematic theologians . . . have become impatient with waiting for the mountains of historical footnotes to give birth to the mouse of theological insight."[21]

In his introduction to a useful reader on *The Theological Interpretation of Scripture*, Stephen Fowl describes theological interpretation in a way that also unveils the challenges before us.

> [T]heological interpretation will be nonmodern in several respects. First, it will be interested in premodern biblical interpretation. Second, it will shape and be shaped by the concerns of Christian communities seeking

19. Kort, *"Take, Read,"* p. 1.
20. Barth, *Church Dogmatics*, 1.1, p. 16.
21. N. T. Wright, "Galatians," p. 206.

to live faithfully before the triune God rather than by the concerns of a discipline whose primary allegiance is to the academy. Third, theological interpretation of scripture will try to reject and resist the fragmentation of theology into a set of discrete disciplines that was the result of the conceptual aims of modernity and the practical result of professionalization. Finally, theological interpretation of scripture will be pluralistic in its interpretive methods; it will even use the interpretative methods of modernity to its own ends.[22]

Set in relation to the history of biblical interpretation, and especially in relation to recent study of the Bible with its primary interest in history, the program Fowl sets forth surfaces a number of important and not a few difficult questions. These would include:

> What is the role of history and historical criticism?
> What are the status and role of the OT in the two-testament canonical Scriptures?
> What is the relationship between exegesis and doctrine?
> What is the nature of the "unity" of Scripture?
> What is the role of the canon in theological interpretation?
> Does theological interpretation extract theological claims or principles from the Bible?
> Does theological interpretation draw up the plans for a theological superstructure towering above a biblical foundation?

And there are many others besides.

With regard to the potential contribution of 1 Peter to the discussion, two questions are of particular importance: What of the OT? What of the relationship between Scripture and Creed? I will discuss these serially.

(1) 1 Peter and the "Problem" of the Old Testament. By "problem of the OT," I could be referring to any of a number of issues. Peter Enns parses "the problem" along three lines: relative to other ancient near eastern literature, the OT lacks the uniqueness allotted it in some traditional notions of inspiration and revelation; theological diversity within the OT does not easily divulge a unitary witness; and the OT is handled by the NT writers in surprising ways (surprising, that is, when compared with the canons of modern exegetical practices).[23] The problem I have in mind, however, is more nar-

---

22. Fowl, "Introduction," p. xvi.
23. Enns, *Inspiration and Incarnation.*

rowly focused on the status and role of the OT within the two-testament, Christian canon — an issue that surfaced prominently in the nineteenth century in the theology of Friedrich Schleiermacher but would subsequently become even more pressing under the hegemony of the historical-critical paradigm in scholarship of the Hebrew Bible.

In an explicit statement on the relation of theology and the Bible appearing at the head of his discussion of "The Formation of the Dogmatic System," Schleiermacher wrote, "All propositions which claim a place in an epitome of Evangelical (Protestant) doctrine must approve themselves both by appeal to Evangelical confessional documents, or in default of these, to the New Testament Scriptures, and by exhibition of their homogeneity with other propositions already recognized."[24] The importance of the issues foregrounded in this statement grows once we remind ourselves of Schleiermacher's status as the "father of Protestant theology." Indeed, reading this methodological axiom some 175 years after its first publication, we can see how Schleiermacher brings into focus questions that continue to trouble us.

At this point, my interest is narrowly construed by Schleiermacher's use of "New Testament" to modify "Scriptures," a methodological move that makes explicit what has been and continues often to be the practice associated with theology in its diminishing or completely negating the status and role of the OT as Christian Scripture. In this, Schleiermacher was heir to the agenda already associated with Gabler, whose influential paradigm for biblical and theological studies accorded privilege to the NT. Schleiermacher thus bears witness to what is almost certainly the inevitable outcome of the impulses of history-oriented analysis. In so far as it requires that the meaning of texts resides at their historical address, historical criticism has no intrinsic need for the theological claim constituted by the location of these two collections together as one "book." What is more, Schleiermacher saw his disjunction of Old and New Testaments as the disjunction of Judaism and Christianity. Admitting the historical connection between Christianity and Judaism "through the fact that Jesus was born among the Jewish people" (§12.1), he nonetheless lumped Judaism together with Heathenism "inasmuch as the transition from either of these to Christianity is a transition to another religion" (§12.2). He continues: "Christianity cannot in any wise be regarded as a remodelling or a renewal and continuation of Judaism" (§12.2). For Schleiermacher, as for Christian theology in his wake, antipathy toward or opacity with regard to the status of the OT is tied to antipathy or opacity toward Israel.

---

24. Schleiermacher, *Christian Faith*, §27, italicized in the original.

This does not mean that supersessionism — that is, that the church has displaced Israel as God's chosen — of necessity requires antipathy toward the OT. Indeed, traditional supersessionism needs the OT in order both to demonstrate the failure of Israel (and hence the need for a replacement people) and to anticipate Christ and the church. Even this tradition marginalizes the OT, however, treating it as a kind of historical prefix to the advent of Christ or relegating it to the status of prophecy in need of fulfillment, rather than as divine revelation in its own right.[25]

From the standpoint of reading the NT, the disestablishment of the place of the OT in the two-testament Christian canon prompts a theological crisis often overlooked, for one of its practical effects is its identification of the OT as simply one of several possible presuppositions for reading the NT. It is "background," with the approximate status of the OT apocryphal and pseudepigraphal books or the texts and artifacts of Greek religion. This is problematic *historically*, since it fails to account for the role of Israel's Scriptures in the formation of Christian self-understanding, and *theologically*, since it makes optional the theological inheritance into which the NT is inscribed.[26]

In some ways, the problem of "unity and diversity" in the Bible reaches its acme here. Prioritizing historical analysis resulted in the splintering of the Bible into multiple voices behind the text, whether as persons (say, John or Paul or Jesus) or as purported sources (J, P, E, and D or Q, L, and M in Pentateuchal and Gospel studies respectively), and into different witnesses to perhaps the same voice (Is it possible to speak of a "Pauline theology," or only of a theology of Romans or Philippians?). The most basic splintering, however, was into two "books," OT and NT. Pressing further, to speak of either an "old" or a "new" presumed the relation of the one to the other. With that relationship rendered problematic or even unnecessary, new labels were required. Enter, then, the language of "Hebrew Bible" (with reference to the OT) and "Greek Scriptures" (with reference to the NT). Never mind the avalanche of anachronisms set off by these new labels, our concern here is that, by adopting the nomenclature of "Hebrew Bible" in opposition to "OT," the question of the status of the first two-thirds of the Christian Bible appears to have been resolved through a process of negation. Although motivated in some circles by a concern to raise the importance of those books as something more than "preface" to the Second Testament, the practical effect is nonetheless to tear the OT from its canonical role in a Christian reading of the Scriptures.

What can be said of a church that has in so many arenas proven itself to

---

25. See B. D. Marshall, "Jewish People," pp. 82-87; cf. Soulen, *God of Israel.*
26. Cf. Stuhlmacher, "Biblical Theology," pp. 176-77.

be Marcion's child and an academy that so easily takes for granted the segregation of biblical studies into testamental specializations? If the tool driving the wedge between Old and New Testaments was the hegemony of historical criticism, the result is a profoundly theological problem now present as a necessary aspect of resolving the estrangement of Bible and theology. All of this means, at least, that, for theological hermeneutics, the role of historical criticism must be recast as servant rather than as master.

How, then, might the status of the OT as Christian Scripture be construed in a theological hermeneutic? For Francis Watson, the Old and New Testaments are two interrelated but separate collections whose identity is derived from its relationship to the figure of Jesus. In one of his most concise statements, he writes, "In relation to Jesus, the OT precedes and the NT follows; the OT prepares the way of the Lord, and the NT proclaims that the Word has become flesh and dwelt among us. . . . As Christian Scripture the OT does not have its center within itself but is in teleological movement towards the time of fulfillment."[27] What holds the entire Christian Bible together, therefore, is its christological focal-point, with the OT conceptually establishing and anticipating the preconditions for the intelligibility of Jesus' person and work, though without assuming that this defines Jesus without remainder.[28] A quite different perspective is offered by Christopher Seitz, for whom it is important to maintain that "the OT's per se voice functions normatively for Christian theological construction."[29] For him, indeed, the OT demands to be heard *as Christian Scripture,* apart from its appropriation in the NT, and this for theological reasons. Because God has spoken and acted in the OT and because the NT affirms and does not challenge this basic theological claim, then the Christian is obliged to hear the OT as a discrete witness irrespective of how NT writers might have understood it. To claim the OT as Christian Scripture in this sense is therefore to recognize that the voice we hear in the OT is neither non- nor pre-Christian.

This introduction to what I have called the "problem of the OT" has thus surfaced two issues, the one related to the other — namely, the status of the OT in a Christian theological hermeneutic and, then, the question of Israel's status vis-à-vis God's elect. Briefly, I have sketched two ways in which the first question has been addressed by two of our contemporaries, Watson and Seitz, both of whom are concerned with theological interpretation of Christian Scripture. How might 1 Peter help our understanding here?

27. Watson, "Confessing Biblical Scholarship," p. 2; cf. idem, "Response."
28. See further, Watson, *Text and Truth.*
29. Seitz, "Two Testaments," p. 209; cf. idem, *Word without End;* idem, *Figured Out.*

It is important to declare straightaway that what Peter most certainly does not provide is a method for resolving these theological-hermeneutical complexities. Indeed, fascination with "method" or "technique" is a manifestation of the modern era. This is not to say that method is a recent invention or is irrelevant. Already in the Reformation era, handbooks emphasizing grammar and philology were produced to guide exegetical performance, and we find in Second Temple Judaism an array of "exegetical rules."[30] It is rather to recognize the cottage industry that has mushroomed around modern fascination with "technique" and the presumption that often trails close behind — namely, that good interpretation is foremost a matter of the right method rightly applied. Peter gives us no four-step process by which to lift ourselves out of the quagmire. His agenda focuses elsewhere, particularly on a basic stance vis-à-vis the Scriptures.

Nor does Peter provide us with what modern biblical scholarship has so desperately sought: the singular meaning of biblical texts. Eco's perspective is pertinent: "no text can be interpreted according to the utopia of a definite, original, and final historical meaning. Language always says more than its unattainable literal meaning, which is lost from the very beginning of the textual utterance." At the same time, as Eco would be the first to admit, a text's potential for multiple meanings is not an open door to unbridled subjectivism or an infinite range of valid readings; rather, for Eco, "the limits of interpretation coincide with the rights of the text."[31] The outstanding issue, which begs for resolution, is how to determine "validity in interpretation." If these texts are capable of a range of interpretations, what interpretations might be classified as "Christian"?

On the question of theological hermeneutics, the point of entry is 1 Pet 1:10-12:

> Concerning this salvation the prophets, who prophesied concerning the grace that has come to you, searched and explored, inquiring into what person or what sort of time was meant when the Spirit of Christ which was in them was testifying in advance to the sufferings coming to Christ and his subsequent glories. It was revealed to them that they were not serving themselves but you in these matters — matters that have now been announced to you through those who evangelized you through the Holy Spirit sent from heaven, matters on which angels yearn to gaze.

Watson refers to this text in support of his position, observing that, "in the light of Easter Day, the law and the prophets can be seen as preparing the way

---

30. On the latter, see Ellis, *Old Testament*, pp. 79-101.
31. Eco, *Limits of Interpretation*, pp. 2, 6-7.

for what has now come to pass. But this only becomes apparent *retrospectively:* the prophets themselves had only the haziest knowledge of the future events to which, for Christian hindsight, they bore witness (1 Pet.1.10-12)." As a consequence, Watson finds in 1 Peter support for his position that a Christian reading of the Jewish Scriptures is actually a *re*reading that clarifies and reorders the first reading. "The second reading does not simply repeat the first reading, but neither does it erase it; it preserves within itself the knowledge that, although the end or goal is now known, that was not the case at first."[32] However true Watson's position might be in the case of the actual practice of Christian readings of Israel's Scriptures, Peter neither supports this practice nor the hermeneutic on which Watson claims it is based. In other words, we would support Watson's hermeneutical role to the degree that we are ill-formed as competent readers of the Christian Scriptures.

Peter does speak of the haziness of the prophets, but this is not the point of Peter's theological hermeneutic. Rather, the character of OT witness is documented in Peter's claim that "the Spirit of Christ which was in them was testifying in advance to the sufferings coming to Christ and his subsequent glories." Authorial awareness, clarity, or intent aside, the status of the OT as Christian witness was and is determined by the testimony of the Spirit of Christ. That is, Peter's theological hermeneutic does not depend on the competence of the prophets but on the animating presence of the Spirit of Christ.

We are right to find in 1:10-12 the "hermeneutical key"[33] or, better, a theological hermeneutic of Scripture, with Peter intimating how the Scriptures must be read: (1) as "testifying in advance to the sufferings coming to Christ and his subsequent glories" and (2) in continuity with the communities comprising Peter's audience, a continuity made possible by the Holy Spirit. Moreover, we are right to find here a theological pattern by which to order the prophetic witness. What is problematic is the suggestion that this theological pattern is the consequence of reading with new lens provided by the advent of Christ. What Peter makes clear, actually, is that this theological pattern is resident already in the Scriptures of Israel themselves. The issue is not that we are taught by the advent of Christ to read the Scriptures retrospectively, but that the Christ in whom Christians place their trust and now worship is the same Christ who long ago revealed the ways of God in the Scriptures. Interpretively, then, Israel's Scriptures are not predictions that Christ would fulfill, but rather testify to the Christ (and none other) who first inspired them.

---

32. Watson, "OT as Christian Scripture," pp. 229-30.

33. So, e.g., Goldingay, *Models for Interpretation,* pp. 146-47, 150-51; Schutter, *Hermeneutics and Composition,* pp. 100-109.

To illustrate, Peter develops the work of Christ in terms of the great act of liberation by which Israel as a people received its call, exodus from Egypt. Christ does not "fulfill" exodus, nor does he displace it in the divine order of things. Rather, both the deliverance manifest in exodus and the deliverance manifest in Christ disclose the one aim of God, reveal the character of God, and thus paradigmatically make known the nature of God's story. To illustrate further, we can recall Peter's claim in 2:21-25 that Christ actualizes the role of Yahweh's Servant in Isa 52:13–53:12. At one level, we can allow that the suffering of Christ serves Peter as a theological assumption from which to read the Scriptures and make sense of them for Christians in the world. However, this is not because Isaiah 53 waited for the advent of Christ in order to be understood in relation to Christ. Nor is it merely that Peter found in Isaiah 53 a "prophecy" awaiting its "fulfilled" in Christ. Instead, the suffering of Christ and the suffering of Yahweh's Servant point to the same reality in God's purpose: God's saving purpose on behalf of a sinful people accomplished in the suffering of Yahweh's righteous servant. Inspired by the Spirit of Christ, Isaiah's text testifies to the saving economy of God, so that the proper context within which to read Isaiah 53 is conceptualized theologically as the terrain in which God actualizes his purpose. From this perspective, we would do violence to the text were we to treat it merely as a literary artifact or historical curiosity, or press it into the service of an agenda other than the outworking of God's aims.[34]

The hermeneutical question that must be resolved resides in the abundance of possible readings of Israel's Scriptures, its surplus of meaning. We cannot escape the multiple expressions of Israel's heritage in the first century, presumably any of which could demonstrate from the Scriptures that their community and its members comprised the heirs of Israel. Are we left to this conclusion: to each community its own valid reading? How might we differentiate among them? How might we know when or that the Scriptures are read aright (i.e., within the context of the divine economy)? Peter's theological hermeneutic rests in a mode of understanding that takes seriously how theological commitments shape or order our reading of Scripture. In this case, the suffering-and-vindicated Christ and the Scriptures of Israel are mutually informing, with the Scriptures demonstrating how to read Christ and Christ demonstrating which reading of Scripture has divine sanction. *Faithful readings of the OT take seriously its witness "in advance to the sufferings coming to Christ and his subsequent glories" and lead to the faithful communi-ties comprising Peter's audience. Why should we trust that such readings are*

34. Rae, "Texts in Context."

divinely sanctioned? We do so not because Peter does historical analysis better than the Pharisees do or because he follows the literary structure of the passages in question better than do the Qumran sectarians (as important as these interpretive procedures might be). Instead, we do so because Peter actualizes the Scriptures in a way that coheres with their generation long ago, a coherence guaranteed by the Spirit of Christ.

This does not mean that the words of the prophets were devoid of revelatory value before Christ; after all, God made known to the prophets that their words were anticipatory (v. 12). It does mean, though, that the prophets lacked the mental equipment, the pattern of thinking, necessary to grasp what was before them. Even more so, it means that Peter finds an essential unity in the outworking of God's purpose, from the Scriptures of Israel to the community of Christ's followers — a unity that coheres in the one God, Yahweh, who raised Jesus from the dead; and in the Holy Spirit, who inspired the prophets of old and the evangelists who proclaimed the message of the prophets as good news.

Once again, we see here the importance of recognizing and embracing the fabula (or story behind the story — i.e., the divine economy; see further, below) of rejection leading to vindication, suffering to glory that underlies the biblical narrative. With it, Peter points to a particular way of articulating the beginning, middle, and end of the biblical story. By it, the story of salvation finds its locus here: the prophets, who prophesied in advance, testified to the sufferings destined for Christ and the subsequent glory. They prophesied through the Spirit, and the gospel message, which embodies this story, was brought by means of the Spirit.

Peter's hermeneutic ties the exemplary and salvific life of Christ into the ancient purposes of God found in Scripture, but also the lives of Christians into the life of Christ. Inexorably linked in Peter's passion theology are the sufferings of Christ and his followers, who are thereby assured that their suffering will have a redemptive effect and will lead to glory and honor from God just as Jesus' suffering did. Peter's theological hermeneutic is thus oriented toward the identity, faith, and practices of the people of God. This is the interpretation of things inspired by the Spirit.

The ramifications of this hermeneutic are numerous, since it insists that, for the theological work of the church, no biblical text ought to be interpreted, as it were, "on its own," but always in relation to its context in the divine order of things. Accordingly, Scripture is not *about* humanity, or even a particular, identifiable segment of humanity, Israel. Nor is Scripture *about* Christ — that is, the Bible is not a christological book. Rather, the economy to which Scripture bears witness and which provides its primary interpretive context is *theo*logically determined. Scripture's subject and focus is God, whose identity is found in three persons, Father, Christ, and Spirit. Yahweh's purpose thus determines the shape of our interpretation of Scripture at the same time that it calls on its readers to identify with his purpose (that is, to choose sides).

Recalling the intimate association of OT and Israel in Schleiermacher's (and others') theological method, we ask, finally, What of the status of Israel as God's people? Peter has studied the past with an eye to serving the present and especially to showing the continuity between followers of Jesus and Israel of old. He has demonstrated a heightened commitment to tracing the heritage of his largely Gentile audience into the story of Israel, thus making the story of his aliens and strangers in the world continuous with that of the people of God formed in God's great act of deliverance from Egypt. It is here that Christians find their true identity and learn the way of faithfulness. With good reason, Achtemeier observes, "In 1 Peter, the language and hence the reality of Israel pass without remainder into the language and hence the reality of the new people of God."[35] Peter collapses the historical distinctives between ancient Israel and contemporary Christians in favor of theological unity. This is not to deny the importance of history but to use history rhetorically as a means of legitimating the status of Peter's harried audience before God.

Naturally, the way in which the heritage of Israel is identified as the heritage of those who follow Jesus raises the question of the ongoing status of Israel in God's purpose. That honorific names given Israel by God are taken over as labels of the community of Christ-followers (2:9-10) presses the issue further. It may not be surprising, then, that supersessionism (or "replacement theology") is attributed to Peter by some commentators, either explicitly or implicitly.[36] The Venerable Bede is more to the point, though, when he observes that Peter is speaking especially of Gentiles "who were once separated from the way of life of the people of God but then through the grace of faith were joined to his people and obtained the mercy which they did not know how to hope for."[37] Unfortunately, little more can be said, for Peter's agenda is

---

35. Achtemeier, p. 69; see further, idem, "Christology"; idem, "Newborn Babies." Note, however, that Achtemeier does not mean by this to suggest that Jews are thereby excluded from God's new people.

36. E.g., Grudem, p. 113; Davids, p. 93.

37. Bede, p. 88; see also p. 86. Similarly Slaughter: "By use of these Old Testament Jewish titles, Peter is not likely to be suggesting that Christians are replacing Jews in God's sight. Rather, he is explaining that they are added on to what God has already begun" (p. 34). See further, Diprose, *Israel*, pp. 52-55.

not so much to work out the relationship between Israel and the church as to clarify, according to God's perspective, the honorable status of the Christian community in the world.

(2) 1 Peter and the Rule of Faith. That the Bible precedes theology, that the Bible should provide the raw materials required for theological work, and, indeed, that the Bible is theology's foundation — such assumptions as these have led students of the Bible to be wary of theological categories and doctrinal systems lest they predetermine what the Bible can or cannot say. To be avoided at all costs is the anachronistic theological framework into which the pluriform message of Scripture might be squeezed. As a result, today, biblical studies seems quite capable of carrying on its work sans any need to draw on or check in with theological studies, and vice versa.

Nevertheless, theological hermeneutics cannot escape the question of the relationship between those ecumenical creeds that define the faith of the church and this canonical collection we embrace as Scripture. For many, the issue here is one of source and continuity: Can these biblical documents, by themselves, support the theological weight placed on them by later creedal formulations? So, for example, study of NT christology has often centered on the question whether we find in the Bible adequate foundation for the later explicit confessional claims of Jesus' divinity.[38] More pressing, however, is that, taken on their own terms and without recourse to a history or community of interpretation, biblical texts are capable of multiple interpretations, not all of which are recognizably "Christian." *Sola Scriptura* cannot guarantee the Christian identity of a person or community or religious claim. Irenaeus (*ca.* AD 130 — *ca.* 202) noted how Gnostics made use of biblical exegesis in their arguments, but insisted that they did not read the Scriptures aright on account of their disregard of the "order and connection" of Scripture. Failing to understand the Bible's true content, he maintained, they put the pieces of the biblical puzzle together in a way that turned a king into a hound or fox (*Adversus Haereses* 1.8.1). The "order and connection" to which Irenaeus referred was the rule of truth, also known as rule of faith, a summary of the Christian kerygma that measured faithful interpretation of Scripture. Writing of this stage in the church's history, William Abraham observes, ". . . the development of a scriptural canon was utterly inadequate to meet the challenge posed by the Gnostics. The Gnostics had no difficulty accepting any canon of Scripture which might be proposed; being astute in their own way and eclectic in their intellectual sensibilities, they simply found ways to use Scripture to express their own theological convictions. *This should come as no surprise*

---

38. See, e.g., Dunn, *Christology in the Making.*

to anyone. A list of diverse books merely by the sheer volume involved is susceptible to a great variety of readings."[39] The church has long recognized the need, then, for a "ruled reading" of its canonical texts, and this presses the question, How does Scripture function vis-à-vis doctrine?

We have just seen one way in which 1 Peter addresses this question. In 1:10-12, Peter recognizes the past testimony of the Spirit of Christ in providing a theological pattern by which to construe the meaning of Scripture. This pattern consisted of the *fabula,* or story behind the story, of the *Vindication of the Suffering Righteous.* What is more, Peter demonstrates that a faithful reading of Scripture traces the story from before creation itself, to the end-time revelation of Christ, *and through the life of the church comprised of aliens and strangers in the world.* Are other readings of the Scriptures possible, even defensible? Of course, but, for Peter, they would not be Christian readings of the Scriptures, since Peter's theological hermeneutic orders our reading of the Bible accordingly. Lest this perspective on Peter's hermeneutic seem overly subjective, let me reiterate what Peter himself claims — namely, that the pattern by which he orders theological exegesis is nothing other than the testimony of the Spirit of Christ, who inspired the prophets of old.

Let me sketch three additional points, two more directly from 1 Peter itself, the third more procedural. First, in our discussion of 3:18-22, we found evidence of an "ordered" reading of Scripture on the part of Peter himself. Clearly, in 3:21, Peter labels the Flood as an antitype of baptism, following the path of early Christian typology, in which interpretive interest moves beyond the analysis of particular words and grammatical relationships in deference to larger, overarching patterns within Scripture. Additionally, we saw that, in 3:18-19, Peter interprets the career of Christ — "put to death as a human but made alive by the Spirit" — in relation to biblical material regarding angels and the deceased in ways not readily supported by a straightforward grammatico-historical analysis. Either this, or within decades of the writing of 1 Peter, Peter's own exegesis was being read according to a theological pattern by which Christians were making sense of the work of Christ in terms of his defeat of Death and evangelization of the inhabitants of Hades. For persons inclined to treat Scripture as the *foundation* for theological claims, an approach like this will seem problematic. However, this interpretation could easily have grown out of Israel's own story. Israel's understanding of Sheol as the place of the dead coheres with the OT distinction between life (lived in this world, before and in relation to Yahweh) and death (in the underworld, separate from Yahweh). And this coheres well with Israel's speech about human experience

---

39. Abraham, *Canon and Criterion,* p. 36; emphasis added.

"in Sheol/in the Pit" and "out of Sheol/out of the Pit," which Brueggemann suggests has been informed by Israel's own life story in and out of bondage in Egypt.[40] Christ's "descent into hell" thus becomes the ultimate expression of life beyond death — that is, of the reach of Yahweh's saving purpose even beyond that most potent of barriers to life, death itself. In the theological hermeneutic of the early church, the witness of 1 Peter would not need to be taken as a foundation for belief in Christ's descent into hell; instead, it would be perfectly natural for the story of exodus, recapitulated again and again in Israel's life and hope, to provide the pattern for comprehending Christ's saving career.

In early patristic exegesis, the notion of "economy" was paramount, for the correct interpretation of Scripture must express its economy — that is, its overall order or structure. For Irenaeus and others, "the true and accurate reading of scripture . . . must follow the divine economy by which God has put together the mosaic of scripture."[41] This perspective is not reserved to the second century. Barth urged that the "whole" within which the parts of the Bible must be comprehended was its unified witness to God.[42] For Peter, unity is above all to be found in the one God, the Father of our Lord Jesus Christ, who raised Christ from the dead, and in his purpose from before creation; and then in the agency of God expressed also in Christ and the Spirit, who share in God's purpose and similarly span the biblical story from creation to final revelation; and then in the one people of God, strangers and aliens in the world, from sojourner Abraham and his clan to the end of all journeying with the "imperishable, uncorrupted, and unfading inheritance."

Second, for Peter all theological interpretation is ordered by its end; in this sense, this hermeneutic is eschatologically determined. We have referred to this perspective in 1 Peter with the narrative-analytical term "backshadowing." Knowledge is asymmetrical with respect to time, so that we experience life as the unfolding of knowledge, the realization of some of the possibilities of what might have been; the present comprises the effects of past causes. So historians make sense of the present by showing how it is contained in the intentions and possibilities of the past. In large part, the theological perspective from which Peter operates, however, can be described as a kind of backward causation — events happen as a consequence of things to come; ". . . the future must already be there, must somehow already exist substantially enough to send signs backward."[43] Knowing the future, even in broad outline, as Peter

40. Brueggemann, *Theology of the OT,* pp. 483-85.
41. O'Keefe and Reno, *Sanctified Vision,* p. 37.
42. Burnett, *Theological Exegesis,* pp. 77-78.
43. Morson, *Narrative and Freedom,* p. 7.

claims, equips him with a remarkable hermeneutical compass, allowing him to proclaim the sovereignty of God as Lord of history (including the history yet to unfold), to assure his audience of the temporal restrictions on the calamities of Christian life, and thus to urge that "time" is not open and choices are not "free" — at least not in an ultimate sense. These struggles will not continue into perpetuity and the injuries of acidic treatment are constrained in both duration and effect. This eschatological perspective orders Peter's hermeneutic.

Third, the choices open to exegetes are more than the two usually supplied — either allow the creeds to overrun the biblical text or hold the creeds at bay so as not to spoil our close reading of the biblical text. As I have urged in my reflections on the triune God and on Peter's understanding of the church, we can inquire into how creedal statements might order our reading of 1 Peter without thereby insisting or assuming either that 1 Peter must provide the foundation for the church's confession concerning its own nature or that it must address each of these issues at all. The earliest creedal traditions (already at work in the earliest NT documents — e.g., from the simple acclamation, "Jesus is Lord" [1 Cor 12:3], to more developed formulas such as 1 Cor 15:3-5 represents) served to unify the Christian movement and to clarify its faith in the context of its challengers, with the result that the ecumenical creeds speak to the integrity of the Christian church and its faith. "The creed provides a measure or rule for the proper reading of Scripture. Such a rule is necessary for a coherent communal understanding of Scripture."[44] Procedurally, then, a theological hermeneutic is well-advised to ask, What do we see in 1 Peter as we read it as Scripture through the prism of the creeds that we would not otherwise see?

"You Must Become Holy in Every Aspect of Life": Anthropology and Salvation in 1 Peter

The questions of what it means to be human and what it means to be saved are close kin, and in Christian theology it is difficult to address the one apart from the other. This is because an understanding of salvation, or soteriology, raises questions about the human condition from which the human family needs to be liberated and the condition to which liberation is directed. The situation of humanity in relation to the rest of the creaturely world is likewise a part of the discussion. In order to get at these issues, my plan is to focus on

44. L. T. Johnson, *Creed*, p. 47.

four aspects of Peter's theological anthropology: the essential nature of the human person, the shaping of human identity, the character of sin and liberation, and holiness as divine gift and charge.

Wholism in Anthropology

Jürgen Moltmann observes that, "from its earliest beginnings, the history of Western anthropology shows a tendency to make the soul paramount over the body, which is thus something from which the person can detach himself [*sic*], something to be disciplined, and made the instrument of the soul. This tendency is an essential element in the history of freedom in the Western world."[45] Moltmann goes on to develop an alternative approach, emphasizing human embodiment within the biblical tradition, but he is well aware that, in doing so, he is swimming against the current.

Theologians ancient and contemporary have found in an anthropology of body-soul dualism either the necessary supposition or corollary of a number of theological loci, including creation in the divine image, a theology of free will and moral responsibility, hope for life after death, and Christian ethics.[46] Even if they would debate the precise *origin* of the soul,[47] as early as the second century of the Christian era it was nonetheless clear to most theologians, as *Epistle to Diognetus* 6 puts it, that "the soul lives in the body, but it does not belong the body"; indeed, "the soul, which is invisible, is put under guard in the visible body" and "the soul is imprisoned in the body, but it sustains the body" (LCL). That these statements provide the basis for a parabolic description of the place of Christians in the world speaks to their status as widely held presuppositions. "Without the soul, we are nothing," wrote Tertullian, adding, "there is not even the name of a human being — only that of a carcass" (*On the Flesh of Christ* 12). Summarizing in his *Treatise on the Soul,* Tertullian writes, "The soul, then, we define to be sprung from the breath of God, immortal, possessing body, having form, simple in its substance, intelligent in its own nature, developing its power in various ways, free in its determinations, subject to changes of accident, in its faculties mutable, rational, su-

---

45. Moltmann, *God in Creation*, p. 244.

46. See, e.g., Cooper, *Body, Soul, and Life Everlasting* (emphasizing eschatological arguments); Moreland and Rae, *Body and Soul* (emphasizing ethics); Jewett with Shuster, *Who We Are,* chapters 1 and 2 (with reference to the image of God).

47. Are souls created by God *ex nihilo* at the moment of their infusion into the body (Lactantius, Aquinas, Peter Lombard)? Are body and soul formed together (Tertullian, Luther)? Are souls preexistent (Origen)?

preme, endued with an instinct of presentiment, evolved out of one (archetypal soul)" (22). Lactantius observed early in the fourth century that the body, formed from the earth, is solid and mortal — "made up of a ponderous and corruptible element," "is tangible and visible, is corrupted and dies"; but the soul "received its origin from the Spirit of God, which is eternal" (*Divine Institutes* 12). He observes, "The body can do nothing without the soul. But the soul can do many and great things without the body" (11). Traditionally, the doctrine of humanity develops the uniqueness of humanity with respect to human creation in the divine image and the human possession of a soul.[48] Often these two affirmations are reduced to one, with the soul understood as the particular consequence of creation in God's image.

Of course, the theological tradition is not univocal on these issues. A dualist anthropology grounds a Christian hope usually articulated in terms of the "immortality of the soul," yet the Christian tradition has stubbornly held to a belief more pointedly focused on the body — that is, the "resurrection of the body." Granted that in Second Temple Judaism talk of "resurrection" and "afterlife" might trigger a range of conceptions: resuscitation of a dead corpse, revivification of the soul, flight of the immortal soul at the moment of death, transformation of the body for afterlife, and more. It is nevertheless true, as Caroline Walker Bynum has demonstrated, that Christian belief in the resurrection has emphasized the physicality of both resurrection and ultimate salvation,[49] and today this interest has led to a renewed emphasis on the resurrection *of the body,* as the Apostles' Creed has it, as opposed to the immortality of the soul. A number of Christian theologians and scientists alike have emphasized that Scripture holds forth no belief that the quality of immortality is inherent in some part of the human person; rather, Scripture teaches that the hope of life after death is rooted solely in the gracious intervention of God to bring forth life.[50] As John Polkinghorne reasons,

> It seems a coherent belief that God will remember and reconstitute the pattern that is a human being, in an act of resurrection that takes place beyond present history. Thus the Christian hope centres on a real death

48. E.g., Robinson, *Doctrine of Man.*

49. Bynum, *Resurrection of the Body.* She concludes ". . . that a concern for material and structural continuity showed remarkable persistence even where it seemed almost to require philosophical incoherence, theological equivocation, or aesthetic offensiveness. . . . The materialism of this [medieval Christian] anthropology expressed not body-soul dualism but rather a sense of self as psychosomatic unity" (p. 11).

50. E.g., Harris, "Resurrection and Immortality"; Longenecker, "Resurrection Thought"; Peters, et al., eds., *Resurrection.*

followed by a real resurrection, brought about through the power and merciful faithfulness of God. Christianity is not concerned with a claim that there is human survival because there is an intrinsically immortal, purely spiritual, part in our being. The ground of hope for a destiny beyond death does not lie in human nature at all, but in divine, steadfast love.[51]

Additionally, in recent decades extraordinary advances in the neurosciences have raised repeated questions about the viability of traditional belief in body-soul dualism;[52] indeed, Pannenberg has observed that advances with regard to the close mutual interrelations of physical and psychological occurrences have robbed of their credibility traditional ideas of a soul distinct from the body that is detached from it in death.[53] The relevance of science in theological discourse has long been recognized. Augustine wrote, "Some people read books in order to find God. But the very appearance of God's creation is a great book." He advised, "Ponder heaven and earth religiously."[54] The concept of God's "two books," the Bible and the natural world, reached proverbial status in seventeenth-century English natural theology. More to the point, both Peter and his interpreters are shaped by the scientific views of their (including our) time, so the influence of science is inescapable. The only question is whether it is acknowledged. The issue is this: scientific experiments, one after the other, have demonstrated that the very capacities traditionally associated with the soul — relationality, affect, memory, empathy, spiritual awareness, volition, self-awareness, and more — have neural substrates; they are functions that depend on neuronal processes.[55] It is not too much to say that, when compared with dominant, traditional views, a dramatically new image of humanity is emerging.[56]

1 Peter enters the fray for two reasons.[57] (A) Environmentally, 1 Peter

51. Polkinghorne, *Science and Theology*, p. 115.

52. The issue has surfaced publicly in the last thirty years, but problems with body-soul dualism were associated with the very beginnings of modern neuroscience in the work of Thomas Willis in the seventeenth century (J. B. Green, "Mind-Brain Problem"; and, more fully, Zimmer, *Soul Made Flesh*).

53. Pannenberg, *Systematic Theology*, 2:181-202. See especially, Murphy, *Bodies and Souls.*

54. Augustine *Sermo Mai* 126; ET in Froehlich, "Take Up and Read," p. 12.

55. The literature is voluminous and growing. For convenient points of entry, see Jeeves, ed., *Changing Portraits;* G. R. Peterson, *Minding God;* Lakoff, "How to Live with an Embodied Mind"; Ramachandran, *Human Consciousness;* Feinberg, *Altered Egos;* Libet, et al., eds., *Volitional Brain.*

56. So Metzinger, "Consciousness Research," p. 6.

57. Cf. Feldmeier, "Seelenheil."

was written at the confluence of a number of streams of tradition, Hebrew and Greek, spread across a continuum with more radical forms of dualism and monism at each pole. I use these two terms, dualism and monism, largely because of their philosophical imprecision. Today, a dizzying array of possibilities are championed,[58] but they presume a measure of analytical precision lost on these ancient texts. Hence, by "dualism" I refer to the view that body and soul are separate entities, with the soul survivable apart from the body; and by monism I refer to nothing more than those portraits of the human person that require no second, metaphysical entity, such as a soul, to account for human capacities and distinctives.

In terms of the philosophical climate in which Peter lived, it is common today to speak of a characteristic dualism among the Greeks and Romans; in fact, however, "Greek thought" cannot be reduced to a single viewpoint. For Aristotle, the soul is that in virtue of which an organism is alive (*On the Soul* 2.1.412a-413a10); even if "soul" is not the same thing as body, neither is it non-matter but can still occupy space. Even Plato thought that the soul was constructed from elements of the world, though he famously argued for a distinction between body and soul. Within Epicureanism, mind and spirit were understood to be corporeal because they act on the body, and all entities that either act or are acted upon are bodies by definition. Stoicism taught that everything that exists, including the human soul, is corporeal; accordingly, only non-existent "somethings" (like imagined things) could be incorporeal. Ancient medical writers emphasized the inseparability of the internal processes of the body (what we today call "psychology") and its external aspects ("physiology"); any differentiation between inner and outer was fluid and permeable. In short, there simply was no singular conception of the soul among the Greeks, and the body-soul relationship was variously assessed among philosophers and physicians in the Hellenistic period.[59] For example, Heinrich von Staden includes in "the belief cluster" shared by philosophers and physicians of the Hellenistic period, among other things, that the "soul" is corporeal, and that the "soul" is generated with the "body" and neither exists before the

---

58. For four views being discussed now in Christian theology, see J. B. Green and Palmer, eds., *In Search of the Soul*. The range of options is extensive — including, e.g., substance dualism, naturalistic dualism, wholistic dualism, emergent dualism, two-aspect monism, constitutional materialism, emergent monism, open-system emergentism, deep physicalism, nonreductive physicalism, and (reductive) materialism — leading Ted Peters to complain that, "when philosophers of religion and their intellectual fingers tapped around on issues such as the human soul, they squeeze out more distinctions than Minute Maid can squeeze out orange juice" ("Soul of Trans-Humanism," pp. 389-90).

59. For a useful survey, see J. P. Wright and Potter, eds., *Psyche and Soma*.

body nor is separable from it after the body's demise. That is, "the soul does not exist independently of the body in which it exists."[60]

The position of Israel's Scriptures is more straightforward. There, the term *nepeš* ("vitality, life," sometimes translated "soul") is used with reference to the whole person as the seat of desires and emotions, not to the "soul" as though this were something separate from one's being. *Nepeš* can be translated in many places as "person," or even by the personal pronoun (e.g., Lev 2:1; 4:2; 7:20). It denotes the entire human being, but can also be used with reference to animals (e.g., Gen 1:21, 24; 2:7; 9:10).[61] From time to time, the Hebrew term *bāśār* ("body, flesh") stands in parallel with but not in contrast to *nepeš* — the one referring to the external being of the person, the other to the internal (e.g., Isa 10:18). Indeed, although *bāśār* frequently refers to the fleshly aspect of a person, this term is also prominent as an expression of the spiritual. *Bāśār* and *nepeš* ". . . are to be understood as different aspects of man's [*sic*] existence as a twofold unity."[62] The Scriptures of Israel employ other terms, too, to speak of humans from the perspective of their varying functions — e.g., *lēb* ("heart") with reference to human existence, sometimes in its totality (e.g., Gen 18:5; Ezek 13:22), sometimes with reference to the center of human affect (e.g., Prov 14:30) or perception (Prov 16:9);[63] and *rûaḥ* ("breath, spirit") with reference to the human from the perspective of his or her having been imbued with life (e.g., Job 12:10; Isa 42:5). In short, Israel's Scriptures project a monist anthropology.[64]

If the possession of a "soul" is not the distinguishing mark of the human person, what is? In general, the Scriptures do not consider the human person in essential terms, bur rather in relational. Human uniqueness vis-à-vis other members of creation, animate and inanimate, is thus measured in terms of humanity having been created by God "in his own image" (Gen 1:26-

---

60. Von Staden, "Body, Soul, and Nerves," p. 79.

61. See Seebass, "נפש‎," and especially his excursus on "The Translation 'Soul'" (pp. 508-10).

62. Bratsiotis, "בשׂר‎," p. 326.

63. See Fabry, "לב‎."

64. See Childs, *Biblical Theology,* pp. 566, 571-72. What of Gen 2:7 ("the Lord God formed the human being of the dust of the ground, breathed into his nostrils the breath of life, and the human being became a living soul [*nepeš*]," my translation)? In fact, the same term is used only a few verses earlier with reference to "every beast of the earth," "every bird of the air," and "everything that creeps on the earth" — that is, to everything "in which there is life *(nepeš)*" (1:30, my translation), demonstrating incontrovertibly that "soul" is not, under this accounting, a unique characteristic of the human person. One might better translate Gen 2:7 with reference to the divine gift of *life:* "the human being became a living person" (my translation). See further, Stone, "Soul."

27). Here, Genesis identifies the human person as Yahweh's partner, and with emphasis on the communal, intersexual character of personhood, the quality of care the human family is to exercise with regard to creation as God's representative, the importance of the human modeling of the personal character of God, and the irrefutable vocation of humans to reflect in their relationships God's own character.[65] The distinguishing mark of *human* existence when compared with other creatures is thus the whole of human existence in relation to God and God's creation, and not some "part" of the individual.

By the time of the writing of 1 Peter, as one might expect, three hundred years of admixture of Greco-Roman and Hebrew perspectives on the nature of humanity had yielded a range of positions. Some would be more clearly dualistic (e.g., the writings of Josephus and Philo), others monist, though with most Jewish writers rejecting body-soul dualism in favor of a more "integrated" anthropology (as Tom Wright recognizes).[66] The question before us is how Peter portrayed the human person, and the significance this has for his theology. Did he lean in a more dualist perspective, or did he situate himself more fully in continuity with the monism of the Scriptures and of parts of the Greco-Roman tradition?

(B) The second reason we have pressed 1 Peter into the fray is that his language usage might invite a dualist reading. If this were the nature of his anthropology, this would have devastating consequences for his theological perspective on suffering, on life in the world, and on eschatology, and it would be hard to square with his particular understanding of sin.

How does Peter deploy those terms associated with the nature of the human person? He uses σῶμα (*sōma*, "body") only once, in 2:24, with reference to Christ's having borne "our sins in his body on the tree." Since this is the very Christ who was present in times past to inspire the prophets (1:11) and who will be revealed in glory (e.g., 1:13; 4:13) — i.e., since Christ is also portrayed as a transcendent figure who shares in the identity of God — then this is a profound affirmation of bodily existence and of the significance of embodied, human suffering. σάρξ (*sarx*, "flesh, body") appears in 1:24 to refer to "humanity," and otherwise with reference to life as a human in 3:18, 21; 4:1 (2x), 2, 6. ψυχή (*psychē*, "life, vitality," sometimes translated as "soul") appears in 1:9, 22; 2:11, 25; 3:20; 4:19. In 2:11, it is set in contrast to σαρκικός (*sarkikos*, "belonging to this world"), but it never appears in relation to *sarx*. (*Sarx* is juxtaposed with πνεῦμα [*pneuma*, "spirit"] in 3:18; 4:6, however.) Christ is the

---

65. See further, below; also Brueggemann, *Theology of the OT*, pp. 451-52; Gunton, "Trinity, Ontology and Anthropology."

66. N. T. Wright, *People of God*, pp. 254-55; more fully, see Warne, *Hebrew Perspectives*.

guardian of the Christian's *psychē* in 2:25, just as God is guarding "you" for a salvation ready to be revealed at the last time (1:5; ὑμᾶς, *hymas,* "for you," from 1:4). Those who suffer entrust their *psychai* (plural) to God (4:19). In 3:20, *psychē* refers to "persons," Noah and his kin, rescued through the flood. In general, then, for Peter, *sarx* concerns "life as it reflects and/or pertains to this world" and *psychē* connotes "life as it reflects and/or pertains to the world to come." The dualism with which Peter operates, then, is eschatological and not anthropological.

In other words, Peter proves himself to be more the heir of the Scriptures of Israel than of Plato in his understanding of the human person. This allows him to take with the utmost seriousness the dire situation in which his audience finds itself; after all, it is not the case for him that they could retreat from physical pain into their genuine selves, their souls, untouched by calamity or suffering, as though their suffering were purely physical. Nor does he offer the related "hope" that, even though they are suffering in their bodies, this does not matter since God is really concerned with and will rescue their souls. His emphasis on embodied existence provides life in this world its fullest significance and it serves as the basis for his emphasis on a faithful "manner of living" in the material world. Human physicality also ties Peter's audience to the rest of creation, thus pressing the question how their suffering participates in the situation of the cosmos and, perhaps more to the point, how their liberation is tied to the fate of the cosmos. Importantly, the work of Christ in death and exaltation has repercussions for humans and for the cosmos.

The Shaping of Identity

This emphasis on human embodiment has immediate ramifications for Peter's structuring of Christian identity, as well as for his perspectives on sin and holiness. A few comments at the interface of theology and neuroscience will help to set the stage.

Contained within the affirmation of human embodiment is the reality that human beings are always in the process of formation. "People don't come preassembled, but are glued together by life."[67] So writes Joseph LeDoux, who describes how, at a basic level, formative influences are encoded in the synapses of the central nervous system, those points of communication among the cells of the brains, or neurons. Though the organization of the brain is hardwired genetically, genes shape only the broad outline of our mental and be-

---

67. LeDoux, *Synaptic Self,* p. 3.

havioral functions, with the rest sculpted through our experiences. From birth, we are in the process of becoming, and this "becoming" is encoded in our brains by means of synaptic activity. Simply put, in our early years, far more synapses are generated than are needed, so that the formation of the brain proceeds under the principle, "Use it or lose it." Those neural connections that are used are maintained and remodeled, while those that fall into disuse are eliminated. Fresh connections are generated in response to our experiences, even into adulthood, until the very moment of death. Hence, both nature and nurture end up having the same effect — namely, shaping our neuronal interactions in ways that form and reform the developing self.

Three consequences immediately follow. First, "who we are" can never be divided into "parts." Transformation of "my inner person" is nothing more or less than transformation of "me." If human identity is grounded in consistency of memory; if the differentiating marks of the human person are the development of consciousness, individuality within community, self-consciousness, the capacity to make decisions on the basis of self-deliberation, planning and action on the basis of that decision, and taking responsibility for these decisions and actions;[68] and if these are neurobiologically supported, then there is no segregating human (trans)formation into bodily and soulish categories. There can be no (trans)formation that is not fully embodied. What is more, if the neurobiological systems that shape how we think, feel, and behave are forever being sculpted in the context of our social experiences, then in a decisive sense we can speak of personal (trans)formation only in relational terms; our autobiographical selves are formed within a nest of relationships, a community.

Second, and closely related, the popular distinction between "being" and "doing" is made problematic, since the "me" who is "being" is nothing other than the "me" implicated in the "doing." This is not to deny the possibility of a disconnection between what one claims to be and what one is, or between what one claims to be and what one does; this is the problem of human integrity implicated in sin (cf. Jas 1:21-27).

Taken together, these first two points urge an understanding of human identity wrapped up in an inescapable network of relationships and interactions, and manifest in behaviors, in performance. Before moving to the third consequence, let me put these first two in perspective by drawing on the work of Pierre Bourdieu.

In his analysis of human interactions, Bourdieu concerned himself with accounting for the practical competence of human agents and the social con-

68. This list is adapted from Hefner, *The Human Factor*, pp. 118-19.

ditions within which those encounters find their meaning. In his theory of practice, he gave special attention to the concept of *habitus,* those dispositions that incline agents to respond and act in certain ways without those actions and responses being ruled by external authorities or even coordinated by thoughtful decision-making. These are

> [s]ystems of durable, transposable dispositions, structured structures predisposed to function as structuring structures, that is, as principles which generate and organize practices and representations that can be objectively adapted to their outcomes without presupposing a conscious aiming at ends or an express mastery of the operations necessary in order to attain them. Objectively "regulated" and "regular" without being in any way the product of obedience to rules, they can be collectively orchestrated without being the product of the organizing action of a conductor.[69]

Dispositions are "embodied history," internalized and so operative at a preconscious level, and practices grow out of the interplay of this "second nature" and specific social contexts. Emending Bourdieu's model for our purposes, we can see how it has immediate implications for human identity — which, then, would grow out of the interrelations among one's theological imagination, dispositions (allegiances, commitments, character), and practices. Why is this important? To start, it helps us to map the chasm between the character of ethical discourse and formation in many churches and church-related institutions today and in Christian Scripture. Whereas the church and its related institutions tend to focus on "moral acts," Scripture, and 1 Peter in particular, is far more concerned with shaping our imaginations, our patterns of thinking — which, inevitably, finds expression in transformed commitments and practices. This means that Peter's repeated directive to "do good" (e.g., 2:14, 15, 20; 3:6, 11, 17; 4:19) cannot be reduced merely to doing the right things; rather, with Peter having defined "good" in terms of God's purpose and plan, it is putting into play "the good."[70] Behavior serves as the display window of one's deepest commitments.

Before developing this further with reference to 1 Peter, recognition of a third implication is necessary. This is that meaning-making is central to our day-to-day experience, and that we will go to great lengths to construct stories

---

69. Bourdieu, *Logic of Practice,* p. 53.

70. Michaels thus erroneously claims that Peter's emphasis is on action — on "doing good," not "being good" (p. lxxiv). The problem here is twofold. First, Michaels too easily allows a division between being and doing. Second, Michaels does not take seriously enough that all "doing good" is cast under the canopy of "being holy" (1:14-16; see further below).

that provide a context for understanding and interpreting what we perceive to be true. My brain imposes structure on the data it receives from its sensory organs, contributing to a baseline conclusion that my sense of reality is both embodied and interpreted within the framework of my formation as a social being. My "perception" of the world is based in a network of ever-forming assumptions about my environment, and in a series of well-tested assumptions, shared by others with whom I associate, about "the way the world works." Ambiguous data may present different hypotheses, but my mind disambiguates that data according to what I have learned to expect to see.

Similarly, we typically explain our behaviors not by physical and chemical chains of cause-and-effect, but through the historical narratives by which we collaborate to create a sense of ourselves as persons and as a people. Memory, then, is not passive chronicling of events, but active reconstruction, through which we seek coherence. Our sense of who we are is intricately woven into and out of our long-term memories, which, then, are the prerequisite for self-representation. We tell stories about ourselves through which we construct our sense of self, and these are woven out of the threads and into the cloth of the stories present to us in our social world and communal traditions. These narratives order our beliefs, setting the terms of what we take to be true, normal, and good. And the inculcation of a new narrative reorders life events, giving them fresh significance within a new structure of beliefs. Human transformation in this sense is a conversion of the imagination. According to one narrative, the majority view, ostracism is a shaming practice designed either to bring people back into line with regard to their behavior or to marginalize them so that their faulty attitudes and behaviors do not contaminate the community; according to another narrative, ostracism is a badge of honor, an indication of the authenticity of one's faith in God. According to one narrative, Christ, the "living stone," "rejected by humans"; according to another narrative, "in God's perspective," "elect, honored" (2:4). Human identity is embodied, comes to expression through behaviors that exhibit one's dispositions, is cultivated relationally, and is structured (and restructured) narratively.

Although I have come at these issues by way of explorations at the interface of theology and science, I need not have done so. Every one of these emphases is embedded in Scripture,[71] and is on display in 1 Peter. Thus:

> A central feature of Peter's letter is its marking of time, its narration of God's work from before creation to the eschaton, and especially its

---

71. See, e.g., Di Vito, "Old Testament Anthropology"; K. Berger, *Identity*, pp. 26-43.

folding of the narrative of Peter's audience into the narrative of Christ's suffering and vindication, itself folded into the narrative of God's dealing with Israel in Israel's Scriptures. Peter is in identity-formation mode as he inscribes the community of Christians, mostly Gentile, into the history of Israel, giving them strong roots in antiquity; and as he accords privilege to the *fabula* or pattern of thinking that both outlines the effective nature of righteous suffering and shows the certain movement of life through righteous suffering to vindication.

With the language of "new birth" and "growth," as well as in his juxtaposition of Roman conventions and God's, Peter highlights the past reality and ongoing necessity of his audience's conversion to new ways of thinking, feeling, believing, and acting. In a society noted for its hyper-concern with social status, Peter urges that what really matters is one's standing before God. Status is measured according to divine standards. This requires new ways of ordering and evaluating life in the world, but also personal reconstruction within a new web of relationships, resocialization within the new community, and the embodiment of a new life-world evidenced in altered dispositions and attitudes.

We find no instruction in 1 Peter for autonomous individuals. Household and kinship language is enmeshed with metaphors of Israel as "a nation" or "people" in ways that accentuate the embeddedness of Christians with others who share their experience of new birth, who therefore share (or are urged to share) a common way of seeing things, who are deeply attached to a common set of beliefs and values, and who, together, seek to live according to the terms of this new life. Within the community, the community itself is formed, as is each of its members, through the practices of unceasing love, hospitality, prayer, joy, and vigilance and through the stewardship of God's grace in service. This is their center of identity, from which they are able to engage with courageous endurance a hostile world.

The Character of Sin and Liberation

Peter's vocabulary of sin is as imaginative as his theology of sin is insightful. Words like "stumble," "transgress," "offend," "wrongdoing," "lost," "hard-hearted," "stiff-necked," "falling short," or "overstepping" are missing from 1 Peter. Instead we find:

references to the former lives of Peter's Christian audience: "no longer being shaped by the desires that marked your former time of igno-rance" (1:14); "you were liberated from the emptiness of your inher-ited way of life" (1:18); "having set aside every evil and every deceit, and pretenses and jealousies and all slander" (2:1); "enough time has been lost discharging the will of the Gentiles, conducting yourselves in acts of unrestraint, lust, drunkenness, carousing, bawdy partying, and unseemly idolatry" (4:3); and "flood of unrestrained immoral-ity" (4:4);

references to behaviors currently to be avoided by Peter's Christian au-dience: "avoid worldly cravings that wage war against life" (2:11); "live your remaining time as a human no longer in accordance with human desires but in accordance with the will of God" (4:2); and "let none of you suffer as a murderer, thief, or evildoer, or as a mischief-maker" (4:15); and

labels for the antagonists of Peter's Christian audience: "disbelievers" (2:8; 3:1; 4:17) and "blasphemers" (4:4).

Additionally, Peter refers once to the "unrighteous" for whom the "Righteous One" suffered (3:18).

What is perhaps most conspicuous about this catalog is its astonishing lack of interest in vilifying the opponents of Christian communities. When Peter comes closest to documenting the sorry behaviors of "the Gentiles" (4:3-4), he stops short, placing the spotlight instead on those Gentile-ish be-haviors that once characterized the lives of his audience. We might justifiably conclude that those vices equally categorize those outside the Christian com-munity, but this is not a step Peter takes. Instead, he models that pattern of Christ on display in 2:21-25 and directs his audience to do the same by refus-ing to engage in reciprocal animosity and slander.

With regard to his understanding of sin, Peter's thought is particularly penetrating. Building on our earlier observations regarding the embodied, communal, and narrative character of human life and identity, we see imme-diately the profundity of Peter's diagnosis. The past, he says, was marked by the work of a sculptor who shaped human life according to the conventions, values, and dispositions of ignorance. Ignorance functions like a master de-termining every thought and move of its slave, or as an artisan creating hu-man life in its own image. Clearly, in such a context, "ignorance" cannot be equated with "lack of data" or "lack of knowledge," in the narrow sense; rather, ignorance is potent as "a faulty pattern of thinking," influential as a mistaken life-world. Ignorance is less "not understanding," more "misunderstanding" — that is, a failure at the deepest level to grasp adequately and thus to participate fully in God's aims. It provides the impetus and muscle for behaviors that Peter catalogs as vices — that is, as outside the boundaries of those whose deepest allegiance is to the God and Father of the Lord Jesus Christ. This perspective is fully at home in our understanding of the embodied nature of human existence, which accounts both for the potency of the narratives by which our lives are structured and for inappropriate desires that spring from natural ones, blossoming as distended and distorted cravings.[72] Needed, then, is a theological transformation, a conversion of the imagination, tied to the reformation of commitments, attitudes, and daily practices. "Sin," then, is inhabiting and executing the muck of a religious and moral climate set against God; it is present as an ethos of unrestrained immorality and craving that cannot but shape persons in its own likeness.

This is simply the way of sin. Sin begets sin, one sinner the next, one sin after the other. Sin in Genesis 3 is like a contagion, transmuting from shame and vulnerability to heightened alienation, even to the point where Yahweh's own voice is no longer invitation but threat. The woman and man learn to deflect responsibility — the man blaming the woman, the woman the serpent — as each assumes the role of victim. Human self-determination leads now to a freedom that exceeds its grasp and a harmony set aside in favor of struggle, hierarchy, and drudgery.[73]

Genesis 3 is only the beginning. Cain's murderous act results in his exile (Gen 4:1-16); a restless, godless society emerges (Gen 4:17-24; 5:28-29); global violence leads to global destruction (Gen 6:1–9:18); sin in Noah's family leads to the enslavement of one people by another (Gen 9:17-27); and finally the imperialism of conquest leads to the confusion of languages (Genesis 11). From Genesis across the whole of the Christian Bible, sin emerges as a characteristic feature of human existence. For Paul, sin "entered the world" (Rom 5:12), "came to life" (Rom 7:9), and now enslaves not only individuals but all of humanity (Rom 1:18-32; 3:23). "Sin" is a power that can lord it over a person (Rom 6:12, 14), a master to whom wages are due (Rom 6:23), an owner to whom people have been sold in the slave market (Rom 7:14). In all this we are not far from Peter. Using different language, the apostle can nonetheless depict sin as a power, as desires and cravings capable of plaguing even the reborn. It is not for nothing that Peter portrays Christians as slaves to God, who

---

72. Williams, *Sociobiology and Original Sin,* pp. 148-52. On this issue more broadly, see now the interchange between Domning (evolutionary biologist) and Hellwig (Catholic theologian) in *Original Selfishness.*

73. W. P. Brown, *Ethos of the Cosmos,* pp. 160-61.

therefore cannot be enslaved to the empty, ancestral ways that shape society at large.

Leaving no doubt but that the capacity for transformation is divine gift, Peter nonetheless addresses his audience as persons capable of choice and responsible for their behavior. Responsibility is not a consequence of intentionality, however. Choices contrary to the will of God in the past were made in ignorance, but this did not make those choices any less sinful.[74] Even for those called to holiness, sin remains an option, a road that need not be taken. But for those who lack the empowering grace of God, what sort of choice is this? If the human family, globally and historically, has embraced sin, apart from divine intervention, what options remain genuinely open? If the narratives around us are implicated in godlessness and our very lives have been sculpted to reflect those narratives, can we even know how to entertain alternatives? If the values and practices honored in the universe of day-to-day existence, the ideals and modes of conduct sanctioned by its systems and institutions, are set in opposition to the ways of God, then the pull of sin's gravity is difficult to escape indeed. Genuine choice can come only in the context of authentic options, and this highlights both the profundity of Peter's diagnosis of sin as power and the importance for him of the work of the Spirit in evangelism and of a community set on following the pattern of Christ and embodying the character of God. Another vision of the world is needed, one that reminds us that the ancestral ways may be common heritage but are not necessarily defining influence. Renewed patterns of thinking must animate the new community oriented toward resisting evil and sin.

Recognition of the oppressive power of the attitudes and practices, the embodied narratives of evil, around us does not excuse sin. Peter never countenances a response like, "I was raised in this world; what did you expect?" any more than he might say "Satan made me do it." The idolatry of life apart from Christ is a sobering recognition of our limits and proclivity to expressions of evil, socially and personally. Reflecting backward on his own rise to power as an officer in the Soviet army, Aleksandr Solzhenitsyn wrote, "Pride grows in the human heart like lard on a pig" — this, as he acknowledged that the demonic "system" that robbed him of so much of his life, that left him cruelly imprisoned, was not an invention of Soviet Russia but the progeny of the human heart.[75]

Yet there is no escaping the reality that human patterns of thinking, feeling, believing, and behaving are cultivated socially. This perspective does

---

74. This is a major thesis of Biddle, *Missing the Mark,* chapter 5.
75. Solzhenitsyn, *Gulag Archipelago,* p. 163.

not spell the loss of freedom to choose, but it does suggest the degree to which our choices are circumscribed already by communities of formation, even formation along evil lines. For this reason Peter urges his audience to be no longer "shaped by the desires that marked your former time of ignorance" and claims for them that "you were liberated from the emptiness of your inherited way of life."

Contrary to the claims of the serpent in the Garden, the concepts of good and evil do not exist in a vacuum. These are not "objective" realities, but must be understood in relation to some instrument of measuring. Living in a world that measures "the good" always in relation to the interests of "my group" or of "people like me" presses upon us choices that perpetuate disobedience, estrangement, disharmony, alienation. In an agonistic society like that of Peter's world, the canons by which "the good" is measured beckon all the more, since failure to line up behind Roman conventions would lead to serious and immediate ramifications. What of "the good" as defined by God's own words spoken over creation? Like those who live with lifelong disease, humans easily adjust their lives to account for their maladies. We can scarcely imagine what the freedom to choose God's "good" would be, so much have we adapted ourselves to estrangement and alienation. We are in need of the medicine of liberation — and this is precisely what God administers, according to Peter: through Christ's defeat of the powers arrayed against God; through his sacrificial death, by which the stain of sin was cleansed; through the power of the Spirit in evangelism and sanctification; through the community of believers, whose mutuality of love provides a new home and family; and through the new identity that comes as believers are written into the eternal narrative of God's merciful agenda.

For Peter, the basic sin appears to be idolatry. Not only does he refer to the idolatrous past of his audience; he also refers to the blasphemy of those who oppose the faith. Blasphemy, it is true, can extend beyond idolatry, but it is hardly unrelated. In his analysis of human sin, Ted Peters refers to two kinds of blasphemy — the overt dishonoring of the name of God or his work and the covert use of the name of God in order to mask evil, the use of God and the things of God in self-justification.[76] Idolatry, Jenson urges, is the primary sin, a counter to the first command, "You shall have no other gods before me" (Exod 20:3). "One can serve the Lord, or one can plunge into the religious world's welter of possibilities and quests, but one cannot do both at once."[77] Either way, humanity is implicated in the use of communal and per-

---

76. Peters, *Sin*, p. 217.
77. Jenson, *Systematic Theology*, 2:134.

sonal projects as deities to our own ends; "we necessarily posit a middle realm in which to meet and negotiate with the deity, and 'idols' are whatever then emerges to conduct the negotiation."[78]

Though without reference to 1 Peter, Jenson names a further sin with which Peter is very much concerned even if he never voices it in quite this way. This is the sin of despair: "acting as if I were not delivered over to the future, as if in what I already am I were my proper self."[79] Two possibilities come to the fore. The first is life lived under the horrific illusion that *this* is the object of our hope, that *this* is the destination for which the journey of faith was begun, and thus that *this* is our genuine home. The second is abandonment of hope in the face of wrongful suffering. The first forgets that this is Babylon, while the second assumes that Babylon has the last word. The first assumes that courageous resistance in the world is unnecessary, while the second assumes that courageous resistance in the world is useless. The effect is the same — capitulation in the face of that temptation so integral to the experience of exile: defection, apostasy. It is no wonder that Peter urges joyful and hopeful responses even in the midst of suffering (e.g., 1:8; 4:13). And it is no wonder that he anticipates the sin of despair with his sharpest imperatives: "Remain vigilant! Stay alert! Your adversary, the devil, like a roaring lion is on the prowl, seeking someone to devour. Resist him, standing firm in the faith, recognizing that the same kind of sufferings are being accomplished in the case of your family of believers throughout the world" (5:8-9).

Being Holy, Being Saved

The goal of faith is salvation (1:9), about which Peter speaks especially though not exclusively in eschatological terms (1:5, 9). Present Christian life is a process of "growing up in salvation" (2:2) as believers grow into the robes of obedience they received with their baptism (3:21). This means that, for Peter, salvation is past, present, and future.

The notion of living into salvation finds its center in 1:14-16, "As obedient children, no longer being shaped by the desires that marked your former time of ignorance, you yourselves must rather become holy in every aspect of life, just as the one who called you is holy, for it is written, 'You shall be holy, because I am holy.'" This directive on Peter's part reaches back into the past of new birth, claiming that holiness is not only divine declaration but also hu-

---

78. Jenson, *Systematic Theology,* 2:137.
79. Jenson, *Systematic Theology,* 2:145.

man vocation. In the language of the Reformers, justification (what Peter would call rebirth) is related to sanctification (what Peter would call becoming holy) as indicative and imperative — or, in the language of Orthodox and Roman Catholic theology, as declaring righteous and making righteous. Wesley, for whom holiness was of paramount importance, spoke of sanctification as the work of God in us by the Spirit by which we are restored to God's image.[80]

This reference to the divine image is of special importance, and this for two reasons. First, the most basic word spoken with reference to the human family was God's decision to create humanity in his own image — a word brought again into the foreground in God's speech, "You shall be holy, because I am holy." Second, at the same time that Peter writes of holiness in imitation of God, he goes on to paint the Christian life as tracing the pattern of Christ, as walking in his footsteps (2:21). The human vocation to reflect the divine image is exegeted in relation to God's holiness and the imitation of Christ.

Gen 1:27 reports the outcome of the divine soliloquy: "God created humankind in his image, in the image of God he created them." Accordingly the embodied existence of human beings has its singular vocation to reflect the image of God. Unfortunately, the relative succinctness of this affirmation in Genesis cannot be equated with clarity, and how best to understand this "image" has long been the focus of diverse interpretations among Jews and Christians — ranging from some physical characteristic of humans (such as standing upright) to a way of knowing (especially the human capacity to know God), and so on. What is obvious is that humanity is thus defined in relation to God in terms of both similarity and difference: humanity is in some sense "like" God, but is itself not divine. Humanity thus stands in an ambivalent position — living in solidarity with the rest of the created order and yet distinct from it on account of humankind's unique role as the bearer of the divine image, called to a particular and crucial relationship with Yahweh and yet not divine.[81] Recent theological study has emphasized relationality as the heart of what it means to reflect God's image, as well as the text's democratized notion of the image of God (all humanity, not an elite subgroup of humans, such as royalty, bears the divine image) and the affirmation of the divine image as divine gift (humanity does nothing to merit its elect status).[82] In a further OT text addressing the nature of humanity, Psalm 8, similar mo-

---

80. Klaiber and Marquardt, *Living Grace,* p. 286.

81. McGrath, *Nature,* p. 197.

82. See Towner, "Clones of God"; Middleton, *Liberating Image;* Grenz, *Social God and Relational Self.*

tifs recur. The psalmist appears baffled that Yahweh's splendor does not completely overshadow the possibility of his attending to mere earthlings: "What are human beings that you are mindful of them?" (Ps 8:4). On the other hand, the psalmist recognizes that the human family finds its true identity only in relation to God. Moreover, in a world that marked differences between royalty and common folk on the basis of family lineage, Psalm 8 disallows any concern with inherited status. Instead, it attributes nobility to every person. Here again, the prominent place of humankind in relation to the rest of creation is accentuated, at the same time that human beings are positioned clearly in relation to God and the heavenly counsel.

Taken within its immediate setting in Genesis 1, "the image of God" in which humanity is made transparently relates to the exercise of dominion over the earth on God's behalf. This dominion is unrelated to superiority or conflict, however; it is not the consequence of a win-lose encounter. God's words thus affirm the creation of the human family in its relation to himself, as his counterpart, so that the nature of humanity derives from the human family's relatedness to God. The concept of the *imago Dei,* then, is fundamentally relational and takes as its ground and focus the graciousness of God's own covenantal relations with humanity and the rest of creation. The distinguishing mark of *human* existence when compared with other creatures is thus the whole of human existence and not some "part" of the individual. Humanity is created uniquely in relationship to God and finds itself as a result of creation in covenant with God. Humanity is given the divine mandate to reflect God's own covenant love in relation with God, within the covenant community of all humanity, and with all that God has created.

Whether one can imagine that all this stands in the background of Peter's directives, it is nonetheless clear that the soteriological journey on which he envisions his audience traveling is a rehabilitation of human relatedness to God and God's creation as this is envisioned in Israel's Scriptures. The existential beginning point of this journey is entry into the new reality to which Peter refers as God's having "given us new birth" (1:3). "New birth" is a dramatic metaphor for the decisive transformation of life that has come in accordance with God's mercy and by means of the resurrection of Jesus. One's relations to the exigencies of life are read according to a radically different pattern of thought — one that grows out of new birth. Eschatological salvation has broken into the mundane world, so that nothing can be the same. As Paul phrased it, "If anyone is in Christ, there is a new creation: everything old has passed away, see, everything has become new!" (2 Cor 5:17). What Peter announces is nothing less than a conversion to a new way of thinking, feeling, believing, and behaving. This is conversion with all that this entails, including the construction of a new autobiography oriented around allegiance to God, the refreshment of personal identity within a new web of relationships, resocialization within the new community, and the embodiment of a new narrative, Israel's own story, evidenced in altered dispositions and attitudes.[83]

In new birth we are "made holy," in the sense that God has called us out. Whoever belongs to God is holy. For the reborn, holiness is also a mandate, for the call to holiness is a call to live in accordance with the will of God or in imitation of God: "you yourselves must rather become holy in every aspect of life, just as the one who called you is holy." What is more, Peter's phrase, "in every aspect of life," is a précis of the text from which he quotes, Leviticus 19, in which holiness extends into what we today might call "inter-human common life within society," "social welfare" within the community of one's neighbors, as well as "the religious-cultic area" and "the area of sexual taboos."[84] Peter's phrase "in every aspect of life" summarizes the concerns of Leviticus 19: family and community respect (vv. 3, 32), religious loyalty (vv. 3-8, 12, 26-31), economic relationships (vv. 9-10), workers' rights (v. 13), social compassion (v. 14), judicial integrity (v. 15), neighborly attitudes and conduct (vv. 11, 16-18), distinctiveness (v. 19), sexual integrity (vv. 20-22, 29), exclusion of the idolatrous and occult (vv. 4, 26-31), racial equality (vv. 33-34), and commercial honesty (vv. 35-36).[85] Within the context of Peter's world, holiness is bi-directional — both the practice of love within the Christian family and the practice of risky resistance vis-à-vis the institutions that define the larger world. Clearly, this is a holiness of engagement, not of withdrawal.

Peter places "becoming holy" together with "no longer being shaped by the desires that marked your former time of ignorance" (1:14-15). This juxtaposition is important, for it marks holiness as a potent sculptor of life just as we earlier found "ignorance" to be. Wesley spoke of this in terms of deliverance from the slavery or dominion of sin. He acknowledges, with Peter, that a tendency to sin remains (Peter thus reminds his audience not to suffer as "a murderer, thief, or evildoer, or as a mischief-maker," 4:15), but even if it remains, it no longer reigns.[86] In the case of 1 Peter, this "making holy" comes in various forms, especially the contrasting but nonetheless formative influences of suffering (the testing of faith as purgation, 1:6-7) and of the unmitigated love practiced within the household of faith (1:22; 2:17; 3:8; 4:8; 5:14).

Though without using the terminology, Peter presents Christ as holy —

---

83. On this model of conversion, see Meeks, *Christian Morality,* pp. 18-36; Snow and Machalek, "Convert"; N. H. Taylor, "Social Nature of Conversion."

84. So Klaiber and Marquardt, *Living Grace,* p. 287.

85. So C. J. H. Wright, "OT Ethics."

86. Collins, *Evangelical Moment,* p. 81.

referring to him in 3:18 as "the Righteous One," sketching the character of his righteousness in 2:21-25, and tying liberation to "the precious blood of Christ, like that of a lamb without blemish or defect" (1:19). Accordingly, Christ in his suffering and resurrection was able to mediate the mercy of God to human beings who, on account of sin, were marked by pollutants; sin, that powerful taskmaster, stains and spoils, but the sacrifice of Christ liberates and cleanses. What is more, in his sufferings Christ modeled holiness for believers by demonstrating the behavior that wells up from holiness. Further, in his sufferings and resurrection, Christ proved the holiness of God, for the holy God is the one who stands by and delivers his people; his faithfulness invites and enables theirs (see 1:5; 4:19).

The imitation of Christ for which Peter calls is thus a second call to holiness. On the one hand, Peter has represented Christ's righteousness in terms so fully oriented toward the condition of his first audience that they can exhibit holiness by doing (almost) precisely as Christ has done. Notice, then, Peter's portrait of Christ's innocent suffering, his refusal to retaliate, and his response to verbal abuse — all reminiscent of the very situation Peter envisions of his audience. On the other, "imitation" has a more expansive sense of "performance" or "putting into play" the character of the person or thing imitated. Thinking of the character and behavior of Christ as a "script" or "score" to be performed, creative fidelity makes immediate sense: "fidelity" in the sense that the notes on the score or words in the script predetermine the parameters of performance, "creative" in the sense that life is too particular and unruly to be carefully scripted, but Christians can nonetheless be shaped by this script and can understand the plotlines of life by it.

Returning to the model I adapted from Pierre Bourdieu, let me draw out two further implications of Peter's instruction to holiness. Dispositions, we may recall, are "embodied history," internalized and so operative at a preconscious level, with practices growing out of the interplay of this "second nature" and specific social contexts. And human identity grows out of the interrelations among one's theological imagination, dispositions (allegiances, commitments, character), and practices. This model, first, suggests how the imitation of Christ might take different forms — not because the pattern of Christ's life has changed, but because the social contexts within which that pattern is imitated vary. What is crucial here, then, is Peter's concern that we internalize or come to embody the pattern of Christ, that our dispositions be conformed to his. Becoming holy in this way, we will also practice holiness in our daily routines. Second, because "doing" and "being" are inseparable and because human identity grows out of the interrelations of imagination, dispositions, and practices, we should not imagine that practices are *only* the outward manifestations of "who we are." The reverse is also true. Practices effect character development. And so, for example, Peter can call upon his audience to practice hospitality, to be good stewards of the grace of God, and to love without pretentiousness, irrespective of whether they want to do so yet or feel like doing so. These are the practices of the family of God, and those who engage in them find that they become more and more that household, the community that embodies in its inner life the holiness of God.

"If, When You Do Good and Suffer, You Endure, This Is Commendable before God": Peter, Politics, and Society

In tandem with Rom 13:1-7, 1 Pet 2:13-17 is a well-worn centerpiece of debate among Christians regarding church-state relations. The outcome of those debates, insofar as they are said to follow the perspective of 1 Peter, is fairly predictable. "The author views the Roman system favorably and encourages cooperation with the Roman authorities," writes Richard Cassidy.[87] Walter Pilgrim queries, "What then should be the attitude of Christians toward those in political power?" He imagines a variety of perspectives. "Some Christians may have strongly advocated political resistance. Perhaps others urged withdrawal and quietness. Still others . . . may have argued for more openness and accommodation with their pagan neighbors. Whatever the arguments, the response of [1 Peter] comes down forcefully on the side of subjection to authorities . . . a willingness to try to get along."[88] Though with more nuance, Wolfgang Schrage concludes that Christians "are free with respect to the authorities, and normally freedom manifests itself in respect and loyalty, submission and honor."[89]

A number of considerations counsel caution with regard to such overly positive constructions of the state and ethics of submission found in these conclusions.[90] For example, for Peter "the will of God" is the umbrella under which any political ethics can be constructed (2:15), dispositions and practices of subordination proceed from freedom rather than coercion (2:16), Christians are enslaved to God rather than to humans or human institutions (2:16), and the honor due the emperor is nothing more or less than the honor due everyone else, including a child or the lowliest slave (2:17). The seeds of

---

87. Cassidy, *Christians and Roman Rule*, p. 78.

88. Pilgrim, *Uneasy Neighbors*, p. 18.

89. Schrage, *NT Ethics*, p. 278.

90. See, e.g., Verhey, *Great Reversal*, pp. 137-40; Achtemeier, pp. 179-88; Cosgrove, *Appealing to Scripture*, pp. 147-48.

these extenuating factors blossom in the *Martyrdom of Polycarp* (ca. 160 AD), in which Polycarp exegetes Rom 13:1 and 1 Pet 2:13 before the proconsul by claiming, "We are taught to render all due honor to rulers and authorities appointed by God, *in so far as it does us no harm*" (10.2, LCL; note, however, that the idea that ruler and authorities are appointed by God derives from Romans, not 1 Peter). Compare the words of the apostles before the Jerusalem Sanhedrin: "We must obey God rather than any human authority" (Acts 5:29).[91] Of course, whatever is said in 1 Peter is also shaped by the reality that the apostle is not developing a theology of the imperial state, nor, for that matter, addressing the ruling authorities, whether local, regional, or imperial. Instead, he addresses a small minority movement of aliens and strangers in the world: his concerns are pastoral.[92]

As important as these considerations might be for a reevaluation of Peter's alleged generous attitude toward the state in 2:13-17, it is even more important that we locate his directives in this single text within the whole of his letter. The debate on this matter has revolved around the disparate perspectives of David Balch and John Elliott, with Balch claiming that Peter encourages his audience on pragmatic and apologetic grounds to integrate themselves into Roman society and Elliott concluding that Peter's is a sectarian audience for whom separation from the world served the author's concern for a unified group identity.[93] Others have waded into the controversy, typically by arguing a via media.[94] Miroslav Volf, for example, introduces into the discussion the category of "soft difference" — not weak, but soft; not hard, but strong. Peter does not envision the changing of social structures but gives the church no less of a social mission. "The distance from society that comes from the new birth into a living hope does not isolate from society. For hope in God, the Creator and Savior of the world, knows no boundaries. Instead of leading to isolation, this distance is a presupposition of mission. Without distance, churches can only give speeches that others have written for them and only to places where others lead them. To make a difference, one must be different."[95] Basing his analysis on more nuanced views of the social-science

---

91. See McDonald, *Biblical Interpretation*, p. 195.

92. McDonald, *Christian Morality*, pp. 176-77.

93. See, e.g., Balch, *Let Wives Be Submissive*; idem, "Hellenization/Acculturation"; Elliott, *Home for the Homeless*; idem, "1 Peter, Its Situation and Strategy."

94. In addition to the two examples that follow, see Bechtler, *Following in His Steps* (who writes of the "liminal existence" of Peter's audience); Richard, "Honorable Conduct" (who emphasizes Peter's assessment of all humans as God's creatures who are therefore worthy of honor).

95. Volf, "Soft Difference," p. 24.

terms "acculturation" and "assimilation" than we find in Balch or Elliott, Torrey Seland concludes that 1 Peter is not interested primarily in the relation of Christians to the world at large; instead, its main strategy is to cultivate the socialization of Christians within the Christian faith and ethos. This includes reference to relations with those outside the Christian community, however, and on this Peter's position is "a rather high acculturation, but with some modifications; it is a modified acculturation where the obedience to Christ is the primary value of life." By acculturation, Seland refers to general attitudes toward such social traits as language, dress, and the like. With regard to "assimilation" — that is, attitudes toward social structures and means by which personal identity is structured — Seland concludes that Peter's stance is negative: "very low, close to non-existent."[96]

I want to approach this issue from a slightly different angle, one that takes seriously the colonial and imperial context within which 1 Peter was written and, therefore, which attempts a greater degree of sensitivity to the potential of Peter's "political voice." In essence, I want to suggest that the categories for our thinking about these issues, that is, our models of social stratification and difference and our regnant typology for thinking about "Christ and culture," have tended to be problematic.

In the modern West, popular opinion has it that society is well-modeled by the image of a pyramid, whether in terms of economic status or the distribution of power. Whatever its utility for comprehending the social world of the modern West, projecting this model onto the world of Roman antiquity introduces significant distortion. For example, the pyramid image assumes a large "middle class," typically measured in economic terms. It assumes a stable increase in proportional and gradually increasing distribution of persons as one moves from the top of the pyramid to the bottom. In its presumption that the upper echelons are available to anyone who works hard enough, it assumes the viability of upward mobility and promotes dreams of rags-to-riches. Moreover, politically, it assumes that the masses located further down the pyramid can exert influence not only on how the "power elite" exercise their power but on which persons are allowed power elite status.[97] Such assumptions make little sense in Roman antiquity, where a more apt image would be a teardrop, which recognizes a relatively small number of elites, no "middle class" to speak of, and little expectation or opportunity for upward

---

96. Seland, *Strangers*, pp. 188, 189.

97. I have borrowed this language from Mills, *Power Elite*; though dated, this analysis is helpful for its discussion of class consciousness in the U.S. and its portrait of the status drama in which those at the pinnacle of power participate.

mobility. In particular, the disjunction between elites and non-elites would be such that options available to persons in the modern West would hardly have been available to persons in antiquity.[98]

How we have come to understand the relationship between Christ and culture has been largely determined by the seminal work of Richard Niebuhr a half-century ago, but not in altogether helpful terms.[99] Even when his influence is unacknowledged, the categories he identified — Christ of culture, Christ against culture, Christ and culture, and so on — are often determinative, prescriptive rather than descriptive. One of the peculiarities of this approach is the way it accords privilege to sociology over theology — that is, the way it assumes the stability of "culture," then parses various ways in which "Christ" might be related to it. What would happen if the opposite were assumed, if the Christian story were assumed to be the stable factor in the equation? In 1 Peter, this story is the exemplar of Christ, whose life, death, and exaltation is read in relation to the story of Israel in the Scriptures, and whose narrative is thus determinative of the lives of those who follow after Christ. Not coincidentally, Luke Johnson finds a similar pattern in the Gospels.

> Their fundamental focus is not on Jesus' wondrous deeds nor on his wise words. Their shared focus is on the *character* of his life and death. They all reveal the same *pattern* of radical obedience to God and selfless love toward other people. All four Gospels also agree that discipleship is to follow the same *messianic pattern.* They do not emphasize the performance of certain deeds or the learning of certain doctrines. They insist on living according to the same pattern of life and death shown by Jesus.[100]

Without doing violence to Johnson's summary, we can easily add that the "messianic pattern" on display in the Gospels includes non-retaliation and the journey through suffering to vindication, emphases so central to the portrait of Jesus in 1 Peter. A further emphasis shared by the Gospels, 1 Peter, and, indeed, the NT materials as a whole is that in his advent Jesus brokered the inauguration of the messianic age, introducing into the cosmos the very conflict that led to Jesus' execution and to the oppressive circumstances that define the lives of Peter's audience. What model befits this reality other than Niebuhr's "Christ *against* culture"? Yet this model too is inadequate since (1) it remains the case that the Spirit of God is presently at work in the world and (2) the inauguration of the messianic age brings with it the mandate not

---

98. Cf. Finley, *Ancient Economy;* Lenski, *Power and Privilege.*
99. Niebuhr, *Christ and Culture.*
100. L. T. Johnson, *Real Jesus,* pp. 157-58.

for declaring war on (or withdrawing from) society at large but for missional engagement.[101]

A further complicating factor is the ease with which moderns in the West have learned to identify church, society, and nation. However difficult this has become in recent years, its lingering presence evidences a history of ecclesial influence that has no analogue for the Christian communities to which Peter addresses his letter. That today we can entertain conversations about the exertion of moral authority by the church on the political scene, whether from the religious right or religious left, is already to introduce choices that could scarcely have entered the thoughts of exilic aliens and strangers. What options are available in a letter concerned with the character of minority Christian life in a manifestly non-Christian and at least at an implicit level anti-Christian world? So accustomed have we become to imagining ourselves in Jerusalem that we are hard-pressed to imagine how to take the measure of faithfulness for persons who find themselves living in Babylon.

For this reason, in his consideration of the "instruction" on church and state in 2:13-17, Volf is right to add three additional considerations to the list of mitigating factors to which we have drawn attention. First, unlike the household codes elsewhere in the NT, the code in 1 Peter pertains to the relation of Christians to unbelievers. Second, Christians find themselves in a conflicted situation that they did not provoke, but from which they cannot escape and in which they are the oppressed party. Third, their communal identity was marked by love of enemies and nonviolence. "Taken together, these three considerations place the 'conservative' exhortation in a new light." Non-retaliation and "doing good" would suppress rather than incite further violence, and thus "break the vicious cycle of violence by suffering violence."[102] What appears to be subjugation, what might be taken as a religious legitimation of oppression, then, is rather a vocation of struggle on the side of the politics of the crucified Christ against the politics of coercion and violence.

One final consideration: The process of colonization requires two parties, the colonizer and the colonized, to achieve a certain and necessary symmetry in attitude and action. Colonizers bring the weapons of military conquest, to be sure, but, over time, must also win the rhetorical — or, better, ideological — war. That is, the conqueror and the conquered must reach an implicit agreement that the new state of imperial affairs is of benefit to all involved. Indeed, God (or the gods) has willed the new arrangement. This means that resistance to the empire can come in the form of active opposition

---

101. See Finger, *Christian Theology,* 2:273-84.
102. Volf, "Soft Difference," p. 22.

but also in the nurturing of an alternative ideology and its concomitant practices. With respect to 1 Peter, it is surely of consequence that Peter's audience is suffering undeservedly, that he qualifies their undeserved suffering in terms of the sufferings of Christ, and that he advises them to engage the wider world in ways that do not lead him to anticipate the termination of hostilities. Instead, he exclaims (as we might paraphrase), "What did you expect? You are following in the footsteps of Christ whose commitments and behaviors similarly won for him opposition and violence" (see 4:12-14). It is hard to imagine, then, Peter anticipating that his instruction might be read as a directive to "fit in" in order to avoid hostility. With his letter, Peter has joined the ideological struggle against the empire and encourages his audience to do the same.

Taken together, these considerations raise the possibility of an engagement in 1 Peter with the social, religious, and political world of significant proportions, but an engagement that can be overlooked by onlookers unfamiliar with an exilic ecclesiology. The canons by which to measure "nonconformity" must be taken in different times and places. Recalling our adaptation of the work of Bourdieu, this is because the dispositions — character, commitments, allegiances — that govern one's life do not give rise to a standard or ahistorical set of practices. The career of Christ through suffering to glory is internalized, becomes our "embodied history," and is operative at a preconscious level, and our practices grow out of the interplay of this "second nature" and the particular social contexts in which we find ourselves.

The question remains, then, whether we can discern in 1 Peter itself the presence of hidden scripts that trace the horizons of resistance against the ways of Roman society, or tactics by which the marginal maintain their identity and live out their lives in environments not of their own making and outside of their control.[103] Let me mention three.

(1) Plotting Time: Whose Narrative? Smith-Christopher recognizes that "a significant strategy of creativity in exile is to do critical historiography."[104] I take it that, by this, he does not refer to that sort of revisionist history writing that creates "events" out of nothing or that conveniently excludes or declares as fictional those events that do not fit one's agenda. Instead, my estimation is that this is the sort of historiography that recognizes, first, that there are multiple ways of construing events, second, that "the best weapon or best defense of the powerless is narrative,"[105] and third, that one of the primary aims of history writing is identity shaping.

---

103. Cf. Scott, *Hidden Transcripts;* de Certeau, *Everyday Life.*
104. Smith-Christopher, *Exile,* p. 200.
105. So Phelan, *Narrative as Rhetoric,* pp. 17, 13.

Reflecting on the contemporary theological problematic in the U.S., McClendon refers to a "contest of stories." From an early age, we learn a consensus story that forms us as Americans, a narrative with such stable elements as these: brave pilgrims set out in search of freedom from tyranny; they find the promised land where they must conquer the indigenous population as well as fight for their independence; they engage in civil war in order to liberate all persons; they move westward across the continent, depending only on themselves, to realize their dreams; and they are blessed by God so that they are able to fight for the liberty of others outside their borders as well. Without wanting to belittle the American Story, which has underwritten hope for millions of families, McClendon nevertheless observes that one of the most visible constants of that story is the violence determined to be necessary in order to overthrow threats to freedom. Contrast this, he says, with a story that pivots upon a savior who comes on a donkey, is acclaimed as the prince of peace, and in whose death peace is won. The pressing question for McClendon is this: "Which story, the cultural or the biblical one, really engages me?"[106]

Rome, of course, has its own story: the conquest of all the inhabited world, to make all people one under Roman rule, with the emperor as lord and savior of all, and with all of this granted by the gods. The Roman system pronounced "peace" *(pax Romana),* but questions quickly follow: Peace experienced by whom? Peace for whose benefit? Peace at what cost? The ideology of the empire was carried through its armies and inculcated through its religion. Caesar was savior of the world, the epoch of empire was the age of salvation, and the life record of the emperor was good news. Caesar owed his own rule to the beneficence of the gods. The glue of Rome and the Roman empire was worship — worship of the Roman emperor as at least son of god if not as god, and of *Roma,* the goddess of Rome; and the matrices of honor and obligation that threaded their way down from the gods through the emperor to the elite and, eventually, to the lowest echelons of the empire.

What is remarkable, then, is the combination of Peter's obvious concern with establishing the identity of his audience and his failure to do so on Roman terms. These Christians, Gentiles mostly, are to trace their history through Christ into the antiquity of God's dealings with Israel. These Christians are not citizens of Rome, then; indeed, they are not citizens at all, but are sojourners whose ultimate loyalty is to God. Like Abraham, that prototypical alien and stranger, these Christians find their identity foremost in their being bound to God and, consequently, within the community of aliens and strang-

---

106. McClendon, *Witness,* pp. 358-62 (362); I have adapted the version of the American Story that McClendon recounts.

ers determined by the liberation won for them by Christ and the pattern of his life, by the evangelizing and sanctifying work of the Spirit, and by the mutual, unceasing love at work among them.

The construction of identity is a process both of affirmation and negation. Christians in the second and third centuries, for example, worked out their identity in part by declaring their differences from Judaism, sometimes in disturbingly acerbic terms, while at the same time codifying the essential beliefs in which the church found its unity. We have already seen that Peter says almost nothing about persons outside of the Christian communities he addresses, but his strategy for shaping Christians' identity nonetheless includes affirmation and negation. Negated is the former life of his audience: "Enough time has been lost discharging the will of the Gentiles, conducting yourselves in acts of unrestraint, lust, drunkenness, carousing, bawdy partying, and unseemly idolatry" (4:3). Affirmed is the location of his audience "in Christ," and, accordingly, "in Israel." But to make this affirmation is to document a further negation: they are not Gentiles. In other words, the boundaries by which identity is constructed include at the same time that they exclude. However, for 1 Peter, it is not the boundary line itself that is solid and fixed, but rather the center that defines the perimeter. Peter sketches a number of characteristic dispositions and behaviors for his readers, but his concern is not so much to segregate Christian communities from the larger world. That is, Peter works less to construct boundaries for the people of God than to define their center, and he does this by locating his audience on the map as persons "in Christ."

To add to the comments on the narrative formation of identity made earlier (see above, pp. 265-69), there is growing empirical evidence that ethical decision-making is tied above all to personal formation (and not, say, to analysis of ethical quandaries and options),[107] urging, once again, the significance of the narrative we inhabit. Without belaboring the point further, we have already seen, more generally, the centrality of narrative in the constructive of identity and, more particularly, Peter's concern to mark the time (see above, pp. 199-202). In his letter, the apostle sets out to recount the lives of his audience so that they see their place within the narrative of God's work from before creation to the glory of the End, and thus he relegates the "eternal glory of Rome" to little more than a short-term, interim arrangement.

(2) Playful Language: Whose Lexicon? Words are important in 1 Peter. The violence directed toward Christians is primarily verbal, at least at present. And Peter seems well-aware of the potential of language to create the experi-

---

107. See the related essays in Fireman, et al., eds., *Narrative and Consciousness*.

enced world. That is, words *do things*. Hence, it is important that we not over-look the surprising lexicon Peter is developing. A few examples will suffice. "Lord" refers to Jesus, not the emperor (nor to local benefactors to whom ob-ligations would be due). "Fear" refers to reverent awe; it is unrelated to intim-idation, anxious dread, or terror, but realized rather in the fundamental ori-entation of one's life toward God, so that one's relationship with God determines all else. "Judgment" is not the prerogative of Rome, is not con-cerned with social standing in one's community, is not based on human valu-ations, and is not a proper motivation for faithful living. Nor are Christians entitled to the exercise of judgment. God has a monopoly on judgment, and his canons are unaffected by human concerns with honor and shame, are guided by his mercy, and are oriented toward the vindication of the righteous. "Endurance" is not realized in long-suffering, passivity, or forbearance, but "unyielding perseverance," "risky engagement," or "courageous steadfastness in the face of opposition." Peter calls for resistance — active not passive, de-termined but not violent. Such words, and others besides, inflect normal us-age in ways that are unobtrusively subversive.

(3) Doing Good and Receiving Honor: Whose Canons? Conventions gov-erning social life in Peter's world were determined by honor and shame. What Peter consistently counsels is "doing good." To "do good" is rather vague since it does not carry within itself the standard by which to measure what is good or right. Similarly, judgments regarding what or who is "honorable" are based on standards that need to be named. Of course, the Roman world had achieved clarity in such matters, so much so that "doing good" could be read almost as a technical term for the exercise of public benefaction.[108] Similarly, one's place in the hierarchy of status stratification and how to behave toward one's betters and one's inferiors — these were the stuff of child-rearing, with the ensuing conventions powerful instruments of social pressure toward be-havioral and attitudinal conformity. But for Peter, "doing good" is nothing other than holiness in every aspect of life and performance of the will of God. As for honor and shame, in 1 Peter what matters is God's choice, itself an ex-pression of God's grace, and then whether one adopts God's valuation of peo-ple and things. God is the arbiter of status, and he refuses to "acknowledge someone's face" — that is, to be swayed by such indices of prestige, sex, age, ancestry, landed wealth, the status of one's circle of friends — accounting in-stead for one's faithfulness in response to the good news of Christ.

Though not a tactic per se, it is important nonetheless that the life to which Peter calls his readers is essentially amphibious. They are not a "third

---

108. As Winter attempts to do ("Public Honoring").

race," neither Jew nor Gentile, but a people whose feet are planted in their culture yet who are outsiders to their own culture. "Their difference is internal to the culture."[109] Their life is a metaphor of ambivalence.[110] They are bicultural, living between two worlds, with the one a source of tension with the other. How they choose to live in that tension, and whether they choose to resolve it by fully withdrawing from one in favor of the other, is the issue to which Peter devotes himself. For this reason, it is impossible to imagine that Peter's theological strategy could be reduced to a concern either for internal cohesion or for external separation. Following the Christ who was crucified on a tree determines both internal and external relations; it is a profoundly political and missiological act (external) and a commitment to indwelling a terrain determined by the sanctifying Spirit and intramural hospitality (internal). The homeless people of God is a temple (rather than a people that has a temple home), a house of God under construction, and a priesthood whose vocation is to mediate God's presence wherever they find themselves (2:4-10). Writing with their lives the next chapter in the Israel-Christ story, empowered by the Spirit to maintain their allegiance to the merciful Father by journeying through suffering in hope of eschatological honor, they bear witness to the coming of the new age.

---

109. Volf, *Exclusion and Embrace*, p. 49; original in italics.
110. Meeks, *Christian Morality*, p. 50.

Bibliography

Commentaries are cited by author's name only, all other works by author's name and short title.

Commentaries on 1 Peter

Achtemeier, Paul J. *1 Peter*. Hermeneia. Minneapolis: Fortress, 1996.

Bede, the Venerable. *The Commentary on the Seven Catholic Epistles*. CSS 82. Kalamazoo, Michigan: Cistercian, 1985.

Bray, Gerald, ed. *James, 1-2 Peter, 1-3 John, Jude*. ACCNT 11. Downers Grove: InterVarsity, 2000.

Brox, Norbert. *Der erste Petrusbrief*. EKK 21. 4th ed. Zürich: Benziger; Neukirchen-Vluyn: Neukirchener, 1993.

Davids, Peter H. *The First Epistle of Peter*. NICNT. Grand Rapids: Eerdmans, 1990.

Elliott, John H. *1 Peter: A New Translation with Introduction and Commentary*. AB 37B. New York: Doubleday, 2000.

Feldmeier, Reinhard. *Der erste Brief aus Petrus*. THKNT 15.1. Leipzig: Evangelische, 2005.

Goppelt, Leonhard. *A Commentary on 1 Peter*. Grand Rapids: Eerdmans, 1993.

Grudem, Wayne. *1 Peter*. TNTC. Downers Grove: InterVarsity, 1988.

Jobes, Karen H. *1 Peter*. BECNT. Grand Rapids: Baker Academic, 2005.

Marshall, I. Howard. *1 Peter*. IVPNTC. Downers Grove: InterVarsity, 1991.

McKnight, Scot. *1 Peter*. NIVAC. Grand Rapids: Zondervan, 1996.

Michaels, J. Ramsey. *1 Peter*. WBC 49. Waco, Texas: Word, 1988.

Schelkle, Karl Hermann. *Die Petrusbriefe, der Judasbriefe*. HTKNT 13.2. 3d ed. Freiburg: Herder, 1976.

Schweizer, Eduard. *Der erste Petrusbrief*. ZBK NT 15. 4th ed. Zürich: Theologischer, 1998.

Selwyn, Edward Gordon. *The First Epistle of St. Peter: The Greek Text with Introduction, Notes, and Essays*. 2nd ed. London: Macmillan, 1947; reprint ed., Grand Rapids: Baker, 1981.

Skaggs, Rebecca. *The Pentecostal Commentary on 1 Peter, 2 Peter, Jude.* Cleveland: Pilgrim, 2004.

Windisch, Hans. *Die Katholischen Briefe.* HNT 15. Tübingen: Mohr, 1951.

Other Works

Aasgaard, Reidar. "Brotherhood in Plutarch and Paul: Its Role and Character." In *Constructing Early Christian Families: Family as Social Reality and Metaphor,* ed. Halvor Moxnes, pp. 166-82. London: Routledge, 1997.

Abraham, William J. *Canon and Criterion in Christian Theology: From the Fathers to Feminism.* Oxford: Clarendon, 1998.

Achtemeier, Paul J. "The Christology of 1 Peter: Some Reflections." In *Who Do You Say That I Am? Essays on Christology Presented to Jack Dean Kingsbury,* ed. Mark Allan Powell and David R. Bauer, pp. 140-54. Louisville: Westminster John Knox, 1999.

———. "Newborn Babes and Living Stones: Literal and Figurative in 1 Peter." In *To Touch the Text: Biblical and Related Studies in Honor of Joseph A. Fitzmyer, S.J.,* ed. Maurya P. Horgan and Paul J. Kobelski, pp. 207-36. New York: Crossroad, 1989.

———. "Suffering Servant and Suffering Christ in 1 Peter." In *The Future of Christology: Essays in Honor of Leander E. Keck,* ed. Abraham J. Malherbe and Wayne A. Meeks, pp. 176-88. Minneapolis: Fortress, 1993.

———, Joel B. Green, and Marianne Meye Thompson. *Introducing the New Testament: Its Literature and Theology.* Grand Rapids: Eerdmans, 2001.

Agnew, Francis H. "1 Peter 1:2: An Alternative Translation." *CBQ* 45 (1983): 68-73.

Aitken, Ellen Bradshaw. *Jesus' Death in Early Christian Memory: The Poetics of the Passion.* NTOA 53. Göttingen: Vandenhoeck und Ruprecht; Fribourg: Academic, 2004.

Allison, Dale C. *The End of the Ages Has Come: An Early Interpretation of the Passion and Resurrection of Jesus.* Philadelphia: Fortress, 1985.

Andersen, Francis I. "Yahweh, the Kind and Sensitive God." In *God Who Is Rich in Mercy: Essays Presented to Dr. D. B. Knox,* ed. P. T. O'Brien and D. G. Peterson, pp. 41-88. Homebush West, New South Wales: Lancer, 1986.

Anderson, Gary A. "Sacrifice and Sacrificial Offerings (Old Testament)." In *ABD* 5:870-86.

Anderson, Kevin L. "The Resurrection of Jesus in Luke-Acts." Ph.D. diss. Brunel University, 2000.

Applegate, Judith K. "The Co-Elect Woman in 1 Peter." *NTS* 38 (1992): 587-604.

Arichea, Daniel C., Jr. "God or Christ? A Study of Implicit Information." *BT* 28 (1977): 412-18.

Arnold, Bill T. *Who Were the Babylonians?* SBLABS 10. Atlanta: Society of Biblical Literature, 2004.

Arnold, Clinton E. *Powers of Darkness: Principalities and Powers in Paul's Letters.* Downers Grove: InterVarsity, 1992.

Baird, William. *History of New Testament Research. 2 vols. Minneapolis: Fortress, 1992/2003.

Baker, William R. *Personal Speech-Ethics in the Epistle of James.* WUNT 2:68. Tübingen: Mohr, 1995.

Balch, David L. "Hellenization/Acculturation in 1 Peter." In *Perspectives on First Peter,* ed. Charles H. Talbert, pp. 79-101. NABPRSS 9. Macon, Georgia: Mercer University Press, 1986.

―――. "Household Codes." In *Greco-Roman Literature and the New Testament: Selected Forms and Genres,* ed. David E. Aune, pp. 25-50. Atlanta: Scholars, 1988.

―――. *Let Wives Be Submissive: The Domestic Code in 1 Peter.* SLBDS 26. Chico, California: Scholars Press, 1981.

Balla, Peter. *Challenges to New Testament Theology: An Attempt to Justify the Enterprise.* WUNT 2:95. Tübingen: Mohr, 1997.

Barclay, John M. G. *Jews in the Mediterranean Diaspora: From Alexander to Trajan (323 BCE–117 CE).* Berkeley: University of California Press, 1996.

Bartchy, S. Scott. *First-Century Slavery and 1 Corinthians 7:21.* SBLDS 11. Atlanta: Scholars, 1973.

Barth, Karl. "The Christian's Place in Society." In *The Word of God and the Word of Man,* pp. 272-327. Gloucester: Smith, 1978.

―――. *Church Dogmatics.* Vol 1, part 1. Edinburgh: Clark, 1975.

Barth, Markus, and Helmut Blanke. *The Letter to Philemon: A New Translation with Notes and Commentary.* ECC. Grand Rapids: Eerdmans, 2000.

Barton, Stephen C. "New Testament Interpretation as Performance." *SJT* 52 (1999): 179-208.

Bassler, Jouette M. *God and Mammon: Asking for Money in the New Testament.* Nashville: Abingdon, 1991.

Bauckham, Richard. *The Fate of the Dead: Studies on the Jewish and Christian Apocalypses.* NovTSup 93. Leiden: Brill, 1998.

―――. *God Crucified: Monotheism and Christology in the New Testament.* Grand Rapids: Eerdmans, 1998.

―――. "Hades, Hell." In *ABD,* 3:14-15.

―――. "James, 1 and 2 Peter, Jude." In *It Is Written: Scripture Citing Scripture: Essays in Honour of Barnabas Lindars, SSF,* ed. D. A. Carson and H. G. M. Willliamson, pp. 303-17. Cambridge: Cambridge University Press, 1988.

―――. "Reading Scripture as a Coherent Story." In *The Art of Reading Scripture,* ed. Ellen F. Davis and Richard B. Hays, pp. 38-53. Grand Rapids: Eerdmans, 2003.

―――. "Spirits in Prison." In *ABD,* 6:177-78.

Bauer, Walter. *Orthodoxy and Heresy in Earliest Christianity.* Philadelphia: Fortress, 1972.

Bauman, Richard. *Women and Politics in Ancient Rome.* London: Routledge, 1992.

Bauman-Martin, Betsy J. "Women on the Edge: New Perspectives on Women in the Petrine *Haustafel.*" *JBL* 123 (2004): 253-79.

Bechtler, Steven Richard. *Following in His Steps: Suffering, Community, and Christology in 1 Peter.* SBLDS 162. Atlanta: Scholars, 1998.

Bellah, Robert N., et al. *The Good Society.* New York: Alfred A. Knopf, 1991.

Berger, Klaus. *Identity and Experience in the New Testament.* Minneapolis: Fortress, 2003.

―――. "χάρις." In *EDNT* 3:457-60.

Berger, Peter L., and Thomas Luckmann. *The Social Construction of Reality: A Treatise in the Sociology of Knowledge.* New York: Doubleday, 1966.

Bertram, Georg. "ὑπερήφανος, ὑπερηφανία." *TDNT* 8:525-29.

Best, Ernst. "1 Peter and the Gospel Tradition." *NTS* 16 (1970): 95-113.

————. "1 Peter II, 4-10: A Reconsideration." *NovT* 11 (1969): 270-93.

Betz, Hans Dieter. "The Concept of the 'Inner Human Being' (ὁ ἔσω ἄνθρωπος) in the Anthropology of Paul." *NTS* 46 (2000): 315-41.

Biddle, Mark E. *Missing the Mark: Sin and Its Consequences in Biblical Theology.* Nashville: Abingdon, 2005.

Bloesch, Donald G. *The Church: Sacraments, Worship, Ministry, Mission.* Christian Foundations 6. Downers Grove: InterVarsity, 2002.

Blommaert, Jan. *Discourse: A Critical Introduction.* New Topics in Sociolinguistics. Cambridge: Cambridge University Press, 2005.

Bockmuehl, Markus. "'To Be or Not to Be': The Possible Futures of New Testament Scholarship." *SJT* 51 (1998): 271-306.

Boers, Hendrikus. *What Is New Testament Theology?* GBS. Philadelphia: Fortress, 1979.

Boff, Leonardo. *Passion of Christ, Passion of the World: The Facts, Their Interpretation, and Their Meaning Yesterday and Today.* Maryknoll: Orbis, 1987.

Boobyer, G. H. "The Indebtedness of 2 Peter to 1 Peter." In *New Testament Essays: Studies in Memory of Thomas Walter Manson 1893-1958,* ed. A. J. B. Higgins, pp. 34-53. Manchester: Manchester University Press, 1959.

Borgen, Peder. *Early Christianity and Hellenistic Judaism.* Edinburgh: Clark, 1996.

Bornemann, W. "Der erste Petrusbrief: Eine Taufrede des Silvanus?" *ZNW* 19 (1919-20): 143-65.

Bourdieu, Pierre. *Language and Symbolic Power.* Cambridge, Massachusetts: Harvard University Press, 1991.

————. *The Logic of Practice.* Stanford: Stanford University Press, 1980.

————. *Practical Reason: On the Theory of Action.* Stanford: Stanford University Press, 1998.

————, and Loïc J. D. Wacquant. *An Invitation to Reflexive Sociology.* Chicago: University of Chicago Press, 1992.

Boyarin, Daniel. *Intertextuality and the Reading of Midrash.* ISBL. Bloomington: University of Indiana Press, 1990.

Boyd, Gregory A. *Satan and the Problem of Evil: Constructing a Trinitarian Warfare Theodicy.* Downers Grove: InterVarsity, 2001.

Bradley, Keith. *Slavery and Society at Rome.* KTAH. Cambridge: University of Cambridge Press, 1994.

Bratsiotis, N. P. "בשׂר." *TDOT* 2:313-32.

Breytenbach, Cilliers. "'Christus litt euretwegen': Zur Rezeption von Jesaja 53 LXX und anderen frühjüdischen Traditionen im 1. Petrusbrief." In *Deutungen des Todes Jesu im Neuen Testament,* ed. Jög Frey and Schröter, pp. 437-54. WUNT 181. Tübingen: Mohr, 2005.

Brown, Jeannine K. "Silent Wives, Verbal Believers: Ethical and Hermeneutical Considerations in 1 Peter 3:1-6 and Its Context." *WW* 24 (2004): 395-403.

Brown, Peter. *Poverty and Leadership in the Later Roman Empire.* The Menahem Stern Jerusalem Lectures. Hanover: The University Press of New England, 2003.

Brown, Roger, and Albert Gilman. "The Pronouns of Power and Solidarity." *AA* 4 (1960): 24-29.

Brown, William P. *The Ethos of the Cosmos: The Genesis of Moral Imagination in the Bible.* Grand Rapids: Eerdmans, 1999.

Bruce, F. F. *Peter, Stephen, James, and John: Studies in Early Non-Pauline Christianity.* Grand Rapids: Eerdmans, 1979.

Brueggemann, Walter. *Theology of the Old Testament: Testimony, Dispute, Advocacy.* Minneapolis: Fortress, 1997.

Bruner, Jerome. *Making Stories: Law, Literature, Life.* New York: Farrar, Straus and Giroux, 2002.

Bryant, David J. *Faith and the Play of Imagination.* Macon, Georgia: Mercer University Press, 1989.

Buchan, Thomas N., III. "'Blessed Is He Who Has Brought Adam from Sheol': Christ's Descent to the Dead in the Theology of Saint Ephrem the Syrian." Ph.D. diss. Drew University, 2003.

Bultmann, Rudolf. "Bekenntnis- und Liedfragmente im ersten Petrusbrief." *ConNT* 11 (1947): 1-14.

———. "New Testament and Mythology." In *Kerygma and Myth,* ed. Hans Werner Bartsch, pp. 1-44. London: SPCK, 1953; reprint ed., New York: Harper and Row, 1961.

Burnett, Richard E. *Karl Barth's Theological Exegesis: The Hermeneutical Principles of the* Römerbrief *Period.* Grand Rapids: Eerdmans, 2004.

Bryant, David J. *Faith and the Play of Imagination: On the Role of Imagination in Religion.* SABH 5. Macon, Georgia: Mercer University Press, 1989.

Bynum, Caroline Walker. *Metamorphosis and Identity.* New York: Zone, 2001.

———. *The Resurrection of the Body in Western Christianity, 200–1336.* New York: Columbia University Press, 1995.

Caird, G. B., and L. D. Hurst. *New Testament Theology.* Oxford: Clarendon, 1994.

Campbell, Barth L. *Honor, Shame, and the Rhetoric of 1 Peter.* SBLDS 160. Atlanta: Scholars, 1998.

Cassidy, Richard J. *Christians and Roman Rule in the New Testament: New Perspectives.* New York: Crossroad, 2001.

Casurella, Anthony. *Bibliography of Literature on 1 First Peter.* NTTS 23. Leiden: Brill, 1996.

Charles, J. Daryl. "Vice and Virtue Lists." In *DNTB,* pp. 1252-57.

Charlesworth, J. H. "Odes of Solomon." In *OTP,* 2:725-71.

———, ed. *The Messiah: Developments in Earliest Judaism and Christianity.* The First Princeton Symposium on Judaism and Christian Origins. Minneapolis: Fortress, 1992.

Chester, Andrew, and Ralph P. Martin. *The Theology of the Letters of James, Peter, and Jude.* NTT. Cambridge: Cambridge University Press, 1994.

Childs, Brevard S. *Biblical Theology of the Old and New Testaments.* Minneapolis: Fortress, 1992.

———. *The Book of Exodus: A Critical, Theological Commentary.* OTL. Philadelphia: Westminster, 1974.

———. *Isaiah.* OTL. Louisville: Westminster John Knox, 2001.

Chin, Moses. "A Heavenly Home for the Homeless: Aliens and Strangers in 1 Peter." *TynB* 42 (1991): 96-112.

Clark, G. R. *The Word* Hesed *in the Hebrew Bible.* JSOTSup 157. Sheffield: Sheffield Academic Press, 1993.

Clarke, Andrew D. "The Healthy Church: Embodying Leadership." *Catalyst* 30/1 (2003): 1-3.

———. *Serve the Community of the Church: Christians as Leaders and Ministers.* FCCGRW. Grand Rapids: Eerdmans, 2000.

Collins, Kenneth J. *The Evangelical Moment: The Promise of an American Religion.* Grand Rapids: Baker Academic, 2005.

Combes, I. A. H. *The Metaphor of Slavery in the Writings of the Early Church: From the New Testament to the Beginning of the Fifth Century.* JSNTSup 156. Sheffield: Sheffield Academic Press, 1998.

Cooper, John W. *Body, Soul, and Life Everlasting: Biblical Anthropology and the Monism-Dualism Debate.* Grand Rapids: Eerdmans, 1989.

Cosgrove, Charles H. *Appealing to Scripture in Moral Debate: Five Hermeneutical Rules.* Grand Rapids: Eerdmans, 2002.

Craigo-Snell, Shannon. "Command Performance: Rethinking Performance Interpretation in the Context of *Divine Discourse.*" *ModT* 16 (2000): 475-94.

Dalton, William Joseph. "1 Peter 3:10 Reconsidered." In *The New Testament Age: Essays in Honor of Bo Reicke,* 2 vols., ed. William C. Weinrich, 1:95-105. Macon, Georgia: Mercer University Press, 1984.

———. *Christ's Proclamation to the Spirits: A Study of 1 Peter 3:18–4:6.* AnBib 23. Rome: Pontifical Biblical Institute, 1965.

———. "The Interpretation of 1 Peter 3,19 and 4,6: Light from 2 Peter." *Bib* 60 (1979): 547-55.

Dana, H. E., and Julius R. Mantey. *A Manual Grammar of the Greek New Testament.* Toronto: Macmillan, 1927.

Daube, David. "κερδαίνω as a Missionary Term." *HTR* 40 (1946): 109-20.

Dautzenberg, P. Gerhard. "Σωτηρία ψυχῶν" (1 Petr 1,9). *BZ* 8 (1964): 262-76.

Davids, Peter H. "The Use of Second Temple Traditions in 1 and 2 Peter and Jude." In *The Catholic Epistles and the Tradition,* ed. J. Schlosser, pp. 409-31. BETL 176. Leuven: Leuven University Press, 2004.

Davis, Patricia M., and Lewis R. Rambo. "Converting: Toward a Cognitive Theory of Religious Change." In *Soul, Psyche, Brain: New Directions in the Study of Religion and Brain-Mind Science,* ed. Kelly Bulkeley, pp. 159-73. New York: Palgrave Macmillan, 2005.

Dawn, Marva J. "Powers and Principalities." In *DTIB,* pp. 609-12.

de Certaeu, Michel. *The Practice of Everyday Life.* Berkeley: University of California Press, 1984.

Deissmann, Adolf. *Light from the Ancient East: The New Testament Illustrated by Recently Discovered Texts of the Graeco-Roman World.* New York: Doran, 1927; reprint ed., Peabody: Hendrickson, 1995.

Denney, James. *The Death of Christ: Its Place and Interpretation in the New Testament.* 3rd ed. New York: Armstrong, 1903.

Derrett, J. Duncan M. "He Descended into Hell." *JHC* 9 (2002): 234-45.

Derrida, Jacques. *Given Time.* Vol. 1: *Counterfeit Money.* Chicago: University of Chicago, 1991.

deSilva, David A. "Honor and Shame." In *DNTB*, pp. 518-22.

———. *Honor, Patronage, Kinship and Purity: Unlocking New Testament Culture.* Downers Grove: InterVarsity, 2000.

Diprose, Ronald E. *Israel and the Development of Christian Thought.* Rome: Istituto Biblico Evangelico Italiano, 2000.

Di Vito, Robert A. "Old Testament Anthropology and the Construction of Personal Identity." *CBQ* 61 (1999): 217-38.

Dixon, Suzanne. *Reading Roman Women.* London: Duckworth, 2001.

Domning, Daryl P., and Monika K. Hellwig. *Original Selfishness: Original Sin and Evil in the Light of Evolution.* Aldershot: Ashgate, 2006.

Dubis, Mark. *Messianic Woes in First Peter: Suffering and Eschatology in 1 Peter 4:12-19.* SBL 33. New York: Peter Lang, 2002.

Dunn, James D. G. *Christology in the Making: A New Testament Inquiry into the Origins and Doctrine of the Incarnation.* 2nd ed. Grand Rapids: Eerdmans, 1989.

———. "Jesus — Flesh and Spirit: An Exposition of Romans 1:3-4." In *Christ and the Spirit*, 2 vols., vol. 1, pp. 126-53. Grand Rapids: Eerdmans, 1998.

———. *Unity and Diversity in the New Testament: An Inquiry into the Character of Earliest Christianity.* Philadelphia: Westminster, 1977.

Eakin, Paul John. *How Our Lives Become Stories: Making Selves.* Ithaca: Cornell University Press, 1999.

Eco, Umberto. *Interpretation and Overinterpretation.* Ed. Stefan Collini. Cambridge: Cambridge University Press, 1992.

———. *The Limits of Interpretation.* Bloomington: Indiana University Press, 1990.

———. *The Role of the Reader: Explorations in the Semiotics of Texts.* Advances in Semiotics. Bloomington: Indiana University Press, 1979.

Eilberg-Schwartz, Howard. *The Savage in Judaism: An Anthropology of Israelite Religion and Ancient Judaism.* Bloomington: Indiana University Press, 1990.

Ellingworth, Paul. *The Epistle to the Hebrews: A Commentary on the Greek Text.* NIGTC. Grand Rapids: Eerdmans, 1993.

Elliott, John H. "1 Peter, Its Situation and Strategy: A Discussion with David Balch." In *Perspectives on First Peter*, ed. Charles H. Talbert, pp. 61-78. NABPRSS 9. Macon, Georgia: Mercer University Press, 1986.

———. "Backward and Forward 'In His Steps': Following Jesus from Rome to Raymond and Beyond: The Tradition, Redaction, and Reception of 1 Peter 2:18-25." In *Discipleship in the New Testament*, ed. Fernando F. Segovia, pp. 184-209. Philadelphia: Fortress, 1985.

———. "Disgraced yet Graced: The Gospel according to 1 Peter in the Key of Honor and Shame." *BTB* 25 (1995): 166-78.

———. *The Elect and the Holy: An Exegetical Examination of 1 Peter 2:4-10 and the Phrase βασίλειον ἱεράτευμα.* NovTSup 12. Leiden: Brill, 1966.

———. *A Home for the Homeless: A Sociological Analysis of 1 Peter, Its Situation and Strategy.* Philadelphia: Fortress, 1981.

———. "Ministry and Church Order in the NT: A Traditio-Historical Analysis (1 Pt 5,1-5 & plls)." *CBQ* 32 (1970): 367-91.

————. "The Rehabilitation of an Exegetical Step-Child: 1 Peter in Recent Research." *JBL* 95 (1976): 243-54.

————. *What Is Social Science Criticism?* GBS. Minneapolis: Fortress, 1993.

Ellis, E. Earle. *The Old Testament in Early Christianity: Canon and Interpretation in the Light of Modern Research.* WUNT 54. Tübingen: Mohr, 1991.

Enns, Peter. *Inspiration and Incarnation: Evangelicals and the Problem of the Old Testament.* Grand Rapids: Baker Academic, 2005.

Evang, Martin. "ἐκ καρδίας ἀλλήλους ἀγαπήσατε ἐκτενῶς: Zum Verständnis der Aufforderung und ihrer Begründungen in 1 Petr 1,22f." *ZNW* 80 (1989): 111-23.

Eyben, Emiel. "Fathers and Sons." In *Marriage, Divorce, and Children in Ancient Rome,* ed. Beryl Rawson, pp. 114-43. Oxford: Oxford University Press, 1991.

Fabry, Heinz-Josef. "לֵב." *TDOT* 7:399-437.

Farrar, Frederic W. *The Life of Christ Represented in Art.* New York: Hodder and Stoughton, 1894.

Fasold, Ralph. *Introduction to Sociolinguistics.* Vol. 2: *Sociolinguistics of Language.* Language in Society 6. Cambridge: Blackwell, 1990.

Fauconnier, Gilles, and Mark Turner. *The Way We Think: Conceptual Blending and the Mind's Hidden Complexities.* New York: Basic, 2002.

Feinberg, Todd E. *Altered Egos: How the Brain Creates the Self.* Oxford: Oxford University Press, 2001.

Feldman, Louis H. *Jew and Gentile in the Ancient World: Attitudes and Interactions from Alexander to Justinian.* Princeton, New Jersey: Princeton University Press, 1993.

Feldmeier, Reinhard. *Die Christen als Fremde: Die Metapher der Fremde in der antiken Welt, im Urchristentum und in 1. Petrusbrief.* WUNT 64. Tübingen: Mohr, 1992.

————. "Seelenheil: Überlegungen zur Soteriologie und Anthropologie des 1. Petrusbriefes." In *The Catholic Epistles and the Tradition,* ed. J. Schlosser, pp. 291-306. BETL 176. Leuven: Leuven University Press, 2004.

————. "Wiedergeburt im 1. Petrusbrief. In *Wiedergeburt,* ed. Reinhard Feldmeier, pp. 75-99. Göttingen: Vandenhoeck und Ruprecht, 2005.

Finger, Thomas N. *Christian Theology: An Eschatological Approach.* 2 vols. Scottdale, Pennsylvania: Herald, 1985, 1989.

Finley, M. I. *The Ancient Economy.* Berkeley: University of California Press, 1973.

————. *The World of Odysseus.* 2d ed. London: Penguin, 1978.

Finn, Thomas M. *From Death to Rebirth: Ritual and Conversion in Antiquity.* New York/ Mahwah, New Jersey: Paulist, 1997.

Fireman, Gary D., et al., eds. *Narrative and Consciousness: Literature, Psychology, and the Brain.* Oxford: Oxford University Press, 2003.

Fishwick, Duncan. *The Imperial Cult in the Latin West: Studies in the Ruler Cult of the Western Provinces of the Roman Empire.* 2 vols. EPROER. Leiden: Brill, 1987-92.

Flanagan, Owen. *The Problem of the Soul: Two Visions of Mind and How to Reconcile Them.* New York: Basic, 2002.

Flemming, Dean. *Contextualization in the New Testament: Patterns for Theology and Mission.* Downers Grove: InterVarsity, 2005.

Foerster, Werner. "κτίζω κτλ." *TDNT* 3:1000-1035.

Fowl, Stephen E. *Engaging Scripture: A Model for Theological Interpretation.* Oxford: Blackwell, 1998.

———. "Introduction." In *The Theological Interpretation of Scripture: Classic and Contemporary Readings,* ed. Stephen E. Fowl, pp. xii-xxx. Oxford: Blackwell, 1997.

———. *Philippians.* THNTC. Grand Rapids: Eerdmans, 2005.

Froehlich, Karlfried. "'Take Up and Read': Basics of Augustine's Biblical Interpretation." *Int* 58 (2004): 5-16.

Furnish, Victor Paul. "Elect Sojourners in Christ: An Approach to the Theology of 1 Peter." *PSTJ* 28, no. 3 (1975): 1-11.

———. *The Love Command in the New Testament.* Nashville: Abingdon, 1972.

Gadamer, Hans-Georg. *Truth and Method.* 2d ed. New York: Crossroad, 2000.

Gamble, Harry Y. *Books and Readers in the Early Church: A History of Early Christian Texts.* New Haven: Yale University Press, 1995.

Gardner, Jane F., and Thomas Wiedemann. *The Roman Household: A Sourcebook.* London: Routledge, 1991.

Gärtner, Bertil. *The Temple and the Community in Qumran and the New Testament: A Comparative Study in the Temple Symbolism of the Qumran Texts and the New Testament.* SNTSMS 1. Cambridge: Cambridge University Press, 1965.

Gaventa, Beverly Roberts. *From Darkness to Light: Aspects of Conversion in the New Testament.* OBT. Philadelphia: Fortress, 1986.

Gehring, Roger W. *House Church and Mission: The Importance of Household Structures in Early Christianity.* Peabody, Massachusetts: Hendrickson, 2004.

Goldingay, John. *God's Prophet, God's Servant: A Study in Jeremiah and Isaiah 40-55.* Carlisle: Paternoster, 1984.

———. *Models for Interpretation of Scripture.* Grand Rapids: Eerdmans, 1995.

Goodman, Martin. *Mission and Conversion: Proselytizing in the Religious History of the Roman Empire.* Oxford: Clarendon, 1994.

Goppelt, Leonhard. *Apostolic and Post-Apostolic Times.* Grand Rapids: Baker, 1970.

———. *Theology of the New Testament.* Vol. 2: *The Variety and Unity of the Apostolic Witness to Christ.* Ed. Jürgen Roloff. Grand Rapids: Eerdmans, 1982.

Green, Gene L. "The Use of the Old Testament for Christian Ethics in 1 Peter." *TynB* 41 (1990): 276-89.

Green, Joel B. *The Death of Jesus: Tradition and Redaction in the Passion Narrative.* WUNT 2:33. Tübingen: Mohr, 1988.

———. "Faithful Witness in the Diaspora: The Holy Spirit and the Exiled People of God according to 1 Peter." In *The Holy Spirit and Christian Origins: Essays in Honor of James D. G. Dunn,* ed. Graham N. Stanton, Stephen C. Barton, and Bruce W. Longenecker, pp. 282-95. Grand Rapids: Eerdmans; Edinburgh: Clark, 2004.

———. "Grace." In *NDBT,* pp. 524-27.

———. "Healing." In *NDBT,* pp. 526-40.

———. "Identity and Engagement in a Diverse World: Pluralism and Holiness in 1 Peter." *ATJ* 55 (2000): 85-92.

———. "Living as Exiles: The Holy Church in the Diaspora in 1 Peter." In *Holiness and Ecclesiology,* ed. Kent E. Brower and Andy Johnson. Grand Rapids: Eerdmans, 2007.

————. "Modernity, History, and the Theological Interpretation of the Bible." *SJT* 54 (2001): 308-29.

————. "Narrating the Gospel in 1-2 Peter." *Int* 60 (2006): 262-77.

————. "Restoring the Human Person: New Testament Voices for a Wholistic and Social Anthropology." In *Neuroscience and the Person*, ed. Robert John Russell et al., pp. 3-22. Scientific Perspectives on Divine Action 4. Vatican City State: Vatican Observatory; Berkeley, California: Center for Theology and the Natural Sciences, 1999.

————. *Salvation.* UBT. St. Louis, Missouri: Chalice, 2003.

————. "Science, Religion, and the Mind-Brain Problem: The Case of Thomas Willis (1621-1675)." *SCB* 15 (2003): 165-85.

————. "Scripture and Theology: Failed Experiments, Fresh Perspectives." *Int* 56 (2002): 5-20.

————, and Stuart L. Palmer, eds. *In Search of the Soul: Four Views of the Mind-Body Problem.* Downers Grove: InterVarsity, 2005.

Greenblatt, Stephen. "Culture." In *Critical Terms for Literary Study*, ed. Frank Lentricchia and Thomas McLaughlin, pp. 225-32. Chicago: University of Chicago Press, 1990.

Grenz, Stanley J. *The Social God and the Relational Self: A Trinitarian Theology of the Imago Dei.* The Matrix of Christian Theology. Louisville: Westminster John Knox, 2001.

————. *Theology for the Community of God.* Grand Rapids: Eerdmans, 1994.

Griffin, Miriam. "*Urbs Roma, Plebs* and *Princeps*." In *Images of Empire*, ed. Loveday Alexander, pp. 19-46. JSOTSup 122. Sheffield: Sheffield Academic Press, 1991.

Gross, Carl D. "Are the Wives of 1 Peter 3.7 Christians?" *JSNT* 35 (1989): 89-96.

Gruen, Erich S. *Diaspora: Jews amidst Greeks and Romans.* Cambridge, Massachusetts: Harvard University Press, 2002.

Grundmann, Walter. "στέφανος, στεφανόω." *TDNT* 7:615-36.

————. "ταπεινός κτλ." *TNDT* 8:1-26.

Gunton, Colin E. *The Actuality of Atonement: A Study of Metaphor, Rationality and the Christian Tradition.* Grand Rapids: Eerdmans, 1989.

————. "Trinity, Ontology and Anthropology: Towards a Renewal of the Doctrine of the Imago Dei." In *Persons Divine and Human: King's College Essays on Theological Anthropology*, ed. Christoph Schwöbel and Colin E. Gunton, pp. 47-61. Edinburgh: Clark, 1991.

Hamel, Gildas. *Poverty and Charity in Roman Palestine, First Three Centuries C.E.* Berkeley: University of California Press, 1990.

Harrill, J. Albert. *The Manumission of Slaves in Early Christianity.* HUT 32. Tübingen: Mohr, 1995.

————. *Slaves in the New Testament: Literary, Social, and Moral Dimensions.* Minneapolis: Fortress, 2006.

Harris, Murray J. "Resurrection and Immortality in the Pauline Corpus." In *Life in the Face of Death: The Resurrection Message of the New Testament*, ed. Richard N. Longenecker, 147-70. MNTS. Grand Rapids: Eerdmans, 1998.

————. *Slave of Christ: A New Testament Metaphor for Total Devotion to Christ.* NSBT. Downers Grove: InterVarsity, 1999.

Hartman, Lars. *'Into the Name of the Lord Jesus': Baptism in the Early Church.* SNTW. Edinburgh: Clark, 1997.

Harvey, A. E. *Strenuous Commands: The Ethic of Jesus.* London: SCM, 1990.

Haskell, Thomas L. "Objectivity Is Not Neutrality: Rhetoric versus Practice in Peter Novick's *That Noble Dream.*" In *Objectivity Is Not Neutrality: Explanatory Schemes in History,* pp. 145-73. Baltimore: The Johns Hopkins University Press, 1998.

Hauerwas, Stanley. *After Christendom?* Nashville: Abingdon, 1991.

————, and William H. Willimon. *Resident Aliens.* Nashville: Abingdon, 1989.

Heckel, Theo K. *Der innere Mensch: Der paulinische Verarbeitung eines platonischen Motivs.* WUNT 2:53. Tübingen: Mohr, 1993.

Hefner, Philip. *The Human Factor: Evolution, Culture, and Religion.* Minneapolis: Fortress, 1993.

Helgeland, John. "Time and Space: Christian and Roman." *ANRW* 23:2:1285-305.

Hemer, Colin J. "The Address of 1 Peter." *ExpTim* 89 (1977-78): 239-43.

Hengel, Martin. *Crucifixion: In the Ancient World and the Folly of the Message of the Cross.* Philadelphia: Fortress, 1977.

————. *The Zealots: Investigations into the Jewish Freedom Movement in the Period from Herod I until 70 A.D.* Edinburgh: Clark, 1989.

Herzer, Jens. *Petrus oder Paulus? Studien über das Verhältnis des Ersten Petrusbriefs zur paulinischen Tradition.* WUNT 103. Tübingen: Mohr, 1998.

Hill, David. "'To Offer Spiritual Sacrifices . . .' (1 Peter 2:5): Liturgical Formulations and Christian Paraenesis in 1 Peter." *JSNT* 16 (1982): 45-63.

Hofius, Otfried. *Der Christushymnus Philipper 2,6-11.* WUNT 17. Tübingen: Mohr, 1976.

————. "The Fourth Servant Song in the New Testament Letters." In *The Suffering Servant: Isaiah 53 in Jewish and Christian Sources,* ed. Bernd Janowski and Peter Stuhlmacher, pp. 163-88. Grand Rapids: Eerdmans, 2004.

Holladay, Carl R. *A Critical Introduction to the New Testament.* 2 vols. Nashville: Abingdon, 2005.

Holloway, Paul A. "*Nihil inopinati accidisse* — 'Nothing unexpected has happened': A Cyrenaic Consolatory *Topos* in 1 Pet 4,12ff." *NTS* 48 (2002): 433-48.

Hornik, Heidi J., and Mikeal C. Parsons. "The Harrowing of Hell." *BRev* 19 (2003): 18-26, 50.

Horrell, David G. "From ἀδελφοί to οἶκος θεοῦ: Social Transformation in Pauline Christianity." *JBL* 120 (2001): 293-311.

————. "The Product of a Petrine Circle? A Reassessment of the Origin and Character of 1 Peter." *JSNT* 86 (2002): 29-60.

————. "Who Are 'the Dead' and When Was the Gospel Preached to Them? The Interpretation of 1 Pet 4.6." *NTS* 49 (2003): 70-89.

————. "Whose Faith(fulness) Is It in 1 Peter 1:5?" *JTS* n.s. 48 (1997): 110-15.

Hurtado, Larry W. "Christology." In *DLNTD,* pp. 170-84.

————. *How on Earth Did Jesus Become a God? Historical Questions about Earliest Devotion to Jesus.* Grand Rapids: Eerdmans, 2005.

————. *Lord Jesus Christ: Devotion to Jesus in Earliest Christianity.* Grand Rapids: Eerdmans, 2003.

Isaac, E. "1 (Ethiopic) Apocalypse of Enoch: A New Translation and Introduction." In *OTP,* 1:5-89.

Janowski, Bernd. "He Bore Our Sins: Isaiah 53 and the Drama of Taking Another's Place."

In *The Suffering Servant: Isaiah 53 in Jewish and Christian Sources,* ed. Bernd Janowski and Peter Stuhlmacher, pp. 48-74. Grand Rapids: Eerdmans, 2004.

Jarick, John. "Questioning Sheol." In *Resurrection,* ed. Stanley E. Porter, Michael A. Hayes, and David Tombs, pp. 22-32. JSNTSup 186. Sheffield: Sheffield Academic Press, 1999.

Jeanrond, Werner G. "After Hermeneutics: The Relationship between Theology and Biblical Studies." In *The Open Text: New Directions for Biblical Studies?,* ed. Francis Watson, pp. 85-102. London: SCM, 1993.

Jeeves, Malcolm A., ed. *From Cells to Souls: Changing Portraits of Human Nature.* Grand Rapids: Eerdmans, 2004.

Jeffers, James S. *The Greco-Roman World of the New Testament Era: Exploring the Background of Early Christianity.* Downers Grove: InterVarsity, 1999.

Jenson, Robert W. "The Religious Power of Scripture." *SJT* 52 (1999): 89-105.

——. *Systematic Theology.* 2 vols. Oxford: Oxford University Press, 1997-99.

Jeremias, Joachim. *The Eucharistic Words of Jesus.* Philadelphia: Westminster, 1966.

Jewett, Paul K., with Marguerite Shuster. *Who We Are: Our Dignity as Human: A Neo-Evangelical Theology.* Grand Rapids: Eerdmans, 1996.

Johnson, Dennis E. "Fire in God's House: Imagery from Malachi in Peter's Theology of Suffering (1 Pet 4:12-19)." *JETS* 29 (1986): 285-94.

Johnson, Luke Timothy. *The Creed: What Christians Believe and Why It Matters.* New York: Doubleday, 2003.

——. *The Real Jesus: The Misguided Quest for the Historical Jesus and the Truth of the Traditional Gospels.* San Francisco: HarperSan Francisco, 1996.

——. *Sharing Possessions: Mandate and Symbol of Faith.* OBT. Philadelphia: Fortress, 1981.

——. *The Writings of the New Testament: An Interpretation.* Philadelphia: Fortress, 1986.

Johnson, Mark. *The Body in the Mind: The Bodily Basis of Meaning, Imagination, and Reason.* Chicago: University of Chicago Press, 1987.

Johnson, Sherman E. "The Preaching to the Dead." *JBL* 79 (1960): 48-51.

Johnston, Philip S. *Shades of Sheol: Death and Afterlife in the Old Testament.* Downers Grove: InterVarsity, 2002.

Jones, F. Stanley. "Freedom." In *ABD* 2:855-59.

Kendall, David W. "1 Peter 1:3-9: On Christian Hope." *Int* 41 (1987): 66-71.

——. "The Literary and Theological Function of 1 Peter 1:3-12." In *Perspectives on First Peter,* ed. Charles H. Talbert, pp. 103-20. NABPRSS 9. Macon, Georgia: Mercer University Press, 1986.

Kiley, Mark. "Like Sara: The Tale of Terror behind 1 Peter 3:6." *JBL* 106 (1987): 689-92.

Kilpatrick, G. D. "1 Peter 1:11 ΤΙΝΑ 'Η ΠΟΙΟΝ ΚΑΙΡΟΝ." *NovT* 28 (1986): 91-92.

Klaiber, Walter, and Manfred Marquardt. *Living Grace: An Outline of United Methodist Theology.* Nashville: Abingdon, 2001.

Klassen, William. "The Sacred Kiss in the New Testament: An Example of Social Boundary Lines. *NTS* 39 (1993): 122-35.

Klijn, A. F. J. "2 Baruch." *OTP* I, 615-52.

Klumbies, Paul-Gerhard. "Die Verkündigung unter Geistern und Toten nach 1 Petr 3,19f. und 4,6." *ZNW* 92 (2001): 207-28.

Koch, Christof. *The Quest for Consciousness: A Neurobiological Approach*. Englewood, Colorado: Roberts, 2004.

Koenig, John. *New Testament Hospitality: Partnership with Strangers as Promise and Mission*. OBT 17. Philadelphia: Fortress, 1985.

Koester, Helmut. *Introduction to the New Testament*. Vol. 2: *History and Literature of Early Christianity*. Philadelphia: Fortress, 1982.

Konstan, David. *Friendship in the Classical World*. KTAH. Cambridge: Cambridge University Press, 1997.

Kort, Wesley A. *"Take, Read": Scripture, Textuality, and Cultural Practice*. University Park: The Pennsylvania State University Press, 1996.

Köstenberger, Andreas J., and Peter T. O'Brien. *Salvation to the Ends of the Earth: A Biblical Theology of Mission*. NSBT. Downers Grove: InterVarsity, 2001.

Kreitzer, Larry J. "'When He at Last Is First!' Philippians 2:9-11 and the Exaltation of the Lord." In *Where Christology Began: Essays on Philippians 2*, ed. Ralph P. Martin and Brian J. Dodd, pp. 111-27. Louisville: Westminster John Knox, 1998.

Kümmel, Werner Georg. *Introduction to the New Testament*. Rev. ed. Nashville: Abingdon, 1975.

Küng, Hans. *The Church*. Garden City, New York: Doubleday, 1976.

Lakoff, George. "How the Body Shapes Thought: Thinking with an All-Too-Human Brain." In *The Nature and Limits of Human Understanding*, ed. Anthony J. Sanford, pp. 49-73. The 2001 Gifford Lectures. London: Clark, 2003.

———. "How to Live with an Embodied Mind: When Causation, Mathematics, Morality, the Soul, and God Are Essentially Metaphorical Ideas." In *The Nature and Limits of Human Understanding*, ed. Anthony J. Sanford, pp. 75-108. The 2001 Gifford Lectures. London: Clark, 2003.

———, and Mark Johnson. *Metaphors We Live By*. Chicago: University of Chicago Press, 1980.

Lane, William L. *Hebrews*. WBC 47a-b. Dallas: Word, 1991.

Lassen, Eva Marie. "The Roman Family: Ideal and Metaphor." In *Constructing Early Christian Families: Family as Social Reality and Metaphor*, ed. Halvor Moxnes, pp. 103-20. London: Routledge, 1997.

Lategan, Bernard. "Intertextuality and Social Transformation: Some Implications of the Family Concept in New Testament Texts." In *Intertextuality in Biblical Writings: Essays in Honor of Bas van Iersel*, ed. Sipke Draisma, pp. 105-16. Kampen: J. H. Kok, 1989.

LaVerdiere, Eugene A. "A Grammatical Ambiguity in 1 Pet 1:23." *CBQ* 36 (1974): 89-94.

LeDoux, Joseph. *Synaptic Self: How Our Brains Become Who We Are*. New York: Viking Penguin, 2002.

LeGuin, Ursula K. *The Telling*. New York: Harcourt, 2000.

Lenski, Gerhard. *Power and Privilege: A Theory of Social Stratification*. 2nd ed. Chapel Hill: University of North Carolina Press, 1984.

Levenson, Jon D. "Exodus and Liberation." *HBT* 13 (1991): 134-74.

Levinskaya, Irina. *The Book of Acts in Its Diaspora Setting*. A1CS 5. Grand Rapids: Eerdmans, 1996.

Levison, John R. "Holy Spirit." In *DNTB*, pp. 507-14.

————. *The Spirit in First Century Judaism*. AGJU 29. Leiden: Brill, 1997.

Lewis, C. S. *The Lion, the Witch and the Wardrobe*. New York: Collier, 1956.

————. *The Magician's Nephew*. New York: Macmillan, 1970.

Libet, Benjamin, et al., eds. *The Volitional Brain: Towards a Neuroscience of Free Will*. Thorverton: Imprint Academic, 1999.

Lindars, Barnabas. *New Testament Apologetic: The Doctrinal Significance of the Old Testament Quotations*. Philadelphia: Westminster, 1961.

Lohfink, Gerhard. *Jesus and Community: The Social Dimension of Christian Faith*. Philadelphia: Fortress, 1984.

Lohse, Eduard. *Märtyrer und Gottesknecht: Untersuchungen zur urchristlichen Verkündigung vom Sühntod Jesu Christi*. 2nd ed. FRLANT 64. Göttingen: Vandenhoeck und Ruprecht, 1963.

————. "Parenesis and Kerygma in 1 Peter." In *Perspectives on First Peter*, ed. Charles H. Talbert, pp. 37-59. NABPRSS 9. Macon, Georgia: Mercer University Press, 1986.

Longenecker, Richard N. "Is There Development in Paul's Resurrection Thought?" In *Life in the Face of Death: The Resurrection Message of the New Testament*, ed. Richard N. Longenecker, pp. 171-202. MNTS. Grand Rapids: Eerdmans, 1998.

Longman, Tremper, III. "Warfare." In *NDBT*, pp. 835-39.

————, and Daniel G. Reid, *God Is a Warrior*. SOTBT. Grand Rapids: Zondervan, 1995.

Lowenthal, David. *The Past Is a Foreign Country*. Cambridge: Cambridge University Press, 1985.

MacIntyre, Alasdair. *Three Rival Versions of Moral Inquiry: Encyclopaedia, Geneaology and Tradition*. Notre Dame, Indiana: University of Notre Dame Press, 1990.

Mantey, J. R. "The Causal Use of *eis* in the New Testament." *JBL* 70 (1951): 45-48.

————. "On Causal *eis* Again." *JBL* 70 (1951): 309-11.

Marcus, Joel. "Idolatry in the New Testament." *Int* 60 (2006): 152-64.

Marcus, Ralph. "The Elusive Causal *eis*." *JBL* 71 (1952): 43-44.

————. "On Causal *eis*." *JBL* 70 (1951): 129-30.

Marincola, John. *Authority and Tradition in Ancient Historiography*. Cambridge: Cambridge University Press, 1997.

Marshall, Bruce D. "Christ and the Cultures: The Jewish People and Christian Theology." In *The Cambridge Companion to Christian Doctrine*, ed. Colin E. Gunton, pp. 81-100. Cambridge: Cambridge University Press, 1997.

Marshall, I. Howard. *New Testament Theology: Many Witnesses, One Gospel*. Downers Grove: InterVarsity, 2004.

————. "Orthodoxy and Heresy in Earlier Christianity." *Themelios* 2, no. 1 (1976): 5-14.

Martin, Clarice J. "The *Haustafeln* (Household Codes) in African American Biblical Interpretation: 'Free Slaves' and 'Subordinate Women.'" In *Stony the Road We Trod: African American Biblical Interpretation*, ed. Cain Hope Felder, pp. 206-31. Minneapolis: Fortress, 1991.

Martin, Dale B. *The Corinthian Body*. New Haven, Connecticut: Yale University Press, 1995.

Martin, Raymond, and John Barresi. "Personal Identity and What Matters in Survival: An Historical Overview." In *Personal Identity*, ed. Raymond Martin and John Barresi, pp. 1-74. Blackwell Readings in Philosophy 11. Oxford: Blackwell, 2003.

Martin, Troy W. *Metaphor and Composition in 1 Peter*. SBLDS 131. Atlanta: Scholars, 1992.

————. "The Present Indicative in the Eschatological Statements of 1 Pet 1:6, 8." *JBL* 111 (1992): 307-12.

————. "The TestAbr and the Background of 1 Pet 3,6." *ZNW* 90 (1999): 139-46.

Mastronarde, Donald J. *Introduction to Attic Greek.* Berkeley: University of California Press, 1993.

Matera, Frank J. *New Testament Christology.* Louisville: Westminster John Knox, 1999.

Matson, David Lertis. *Household Conversion Narratives in Acts: Pattern and Interpretation.* JSNTSup 123. Sheffield: Sheffield Academic Press, 1996.

Maurer, Christian, and Wilhelm Schneemelcher. "The Gospel of Peter." In *New Testament Apocrypha,* 2 vols., by Edgar Hennecke, ed. Wilhelm Schneemelcher, rev. ed., 1:216-27. Philadelphia: Westminster, 1991.

McCartney, Dan G. "Atonement in James, Peter, and Jude." In *The Glory of the Atonement: Biblical, Theological and Practical Perspectives: Essays in Honor of Roger Nicole,* ed. Charles E. Hill and Frank A. James III, pp. 176-89. Downers Grove: InterVarsity, 2004.

————. "λογικός in 1 Peter 2,2." *ZNW* 82 (1991): 128-32.

McClendon, James Wm., Jr. *Systematic Theology,* vol. 1: *Ethics.* Nashville: Abingdon, 1986.

————. *Systematic Theology,* vol. 3: *Witness.* Nashville: Abingdon, 2000.

McDonald, J. Ian H. *Biblical Interpretation and Christian Ethics.* New Studies in Christian Ethics. Cambridge: Cambridge University Press, 1993.

————. *The Crucible of Christian Morality.* London: Routledge, 1998.

McGrath, Alister E. *Scientific Theology.* Vol. 1: *Nature.* Grand Rapids: Eerdmans, 2001.

McKelvey, R. J. *The New Temple: The Church in the New Testament.* Oxford: Oxford University Press, 1969.

————. "Temple." In *NDBT,* pp. 806-11.

McKnight, Scot. *Jesus and His Death: Historiography, the Historical Jesus, and Atonement Theory.* Waco, Texas: Baylor University Press, 2005.

Meeks, Wayne A. *The Origins of Christian Morality: The First Two Centuries.* New Haven, Connecticut: Yale University Press, 1993.

Mendenhall, George E. "From Witchcraft to Justice: Death and Afterlife in the Old Testament." In *Death and Afterlife: Perspectives of World Religions,* ed. Hiroshi Obayashi, pp. 67-81. New York: Greenwood, 1992.

Metzger, Bruce M. *A Textual Commentary on the Greek New Testament.* London: UBS, 1975.

Metzinger, Thomas. "Introduction: Consciousness Research at the End of the Twentieth Century." In *Neural Correlates of Consciousness: Empirical and Conceptual Questions,* ed. Thomas Metzinger, pp. 1-12. Cambridge, Massachusetts: The MIT Press, 2000.

Metzner, Rainer. *Die Rezeption des Matthäusevangelium im 1. Petrusbrief: Studien zum traditionsgeschichtlichen und theologischen Einfluß des 1. Evangeliums auf den 1. Petrusbrief.* WUNT 2:74. Tübingen: Mohr, 1995.

Meyers, Carol. *Exodus.* NCBC. Cambridge: Cambridge University Press, 2005.

Michaels, J. Ramsey. "Catholic Christologies in the Catholic Epistles." In *Contours of Christology in the New Testament,* ed. Richard N. Longenecker, pp. 268-91. MNTS. Grand Rapids: Eerdmans, 2005.

————. "Eschatology in I Peter III.17." *NTS* 13 (1967): 394-401.

———. "Going to Heaven with Jesus: From 1 Peter to Pilgrim's Progress." In *Patterns of Discipleship in the New Testament,* ed. Richard N. Longenecker, pp. 248-68. MNTS. Grand Rapids: Eerdmans, 1996.

Middleton, J. Richard. *The Liberating Image: The* Imago Dei *in Genesis 1.* Grand Rapids: Brazos, 2005.

Milgrom, Jacob. *Leviticus.* 3 vols. AB. New York: Doubleday, 1991-2001.

———. *Studies in Cultic Theology and Terminology.* SJLA 36. Leiden: E. J. Brill, 1983.

Mills, C. Wright. *The Power Elite.* London: Oxford University Press, 1956.

Moberly, R. W. L. *The Bible, Theology, and Faith: A Study of Abraham and Jesus.* Cambridge: Cambridge University Press, 2000.

Moltmann, Jürgen. *God in Creation: A New Theology of Creation and the Spirit of God.* The Gifford Lectures 1984-1985. San Francisco: Harper and Row, 1985.

———. *The Spirit of Life: A Universal Affirmation.* Minneapolis: Fortress, 1992.

———. *Theology of Hope: On the Ground and Implications of a Christian Eschatology.* New York: Harper and Row, 1967.

———. *The Trinity and the Kingdom: The Doctrine of God.* San Francisco: Harper and Row, 1981.

Moreland, James Porter, and Scott B. Rae. *Body and Soul: Human Nature and the Crisis in Ethics.* Downers Grove: InterVarsity, 2000.

Morson, Gary Saul. *Narrative and Freedom: The Shadows of Time.* New Haven: Yale University Press, 1994.

Moule, C. F. D. *The Birth of the New Testament.* 3rd ed. San Francisco: Harper and Row, 1982.

———. *An Idiom Book of New Testament Greek.* 2nd ed. Cambridge: Cambridge University Press, 1959.

Moxnes, Halvor, ed. *Constructing Early Christian Families: Family as Social Reality and Metaphor.* London: Routledge, 1997.

———. "Honor and Shame." In *The Social Sciences and New Testament Interpretation,* ed. Richard Rohrbaugh, pp. 19-40. Peabody, Massachusetts: Hendrickson, 1996.

Moy, Russell G. "Resident Aliens of the Diaspora: 1 Peter and Chinese Protestants in San Francisco." *Semeia* 90-91 (2002): 51-67.

Murphy, Nancey. *Bodies and Souls, or Spirited Bodies?* Current Issues in Theology. Cambridge: Cambridge University Press, 2006.

Nestle, Dieter. *Eleutheria: Studien zum Wesen der Freiheit bei den Griechen und im Neuen Testament.* Vol. 1: *Die Griechen.* HUT 6. Tübingen: Mohr, 1967.

Neusner, Jacob, et al., eds. *Judaisms and Their Messiahs at the Turn of the Christian Era.* Cambridge: Cambridge University Press, 1987.

Nickelsburg, George W. E., Jr. *Ancient Judaism and Christian Origins: Diversity, Continuity, and Transformation.* Minneapolis: Fortress, 2003.

———. *Resurrection, Immortality, and Eternal Life in Intertestamental Judaism.* HTS 26. Cambridge, Massachusetts: Harvard University Press, 1972.

Nicolet, Claude. "The Citizen: The Political Man." In *The Romans,* ed. Andrea Giardina, pp. 16-54. Chicago: University of Chicago Press, 1993.

Niebuhr, H. Richard. *Christ and Culture.* New York: Harper and Row, 1951.

Noll, Stephen F. *Angels of Light, Powers of Darkness: Thinking Biblically about Angels, Satan, and Principalities.* Downers Grove: InterVarsity, 1998.

O'Collins, Gerald, and Daniel Kendall. *The Bible for Theology: Ten Principles for the Theo-logical Use of Scripture.* New York: Paulist, 1997.

Oden, Thomas C. *Agenda for Theology.* San Francisco: Harper and Row, 1979.

Okeefe, John J., and R. R. Reno. *Sanctified Vision: An Introduction to Early Christian Inter-pretation of the Bible.* Baltimore: The Johns Hopkins University Press, 2005.

O'Neil, Edward N. "Plutarch on Friendship." In *Greco-Roman Perspectives on Friendship,* ed. John T. Fitzgerald, pp. 105-22. SBLRBS 34. Atlanta: Scholars Press, 1997.

Osiek, Carolyn, and David L. Balch. *Families in the New Testament World: Households and House Churches.* The Family, Religion, and Culture. Louisville: Westminster John Knox, 1997.

Paden, William E. *Religious Worlds: The Comparative Study of Religion.* Boston: Beacon, 1994.

Padgett, Alan G. "The Body in Resurrection: Science and Scripture on the 'Spiritual Body' (1 Cor 15:35-58)." *WW* 22 (2002): 155-63.

Pannenberg, Wolfhart. *Systematic Theology.* 3 vols. Grand Rapids: Eerdmans, 1991-98.

Patzia, Arthur G. *The Emergence of the Church: Context, Growth, Leadership, and Worship.* Downers Grove: InterVarsity, 2001.

Pearson, Sharon Clark. *The Christological and Rhetorical Properties of 1 Peter.* SBEC 45. Lewiston: Edwin Mellen, 2001.

Pesch, Rudolf. *Das Abendmahl und Jesu Todesverständnis.* QD 80. Freiburg: Herder, 1978.

Peters, Ted. *Sin: Radical Evil in Soul and Society.* Grand Rapids: Eerdmans, 1994.

————. "The Soul of Trans-Humanism." *Dialog* 44 (2005): 381-95.

————, et al., eds. *Resurrection: Theological and Scientific Assessments.* Grand Rapids: Eerdmans, 2002.

Peterson, David. *Possessed by God: A New Testament Theology of Sanctification and Holi-ness.* NSBT. Grand Rapids: Eerdmans, 1995.

Peterson, Gregory R. *Minding God: Theology and the Cognitive Sciences.* Minneapolis: For-tress, 2003.

Phelan, James. *Narrative as Rhetoric: Technique, Audiences, Ethics, Ideology.* Columbus: Ohio State University Press, 1996.

Pierce, C. A. *Conscience in the New Testament: A Study of* Syneidesis *in the New Testament; in the Light of Its Sources, and with Particular Reference to St. Paul: With Some Obser-vations regarding Its Pastoral Relevance Today.* SBT 15. London: SCM, 1955.

Pilgrim, Walter E. *Uneasy Neighbors: Church and State in the New Testament.* OBT. Minne-apolis: Fortress, 1999.

Pilhofer, Peter. *Presbyteron Kreitton: Der Altersbeweis der jüdischen und christlichen Apologeten und seine Vorgeschichte.* WUNT 2:39. Tübingen: Mohr, 1990.

Piper, John. *'Love Your Enemies': Jesus' Love Command in the Synoptic Gospels and in the Early Christian Paraenesis: A History of the Tradition and Interpretation of Its Uses.* SNTSMS 38. Cambridge: Cambridge University Press, 1979.

Pobee, John S. *Persecution and Martyrdom in the Theology of Paul.* JSNTSup 6. Sheffield: JSOT Press, 1986.

Pohl, Christine D. "Hospitality." In *NDBT,* pp. 561-63.

————. *Making Room: Recovering Hospitality as a Christian Tradition.* Grand Rapids: Eerdmans, 1999.

Polkinghorne, John. *Science and Theology: An Introduction.* Minneapolis: Fortress, 1998.

Pomerey, Sarah B. *Goddesses, Whores, Wives, and Slaves: Women in Classical Antiquity.* New York: Schocken, 1975.

Prasad, Jacob. *Foundations of the Christian Way of Life according to 1 Peter 1,13-25: An Exegetico-Theological Study.* AnBib 146. Rome: Pontifical Biblical Institute, 2000.

Procksch, Otto. "ἁγιάζω." *TDNT* 1:111-12.

Raaflaub, Kurt. "Freedom in the Ancient World." In *OCD*, pp. 609-11.

Rabinowitz, Peter J. "Reader-Response Theory and Criticism." In *The Johns Hopkins Guide to Literary Theory and Criticism,* ed. Michael Groden and Martin Kreiswirth, pp. 606-08. Baltimore: The Johns Hopkins University Press, 1994.

Radl, Walter. "ὑπομένω." *EDNT* 3:404-5.

Rae, Murray. "Texts in Context: Scripture and the Divine Economy." *JTI,* forthcoming.

Räisänen, Heikki. *Beyond New Testament Theology: A Story and a Programme.* London: SCM, 1990.

Ramachandran, V. S. *A Brief Tour of Human Consciousness: From Imposter Poodles to Purple Numbers.* New York: Pi, 2004.

Rawson, Beryl. "Adult-Child Relationships in Roman Society." In *Marriage, Divorce, and Children in Ancient Rome,* ed. Beryl Rawson, pp. 7-30. Oxford: Oxford University Press, 1991.

———. "The Roman Family." In *The Family in Ancient Rome: New Perspectives,* ed. Beryl Rawson, pp. 1-57. Ithaca, New York: Cornell University Press, 1986.

Reicke, Bo. *The Disobedient Spirits and Christian Baptism: A Study of 1 Pet. III.19 and Its Context.* ASNU 13. Copenhagen: Ejnar Munksgaard, 1946.

Reid, Daniel G. "Principalities and Powers." In *DPL,* 747-52.

Reyna, Stephen P. *Connections: Brain, Mind, and Culture in a Social Anthropology.* London: Routledge, 2002.

Richard, Earl J. "The Functional Christology of First Peter." In *Perspectives on First Peter,* ed. Charles H. Talbert, pp. 121-39. NABPRSS 9. Macon, Georgia: Mercer University Press, 1986.

———. "Honorable Conduct among the Gentiles — A Study of the Social Thought of 1 Peter." *WW* 24 (2004): 412-20.

Richards, E. Randolph. *Paul and First-Century Letter Writing: Secretaries, Composition and Collection.* Downers Grove: InterVarsity, 2004.

———. *The Secretary in the Letters of Paul.* WUNT 2:42. Tübingen: Mohr, 1991.

———. "Sylvanus Was Not Peter's Secretary: Theological Bias in Interpreting διὰ Σιλουανοῦ . . . ἔγραψα in 1 Peter 5:12." *JETS* 43 (2000): 417-32.

Ricoeur, Paul. *Interpretation Theory: Discourse and the Surplus of Meaning.* Fort Worth: Texas Christian University Press, 1976.

Robinson, H. Wheeler. *The Christian Doctrine of Man.* 3rd ed. Edinburgh: Clark, 1926.

Rodgers, Peter R. "The Longer Reading of 1 Peter 4:14." *CBQ* 43 (1981): 93-95.

Rorty, Amélie Oksenberg, ed. *The Identities of Persons.* Topics in Philosophy 3. Berkeley: University of California Press, 1976.

Rosner, Brian S. "Idolatry." In *NDBT,* pp. 569-75.

Rousseau, Philip. "Conversion." In *OCD,* pp. 386-87.

Rudman, Dominic. "1 Peter 3–4 and the Baptism of Chaos." In *The Catholic Epistles and the*

Tradition, ed. J. Schlosser, pp. 397-405. BETL 176. Leuven: Leuven University Press, 2004.

Ruppert, Lothar. *Jesus als der leidende Gerechte? Der Weg Jesu im Lichte eines alt- und zwischentestamentlichen Motivs*. SBS 59. Stuttgart: Katholisches Bibelwerk, 1972.

―――. *Der leidende Gerechte: Eine motivgeschichtliche Untersuchung zum Alten Testament und zwischentestamentlichen Judentum*. FB 5. Würzburg: Echter, 1972.

―――. *Der leidende Gerechte und seine Feinde: Eine Wortfelduntersuchung*. Würzburg: Echter, 1973.

Russell, D. S. *The Method and Message of Jewish Apocalyptic: 200 BC–100 AD*. London: SCM, 1964.

Sahlins, Marshall. *Stone Age Economics*. London: Routledge, 1972.

Said, Edward W. *Culture and Imperialism*. New York: Knopf, 1993.

Sanders, E. P. *Jesus and Judaism*. London: SCM, 1985.

Sandnes, Karl Olav. "Equality within Patriarchal Structures: Some New Testament Perspectives on the Christian Fellowship as a Brother- or Sisterhood and a Family." In *Constructing Early Christian Families: Family as a Social Reality and Metaphor*, ed. Halvor Moxnes, pp. 150-65. London: Routledge, 1997.

Sandys-Wunsch, John, and Laurence Eldredge. "J. P. Gabler and the Distinction between Biblical and Dogmatic Theology: Translation, Commentary, and Discussion of His Originality." *SJT* 33 (1980): 133-58.

Scalise, Charles J. *From Scripture to Theology: A Canonical Journey into Hermeneutics*. Downers Grove: InterVarsity, 1996.

Schacter, Daniel L., and Elaine Scarry, eds. *Memory, Brain, and Belief*. Cambridge, Massachusetts: Harvard University Press, 2000.

Schleiermacher, Friedrich. *The Christian Faith*. Philadelphia: Fortress, 1928.

Schlosser, Jacques. "Guide Lines for Christian Suffering: A Source-Critical and Theological Study of 1 Peter 2,21-25." *Bib* 64 (1983): 381-410.

―――. "La Résurrection de Jésus d'après la *Prima Petri*." In *Resurrection in the New Testament: Festschrift J. Lambrecht*, ed. B. Bieringer, V. Koperski, and B. Lataire, pp. 441-56. BETL 165. Leuven: Leuven University Press, 2002.

Schmidt, Francis. *How the Temple Thinks: Identity and Social Cohesion in Ancient Judaism*. BSem 78. Sheffield: Sheffield Academic Press, 2001.

Schnabel, Eckhard J. *Early Christian Mission*. 2 vols. Downers Grove: InterVarsity, 2004.

Schrage, Wolfgang. *The Ethics of the New Testament*. Philadelphia: Fortress, 1988.

Schreiner, Thomas R. "Election." In *NBDT*, pp. 450-54.

Schreiter, Robert J. *Constructing Local Theologies*. Maryknoll, New York: Orbis, 1985.

Schrenk, Gottlob. "ὑπογραμμός." *TDNT* 1:772-73.

Schulz, Siegfried. *Neutestamentliche Ethik*. ZGB. Zürich: Theologischer, 1987.

Schutter, William L. *Hermeneutic and Composition in 1 Peter*. WUNT 2.30. Tübingen: Mohr, 1989.

Schweizer, Eduard. *Church Order in the New Testament*. London: SCM, 1961.

Scott, James C. *Domination and the Arts of Resistance: Hidden Transcripts*. New Haven: Yale University Press, 1990.

Seebass, H. "נפשׁ." *TDOT* 9:497-519.

Seitz, Christopher R. "Christological Interpretation of Texts and Trinitarian Claims to Truth: An Engagement with Francis Watson's *Text and Truth.*" *SJT* 52 (1999): 209-26.

———. *Figured Out: Typology and Providence in Christian Scripture.* Louisville: Westminster John Knox, 2001.

———. "Two Testaments and the Failure of One Tradition History." In *Biblical Theology: Retrospect and Prospect,* ed. Scott J. Hafemann, pp. 195-211. Downers Grove: InterVarsity, 2002.

———. *Word without End: The Old Testament as Abiding Theological Witness.* Grand Rapids: Eerdmans, 1998.

Seland, Torrey. "πάροικος καὶ παρεπίδημος: Proselyte Characterizations in 1 Peter?" *BBR* 11 (2001): 239-68.

———. *Strangers in the Light: Philonic Perspectives on Christian Identity in 1 Peter.* BibIntS 76. Leiden: Brill, 2005.

Senior, Donald. "The Conduct of Christians in the World (2:11–3:12)." *RevExp* 79 (1982): 427-38.

Senior, Donald, and Carroll Stuhlmueller. *The Biblical Foundations for Mission.* Maryknoll: Orbis, 1983.

Seymour-Smith, Charlotte. *Macmillan Dictionary of Anthropology.* London: Macmillan, 1986.

Siegel, Daniel J. *The Developing Mind: How Relationships and the Brain Interact to Shape Who We Are.* New York: Guilford, 1999.

Sly, Dorothy I. "1 Peter 3:6b in the Light of Philo and Josephus." *JBL* 110 (1991): 126-29.

Smith-Christopher, Daniel L. *A Biblical Theology of Exile.* OBT. Minneapolis: Fortress, 2002.

Snodgrass, Klyne R. "1 Peter II.1-10: Its Formation and Literary Affinities." *NTS* 24 (1977-78): 97-106.

Snow, David A., and R. Machalek. "The Convert as a Social Type." In *Sociological Theory 1983,* ed. R. Collins, pp. 259-89. San Francisco: Jossey Bass, 1983.

Snyder, Scot. "Participles and Imperatives in 1 Peter: A Re-Examination in the Light of Recent Scholarly Trends." *FilNT* 8 (1995): 187-98.

Solzhenitsyn, Aleksandr I. *The Gulag Archipelago: 1918-1956.* London: Book Club, 1974.

Soulen, R. Kendall. *The God of Israel and Christian Theology.* Minneapolis: Fortress, 1996.

Spencer, Aída Besançon. "Peter's Pedagogical Method in 1 Peter 3:6." *BBR* 10 (2000): 107-19.

Spivey, Robert A., and D. Moody Smith. *Anatomy of the New Testament: A Guide to Its Structure and Meaning.* 3rd ed. New York: Macmillan, 1982.

Squires, John T. *The Plan of God in Luke-Acts.* SNTSMS 76. Cambridge: Cambridge University Press, 1992.

Stendahl, Krister. "Biblical Theology, Contemporary." In *IDB,* 1:418-32.

Stone, Lawson G. "The Soul: Possession, Part, or Person? The Genesis of Human Nature in Genesis 2:7." In *What about the Soul? Neuroscience and Christian Anthropology,* ed. Joel B. Green, pp. 47-61. Nashville: Abingdon, 2004.

Strawn, Brent A. *What Is Stronger Than a Lion? Leonine Imagery and Metaphor in the Hebrew Bible and the Ancient Near East.* OBO 212. Fribourg: Academic; Göttingen: Vandenhoeck und Ruprecht, 2005.

Strecker, Georg. *Theology of the New Testament.* New York: Walter de Gruyter, 2000.

Stuckenbruck, Loren T. "Johann Philipp Gabler and the Delineation of Biblical Theology." *SJT* 52 (1999): 139-57.

Stuhlmacher, Peter. *Biblische Theologie des Neuen Testaments.* Vol. 1: *Grundlegung: Von Jesus zu Paulus.* Göttingen: Vandenhoeck und Ruprecht, 1992.

————. "Isaiah 53 in the Gospels and Acts." In *The Suffering Servant: Isaiah 53 in Jewish and Christian Sources,* ed. Bernd Janowski and Peter Stuhlmacher, pp. 147-62. Grand Rapids: Eerdmans, 2004.

————. "My Experience with Biblical Theology." In *Biblical Theology: Retrospect and Prospect,* ed. Scott J. Hafemann, pp. 174-91. Downers Grove: InterVarsity, 2002.

————. "Vicariously Giving His Life for Many, Mark 10:45 (Matt. 20:28)." In *Reconciliation, Law, and Righteousness: Essays in Biblical Theology,* pp. 16-29. Philadelphia: Fortress, 1986.

Swete, Henry Barclay. *The Holy Spirit in the New Testament: A Study of Primitive Christian Teaching.* London: Macmillan, 1919.

Talbert, Charles H. *Learning through Suffering.* Collegeville: Liturgical, 1991.

————. "Once Again: The Plan of 1 Peter." In *Perspectives on First Peter,* ed. Charles H. Talbert, pp. 141-51. NABPRSS 9. Macon, Georgia: Mercer University Press, 1986.

Taylor, Charles. *Sources of the Self: The Making of the Modern Identity.* Cambridge, Massachusetts: Harvard University Press, 1989.

Taylor, Nicholas H. "The Social Nature of Conversion in the Early Christian World." In *Modelling Early Christianity: Social-scientific Studies of the New Testament in Its Context,* ed. Philip F. Esler, pp. 128-36. London/New York: Routledge, 1995.

Taylor, Vincent. *The Atonement in New Testament Teaching.* 2nd ed. London: Epworth, 1945.

Thébert, Yvon. "The Slave." In *The Romans,* ed. Andrea Giardina, pp. 138-74. Chicago: University of Chicago Press, 1993.

Thielicke, Helmut. "Out of the Depths." In *A Thielicke Trilogy,* pp. 199-285. Grand Rapids: Baker, 1980 (1962).

Thompson, Marianne Meye. *The God of the Gospel of John.* Grand Rapids: Eerdmans, 2001.

————. *The Promise of the Father: Jesus and God in the New Testament.* Louisville: Westminster John Knox, 2000.

Thurén, Lauri. *Argument and Theology in 1 Peter: The Origins of Christian Paraenesis.* JSNTSup 114. Sheffield: Sheffield Academic Press, 1995.

Tite, Philip L. "The Compositional Function of the Petrine Prescript: A Look at 1 Pet 1:1-3." *JETS* 39 (1996): 47-56.

————. *Compositional Transitions in 1 Peter: An Analysis of the Letter-Opening.* San Francisco: International Scholars, 1997.

Towner, W. Sibley. "Clones of God: Genesis 1:26–28 and the Image of God in the Hebrew Bible." *Int* 59 (2005): 341-56.

Trebilco, Paul. "Asia." In *The Book of Acts in Its Graeco-Roman Setting,* ed. David W. J. Gill and Conrad Gempf, pp. 291-362. A1CS 2. Grand Rapids: Eerdmans, 1994.

Turner, Mark. *The Literary Mind: The Origins of Thought and Language.* New York: Oxford University Press, 1996.

Vanhoozer, Kevin J. "The Reader in New Testament Interpretation." In *Hearing the New Testament: Strategies for Interpretation,* ed. Joel B. Green, pp. 301-28. Grand Rapids: Eerdmans, 1995.

309

————. "What Is Theological Interpretation of the Bible?" In *DTIB*, pp. 19-25.

Van Rensburg, Fika J. "Christians as 'Resident and Visiting Aliens': Implications of the Exhortations to the πάροικοι and παρεπίδημοι in 1 Peter for the Church in South Africa." *Neot* 32 (1998): 573-83.

————. "Metaphors in the Soteriology in 1 Peter: Identifying and Interpreting the Salvific Imageries." In *Salvation in the New Testament: Perspectives on Soteriology*, ed. Jan G. Van der Watt, pp. 409-35. NovTSup 121. Leiden: Brill, 2005.

————. "The Old Testament in the Salvific Metaphors in 1 Peter." In *The Catholic Epistles and the Tradition*, ed. J. Schlosser, pp. 381-96. BETL 176. Leuven: Leuven University Press, 2004.

Van Unnik, W. C. "The Critique of Paganism in 1 Peter 1:18." In *Neotestamentica et Semitica: Studies in Honour of Matthew Black*, ed. E. Earle Ellis and Max Wilcox, pp. 129-42. Edinburgh: Clark, 1966.

————. "The Teaching of Good Works in 1 Peter." *NTS* 1 (1954-55): 92-110.

Verhey, Allen. *The Great Reversal: Ethics and the New Testament*. Grand Rapids: Eerdmans, 1984.

Vermes, Geza. *The Complete Dead Sea Scrolls in English*. New York: Penguin, 1997.

Volf, Miroslav. *Exclusion and Embrace: A Theological Exploration of Identity, Otherness, and Reconciliation*. Nashville: Abingdon, 1996.

————. "Soft Difference: Theological Reflections on the Relation between Church and Culture in 1 Peter." *Ex Auditu* 10 (1994): 15-30.

von Staden, Heinrich. "Body, Soul, and Nerves: Epicurus, Herophilus, Erasistratus, the Stoics, and Galen." In *Psyche and Soma: Physicians and Metaphysicians on the Mind-Body Problem from Antiquity to Enlightenment*, ed. John P. Wright and Paul Potter, pp. 79-116. Oxford: Oxford University Press, 2000.

Vouga, François. "La christologie de la Première de Pierre." In *The Catholic Epistles and the Tradition*, ed. J. Schlosser, pp. 307-25. BETL 176. Leuven: Leuven University Press, 2004.

Wainright, Geoffrey. *Doxology: The Praise of God in Worship, Doctrine and Life: A Systematic Theology*. New York: Oxford University Press, 1980.

Wall, Robert W. "The Canonical Function of 2 Peter." *BibInt* 9 (2001): 64-81.

Wallace, Daniel B. *Greek Grammar beyond the Basics: An Exegetical Syntax of the New Testament*. Grand Rapids, Michigan: Zondervan, 1996.

Walton, Steve. "ὁμοθυμαδόν in Acts: Co-location, Common Action, or 'Of One Heart and Mind'?" In *The New Testament in Its First Century Setting: Essays on Context and Background in Honour of B. W. Winter on His 65th Birthday*, ed. P. J. Williams, et al., pp. 89-105. Grand Rapids: Eerdmans, 2004.

————. "Sacrifice and Priesthood in Relation to the Christian Life and Church in the New Testament." In *Sacrifice in the Bible*, ed. Roger T. Beckwith and Martin J. Selman, pp. 136-56. Grand Rapids: Baker, 1995.

Warden, Duane. "The Prophets of 1 Peter 1:10-12." *ResQ* 31 (1989): 1-12.

Warne, Graham J. *Hebrew Perspectives on the Human Person in the Hellenistic Era: Philo and Paul*. Lewiston, New York: Mellen, 1995.

Watson, Francis. "The Old Testament as Christian Scripture: A Response to Professor Seitz." *SJT* 52 (1999): 227-32.

————. "A Response to John Riches." *BibInt* 6 (1998): 235-42.

————. "The Task for a Confessing Biblical Scholarship." *Catalyst* 23, no. 3 (1997): 1-3.

————. *Text and Truth: Redefining Biblical Theology.* Grand Rapids: Eerdmans, 1997.

————. *Text, Church and World: Biblical Interpretation in Theological Perspective.* Grand Rapids: Eerdmans, 1994.

Webster, John. *Holy Scripture: A Dogmatic Sketch.* Current Issues in Theology. Cambridge: Cambridge University Press, 2003.

Westfall, Cynthia Long. "The Relationship between the Resurrection, the Proclamation to the Spirits in Prison and Baptismal Regeneration: 1 Peter 3:19-22." In *Resurrection,* ed. Stanley E. Porter, Michael A. Hayes, and David Tombs, pp. 106-35. JSNTSup 186. Sheffield: Sheffield Academic Press, 1999.

Williams, Patricia A. *Doing without Adam and Eve: Sociobiology and Original Sin.* Minneapolis: Fortress, 2001.

Wink, Walter. *Naming the Powers: The Language of Power in the New Testament.* Philadelphia: Fortress, 1984.

Winter, Bruce W. "The Public Honoring of Christian Benefactors: Romans 13.2-4 and 1 Peter 2.14-15." *JSNT* 34 (1988): 87-103.

————. *Roman Wives, Roman Widows: The Appearance of New Women and the Pauline Communities.* Grand Rapids: Eerdmans, 2003.

————. *Seek the Welfare of the City: Christians as Benefactors and Citizens.* FCCGRW. Grand Rapids: Eerdmans, 1994.

Wolterstorff, Nicholas. "Living within a Text." In *Faith and Narrative,* ed. Keith E. Yandell, pp. 202-13. Oxford: Oxford University Press, 2001.

Wood, Charles M. *The Formation of Christian Understanding: An Essay in Theological Hermeneutics.* Philadelphia: Westminster, 1981.

Woyke, Johannes. *Die neutestamentlichen Haustafeln: Ein kritischer und konstruktiver Forschungsüberblick.* SBS 184. Stuttgart: Katholisches Bibelwerk, 2000.

Wright, Christopher J. H. "Old Testament Ethics: A Missiological Perspective." *Catalyst* 26, no. 2 (2000): 5-8.

Wright, John P., and Paul Potter, eds. *Psyche and Soma: Physicians and Metaphysicians on the Mind-Body Problem from Antiquity to Enlightenment.* Oxford: Clarendon, 2000.

Wright, N. T. *Christian Origins and the Question of God,* vol. 1: *The New Testament and the People of God.* Minneapolis: Fortress, 1992.

————. *Christian Origins and the Question of God,* vol. 3: *The Resurrection of the Son of God.* Minneapolis: Fortress, 2003.

————. "The Letter to the Galatians: Exegesis and Theology." In *Between Two Horizons: Spanning New Testament Studies and Systematic Theology,* ed. Joel B. Green and Max Turner, pp. 205-36. Grand Rapids: Eerdmans, 2000.

Wuthnow, Robert. *Communities of Discourse: Ideology and Social Structure in the Reformation, the Enlightenment, and European Socialism.* Cambridge: Harvard University Press, 1989.

Yandell, Keith E., ed. *Faith and Narrative.* Oxford: Oxford University Press, 2001.

Zimmer, Carl. *Soul Made Flesh: The Discovery of the Brain — and How It Changed the World.* New York: Free, 2004.

Index of Authors

Index of Subjects

Index of Scripture and Other Ancient Writings